MINDFUL OF WORDS

Also from Kathy Ganske

Comprehension Across the Curriculum: Perspectives and Practices K–12
Edited by Kathy Ganske and Douglas Fisher

Word Journeys, Second Edition:
Assessment-Guided Phonics, Spelling, and Vocabulary Instruction
Kathy Ganske

Word Sorts and More, Second Edition:
Sound, Pattern, and Meaning Explorations K–3
Kathy Ganske

Mindful of Words

Spelling and Vocabulary Explorations, Grades 4–8

SECOND EDITION

Kathy Ganske

THE GUILFORD PRESS

New York   London

Copyright © 2021 The Guilford Press
A Division of Guilford Publications, Inc.
370 Seventh Avenue, Suite 1200, New York, NY 10001
www.guilford.com

Printed in the United States of America

This book is printed on acid-free paper.

Last digit is print number: 9   8   7   6   5   4   3   2   1

Library of Congress Cataloging-in-Publication Data

Names: Ganske, Kathy, author.
Title: Mindful of words : spelling and vocabulary explorations, grades 4–8 / Kathy Ganske.
Description: Second edition. | New York, NY : The Guilford Press, [2021] | Includes
    bibliographical references and index.
Identifiers: LCCN 2020028898 | ISBN 9781462544288 (hardcover) | ISBN
    9781462544271 (paperback)
Subjects: LCSH: English language—Orthography and spelling—Study and teaching. |
    Vocabulary—Study and teaching.
Classification: LCC LB1574 .G35 2021 | DDC 372.63/2044—dc23
LC record available at https://lccn.loc.gov/2020028898

About the Author

Kathy Ganske, PhD, is Research Professor, Retired, in the Department of Teaching and Learning at Vanderbilt University. She has been involved in researching, using, refining, and teaching about word study practices since the 1990s. Dr. Ganske's work is grounded in extensive teaching experience in elementary classrooms. Her recent research interests include vocabulary development during small-group word study instruction and literacy reform in challenging schools. Dr. Ganske is the author, coauthor, or editor of several books, including *Word Journeys, Second Edition; Word Sorts and More, Second Edition*; and *Comprehension Across the Curriculum,* as well as numerous articles and book chapters.

Preface

Mindful of Words, Second Edition: Spelling and Vocabulary Explorations, Grades 4–8 is written as a practical resource and guide for classroom teachers and others to engage students in upper-level word study activities that are challenging, interactive, and inquiry-based. The work is grounded in research on developmental spelling and vocabulary learning, with careful consideration to motivation and intellectual stimulation, as well as to meeting the different needs of students and teachers. This second edition also includes a new chapter of contributions by several key vocabulary researchers and scholars who recognize the importance of motivation in learning, and whose cutting-edge work targets students in the upper elementary grades and beyond, including language-minority learners and students with disabilities. Furthermore, in this edition, I describe how teachers can leverage word study instruction through the SAIL lesson design (*survey, analyze, interpret, link*) to advance students' knowledge and use of academic vocabulary. To support instruction, lists of academic vocabulary words in English and Spanish, as well as a lesson plan template, have been added to the Appendices. Finally, as with the first edition, a secondary but important aim of the text is to develop an enduring interest among students and teachers alike in savoring, puzzling over, and coming to know the language we call English.

Mindful of Words, Second Edition, may supplement or complement an existing reading, spelling, vocabulary, or writing program. It may also serve as an adjunct to a resource such as *Word Journeys: Assessment-Guided Phonics, Spelling, and Vocabulary Instruction, Second Edition* (Ganske, 2014). Although they are separate, stand-alone works, *Mindful of Words* picks up where *Word Sorts and More: Sound, Pattern, and Meaning Explorations K–3, Second Edition* (Ganske, 2018), ends. The latter book covers the early spelling phases—emergent, letter name, and within word pattern—whereas this book addresses the needs of more mature spellers at the syllable juncture and derivational constancy stages.

This second edition is divided into three parts. In Part One, "Introduction to Word Study," Chapter 1 sets the stage by presenting background information relevant to the rest of the book. In this chapter, I discuss the book's grounding in research; define *word study* in terms of elements I believe are important for effective instruction; briefly outline historical influences on the English spelling system; describe considerations for developing students' spelling and vocabulary knowledge; and introduce the SAIL instructional framework.

Part Two, "The Voices of Researchers and Teachers," consists of two chapters—one focusing on researcher/scholar perspectives, the other providing teacher/administrator tips. Chapter 2 is composed of short pieces written especially for this volume by six vocabulary experts: Michael J. Kieffer, Emily Phillips Galloway, Dianna Townsend, Michael J. Kennedy, Beth Lawrence, and Amanda P. Goodwin (with colleagues). Chapter 3, "Teacher to Teacher," presents the voices of six classroom teachers from grade 4 through middle school who provide glimpses of upper-level word study in action. These authors share a variety of ideas about assessment, classroom management, motivation, teaching techniques, and activities they use. The chapter ends with a former principal's recounting of the journey to upper-level word study in her school.

Part Three, "Word Study Instructional Activities," also consists of two chapters—one focused on the syllable juncture (or syllables and affixes) phase of spelling development, and the other on the derivational constancy (or derivational relations) phase. Categorizations and suggestions for using the sorts are incorporated. For each categorization, there is a template of 21–24 reproducible words and an answer key. Answer keys identify the aim of the sorting activity—sorting by sound, by pattern, by pattern and sound, by meaning, and so forth. Templates include boldfaced category headers at the top to guide teaching and learning; key words follow the headers. Headers may be removed before photocopying for a greater challenge to the students. Descriptions of six additional supports follow:

- "What Is Known" and "What Is New" sections for each feature or sort highlight prior knowledge students are assumed to have, and they detail new concepts being introduced, so that teachers may use the sorts out of order (if desired).
- "Considerations" offer guidance and suggestions for teaching the sort.
- "Talking Points" summarize principles/rules related to spelling features targeted in the sort; they are included with all but the root-focused sorts in Chapter 5.
- "Integrating Idioms" present one of the sort words (or, in a few instances, a related word) in an idiomatic phrase. The word's literal and figurative meanings are briefly discussed. "Integrating Idioms" discussions are included throughout the word studies in Chapter 4 and phased out in Chapter 5.
- "Did You Know?" sections aim primarily to excite students' (and teachers') interest in and appreciation for words. The history of one of the sort words (or a related word) is presented for each of the word studies in Part Three.
- "Literature Links," included for numerous word studies, suggest relevant books.

The first chapter of Part Three, "Word Study for Syllable Juncture Spellers" (Chapter 4), focuses on instructional activities for students with well-developed understandings of single-syllable words, who are ready to explore longer and more complex words and the spelling issues they involve. Nearly all of the targeted words in this chapter are two-syllable words. This length provides opportunities for students to examine many new spelling issues, but without the potential compounded difficulties presented by the three-, four-, and five-syllable words that characterize Chapter 5. At this stage, students examine compound words, inflectional endings and other affixation, open and closed syllables, syllable stress, vowel patterns in stressed and unstressed syllables, and confusing consonant patterns. Sixty-three categorization activities are included in this part, including card games to encourage repeated reinforcement of homophones and homographs. Many students in grades 4–6 will be ready for the challenges of the syllable juncture stage, and, as pointed out in Part One, some older and younger students may also benefit from these studies. Informal assessment and observation should guide teachers' decision making.

The second chapter of Part Three, "Word Study for Derivational Constancy Spellers" (Chapter 5), explores families of sophisticated words of relatively low frequency. Students learn to use their knowledge of one word to spell other words in a family, and they learn that although pronunciation may differ from one related word to another, the spelling tends to remain constant as a visible reminder of the family or meaning relationship (e.g., *geometry* becomes *geometric* rather than *geametric*, as the sound might suggest, because it is in the family of words derived from the Greek *geo-*, or "earth"). This part introduces students to several new concepts. They learn to add inflected endings to polysyllabic base words; advance their knowledge of other affixation, including the assimilation of prefixes; and come to understand the concepts of consonant and vowel alternations. In addition, substantial attention is given to developing students' knowledge of Greek and Latin prefixes and roots as an aid not only to spelling low-frequency words, but also to understanding their meanings. Fifty-eight word explorations are included in this part; 34 of these target Greek and Latin elements. Each of the latter explorations is focused on a particular theme, such as body language or ruling and governing.

The Appendices provide support and extension materials, including lists of 100+ important vocabulary words for social studies, science, and math, and charts for recording student performance on any of the more than 120 word studies, as well as the previously mentioned SAIL lesson framework and the lists of academic vocabulary. Appendices J and K in this edition provide a discussion and examples of the use of Spanish cognates, thanks to Anita C. Hernández and José A. Montelongo, whose work focuses on cognates.

The stories and histories presented in the "Did You Know?" sections in Chapters 4 and 5 were garnered from a variety of sources, with a strong effort made to find the information in multiple texts and/or websites; references are cited if only one source was found. Websites such as Wikipedia (*www. en.wikipedia.org*), an online encyclopedia, and Answer.com, an online dictionary, provided a wealth of information and leads to other online resources. Three valuable texts were *Chambers Dictionary of Etymology* (Barnhart, 2005); *The Merriam-Webster New Book of Word Histories* (1991); and *The American Heritage Dictionary,* which includes a word history every few pages in both its college edition (2004) and the larger edition (1996). The etymology sections of both American Heritage dictionaries were used, as well as the online version (*www.ahdictionary.com*) and the online edition of the *Oxford English Dictionary* (*www.oed.com*). Checks on word frequency were made with *The Educator's Word Frequency Guide* (Zeno, Ivens, Millard, & Duvvuri, 1995) as well as the online Corpus of Contemporary American English (*www.wordfrequency.info/free.asp*).

Acknowledgments

I want to thank the teachers, principal, and researchers/scholars who so generously shared their expertise and time in Chapters 2 and 3. I would also like to thank Craig Thomas, Senior Editor; Anna Brackett, Editorial Project Manager; Paul Gordon, Art Director; Marie Sprayberry, Copy Editor; Judith Grauman, Managing Editor; and the rest of The Guilford Press staff for their insights and careful attention during the production process. Finally, special thanks to friends and colleagues for the generous support and encouragement they have provided along the way, and to Chris Jennison, former editor and publisher at Guilford, who started me on my first word journey.

I wish the reader many thought-provoking and invigorating investigations into the realm of upper-level word study. As Aristophanes noted, "By words the mind is winged." May this text take you and your students to new heights of learning.

Contents

3. Teacher to Teacher: Tips from Teachers for Teachers

Part Three

Word Study Instructional Activities

4. Word Study for Syllable Juncture Spellers

List of Reproducible Pages

5. Word Study for Derivational Constancy Spellers

Appendices

The Idiom Scavenger Hunt and Appendices A–I and K can be downloaded
and printed by purchasers at *www.guilford.com/ganske3-forms*.

Part One

Introduction to Word Study

1 Setting the Stage

Background

Reading and writing are complex processes that involve, among other things, knowledge of letters, sounds, and meaning units; vocabulary; strategies for monitoring for understanding; background knowledge; and motivation. Knowledge of the sounds, patterns, and meaning units of the English spelling system, or *orthographic knowledge,* falls along a continuum that is often summarized in five stages or phases—*emergent, letter name* or *letter name alphabetic, within word pattern, syllable juncture* or *syllables and affixes,* and *derivational constancy or derivational relations* (e.g., Bear, Templeton, Invernizzi, & Johnston, 2016; Ganske, 2014). Although students at a certain grade may tend to be at a particular stage of development, there is much variation across any given class.

This book focuses on instruction at the final two stages of development; *Word Sorts and More: Sound, Pattern, and Meaning Explorations K–3, Second Edition* (Ganske, 2018), attends to instruction at the first three stages. As students progress along the continuum, their attention to words shifts from a focus on sound, to patterns, and finally to meaning. Skilled writers and readers, aided by their orthographic knowledge, easily spell and recognize words, freeing up their cognitive energy for meaning making (e.g., Carlisle, 2010; Graham, 2013; Snow, Griffin, & Burns, 2005). And they not only have well-developed orthographic knowledge; they also have well-developed vocabularies, an attribute deemed critical for success in reading and school, as well as college readiness (e.g., National Governors Association Center for Best Practices & Council of Chief State School Officers, 2010; National Reading Panel, 2000b). Although meaning plays a role in earlier phases of orthographic knowledge development, such as plural and inflectional endings and *homophones,* at the derivational constancy stage, meaning becomes the key factor. During this phase, students engage in morphological studies with prefixes, suffixes, word roots, and base words, knowledge of which can make word learning more efficient.

Vocabulary knowledge is critical for reading comprehension and can fuel a cycle of success. Knowing words makes it easier to comprehend text; in turn, better comprehension of text makes it easier to acquire new words (e.g., Nagy, 2005; Stanovich, 1986). However, it's more than that proficient readers acquire new word meanings more easily; they also learn the words better by developing understandings of their sounds and spellings (Perfetti, 2007). Furthermore, their knowledge of the phonic, graphic, semantic, and syntactic representations of words facilitates their retrieval of the words. This scenario contrasts with that of students whose connections for words are not so developed, and who therefore may require cuing (Perfetti & Hart, 2002). We might best consider the importance of vocabulary knowledge by bearing in mind that words, along with oral language, are the tools that enable children to think (Bruner, Goodnow, & Austin, 1986).

While vocabulary knowledge in general plays a key role in the cycle of success experienced by proficient readers, knowledge of academic vocabulary in particular is crucial. *Academic vocabulary* is the sophisticated vocabulary used in schools and found in school texts. Students need to know this type of vocabulary in order to understand the content (e.g., Nagy & Townsend, 2012), and it might be argued, to understand learning-related talk in the classroom. Two types of academic vocabulary are often distinguished—*general academic vocabulary* and *domain-specific academic vocabulary* (see Figure 1.1). The former type includes words such as *analyze, synthesize,* and *factor,* which tend to cross content areas. We can *analyze* story elements, or a math problem, or the make-up of a liquid solution in science. Similarly, there are *factors* that contribute to a character's actions; 6 and 56 are *factors* in the math problem 56 × 6 = 336; and there were certain *factors* that led to the Revolutionary War. By contrast, domain-specific academic vocabulary words (*photosynthesis, equation, genre, prepositions, mercenary,* etc.) are situated in particular content areas—science, math, language arts, social studies. The two types relate to the Tier Two and Tier Three words, respectively, described by Beck, McKeown, and Kucan (2013).

Academic vocabulary can be particularly challenging, because the words often have numerous affixes. This sometimes occurs through the addition of suffixes, as with *analyze: analyzed, analyzer, analyzing, analyzes, analysis, analyses, analyst, analytic, analytical,* and *analytically.* However, sometimes the formation route is more complex and the results more abstract. This is the case with *nominalization,* the process of forming a noun from another part of speech. *Nominalization* is itself an example of a nominalization; it is formed from word elements meaning "the process of making into a noun." *Democratization* is another example (from *democracy*), meaning "the process of becoming or making a democracy," as is *destabilization* (from *de-* [opposite of] + *stable* + *-ize* [to cause to be/become] + *-tion* [state or condition]). As you can tell, you can understand nominalizations by using morphology, that is, the meanings of the separate chunks (prefixes, suffixes, base word, root) that make up these words—*if* you know how to use morphology. However, nominalizations are very long (13–15 letters in my two previous examples), the meaning abstract, the tone impersonal, and the language very dense.

FIGURE 1.1. Two types of academic vocabulary.

Remember, nominalizations pack entire phrases into a single word! The result? Readers may be intimidated and give up trying to figure out the word, or they may lose the thread of meaning of what they were reading. In grades 3–8, nominalizations are more prevalent in science than in narratives or spoken language (Fang, Lamme, & Pringle, 2010). For science writing, abstraction and impersonalizing are desirable (Baratta, 2010), and few publishers are likely to argue against the space-saving attribute of the conciseness of nominalizations. A recent study of nominalizations in science texts in elementary and middle school revealed that nominalizations were present already in the primary grades; by upper elementary, they made up about 4–4.5% of the vocabulary, and by middle school 5.5% (Mueller, 2015).

It would be great if all students experienced the kind of cycle of success that proficient readers experience. As suggested above, they do not. Children from economically disadvantaged backgrounds and language minority students often lack the kind of academic vocabulary knowledge just described (August, Carlo, Dressler, & Snow, 2005; Graves, August, & Mancilla-Martinez, 2013; Hart & Risley, 1995). They face vocabulary demands in school that can present barriers to their learning. Similar types of challenges can confront those who have had difficulty learning to read. The difficulties of these students tend to increase over time. The end result? They seldom catch up to their peers (Francis, Shaywitz, Stuebing, Shaywitz, & Fletcher, 1996; Torgesen & Burgess, 1998). Recent results from the National Assessment of Educational Progress (NAEP; National Center for Education Statistics, 2015) show that only about a third of the students in grades 4 and 8 achieved proficient ratings for reading, with the performance of Black and Hispanic populations about half that of Whites. Data disaggregated by status of free/reduced price lunch (FRPL) are also troubling: Fewer than half as many students receiving FRPL met or exceeded standards for proficient reading, compared to those not on the National School Lunch Program. Because these students may have few opportunities outside of school to advance their understandings of academic vocabulary (Schleppegrell, 2004), vocabulary instruction in school is critical. Yet, despite the need, research for over 40 years has documented inadequate or ineffective vocabulary instruction across the grades (Durkin, 1978; Lawrence, White, & Snow, 2010; Nelson, Dole, Hosp, & Hosp, 2015; Scott, Jamieson-Noel, & Asselin, 2003; Spear-Swerling & Zibulsky, 2014; Watts, 1995; Wright & Neuman, 2014).

Although the value of spelling instruction for young children is well established (National Reading Panel, 2000a; Snow, Burns, & Griffin, 1998), there has been less evidence related to instruction for older students. A meta-analysis of some 53 studies involving over 6,000 students from kindergarten through 12th grade helps to fill this gap: The synthesis confirms the benefits of spelling instruction across the grades and literacy levels (Graham & Santangelo, 2014), revealing persistent gains in spelling performance across time, with carry-over to writing and advances in phonological awareness and reading ability. The very nature of the English spelling system provides further evidence for the potential of upper-level word study instruction to significantly support students' vocabulary and spelling development and to increase their ability to use the words that are studied (Adams, 2004; Ehri & Rosenthal, 2007; Moats, 2005–2006).

Whereas word study in the primary grades focuses on consonant- and vowel-pattern associations in single-syllable words (see Ganske, 2018), the more advanced word study of this text explores pattern–sound relationships in the context of polysyllabic words and through open and closed syllables, doubling, and syllable stress. The role of meaning becomes prominent as students examine pattern–meaning connections among families of related words, such as *inspire/inspiration* or *discuss/discussion* (Templeton, 1983), and as they delve into the meanings of prefixes, suffixes, and roots and how they combine.

To aid students' understanding of word meanings and to pique their curiosity and appreciation for words, this volume also provides suggestions for developing students' *word consciousness*—their awareness and interest in word learning (Anderson & Nagy, 1992). These suggestions include discussions of word origins; talk about the development of English as a language; and use of word plays, such as idioms and puns (see, e.g., the visual puns at *catchymemes.com/tagged/koalition*). Igniting interest in words is especially important for English language learners, who must devote much energy to learning words (Graves et al., 2013).

Word histories are easy to find online, as well as in some print dictionaries and other word-related resources. As an example of a word history, upper elementary and middle school students typically are surprised to discover that *school* originally meant "leisure" and wonder about the connection, which stems from the fact that at one time, only those with leisure time got to be schooled. Some word histories reveal meanings today that are the opposite of those originally associated with them. This is the case with *egregious,* which means "offensive" but once meant "outstanding," and *nice,* which originally meant "ignorant." The marvel of other words sometimes lies in the meanings of their word parts. *Disaster* quite literally means "bad star" (*dis/aster*), so called because ancient Greeks attributed catastrophes to how the planets were aligned; *malaria*—"bad air" (*mal/aria*)—is so named because Romans thought the disease was caused by the air of the marshes near Rome, not the mosquitoes that bred in this type of environment. Examination of word histories can add a whole new dimension to students' perception of just what words are. They are ever so much more than letters on a page or meanings, and thus can ignite an abiding love for words and language.

Despite the potential benefits of upper-level word study, in my work with teachers I frequently hear concerns expressed by those who teach students at the upper stages of spelling development—syllable juncture and derivational constancy. Some question whether they know enough to teach others about the nature and structure of the English spelling system at these levels. Others worry about lack of time or materials. Curricular demands can indeed fill the school day, making time a precious resource. This is especially true in middle school, where the language arts block may be only 60–75 minutes. Being able to allocate time for word study and other critical elements, such as read-alouds and independent reading, in the middle grades can require creative problem solving, but it is well worth the effort. It necessitates a can-do mindset that reflects the view "This is really important; let's find a way to make time."

My hopes in writing this book are twofold: to provide materials to make upper-level word study instruction easier for teachers, and to cultivate students' and teachers' interest and curiosity in learning about words. Words are central to our everyday lives: We read words, we write words, we talk with words, we listen to words, and we think with words. Words can open doors of opportunity or keep them closed. As philosopher Ludwig Wittgenstein put it, "The limits of my language mean the limits of my world." Clearly, we have every reason to help students become mindful of words.

The Context: What Is Word Study?

Despite widespread use of the term *word study* (a recent Google search generated some 5,000,000 results!), interpretation varies. When someone says, "We just finished word study," it is impossible to know what the person really means, other than that instruction related to some type of word learning occurred. In this text, *word study* refers to the active exploration of the sound, pattern and meaning connections of words through categorizations (word sorts) and collaboration/discussion, with students' orthographic knowledge used as the basis for determining timely instruction. I have long used the mnemonic "THAT'S Word Study" (Ganske, 2006, 2014, 2018) to describe what I believe to be the elements of effective word study:

    T = Thinking
    H = Humor
    A = Appropriate instruction

T = Talk

S = Systematic approach and some sorting

Thinking

There are various ideas as to what *thinking* means. In the context of this text, it is the mental activity of problem solving, of cognitive engagement. *Cognitive engagement* is characterized by effort and persistence to understand or figure out something (Rotgans & Schmidt, 2011). Cognitive engagement, along with behavioral and emotional engagement, can predict academic achievement (Gunuc, 2014), and effective teachers know how to engage students cognitively (Knapp & Associates, 1995; Taylor, Pearson, Peterson, & Rodriguez, 2003). In fact, what teachers do to maximize students' cognitive engagement in literacy activities is just as consequential as what they cover in their instruction (Taylor et al., 2003).

During word study, students actively engage in thinking and questioning as they increase their awareness of word meanings and spellings. They use inquiry to identify common characteristics among words, so that they can generalize their understandings to other words and be efficient in their word learning. Although estimates vary, depending on whether they include proper nouns and count the various forms of a word as a single word or multiple words, during their schooling, students are exposed to some 88,000–180,000 words (Nagy & Anderson, 1984; Anderson & Nagy, 1992)! Clearly, being able to generalize understandings across words is critical.

In word study, *non-examples* (words that do not fit the pattern, sound, or meaning focus) can play an important role in categorizations, because they encourage thinking; they also alert teachers to students who are not thinking, but instead are simply taking their cues from one aspect of the word while ignoring others. This "automatic-pilot" approach causes students difficulties with words like *relish*, which might appear to have a prefix (*re-*) but does not, or *dem-*, a root meaning "people" in *democracy*, *demographic*, and *democratic* but not in *demonstrate*.

Teachers can encourage students' thinking through the kind of support and guidance they provide. In fact, teachers' interactions with students are crucial to their engagement. Students need situations in which they can have a "developmentally calibrated sense of control, autonomy, choice, and mastery" (Pianta, Hamre, & Allen, 2012, p. 370). If this is lacking, or if a teacher's approach is overly top-down or overly passive (leading to teacher over- or underinvolvement), the likelihood of engaging students is little to none (Pianta et al., 2012). With too much teacher direction and too little incentive to problem-solve, students are likely to become disengaged; with too little guidance, they may become frustrated or go off task. When the amount of support is appropriate, students are likely to be actively involved and conjecturing about the words.

Part Three (Chapters 4 and 5) of *Mindful of Words* includes special sections to aid teachers in appropriately supporting students as they engage in the syllable juncture and derivational constancy categorizations. The introduction of each new word feature includes discussion of "What Is Known" and "What Is New." The information presented alerts teachers to what students are assumed to know already and to what they will be learning. If teachers believe it unlikely that the students will have these understandings, they will need to develop this background knowledge. Additionally, for each categorization activity, "Considerations" and "Talking Points" are explained. Details of the latter are included in the Talk portion of this THAT'S Word Study discussion. The "Considerations" sections provide teaching suggestions for the sort. The recommendations are just starting points and may need to be adjusted in terms of teacher involvement, depending on student engagement and motivation. For example, one group of students may require considerable teacher support to scaffold their understandings, so the teacher guides them through the activity by modeling the placement of several word cards and by thinking aloud to reveal the category traits. By contrast, another group may need little guidance to categorize the words, so the teacher simply shows students the key words as guides and prompts them to sort, asking them to take into consideration certain sound, pattern, and/or meaning criteria as they sort, and then follows up with discussion of what they did. Careful observation and talk and listening with students will aid in the determination of how much support a group needs.

Humor

Wit can be a powerful tool in the classroom. Relevant and respectful humor can defuse tensions, build students' confidence and willingness for risk taking, capture their attention and thinking, ignite curiosity, and foster a sense of camaraderie between students and teachers (Cary, 2000; Herbert, 1991; Jeder, 2015). Recent brain research reveals that humor actually activates more of the brain (McNeely, n.d.). It may come as little surprise, then, that one of the characteristics of effective teachers is a sense of humor (Block & Mangieri, 2003; McDermott & Rothenberg, 1999). Humor is a natural partner for word study, because English has given rise to many plays on words—idioms, puns, oxymora (phrases that use contradictory words), and other forms of ludic (playful) language that tend to surprise and amuse us, as in these examples:

How do turtles talk to each other? By using shell phones. (pun)
Why did the spider go to the computer? To check her website. (pun)
What do we call an alligator in a vest? An investigator. (pun)
Dad said that it's going to be a working vacation. (oxymoron)
That was clearly misunderstood. (oxymoron)
The movie is going to cost us an arm and a leg. (idiom)
It's getting quite late, so I'm going to hit the hay. (idiom)

More puns and idioms may be found at the following websites:

- Pun of the Day—*www.punoftheday.com*
- LaffGaff—*http://laffgaff.com*
- Education First: English Idioms—*www.ef.edu/english-resources/english-idioms*

Although use of figurative language can add levity to the daily routine, twists of phrases such as those just described can be confusing, especially to students who are learning English; thus it is important to discuss both the literal and nonliteral senses of the expressions. To incorporate word play and support students in learning figurative language, each of the word studies in Chapter 4 includes an "Integrating Idioms" section, in which an idiom is presented and discussed; this feature is gradually phased out in Chapter 5.

Appropriate Instruction

Spelling knowledge develops from straightforward letter–sound correspondences (*mat*) to increasingly abstract pattern–sound relationships (*break, soil, focus, severe*) and eventually to complex interactions involving sounds, patterns, and meaning (*design, designate; corpse, corporation, corpulent;* and *inspire, inspiration*), as well as relationships involving combinations of meaning elements (*demographics, octogenarian, uncooperative*). Because the sophistication of students' spelling knowledge is likely to differ from student to student within a given class, observation and informal assessments such as the Developmental Spelling Analysis (DSA; Ganske, 2014) are used to determine appropriate instruction. Although syllable juncture spellers tend to be students in grades 4–6, some students at these grade levels may still be grappling with issues from earlier stages (within word pattern or even letter name), whereas others may be ready to take on the challenges of the final stage, derivational constancy (Ganske, 1999). The same is true for students in grades 7 and 8; although most are likely ready to explore issues at the derivational constancy stage, some may still be solidifying understandings from an earlier stage. Likewise, certain students in earlier grades may be ready for some of the more sophisticated upper-level word studies. Assessment helps to ensure that word study instruction is timely.

Talk

The ease or difficulty with which children and adolescents navigate the challenges of learning depends to a considerable extent on their language abilities, which in turn depend on their opportunities to use language. Effective teachers share the classroom talking space: They intentionally encourage students' language use, including meaningful student-to-student interactions (Pianta et al., 2012). During word study, middle-grade learners discuss how categories of words are alike and different, as they share their thinking about how words work and ponder the meanings and origins of words and idioms. Talk becomes a vehicle for them to clarify and expand their ideas, and the interacting with and learning from peers can be motivating (Oldfather, 1995). Student exchanges also create opportunities for attentive teachers to gain insights about the students' understandings—insights that can make it easier to meet the instructional needs of individual students. With the exception of the word studies focused on Greek and Latin roots, each word exploration in this book includes the previously mentioned "Talking Points." These bulleted points highlight spelling generalizations and other information relevant to the features studied. In essence, they are the lesson take-aways. As students discuss their understandings, they may generate similar or other talking points. Any listed generalization that students do not mention during their discussion, teachers may note before the session ends. Attention to talking points is important, as this will help to solidify students' new learning and will bring meaningful closure to each lesson (Ganske, 2017).

Systematic Approach and Some Sorting

In this book, *systematic* refers to instruction that builds on what students already know and that is preplanned and purposeful. Assessment data and ongoing observations of students' performance, rather than lockstep decision making, guide instruction. Teachers focus instruction on features that students need to understand, rather than feeling obligated to have students complete all of the word studies. The previously mentioned "What Is Known" and "What Is New" sections related to teaching word features are there to assist teachers' decision making. Students who have previously engaged in developmentally appropriate word study are likely to have the background indicated. When this is not the case, or when the sorts are used in a different order, scaffolding may be needed to prevent problems from gaps in understanding.

Sorting activities play a strong role in *Mindful of Words*. Categorizing is one of our most basic cognitive abilities (Bruner, Goodnow, & Austin, 1956). We use it to develop concepts and to order the world in which we live. In fact, as we begin to think about it, there is very little we do not categorize; we categorize animals, plants, rocks, books, architectural styles, furniture types, clothing makers and styles, automobiles, foods, age groups of people, hair types . . . and the list goes on. Categorizing helps us to make sense of new information by comparing the new to the known, and to retrieve the information in an efficient manner. As we consider the role of categorizing in learning about words, we need to consider that English is a complex language, with borrowings from many other languages. By categorizing words according to their features, students are able to notice similarities and differences within and across categories that can help them to formulate generalizations about how the words work.

A Word about History

Many of the complexities involved in English spelling are the result of the influences of other languages, primarily Anglo-Saxon English (also known as Old English); an older form of French; and Greek and Latin. For example, consider the letter *c* and the /k/ sound: The hard *c* in *cat* is of Old English origin, whereas the soft *c*, as in *cent*, is from Old French (though the French got the word from Latin). The French gave us /k/ spelled as *que*, as in the final position in *antique* and *boutique*, and from the Greeks we got /k/ spelled with *ch*, as in *chorus* and *chronicle*.

Old English was the language of England from the 6th century to the middle of the 11th. The letter–sound correspondences of Old English are remarkably regular. In fact, young children who tend to rely on sound when spelling words have been said to spell like the Saxons of England (Henderson, 1981), as in *wif* for *wife* and *hus* for *house*. Old English gave us many of our most common words. In fact, the 100 most frequently occurring words in English all have an Anglo-Saxon origin (Moats, 2005–2006).

With the Norman Conquest in 1066 came a tremendous influx of French words into the language. Over time, Old English and Norman French merged into what is now Middle English. New spelling complexities in the form of patterns resulted from the amalgamation of the languages—among them, the existence of:

- Both hard and soft *c* and *g* (*cat, come, cup* but *cent, city cycle*; and *game, got, gut* but *gentle, gym,* and *magic*).
- Many long-vowel patterns, such as the *ea* vowel team with its long and short variations (*reach* and *measure*).
- Abstract vowels, such as the *ou* and *oy* in *country* and *royal*.

During the Renaissance of the 16th century, as interest in the classics revived and explorations and discoveries were made that led to a need for naming, many words of Greek and Latin origin were added to the English language. Because a lot of these borrowings and newly coined words included roots, prefixes, and suffixes, today we have many families of words that relate in spelling and meaning. This spelling–meaning connection can help students to spell words that on the surface level of pronunciation appear unrelated, such as *sign, signature,* and *resignation.* Moreover, awareness of morphological relationships may enable students to infer meanings of new words, as, for example, deducing what *telepathy* means from an understanding of **telegraph** and *sympathy* (Adams, 2004). The benefit of morphological knowledge—being able to recognize and understand prefixes, suffixes, and roots—for developing students' vocabulary knowledge is widely recognized (e.g., Baumann et al., 2002; Bowers, Kirby, & Deacon, 2010; Goodwin & Ahn, 2010). This includes benefits for English learners and struggling readers (e.g., Goodwin & Ahn, 2013; Harris, Schumaker, & Deshler, 2011; Silverman et al., 2013).

Since the Renaissance, English has continued to borrow words from other languages. Table 1.1 shows numerous examples of these borrowings. With some initial guidance in interpreting the etymological information that is part of a word's entry in an unabridged dictionary, students can easily identify additional words from other languages. For example, here is the etymology for *stomach* from the online version of *The American Heritage College Dictionary* (2020): "Middle English, from Old French *stomaque, estomac,* from Latin *stomachus,* from Greek *stomakhos,* gullet, from *stoma,* mouth."

We can interpret the information as follows: The word is most recently derived from Middle English, which borrowed the word from the Old French words *stomaque* and *estomac.* These had been borrowed from the Latin word *stomachus,* which in turn came from the Greek word *stomakhos,* meaning "gullet," and referring to the throat. This word had evolved from another Greek word, *stoma,* meaning "mouth." Although exploring etymologies in hard-copy dictionaries can be a little more challenging—the languages or origin are often abbreviated, and the symbol < is used for "derived

TABLE 1.1. Word Borrowings from Other Languages

Origin	Words	Origin	Words
Aboriginal Australian	*boomerang, kangaroo*	Hawaiian	*hula, ukulele*
American Indian	*chocolate, tepee*	Hebrew	*kosher, schwa*
Arabic	*coffee, monsoon*	Italian	*piano, spaghetti*
Celtic	*heather, plaid*	Japanese	*haiku, emoji*
Chinese	*ketchup, tea*	Russian	*mammoth, parka*
Dutch	*boss, coleslaw*	Sanskrit	*cheetah, yoga*
French	*à la mode, garage*	Scandinavian	*ski, hug*
German	*hamburger, kindergarten*	Spanish	*patio, ranch*
Greek	*chaos, dialogue*	West Africa, Congo	*banana, chimpanzee*

from"—with a couple of walk-throughs and knowledge of where to find the list of language abbreviations, the process is actually quite easy. You can often skim most of the history and get to the origin of the word, which for the preceding example is *stoma*, meaning "mouth." Students might then speculate how a word meaning "mouth" came to be associated with the place where food is digested. Here are several good online sites for learning about other etymologies, including the origins of first names:

- Online Etymology Dictionary—*www.etymonline.com*
- Oxford English Dictionary (OED)—*www.oed.com*
- Wiktionary (choice of 10 languages)—*www.wiktionary.org*
- Google Books Ngram Viewer (graphs of frequency of words in literature across time)—*www.books.google.com/ngrams*
- Wordorigins.org (list of some 400 words/phrases, chosen because of their interesting etymologies)—*www.wordorigins.org/index.php/big_list*
- Inklyo: 20 English Idioms with Surprising Origins—*www.inklyo.com/english-idioms-origins*
- Behind the Name: The Etymology and History of First Names—*www.behindthename.com*

As students explore the etymologies of words, you might also ask them to consider just what *language* is, and to think about or research its beginnings. To learn more about the history of the English language, check out one of the many resources listed at The History of English website (*www.thehistoryofenglish.com/sources.html*).

In an effort to encourage students' interest in word learning and their appreciation for language, each of the word studies in Chapters 4 and 5 includes a "Did You Know?" section in which the story of a word or its history is presented. These sections are written with a student audience in mind, so that they may be read aloud to students if desired. Besides arousing interest, this type of activity provides rich instruction for fostering vocabulary knowledge—instruction that goes beyond definitions and encourages students to think about words and to form connections with them (Beck et al., 2013).

Teaching Considerations

Word Sorts

Categorization activities play a key role in this text. Teachers can conduct the sorts in a variety of ways and with varying support. For instance, students might sort words under exemplars or key words according to common sounds, patterns, or meaning units, with greater or lesser teacher guidance; or they might sort them according to their own ideas, without the benefit of key words. They might also categorize the words as listening sorts, with partners reading the words and making their placement decisions without looking at the words. This last type of activity works well when there are contrasting sounds in the sort and obvious visual patterns, such as with open and closed syllables (*meter* and *matter* or *hoping* and *hopping*). It is not a good choice when a sound has multiple patterns in the sort that represent it. When appropriate, the listening sort format encourages students to think about sound as well as pattern, and it affords opportunity for students to sort the words in multiple ways, such as by sound, by pattern, or with both sound and pattern in mind. Because groups of words can be sorted in multiple ways, answer keys in *Mindful of Words* are labeled to show what type of sort each one is, such as "Sorting by Sound and Pattern" or "Sorting by Pattern and Meaning."

Practice activities, such as those described next, are important for reinforcing student learning.

Speed sorts encourage automatic recall of patterns being studied. Students categorize the words consecutive times, striving to increase their sorting speed while also increasing or maintaining their accuracy. Some teachers like to use a partner format for this activity and may even provide a stopwatch to aid students in tracking their progress. Sometimes students set personal goals and graph their results.

Word hunts are another type of upper-level word study activity. Here, students apply new understandings by searching through texts for sort words and other words with the features they are studying. They complete word hunts after they have considerable familiarity with the patterns, not on the first day they learn about a feature. Many of the word studies in Chapter 4, and some of those in Chapter 5, lend themselves to word hunting because the patterns are common to many words. When related words are the focus of study, as in consonant alternations (*disrupt/disruption* or *discuss/discussion*), teachers encourage students to find *one* of each pair and then generate the related word. This same approach works well for word hunts involving homophones. For some studies, word hunting may not be feasible. For instance, explorations with Greek and Latin roots may involve low-frequency roots, which would make the task of finding multiple words with the same roots nearly impossible. Instead, groups of students might try to brainstorm other words with the roots or to search in dictionaries for further examples.

Many other activities are possible. Students can record the results of their speed sorts and word hunts in a journal, along with personal reflections or other information, as described in the "Teacher to Teacher" tips in Chapter 3 of this book. In small groups, or with partners, students also might generate synonyms or antonyms for some of the words, explore etymologies and word meanings with an unabridged dictionary or online, and record questions and talking points that arise from their explorations of words. As they study roots, they might coin new words with the roots, as described in *Word Journeys* (Ganske, 2014, Chapter 8).

Scheduling

Typically, students work with a set of words for about a week, although scheduling and students' ease in grasping the features can affect this. Teachers are directly involved when introducing a set of words to students, so they can monitor students' understandings, adjust instruction and troubleshoot problems, and perhaps actually guide students through a sort. This type of small-group, focused instruction usually targets specific student needs revealed through assessment data, such as that gathered from the DSA (Ganske, 2014) or other dictated word inventory. Within a given classroom, students' orthographic knowledge will vary. By working regularly with small groups on targeted features, teachers help to ensure that all students build foundational knowledge about how the English orthographic system works. Without such focused instructional attention, some students may end up with a mishmash of knowledge that can negatively affect their reading and writing of words.

For each set of words, groups typically meet once a week with the teacher for explicit instruction and then follow up with 3–4 days of independent, partner, or small-group practice that includes teacher monitoring (but generally not direct teacher involvement). Sometimes teachers build the small-group explicit instruction into the reading block, working with a group of students while others complete independent reading or other meaningful reading-related activities. Other teachers pull students aside for the instruction during a portion of writing workshop. Some are fortunate in having a dedicated word study time. Upper elementary and middle school teachers may teach small groups about affixes and Greek and Latin roots, or they may do this by developing a whole-class routine that includes a 5- to 10-minute mini-lesson on affixes or word roots two to three times a week. Then they pull focus groups for targeted small-group instruction on the other days. They may work with different groups on different days (15–20 minutes each in the upper elementary grades and 10–15 minutes each in middle school), or they may choose to schedule small-group word study instruction all in one day. This may sound like a squeeze on the schedule, but students need to have the necessary orthographic knowledge to read the words and to be able to build on that knowledge in the future to develop understandings that are more sophisticated. While vocabulary instruction and word-reading ability cannot ensure reading success, shortfalls in either promise reading failure (Biemiller, 2005, p. 223). So the key point to bear in mind when faced with the challenge of scheduling is this: *Teachers make time for this instruction because they realize its importance for students' reading and writing.*

When addressing affixes and Greek and Latin roots through whole-class mini-lessons, teachers should start with the most common prefixes and suffixes, and those with transparent meaning. For example, when teaching the *in-* prefix, meaning "not," they should use examples such as *incorrect* and *incapable*, rather than *illegible*, *impossible*, *immobile*, or *incognito*, all of which also include the prefix but are not transparent (due to absorption of the *n* by the following consonant, or attachment of the prefix to a root rather than a base word). The students gradually work on those of lower frequency and of less transparency. The same approach is followed with the study of Greek and Latin roots: Teachers begin with the most common and those whose meanings are the most transparent, then move on to roots with less transparency. Generally, Greek roots are more transparent than those of Latin origin. Teachers should monitor the challenge level presented by the transparency of the root and the prefixes or suffixes added to it. For example, the root *aud* and its meaning "to hear" are quite transparent in *audible*, *auditorium*, and *audience*, but in *status*, *station*, *state*, and *statue*, despite the frequency of the root *stat*, the meaning "to stand" is much less obvious.

Teachers gauge students' performance with a set of words through (1) observing and listening to the students' discussions about the words and anecdotal notes; (2) reading students' word study journals or notebook work, including reflections; and (3) conducting informal assessments over 10–15 of the words. Informal assessments may be teacher-dictated, partner-completed, or carried out at listening stations with prerecorded quiz words. Two popular quiz formats include a traditional dictation and a dictation that requires students to categorize, as well as spell, the words (in other words, a listening written sort). Teachers sometimes incorporate a sentence dictation that includes review words.

Teachers and others often ask me about the use of *transfer words* in quiz dictations. Transfer words—words that have not been studied but that include the pattern—are fine to include, with a caveat. Many words have alternate spelling patterns for the same sound; if a student does not have prior knowledge of the word, an alternative spelling that is legitimate though incorrect may be used, as, for instance, the spelling of *remoat* for *remote*. Some credit should be allowed in such cases, or else transfer words should not be used when a sound can be spelled several ways, unless meaning makes clear the correct spelling, as in *helthy* for *healthy* (the *ea* must be used because it reveals the word's relationship to the meaning "heal"). For convenience in keeping track of students' performance and completion of sorts, Performance Records are included in Appendix A.

Vocabulary Knowledge

As students work with words, they not only examine the sound, pattern, and meaning relationships of their spellings, but they come to understand and use the words. This is important, considering the advantage well-developed vocabulary knowledge affords students in comprehending what they read (Stanovich, 2000). For instance, try comprehending the following well-known piece of literature in its "weighty-word" format:

> Two juvenescent members of the *Homo sapiens* species hied to the apex of a well-defined natural mass, which deviated considerably from the horizontal. Their categorical intention was to acquire an aqueous substance for a cylindrical vessel in their possession. However, the juvenescent male precipitously pitched to a supine position with a consequent cranial fissure, and an ensuing vertiginous plummet by the juvenescent female conveyed her to a state of proximity.

Words like *juvenescent, Homo sapiens, hied, apex, precipitously, supine, cranial,* and *vertiginous,* though perhaps previously heard by students, may not be well enough known to assist readers in identifying the passage as the "Jack and Jill" Mother Goose rhyme: *Jack and Jill went up a hill to fetch a pail of water; Jack fell down and broke his crown, and Jill came tumbling after.* Thinking of known words that derive from the same root as some in the passage, such as *juvenile, aquarium, precipice, cranium,* and *vertigo,* can provide clues to the meanings of words in the passage and thus aid students in deciphering the gist of the paragraph. The passage also illustrates the importance of providing students with texts that do not contain too many unfamiliar words. Eight likely unfamiliar words/phrases out of 70 accounts for about 11–12% of the total words, making the passage far more challenging than if it contained just two or three unfamiliar words (3–4% of the text).

   As students move through the upper grades, they are likely to encounter many unfamiliar words. As previously noted, morphology is an important avenue for helping students to develop understanding of unfamiliar words, and thus their vocabulary knowledge. How important? Consider the following estimate: About 60% of the unfamiliar words that students encounter in their reading can be analyzed into parts—base words, roots, prefixes, and suffixes—to help figure out their meanings (Nagy & Scott, 2000). A limited number of prefixes and suffixes (see Table 1.2) make up 76% of all prefixed words and 80% of all suffixed words (White, Sowell, & Yanagihara, 1989). Similarly, a set of just 14 roots (those shown in Table 1.3 are primarily of Latin origin), used in conjunction with other morphemes, can unlock the meanings of some 100,000 words (Brown, 1947)! But caution is in order: Some of these roots are quite obscure, and therefore not the ones with which to begin a study of word roots.

TABLE 1.2. "Gotta-Know" Prefixes and Suffixes

Prefixes	Suffixes
un- (not, opposite of)	*-s, -es*
re- (back, again)	*-ed*
in- (not) [also as *im-, il-, ir*]	*-ing*
dis- (opposite of)	*-ly*
en- (put into) [also as *em-*]	*-er, -or* (agent)
non- (not)	*-ion, -tion, -ation, -ition*
in- (in, into) [also as *im-, il-, ir*]	
over- (too much)-	
mis- (badly, wrongly)	

TABLE 1.3. Power-Packed Word Roots: 14 Roots That Can Unlock 100,000 Words

Roots	Definitions	Word examples
tain, tent, ten, tin	to have, hold	*obtain, contain, maintain*
mit, miss, mitt	to send	*transmit, admission*
cap, capt, cip, cept	to take, seize	*capital, captain*
fer	to bear, carry	*transfer, conifer*
sta, stat, sist	to stand	*stand, statue*
graph, gram	to write	*autograph, telegram*
log, ology	to speak, study of	*prologue, geology*
spect	to look, see	*spectator, inspection*
plic, plex, ply	to fold, bend	*plywood, complex*
tens, tend, tent	to stretch	*tendril, extension*
duc, duct	to lead, make	*conduct, production*
pos, pon	to put, place	*position, composure*
fac, fic, fact	to do, make	*factory, facsimile*
scribe, script	to write	*postscript, describe*

Reflective of the importance of morphology in understanding and using words, Chapters 4 and 5 of this book include over 60 word studies focused on prefixes, suffixes, and/or roots.

In addition to the emphasis on morphology, each of the word sorts provides an opportunity to expand students' vocabulary knowledge through discussion of the meanings of some of the less familiar sort words. Words that lend themselves to focused talk include those whose meanings are unknown to students; words that students may confuse with other words; and words with multiple meanings, some of which students may know and others they may not. For many of the word sorts, suggestions of words to consider are offered, but not with the expectation that all be highlighted. In fact, students might benefit from discussion of words other than those targeted. Discussion might include talk about word meanings; generation of sentences with the words; brainstorming antonyms or synonyms for the words; creating word webs; developing "Would You?" riddles, as described in Chapter 4, Sorts 60 and 62; and so forth. Follow-up questions can provide teachers with insights about the depth of students' understandings and extend students' learning about the words. The following three short excerpts from discussions about word meanings by small groups of upper elementary students provide examples. (Note that in each excerpt, the teacher's query follows students' identification of the word. Also, despite the label "Student" used below, multiple students are involved in each interaction.)

TEACHER: What's an *athlete*?

STUDENT: It's somebody that does a sport; they play a sport like tennis or football.

TEACHER: Are you an athlete?

STUDENT: Yes.

TEACHER: Okay. Some people are professional athletes, and some are amateurs.

*   *   *

TEACHER: What does *possess* mean?

STUDENT: You own it.

TEACHER: What do you possess?

STUDENT: Clothes.

TEACHER: Do you possess a Mercedes-Benz?

STUDENT: No, I don't.

TEACHER: Do you possess a pencil?

STUDENT: Yes.

TEACHER: Do you possess a pair of pump tennis shoes?

STUDENT: Yes.

TEACHER: Okay, good. Do you think you have to own it?

STUDENT: No, but you might have it. But it's not quite yours.

TEACHER: It's in your possession. It's with you right then. . . . Good ideas.

*   *   *

TEACHER: How about *expert*?

STUDENT: It's like to be real good at something. Perfect or been doing it for a while.

STUDENTS: Not perfect; you're just great at it. Like writing.

TEACHER: Okay, are you an expert at writing?

STUDENT: No.

TEACHER: Trying to be an expert at writing?

STUDENT: Yes.

For some of the Greek and Latin root sorts in Chapter 5, as well as other word sorts that include several unfamiliar words, you might introduce the words by asking students to evaluate how well they know them. To accomplish this, provide students with 8.5- × 11-inch sheets of paper, and ask them to fold them in half along the width and then repeat the process, so that unfolding the paper will reveal four rectangular boxes. Next, ask the students to label each box as shown below (adapted from Blachowicz, 1986; Dale, 1965; Allen, 1999). Then ask them to categorize the sort words according to their level of understanding by writing each word in an appropriate box. As an alternative, provide students with category header cards labeled as each box title, and ask them to categorize their word cards in the appropriate column. Discuss the results. This same process can be used to check understanding after the words have been explored; as an addition, students might be asked to provide an oral or written sentence for some of the words listed under *Could use or define the word*.

Don't know it	Have seen or heard but don't know meaning
Think I know the meaning	Could use or define the word

Certain unfamiliar words from word study or from classroom conversations, read-alouds, or content-area reading (such as those from Appendices B–D) may be deemed worthy of students' *owning*; in other words, they understand the words but also are able to use them. This generally requires 7–10 meaningful encounters with the words. A *teacher's word wall* (Ganske, 2018) can help to make this happen. The word wall reminds busy teachers of the need to bring targeted words into classroom conversation and activities. A few words of interest (10 is a good maximum to ensure prominent visibility) are posted on a wall facing a common teaching location within the classroom. The words are written on sentence strips or large note cards, so they can be seen from anywhere in the classroom. As students begin using the words, teachers replace them with new words.

SAIL: A Word Study Framework

Since the first edition of *Mindful of Words* was published, I've observed and researched the word study practices of many teachers, and have talked to them extensively about these. While it's been great to see word study happening in so many classrooms, too often the small-group meetings have been hurried times with limited cognitive engagement and student talk. In middle school settings, word study instruction was often absent altogether. With these contexts in mind, the concerns often expressed by teachers about a lack of carry-over to writing are not surprising. The need for a structure to better guide teachers in effective word study instruction seemed important. SAIL is my response. I've explored the SAIL framework in classrooms the past several years, and I'm excited about its potential.

The SAIL small-group meeting framework includes four components—*survey, analyze, interpret,* and *link*. Rather than simply telling students how a sound, pattern, or meaning feature works, SAIL involves questioning, talk, and a focus on cognitive engagement. In these ways, students expand their understandings of English orthography and vocabulary more effectively than through the types of word study sorts that often become routinized and mechanical. SAIL also includes a whole-class mini-lesson prior to the small-group meetings to teach a general academic vocabulary word. Once the word is taught, teachers integrate it, along with any previously taught academic vocabulary words, into the talk of the small-group meetings and other parts of the school day. A discussion of the whole-class mini-lesson and the four small-group components follows.

Academic Vocabulary Mini-Lesson

Teaching of the academic vocabulary word is carried out primarily through inquiry and discussion, which are brief (about 5 minutes). There are various lists of academic vocabulary words; the Coxhead (2000) Academic Word List (AWL) is one of the most well known. The AWL includes 570 families of words that are common in academic texts, excluding the 2,000 most frequently occurring words. Table 1.4 includes a sampling of frequently occurring words that teachers might consider for academic vocabulary mini-lessons in upper-level word study. The words are categorized by the component where opportunity to apply the words during small-group word study might be greatest. However, teachers may adjust both the categorization and the selection of words to fit specific classroom needs. Table 1.5 also includes a sampling of easier academic words for mini-lessons.[1] Although teachers have used the words with children in the early grades (see Figure 1.2), they are still appropriate for upper-level word study, if the learners do not already know them. If students do know them, teachers still integrate them into the word study and classroom talk. A mini-lesson should:

---

[1] See additional Coxhead AWL words at *http://wgtn.ac.nz/lals/resources/academicwordlist/publications/AWLmostfreqsublists.pdf*. Appendix K of this book provides Spanish translations of the words in Tables 1.4 and 1.5.

TABLE 1.4. Academic Vocabulary Relevant to Specific SAIL Components—More Difficult

Survey	Analyze	Interpret	Link
academic	adjacent	abstract	compiled
analogous	alter	acknowledged	differentiation
approach	analysis	adequate	facilitate
aspects	apparent	affect	generated
collapse	assume	alternative	integration
complex	coincide	ambiguous	link
components	comprise	arbitrary	option
contribution	confirmed	attributed	relevant
definite	consistent	clarity	response
denote	convinced	conceived	substitution
derived	criteria	contrary	sufficient
distinction	detected	conversely	ultimately
elements	deviation	deduction	
explicit	eliminate	encountered	
indicate	excluded	factors	
monitoring	incompatible	impact	
notion	incorporated	isolated	
precise	modified	implications	
previous	predominantly	implies	
prior	presumption	inclination	
scenario	stress	interpretation	
specified		justification	
survey		nonetheless	
		notwithstanding	
		perceived	
		perspective	
		preliminary	
		primary	
		principle	
		process	
		rejected	
		solely	
		straightforward	
		theory	
		thereby	
		underlying	

TABLE 1.5. A Sampling of Academic Vocabulary Relevant to Specific SAIL Components—Easier

Survey	Analyze	Interpret	Link
definitely	accurate	alters	apply
definition	agree	appropriate	challenge
describes	agreement	clarify	compare
descriptive	analyze	common	context
different	categories	consider	decide
differs	column	consult	demonstrate
disagree	confer	evidence	difficult
discussion	correspond	highlight	discovered
exactly	definitely	insights	expression
explain	detect	interpret	focus
identify	detectives	justify	imagine
illustrate	determine	observations	reasoning
interruption	examine	overlaps	record
obvious	features	understanding	strategies
provide	located		transfer
refer	refine		
specifics			
survey			

1. Engage students in thinking, discussing, and sharing.
2. Uncover and clarify misconceptions and deepen understandings.
3. Connect the word to what students know.
4. Provide numerous examples of the word's use.
5. Leave students with a beginning working understanding of the word's meaning.
6. Integrate previously taught academic vocabulary, as appropriate.
7. Respect and encourage participation.

SAIL Small-Group Lesson

Below is a small-group SAIL lesson, conducted with three grade 5 students (B, J, and R) who lag behind their peers in literacy learning. This 15-minute lesson focusing on prefixes is the students' first experience with word sorting. B and J are language minority students. All attend a school where nearly all of the students are from economically disadvantaged backgrounds. (For examples from the early grades, see Ganske, 2018.) The first academic vocabulary word—*definitely*—has been introduced the day before.

Survey (and Sort)

During the first component, the teacher checks to see that the students can identify and understand the words they are working with. Developing vocabulary knowledge is just as important as developing orthographic knowledge. Part of this process is guiding students to categorize the words—in this case, by prefix *un-*, by prefix *re-*, or as *oddball.* The teacher begins by setting the purpose of the lesson, so that the students clearly understand why they are doing the activity.

MS. PHASIO: When something is *accurate,* it is free of errors, mistakes. What do you think I mean by that? *Accurate.* Turn and talk with your buddies around you.

STUDENTS: (*Talking among themselves; some of their conversation is inaudible*) That means it's right. . . . If it's right, it's accurate. . . . I think *accurate* means that you accidentally make a mistake. . . . If somebody says it's not accurate, that means it's not right. . . . You make a mistake with a phone, and you can't erase it. . . .

MS. PHASIO: Okay. Let's come back to the center. So what are our ideas about the word *accurate?* I heard making mistakes, something about friends and being kind to friends. I heard all these great ideas about what we think *accurate* means, what we think being free of errors means. So let's talk it out a little bit. Kelsey, what are you thinking?

KELSEY: I think *accurate* means, like, free to make a mistake.

MS. PHASIO: Free to make a mistake? Say a little more about that.

KELSEY: I did something and accidentally made a mistake. Like, if it's a marker and I accidentally called it a pen.

MS. PHASIO: So it's okay to make that little mistake. Using your example, what if I said, "You know what, Kelsey, be more accurate. What is this? Is it a marker or a pen?"

KELSEY: I'd say a marker.

MS. PHASIO: Okay, thinking about that, class, what do we think that *accurate* means? "Okay, Kelsey, be more *accurate.* It's not a pen; it's a marker." Tell us more about that, Justin.

JUSTIN: I think what *accurate* means is if someone makes a mistake, it's not right. Like, if you don't get it right, you would say that it's not accurate.

MS. PHASIO: Kind of like what Kelsey was saying. If you don't get it right, it's not accurate. Okay. (*To the class*) Say more. We're on the right track.

REID: If the answer is right. If someone said, "How do you spell *because?*", and I said, "*B-e-c-a-u-s-e,*" that would be accurate.

MS. PHASIO: We're getting it. That was really good. Who can repeat what Reid was saying to us? Go for it, Izzy.

IZZY: If he's trying to spell, and he says, "*b-e-c-a-u-s-e,*" that was accurate.

MS. PHASIO: What if I said, "The accurate way to spell *cat* is *c-o-t*"?

STUDENTS: (*Rejecting the answer*) Not *c-o-t! C-a-t!*

MS. PHASIO: Why do you disagree? Evie?

EVIE: Because *cat* should be *c-a-t.*

MS. PHASIO: So was I accurate? Justin, say more.

JUSTIN: You're not accurate, because *c-o-t* would be *cot.*

MS. PHASIO: I was *not* accurate. Say that again.

STUDENTS: (*Together*) I was not accurate.

JUSTIN: It's *cat,* not *cot.*

MS. PHASIO: What is the accurate spelling of *cat?*

JUSTIN: *C-a-t.*

MS. PHASIO: What is the accurate way of spelling *cat,* Ariana?

ARIANA: *C-a-t.*

MS. PHASIO: What is the accurate way of spelling *bat,* Evie?

EVIE: *B-a-t.*

MS. PHASIO: What if I said to you 2 + 3 = 6?

GRAYSON: That is not accurate.

FIGURE 1.2. A first-grade teacher's academic vocabulary mini-lesson with the word *accurate.*

MS. PHASIO: Say more, Grayson.

GRAYSON: That is not accurate, because I think *accurate* means right, and you were not right, because 2 + 3 = 5, because the hundreds chart shows it.

MS. PHASIO: You want to go prove it on the hundreds chart? Let's look for evidence? He's going to go show us some evidence. (*Grayson goes to hundreds chart.*)

GRAYSON: (*Pointing to numbers on the chart*) 1, 2, 3.

MS. PHASIO: Could you justify your answer a little bit more? So explain your idea. Justify it a little bit more.

GRAYSON: So I'm at 2, and I jump 2 more, and I landed on 5.

MS. PHASIO: So what should the equation be, Grayson?

GRAYSON: 2 + 3 = 5.

MS. PHASIO: (*To the class*) Is Grayson accurate?

STUDENTS: Yes. (*One student qualifies this.*) Not all the time. (*Laughter*)

MS. PHASIO: No, just now. We're never accurate all the time, any of us. We all make mistakes. But was Grayson accurate right now?

STUDENTS: Yes.

MS. PHASIO: I noticed that Grayson didn't just say 2 + 3 = 5. He actually proved it. He found evidence, and he justified his answer. So today and every day when you're doing word study, I'm going to ask you to be accurate. I'm going to ask you to find evidence about which word should be in which category. I'm going to ask you to justify your answers. (*Lesson ends.*)

TEACHER: Today we're going to talk about prefixes, and we're going to try to think about using our new academic vocabulary word. Who remembers what word that is?

STUDENTS: *Definitely!*

TEACHER: Great! To start our lesson, I want you to think about what a prefix is. (*B raises his hand.*) B, what do you think a prefix is?

B: I think a prefix is a word that gives the meaning of a root word.

TEACHER: Okay. So we kind of have a little bit of an idea about it, but not quite, right. It will be good to figure it out. Everyone, tell me, what's this word? (*Holds up a word card and pans it for everyone to see.*)

STUDENTS: *Unwrap.*

TEACHER: So I'm going to put the card there. (*Places it on the table in front of the children at the top of what will become a column of words with the same prefix.*) What's this word?

S: *Rebuild.*

TEACHER: All right. I'm going to put *rebuild* here, because *rebuild* has a different prefix from *unwrap*. Okay? (*Students nod approval.*) If we think a word doesn't have *this* prefix (*points to the* un- *in* unwrap), and we think it doesn't have *this* prefix (*points to the* re- *in* rebuild), we're going to put it over here (*points to the* oddball *card*). Have you done any categorizing? Have you done this sort of thing? Have you worked with little strips and sorted words?

STUDENTS: (*Shaking their heads no*) Unh-unh.

TEACHER: So what we are going to do is we're going to sort these by prefix. I'm going to start. Watch and listen. When you think you know where a word should go—if you think it should go here under—what is this word . . . ?

STUDENTS: *Unwrap.*

TEACHER: . . . under *unwrap* or under *rebuild,* we're going to place the card there. Otherwise, we're going to put it over here (*points to the* oddball *card*). After we sort the cards, we're going to talk about where we placed them and see if we can figure out more about prefixes, so that you leave today knowing more about prefixes than you do right now. Does that sound good? (*Students nod.*) Okay?

STUDENTS: (*Looking at each other*) Definitely!

TEACHER: If I put a card where you think it shouldn't go, say to me, "No, don't put it there." Okay?

STUDENTS: (*Smiling and showing thumbs up*) Okay.

TEACHER: So what's this word?

STUDENTS: *Unable.*

TEACHER: *Unable.* We know what that means. *Unable.* Okay, let's see . . . I think *unable* goes with *unwrap.* So I'm going to put the word there, not under *rebuild.* And what's this word?

STUDENTS: *Recycle.*

TEACHER: Tell me about *recycle.* What is *recycle?* Who wants to tell us what that means? J? Excellent. Tell us about *recycle.*

J: It's like when you recycle . . . like when you drink a can of soda, and then you have a recycle bin and you throw the can inside.

TEACHER: Okay, here's something I'm going to ask you as we talk about the words. I'm going to ask you to use other words, not the word on the card. That's harder, but it will help us to use language. So I want you to tell me about it, but I don't want you to use *recycle.* Do you want to try again, or do you want someone to help you out, 'cause I just changed the rules of the game, didn't I? You want to try again? Tell us about *recycle.* What do you think about *recycle?*

J: You can do it with aluminum foil, plastic, or cans.

TEACHER: And what do we do with the foil, plastic, or cans when we recycle? R?

R: You use it again, to make something new.

TEACHER: Okay. Let's imagine this: If I take a piece of paper, and I write a letter on it, and then I decide to make a paper airplane out of it. Would that be recycling?

STUDENTS: Kind of. No. Unh-unh. Uh-huh.

TEACHER: What do you think, B?

B: I definitely think yes, because you're using it again and again.

TEACHER: Is that the kind of meaning we usually think of with *recycling?* Or do we think of it a little bit differently? (*Pause*) Thinking is hard work, isn't it? I can just feel your thinking. Do you recycle at home . . . ? Does that mean that you take papers and make paper airplanes out of them, or do you do something different when you recycle?

R: We do something different.

TEACHER: Okay, and it's like what J was telling us, right, where you sort maybe—this is metal, or these are cans and these are glass containers, and we sort them, and then they get remade oftentimes into something different or remade into those same products. All right, *recycle . . .* I don't think I'm going to put it under *unwrap.* I think I'm going to put it under *rebuild.* So if you disagree, let me know. (*Places the card.*) What's this word?

STUDENTS: *Unusual.*

TEACHER: Does anybody think they know where it goes? Who wants to try? (*Hands go up.*) You want to try, B? Tell us where you're putting it.

B: Under *unwrap* and *unable*.

TEACHER: Okay, so we've got *unusual, unwrap* and *unable*. (*To J and R*) Do you agree with that, or do you disagree?

J AND R: Agree.

TEACHER: All right; what's this word?

STUDENTS: *Unhappy*.

TEACHER: Okay, who thinks they know where *unhappy* goes? J, do you want to do that one? Tell us each time which word you're putting it under.

J: I'm putting it under *unwrap, unable, unusual*.

TEACHER: Are we okay with that?

B AND R: Definitely okay.

TEACHER: Okay? What's this word?

STUDENTS: *Reread*.

TEACHER: Okay. What do you want to do with that one?

R: I'm putting it under *rebuild* and *recycle*.

TEACHER: All right. What do you think? (*Looks at B and J*) Okay?

B AND J: Yes.

TEACHER: What's this word?

STUDENTS: *Reel-ect*.

TEACHER: What is it?

STUDENTS: *Reelect*.

TEACHER: *Reelect*. What does that mean? What does *reelect* mean?

R: It means to elect again. Like the president. He has to be reelected again.

TEACHER: Okay, so can we use other words besides *reelect* or *elect* to talk about that? J?

J: He was voted again.

TEACHER: Oh, I love it! Because when we elect somebody, we vote for them, right? So he was voted in again. Who was doing that? (*To R*) Were you doing that one?

R: Yes.

TEACHER: Tell us where you think that one should go?

R: Under *recycle, rebuild,* and *reread*.

TEACHER: What do we think about that? Is that a good choice? (*Students nod yes.*) Okay, how about this one? What's this word?

STUDENTS: *Unsure*.

TEACHER: Who knows a synonym for *unsure*? Raise your hand. (*Pause*) J?

J: Not reasonable.

TEACHER: Not reasonable. If we're unsure about something . . .

B: Not positive.

TEACHER: "Not positive"; we're just not quite sure, right. We're uncertain; we could say we're uncertain. And we might use this word—*tentative*. Have you ever heard of *tentative*? *Tentative* means we're unsure. I want you to tuck that word away, because I might ask you about that word before we're finished. *Tentative*. And where should we put *unsure*?

STUDENTS: Under *unwrap*.

TEACHER: Okay. How about this one?

STUDENTS: *Review.*

TEACHER: *Review.* What does *review* mean? B?

B: Like seeing it again and again.

TEACHER: Oh! I love the way he used the *view* part, which means "to see," and then the *re-* part means "again," so we're seeing it again and maybe again. So where does *review* go?

STUDENTS: Under *rebuild.*

TEACHER: (*Continues in like manner with* remove *and* reorder, *and then takes the remaining cards.*) I'm going to divide these up and give you each two, maybe even three cards. . . . Let's take a look at them, and I want you to pick one that you're ready to tell us where it goes. Be prepared to tell us what it means, if I ask you. Who's going to start? J? What's your word?

J: *Unite.*

TEACHER: *Unite.* And where are you putting it?

J: Under the question mark.

TEACHER: Okay. What do we think of that?

R: I think no.

TEACHER: You think no?

R: Because it has the prefix *un-,* and we have a category for *un-.*

TEACHER: Uh-huh? What do you think, B?

B: I think yes. Because this looks like a root word.

TEACHER: You think the whole thing is just a word, that it doesn't have a prefix? (*To J*) Is that what you were thinking? (*J nods her head yes. Then to R*) But you're not sure yet, right? Okay. How about if we leave it here, but we're going to talk about it before we're finished. Does that sound like a deal? Okay?

STUDENTS: Uh-huh.

TEACHER: So who did that one? J? (*J raises her hand.*) Who's next? B?

B: *Unkind.*

TEACHER: *Unkind* goes under . . . ?

B: *Unwrap.*

TEACHER: Okay. (*To R*) Next one is yours.

R: My word is *replace,* and I'm putting it under *rebuild.*

TEACHER: All right, and what does *replace* mean? But don't use the word, though.

R: It's like when I'm changing a light bulb.

TEACHER: All right. J?

J: *Unfair.* (*She places* unfair.) Are we okay with where these are being put? (*Students nod their approval.*) If you had to give a synonym for *unfair,* what would that be?

J: It's like when another person gets something, and then you get mad and you say, "That's not fair."

TEACHER: All right, but can you tell me what that means without using *fair* and with just one word? If something is unfair, is there another way to say that?

B: Unequally.

TEACHER: If something was unequal, it would make us feel like it was unfair. Right? If one of your friends or somebody else in your family got this much of a candy bar (*shows a large amount with her hands*), and you got this much of the candy bar (*shows a much smaller amount*), would you feel like that was unfair? (*Students vigorously nod their heads.*) Okay, unless you didn't like chocolate, you probably would. (*Children chuckle.*) Whose turn? (*B raises his hand.*) Okay, go for it, B.

B: *Rewind.*

TEACHER: Okay, and what does that mean? *Rewind.* (*Long pause; R raises her hand. To R*) Okay, and I appreciate that. Help him out.

R: It means to like "to return to something" or "to go back."

TEACHER: Hmm, like what might we rewind? J? (*Students respond enthusiastically.*)

J: A power cord before we put it away.

TEACHER: We might do that. (*To B*) You thought of something?

B: A clock.

TEACHER: We might rewind a clock.

R: A movie.

TEACHER: Excellent. All of those are good examples. (*To R*) Is it your turn?

R: Uh-huh. My word is *unclean.* And I'm putting it with *unwrap.*

TEACHER: And we know what that word means, right? (*Students nod yes.*) Good.

J: My word is *uneven,* and I'm putting it under *unwrap.*

TEACHER: And I think we all know what that word means. B?

B: *Return.* I'm putting it with *unwrap*; I mean *rebuild.*

TEACHER: Okay. And *return,* I think you know what that means. Last one.

R: *Relish,* and I'm putting it here.

TEACHER: You're placing *relish* under the question mark. Sometimes we call the words under the question mark "oddballs." Good.

Analyze

The teacher guiding this sort has already integrated some analysis into the talk by asking students whether they agree or disagree with various word placements, and also through the brief discussion of *unite,* to which she plans to return. Typically, during the analyze component, students consider the placement of their word cards and whether they need to move any words to a different category. They might discuss this in pairs and then share their ideas with the whole group. The small-group interaction here has stronger teacher guidance, due to its being the first time for students and due to their varying language proficiency. Knowing students enables teachers to optimally meet their instructional needs. Further analyzing follows:

TEACHER: (*Points to the two oddball placements.*) So let's talk about these. (*To B and J*) How do you two feel about *relish* going here?

B AND J: Good. (*Looking at each other, then smiling*) We definitely feel good about that.

TEACHER: First of all, what is *relish*?

R: It's like something people like to put on a hot dog.

TEACHER: Okay. Do you know what's in relish?

R: Pickles.

TEACHER: Pickles, for one thing. Uh-huh. Sometimes there are other things. Sometimes relish can be made out of peppers. It can be made out of different things. There's another meaning for it, too. I can say, "I don't relish having to take out the trash." What do I mean by that, if I say, "I don't relish having to do that"?

R: You don't like taking the trash out.

TEACHER: Yes, so maybe I really like relish on my hot dog, and maybe that's why the word is sometimes used that way. Because I love relish on my hot dog, I can say I relish it; I don't have the same feelings for taking the trash out that I do have when I eat my hot dog. Why do we put this here? Why do we think *relish* goes under the oddballs? (*Pause*) What do you think? You can jump in; just don't talk over each other.

J: Because it does not have a prefix.

TEACHER: And how do you know it doesn't have a prefix?

J: It doesn't say *un-* or *re-*.

TEACHER: Okay. But it has *r-e*.

B: It's actually just one word.

TEACHER: Oooh! It's just one word by itself? So even though it has the letters *re-*, they're not acting like a prefix? What does the prefix *re-* mean in all of these—*rebuild, recycle, reread, reelect, review, remove, reorder, rewrite, replace, rewind,* and *return?* Anybody?

B: You're doing it again.

TEACHER: "Doing it again." Or sometimes it means "back" as in *return*—"return the book," or turn the book back to where you got it. Right? But *relish* is not *re-* something, is it? Excellent observation. Okay, let's return to this word (*points to* unite), because J, you and B thought *unite* belonged here with the oddballs, but R, you thought it didn't.

R: I think it does now.

TEACHER: R, you're changing your mind?

R: Yes.

TEACHER: So why do you think *unite* belongs here?

R: I think it belongs there because *unite* is like when something comes together.

TEACHER: Like we might unite for a cause, right? And we can think of the *United* States, which is a pretty good phrase to describe our country, right—*United* States? So why does *unite* belong over here with the oddballs?

R: It definitely belongs right there because it's like one word together.

TEACHER: All right. It's just an intact word. It's an intact root word, or we can call it an intact *base word,* also. So when we add a prefix, we want to add it to an actual word.

Interpret and Link

During the interpret component, the teacher guides students to understandings from their sorting activity that will help them in their reading and writing. The link component is the portion of SAIL when that learning is applied through authentic reading or writing. The interpret and link components are sometimes integrated, as in the discussion that follows. At other times, teachers use link as a separate component to bring closure to the lesson. What is important is that students come away with new understandings that can help them with reading and/or writing of words, and that they have opportunity to apply understandings through contextual reading or writing.

> TEACHER: Now let's consider a tricky word (*passes out a whiteboard and pencil to each student and herself*). The word doesn't have either of our prefixes, but does have a prefix that is found in a lot of words. It's *mis-, m-i-s*. Can you think of some words that have *m-i-s*? Let's see if we can all think of one, where the *m-i-s* is a prefix. (*To R*) What do you have?

> R: *Misunderstood?*

> TEACHER: Definitely! (*To J*) Do you have one? (*Long pause*) Sometimes it's hard to just think of one. Let me come back. B?

> B: *Misplaced.*

> TEACHER: *Misplaced.* Good one. Sometimes you can think of a word by adding a new prefix onto the base word of a word with a different prefix, such as *replace*. (*To J, who has raised her hand*) You have one now, J?

> J: *Misread.*

> TEACHER: *Misread!* Excellent! Now the reason I brought up *mis-* is because *misspell* is a word that gets incorrectly written a lot—*misspell.*

> B: I was just thinking of that word!

> TEACHER: Were you?!

> B: (*Smiling*) Definitely!

> TEACHER: Okay, I'd like us all to write this sentence on our whiteboards: *I sometimes misspell a word in my paper and have to fix it.* (*Pauses while the students write the sentence, then continues.*) Okay, let's talk about what you wrote. How is *misspell* spelled?

> B: *M-i-s-p-e-l-l* . . .

> TEACHER: *M-i-s-p-e-l-l,* is that what you said?

> B: *M-i-s-p-e-l-l-e-d,* I think?

> TEACHER: For *misspelled*? But is that right? *M-i-s-p-e-l-l-e-d.* Is that how we spell it?

> R: I think no. Because *mis-* is *m-i-s*, and then he missed the *s* for *spell*.

> T: Ooooh! I think that is an excellent observation. So what's our prefix? (*Writes on her whiteboard and then turns it around.*)

> STUDENTS: *M-i-s.*

> TEACHER: *M-i-s.* Right? And what are we adding it onto?

> STUDENTS: *Spell.*

> TEACHER: *S-p-e-l-l.* (*Adds* spell *to* mis- *and then turns the board around to show the students.*) So we

have to have that (*points to* mis-), plus we have to have that (*points to* spell), all of it. Because that gives us *m-i-s-s-p-e-l-l*. Does that look kind of strange? Those two *s*'s there?

STUDENTS: Yes.

TEACHER: Right. Kind of strange. Look back at what you wrote, and fix the spelling if you need to. (*Pause*) Is there a word here in our sort that also looks a little strange because of how the prefix joins? (*Points to the categories in the sort. B points to* reelect.) Yes. Look at the word *reelect*. It kind of looks like its *reel-ect*, doesn't it? Like it's *r-e-e-l*. You have to be on the lookout for letter groups that look like prefixes but really are not. That can mislead you. You need to make sure that you've included the prefix *and* you've included the actual base word that's part of it. Even though *reelect* or *misspell* may look kind of strange with the double letters, you have to have both meaning parts there to make up the whole word. Now let's cycle back to what B said earlier about *misspelled*. If I add *-ed* onto *misspell* (*writes* misspelled *and points to the* -ed), is the *-ed* also a prefix?

STUDENTS: (*Varied answers*)

TEACHER: It's not a prefix; it's a suffix. We have prefixes, but we also have suffixes (*writes the words*). An easy way to remember which meaning unit is a prefix and which is a suffix is to think about this: Did you go to preschool? Preschool isn't *after* you start school. Preschool is school that you go to *before* you start regular school. *Pre-* means "before." So prefixes all come before the base word. Suffixes come at the end, after the base word. So *-ed* is a suffix. Do you know any other suffixes?

J: *-Es*.

T: *-Es* is an excellent example of a suffix.

B: *-S*.

TEACHER: *-S* is another excellent example. *-Ing* and *-ly* are also suffixes. Okay, we need to wrap up. Tell me something you learned today; let's just go around the group.

R: I learned that prefixes are at the beginning of words and suffixes are at the end.

J: I learned that all prefixes start at the beginning.

B: I learned how to put prefixes and suffixes in order, and I learned how to remind myself if I forget about how they go with the rest of the word.

TEACHER: Okay. In other words, you learned that you have to have the whole part of the prefix, plus the word that it is attaching to, right? Knowing this can help you to read and write and understand words that have prefixes or suffixes, or that look as though they have a prefix or suffix. (*Pause*) Now . . . what was that word I was going to ask you about at the end? Do you remember it? It means "unsure." (*Pause*) It's *tentative*. I'm going to show you what that word looks like, because if you're like me, I remember better if I see it. (*Writes the word on the whiteboard.*) What's this word?

STUDENTS: *Tentative.*

TEACHER: That's a big word. It's sort of a "$100 word." We call big words like *tentative* $100 words. *Tentative.* And what does it mean?

STUDENTS: That you're unsure.

TEACHER: Yes. So if someone asks you to go to the movies, you can say, "Tentatively, yes," meaning you're not quite sure. Wow! Excellent work today!

A Small-Group Discussion of the Word Root *Scope,* with Four Middle School Students

The following is an excerpt from a focus lesson with four middle school students (M, J, L, and N) who are meeting with their teacher to learn about Greek and Latin roots. Here they discuss *scope* words in one of the categories they have created after being asked by their teacher to sort words by their meaning units.

TEACHER: Do you know where we got these words?

STUDENTS: Where?

TEACHER: We got these words from a Latin—have you ever heard of Latin?

STUDENTS: Yup. Yes.

TEACHER: These words have a Latin background. This word has a Greek background. What is this word?

STUDENTS: *Kaleidoscope.*

TEACHER: What is that? What is a *ka-lei-do-scope?* (*Pause*) Do you know, L, what it is? (*L shakes her head no.*) Well, you're going to love this, then.

M: I know what it is.

TEACHER: Do you know what it is?

M: Yes, I do.

TEACHER: Okay, M, tell us. What is it?

M: A kaleidoscope is like a bunch of pieces of paper stapled to a small tube, and when you roll it, it changes the pictures.

J: Like a video.

TEACHER: They use other things in there, too. This is a kaleidoscope.

STUDENTS: Oh, yeah! All right! I forgot! That's what I was talking about!

TEACHER: It has a little hole here, and you put it up to your eye and see this thing down here? There's like a glass or plastic piece on the end. And I turn this end, and do you know what it does? (*Demonstrates*) It makes things like this happen, and the next time it might make it look like that, and the next time it might make it look like that. Kaleidoscopes are really cool!

M: (*Pointing to one of the images*) That's a rainbow . . . I think that's a pentagon shape.

TEACHER: Yeah. So let's look at the word *kaleidoscope.* Okay? So *scope* means what?

N: Like "something you see."

TEACHER: So we had *vis,* meaning "to see." But that came to us from the Latin. This comes to us from the Greek, and *scope* means "to see." So let's look at our *scope* words. Okay. So we're seeing colors with a kaleidoscope. Now let's try another word. What is a *stethoscope?* What are we seeing?

M: We're not seeing . . .

TEACHER: Well, in a way we are. But not exactly; that's right. J?

J: I think it's like videos.

TEACHER: No, that is not a stethoscope. But good try. What is a stethoscope?

M: A stethoscope is like two pieces of metal where you put it up to someone's chest to listen to their heart.

N: Oh, yeah!

TEACHER: You've been to the doctor, and he puts those two things in his ears that are connected to it, and he listens. (*Students nod.*) All right; that's a stethoscope. And this (*points to* scope) means "seeing," and *stetho* means "chest." So it's the way he's able to see sort of what's happening in your chest.

J: It tells if it's blocked up, like if you have an infection. Do you know what my little brother did? He actually yelled into one end.

TEACHER: All right; how about this one? What is this word?

N: Oh, I've heard of that before! I just can't remember what it is.

TEACHER: What is this word?

N: Oh! *Periscope.*

TEACHER: Yes. What's a periscope? I should probably have gotten a picture.

J: It's kind of like a telescope?

TEACHER: How is it different from a *telescope*?

J: It sees even farther.

TEACHER: Where do you find a periscope?

N: At the mall.

TEACHER: No, not at the mall. But good try.

L: At the Visual Arts?

TEACHER: No.

M: Like in an astronomy lab.

TEACHER: No, probably not. On a submarine, a periscope extends up.

STUDENTS: Oh, yeah! It has a mirror; it has mirrors inside of it.

TEACHER: Because *peri* means "around," so it means "looking around." That's what a periscope does.

Through upper-level word study discussions, students can learn much about vocabulary as well as orthographic features such as word roots, but teachers can also gain insights about the students' understandings that can inform their teaching and questioning to deepen and advance student learning. In Part Two of this book, researchers (Chapter 2) and teachers (Chapter 3) from fourth grade through middle school present more ideas for effectively engaging upper elementary and middle school students about vocabulary and how words work. Also, because administrators are crucial for effective teaching and learning (Branch, Hanushek, & Rivkin, 2013; Copland, 2004; Cotton, 2003; Sebastian, Allensworth, & Huang, 2016)—second only to teachers as factors that contribute to learning and "catalysts" for school turnaround (Leithwood, Seashore Louis, Anderson, & Wahlstrom, 2004, p. 7)— Chapter 3 ends with a retired principal's vignette about how word study started in her school.

Part Two

The Voices of Researchers and Teachers

2 Researcher Perspectives

The six short pieces in this chapter are the contributions of individuals well known for their vocabulary and language work. We begin with Michael J. Kieffer, who shares his thoughts about the importance of talk in the classroom and the difficulty teachers can have with increasing talk in their classrooms. He offers suggestions for greater student involvement through talk. Emily Phillips Galloway then discusses how to use talk to build academic languages; she emphasizes the need for *academic metalanguage* (language used to talk about language) and for opportunities to discuss conceptually rich curricular topics. In the third piece, Dianna Townsend provides guidance for helping students learn academic vocabulary in their disciplinary texts, by exploring the how and why of use of these words. The next two contributions provide insights on helping students with disabilities or speech difficulties learn vocabulary. Although these suggestions target special populations, teachers can use the techniques described with all students. Michael J. Kennedy first describes situations that can make it difficult for students with disabilities to be successful in learning vocabulary; he then goes on to highlight effective practices that teachers can use to help ensure student success in learning vocabulary. Drawing on her work as a speech–language pathologist, Beth Lawrence provides a rationale and process for using vocabulary interventions that develop knowledge of semantic relationships and semantic reasoning ability. This chapter closes with a piece written by Amanda P. Goodwin and others, in which they describe their work to develop a tool to assess morphological knowledge in order to uncover deeper understandings and instructional insights.

Learning Language Requires Using It

Michael J. Kieffer, New York University

My title may seem flippant or self-evident. However, as I sit in the backs of classrooms or watch videos of student teachers, I am consistently struck by how little students are talking. The teachers are continuing the long tradition of being the "sage on the stage" while their students are silent listeners. Research confirms my observations—that there is very little student talk across classrooms (e.g., Applebee, Langer, Nystrand, & Gamoran, 2003). When individual students do get an opportunity to talk, they are usually responding to a teacher's question with a single word or phrase. After this, the teacher starts talking again, praising or correcting the answer, and moving on. This is the familiar *initiate–respond–evaluate* (IRE) pattern identified by Cazden (2001) and others as the default structure that too many teachers fall into. Breaking out of this pattern is not easy, because it is so ingrained in education and in how we think about teaching and learning. However, promoting more student talk is not just useful but essential for those students who are in the most need of language development, including English learners.

Recent research on rich vocabulary instruction puts student talk at the center of instruction.

Although the specifics of these approaches differ, they share an emphasis on breaking the traditional IRE format and increasing students' vocabulary learning by encouraging their talk with new words. For instance, Academic Language Instruction for All Students (ALIAS; Kelley, Lesaux, Kieffer, & Faller, 2010; Lesaux, Kieffer, Faller, & Kelley, 2010; Lesaux, Kieffer, Kelley, & Russ, 2014) is one approach that aims for students to develop productive use of new academic words. In this approach, depth is prioritized over breadth: Students engage in a variety of activities that integrate speaking, listening, reading, and writing with the same new words. These activities include partner discussions before answering text questions, mock interviews in which students assume characters and ask each other questions containing the target words, whole-class discussions to create personal target word definitions, and regular think–pair–shares (Kelley et al., 2010). Students have reported that the variety of activities helped them feel ownership over the words, while the results from quasi-experimental and experimental tests have confirmed that the approach improved deep knowledge of the words for both monolingual students and English learners.

Similarly, Word Generation (Lawrence, Crosson, Paré-Blagoev, & Snow, 2015; Snow, Lawrence, & White, 2009) is an approach to language and knowledge development that involves students in texts and activities "organized around engaging and discussable dilemmas" (Lawrence et al., 2015, p. 750). Focused on middle school, Word Generation is cross-curricular, with teachers in different content areas teaching a common set of high-utility academic words. Research on this approach has demonstrated that a necessary condition for promoting discussion is giving students something worth talking about, in the form of texts and activities that focus on stimulating and controversial topics. At the same time, such texts are not sufficient without space and opportunity for discussion. An experimental study (Lawrence et al., 2015) demonstrated that Word Generation promoted much richer discussion than that in control classrooms. Moreover, the authors found that improved discussion was a key ingredient in producing gains in academic vocabulary.

Robust Academic Vocabulary Encounters (RAVE; McKeown, Crosson, Moore, & Beck, 2018) emphasizes active processing of new vocabulary through various types of student talk and activity. RAVE aims to teach general academic vocabulary by providing multiple and varied contexts; active processing of words and word uses; and attention to morphology, particularly Latin roots. The active processing element is where promoting student talk is most essential, through activities the range from simpler processing (e.g., choosing a context that fits a word) to more complex activities (e.g., asking about relationships between words). Recent research suggests the promise of this approach for improving not only vocabulary, but reading comprehension as well.

These approaches and others integrate easy-to-use routines for encouraging student talk, such as *think–pair–share* and *turn-and-talk*. In think–pair–share, students are asked to think (ideally about a challenging question) and given wait time to process their answers; each student next turns to a partner to discuss, and then the pairs share their answers with the whole group. In a particularly effective variation, students are asked to share what their partners told them, rather than their own answers, to promote accountability for listening and to facilitate sharing of ideas from all students. In another variation (*think–write–pair–share*), students think and then do some quick writing on the question before talking to their partners, to promote writing practice and provide a different avenue for processing the questions. Turn-and-talk is a related routine that may or may not include the sharing component. The fundamental advantage of both these routines is that all students are talking simultaneously (while engaging in active processing of the material), whereas IRE classrooms have only one student participate at a time. These routines also leverage students' natural orientation toward their peers. For adolescents in particular, talking with peers is going to be far more engaging than answering their teachers' questions.

Most teachers have heard of these routines or seen them in action in professional development sessions. Why, then, are they implemented so rarely and inconsistently? I would argue that they challenge the traditional authority of the teacher as controlling the "floor"—that is, determining who gets to speak and what to speak about. Shifting to noisier classrooms with open-ended student talk can be threatening to teachers. They can frighten not only new teachers who are still developing their confidence with classroom management, but more experienced teachers who may be set in their ways of managing students.

The first step to increasing student talk is realizing that it is important—that students' production of language is the key to their success. To encourage this realization, I ask the teachers I work with to record and transcribe their teaching and analyze their talk and their students' talk. This helps them realize for themselves the lost opportunities for richer discussion. Once educators embrace this new mindset, the second step is to find a way to fit routines that promote student talk into their own teaching and management styles. For instance, many of the teachers I work with find that having students talk in pairs for short periods of time, heavily structured by the teachers, is more manageable as a first step than full-fledged cooperative four-person groups. These routines are tightly controlled by the teachers in terms of time and focus of the student talk, even while the questions and prompts are open-ended. Training students in these routines can also help with management concerns. Like any behavior that teachers want to see, a successful think–pair–share requires explicit teaching and guided practice in the requisite steps, even in the upper elementary and middle school grades.

Another pitfall that may prevent wider implementation of these routines is the myth that increasing student talk is at odds with explicit instruction in vocabulary and other skills. All of the research approaches described above used direct and explicit vocabulary instruction, including providing clear student-friendly definitions, explaining word parts and how they work together, and drawing students' attention to contextual information. The difference was that after each segment of direct and explicit instruction, students also engaged in talk that promoted their active processing of the new material. Of course, a think–pair–share or similar routine takes time, but this investment in time pays off in terms of deeper student learning.

These routines are useful for all students, but are especially essential for English learners. English learners enter classrooms with myriad strengths, but also face the daunting task of acquiring the breadth and depth of English vocabulary needed to comprehend sophisticated texts. Approaches such as ALIAS have confirmed that increasing opportunities for students to actively use the new language they are acquiring is fundamental to their deep learning. Opportunities to process new material in their first language or a combination of their languages through these routines can also produce useful student talk. For instance, multilingual think–pair–shares can facilitate rich concept development, which is the basis for learning vocabulary.

Like many changes to educational practice, increasing student talk is easy to describe and hard to do. It requires a shift in mindset for teachers who have become comfortable with IRE interactions. It requires planning and teaching students how to implement the new routines. It also requires a shift in students' mindsets as they become more active participants in the classroom discourse and can no longer sit as silent listeners. However, research tells us that this hard work can make an important difference in promoting students' vocabulary and language development.

More Than Print Exposure:
Using Talk to Build Knowledge of Academic Languages

Emily Phillips Galloway, Vanderbilt University

To comprehend text, our students must develop the skills to understand the language of print. A reader's knowledge of spoken language—including phonology (language's sound structure), syntax (word order, sentence structures), morphology (structure of words), semantics (word meanings), and pragmatics (the interactional rules of language use, such as when to pause and listen)—readily supports his or her comprehension of the written word. Nevertheless, the transfer of spoken to written language comprehension is less straightforward for upper elementary and middle school readers, who routinely encounter language in text to which they have likely had little (if any) oral exposure. Imagine, for example, the students in your own classroom. For many middle graders, words like *therefore, however,* and *consequently* occur less frequently in our and their conversations, and so the students may first learn these when they are encountered in print.

This reality has led to the increasing focus on creating opportunities for students to use academic languages (ALs) in upper elementary and middle school instruction. Learning is a social activity. That is, we learn through interacting with others—both teachers and classmates—who support and push our thinking. Nevertheless, in order to think together about abstract concepts, we need language that can help us to make our thinking visible to others; this is the role of academic languages. ALs are specialized words and sentence/language structures that support participation in these learning activities (alongside other communicative resources, which include gestures, gaze, and material resources like texts, diagrams, or objects). In fact, it is their usefulness for communicating abstract relationships and ideas that makes ALs so common in classrooms and in informational texts.

Admittedly, it would be challenging to delineate a set of language features that are solely "academic." Drawing from functional linguistics, Snow and Uccelli (2010) argue that although ALs do not exist as categorically distinct from language types used in other contexts, they are more likely to co-occur with school learning tasks. ALs include content-area language for conveying concepts (*photosynthesis, titration, exponent, fertile crescent*), as well as the cross-content language that supports the communication of how these concepts are related (e.g., connective words such as *however* and *therefore*; epistemic markers such as *It may be the case . . .* ; and complex sentence structures such as embedded clauses and nominal phrases). In my own work, I focus on measuring and studying the development of middle graders' cross-disciplinary school language skills, which I refer to as Core Academic Language Skills (CALS; see Figure 2.1).

Here, I share a short summary of this research with the goal of informing instructional practice. I also draw on my own experiences as a middle-grade educator and from my work alongside educators in U.S. schools. In particular, I argue that while we often make use of text-focused instruction to support middle-grade students' learning of ALs, there is a reason to reconsider the important role of talk. These experiences are particularly important for students reading below grade-level expectations—those classified as English learners, and students still developing foundational reading skills—who may not be able to access grade-level texts independently. Indeed, students still developing foundational skills *can and should* be afforded opportunities to work with tasks that ask them to engage with age-appropriate ideas and concepts, as well as the languages for communicating them. This suggests the need for a pedagogical approach that does not hinge solely on students' being able to access print independently, but also leverages talk.

That said, the practice of using text and writing in order to teach ALs is indeed a beneficial practice. My own research has linked students' knowledge of CALS to skill in both comprehending and producing academic texts. These studies suggest that a paradox is at play: While CALS features are meant to support precise communication in texts and do help skilled readers to understand them, they seem to pose major obstacles for text comprehension among developing middle-grade readers. In fact, in studies conducted with my colleague Paola Uccelli and others, we found that even very common phrases used to connect ideas in texts were unfamiliar to most adolescents attending middle schools in large U.S. metropolitan areas. For example, in our sample of nearly 7,000 students, only 15% of fourth graders and 46% of eighth graders were familiar with the phrase *in contrast.* Among students classified as English learners, these percentages were even lower, suggesting that CALS must be the

Domain 1: Unpacking dense information in texts
A. *Skill in unpacking dense morpho-syntactic structures*
Words that have complex morphology (consist of many word parts) are common in academic texts, and so developing knowledge of how to apply knowledge of roots, affixes, and suffixes supports young students as both readers and writers (***Examples:*** *democratization, titration, personalize*).

B. *Unpacking complex sentences / Skill in understanding complex syntax*
For students, navigating center-embedded clauses and other more complex sentence structures, widely used in academic texts in an attempt to achieve concision, often requires additional instruction (***Example:*** "The conflict in the Middle East began as a result of a host of factors, including . . . ").

Domain 2: Connecting ideas in texts logically | Like signposts, connectives and discourse markers are used by academic writers to tell readers how to connect ideas across a text. However, students require support in learning the meaning of these words (***Examples:*** *however, therefore, as a result*).

Domain 3: Tracking participants and ideas through text | To avoid repetition, academic writers vary the language used to refer to a single participant or idea. As a result, readers must track people and ideas through a text as part of routine comprehension (***Example:*** "World War II was preceded by a series of other conflicts. These events . . . ").

Domain 4: Navigating a text by using its structure | Knowledge of how written expository discourse is generally organized is still developing in the middle grades; however, knowledge of these structures simplifies the process of understanding text and communicating clearly in writing (***Example:*** argumentative text structure).

Domain 5: Understanding words that convey thinking and learning processes in texts (and tasks) | Frequently, we use language in classrooms that cues ways of thinking (***Examples:*** hypothesize, make a reasoned argument) and refers to learning tasks (***Examples:*** write a thesis statement or argument). This is called *metalinguistic academic vocabulary,* and should be taught to support full participation in the learning community.

Domain 6: Understanding the writer's viewpoint | All academic knowledge (including that which appears in textbooks) is constructed, and those generating knowledge rarely agree. For this reason, academic writers often convey a perspective (***Examples:*** "It is common sense that . . . ," "Most in the field agree that . . . ") or a sense of certainty or uncertainty about the information presented (***Examples:*** "It is likely the case that . . . ," "Most often . . . "). For students, understanding these subtle ways of communicating a perspective is essential to comprehension of text-based evidence.

Domain 7: Recognizing when academic language is being used in a text | How do readers know when to make use of academic register skills? We hypothesize that skill in identifying more academic forms of discourse, in comparison to more conversational alternatives, may be key to aiding readers in activating their academic register knowledge.

FIGURE 2.1. Core Academic Language Skills (CALS).

focus of instruction for students who do not speak English at home. It is unsurprising in light of these results that many middle graders also struggle to use this language in writing. In my own studies, students with higher levels of CALS knowledge produced higher-quality texts that often contained more connectives, which helped their readers to understand how to connect the ideas and propositions presented in their essays. In sum, texts often provide students necessary first exposures to ALs, and writing is a valuable activity for practicing the use of ALs.

Yet, beyond experiences with reading and writing text, ALs also appear to be learned through talk. My studies examine two types of classroom talk that foster learning of ALs: (1) talk that equips students with language to talk about language—or what we call *academic metalanguage*; and (2) discussions of content and concepts that are supported by the use of ALs. These content discussions provide authentic opportunities to practice using ALs. As described below, both of these types of talk serve important, but distinct functions for fostering our students' ALs development.

In a series of my own studies situated in classrooms in which students were learning ALs, I noted an interesting trend: Students and their teachers were often using metalanguage to make ALs' characteristics visible. For example, teachers and their students might talk about "big words" to describe morphologically complex words, which often contain prefixes and suffixes (e.g., *pre-, non-, -tion*), or "lots of commas" to describe a sentence that contains embedded clauses (Phillips Galloway & Uccelli, 2019; Phillips Galloway, Uccelli, Aguilar, & Barr, 2020). This metalinguistic reflection serves an important function: It develops students' awareness of the ways in which the language used for communication with an academic audience differs from the language used in everyday conversations, and it builds an understanding of the function of different aspects of the language system. For example, in my collaborations with middle-grade teachers, we often focus on selecting short segments of authentic, rich texts as jumping-off points for teaching ALs. Through unpacking language choices in these short text segments—"What does *consequently* tell us about how this sentence and the one before are connected? Why did the author use a comma here? What does the phrase *strongly agree* tell us?"—we can assist our students in focusing on language in the service of making meaning from a text. A far cry from traditional grammar exercises, this work is rooted in meaningful texts that students are reading in the classroom.

An important finding from my studies that have examined metalinguistic talk is that teachers who use this talk successfully in their classrooms build on students' everyday ways of talking about language. This practice recognizes and affirms the linguistic understandings that students have learned as they move between inside-of-school and outside-of-school settings (Phillips Galloway, Dobbs, Olivo, & Madigan, 2019). It is often the case that the complex ways of using language to engage in humor, storytelling, and explaining concepts are useful in academic communications. In particular, for students classified as English learners, this talk recognizes the complex linguistic tasks accomplished by multilingual students each day (see Figure 2.2). For instance, in Figure 2.2, both educators build on students' existing knowledge of language (in English and in Spanish) and seek through talk to co-construct a shared knowledge of the function of morphologically complex words (Example 1) and of connective words (Example 2), respectively. In the first example, Ms. Martinez acknowledges and builds from her students' language skills, all the while further developing their understanding of how ALs "work":

> "Okay, so that's really good word solving, using what you know to get to a meaning. *Preemptive attack,* what could that mean? Think, using Caro's clue that *pre-* means 'before.' Can anyone think of any words that might be related to this one that we've seen before, and what we know about the parts of those words, what those parts mean? Remember, when we see longer words, we will think about whether we can use our morphology skills, because longer words are most of the time going to be morphologically complex."

Indeed, we should not expect our students to bring formal labels used by linguists to reflect on language; nor should having this language be a precondition for talking about language in the classroom. In fact, as illustrated in Figure 2.2, student-generated linguistic terms are equally powerful for making language visible. Talking about "bigger words" and "longer sentences," as well as unpacking why academic writers employ these features, does not require teaching linguistic labels. In addition, as students grapple with new concepts and ideas in the classroom, all of the students' language resources should be put to use.

What Does Metalinguistic Talk Sound Like?

Example 1:

Ms. Martinez and her fifth-grade students, including many classified as English learners, are examining a blog post written by a teen for a peer audience and an editorial that appeared in a national newspaper, both written about the recent presidential election.

MS. MARTINEZ: So what do you notice specifically about the words and sentences—um, the language—that is different between the two of them?

CAROLINA: Well, it's like, you know this one is for a friend, I think . . . because the words are more like what you say to a friend, like casual, and smaller words, the words are not as long.

MS. MARTINEZ: Okay, the newspaper article seems to have longer words. Can you show us what you mean? It's like we talked about—longer words are very common in academic texts, because they help writers to pack lots of information in a single word.

CAROLINA: Like this one here. I think it's, like, Latin or Spanish, maybe, like *preventive* . . . the word has *pre-*. That's, like, telling it's before. (*Points to* preemptive *in the newspaper article.*)

MS. MARTINEZ: Okay, so that's really good word solving, using what you know to get to a meaning. *Preemptive attack,* what could that mean? Think, using Caro's clue that *pre-* means "before." Can anyone think of any words that might be related to this one that we've seen before, and what we know about the parts of those words, what those parts mean? Remember, when we see longer words, we will think about whether we can use our morphology skills, because longer words are most of the time going to be morphologically complex.

Example 2:

Mr. Morris and his seventh graders are reading a social studies informational text explaining causes of water shortages in the Las Vegas metro area.

TOMAS: I've seen this before—this word, *however*—but I don't know, like, what it means, really.

MR. MORRIS: So what might that mean? Do we know what *however* might be doing in these sentences? What is the function—what is the writer saying about how the two sentences relate?

CARLA: It's a connecting word. It's a word that tells me how to connect the two sentences. Like, it says, "They have some water, but it's maybe not getting to people?"

MR. MORRIS: All right, so we are thinking it is a connective, and we know that connectives can do a few things, like signal that an idea is being added or that the author is giving an example. . . . *However* is being used here to tell us that this sentence contrasts with this one. Carla shows us that you can replace it with *but.* So, Carla, can you help me to paraphrase what these two sentences mean, again?

FIGURE 2.2. Metalinguistic talk in the classroom.

The second category of talk that fosters skills in ALs consists of discussions focused on conceptually rich curricular topics that are often expressed through ALs. Like metalinguistic talk, these discussions recognize students' agency and promote the use of all of their language resources in order to communicate thinking and ideas. When these discussions are of high quality, they allow multiple opportunities for students to build on the language of peers and teachers, and educators serve as skilled facilitators supporting students to produce more talk. In addition, talk that involves peers allows students to be exposed to authentic language models. In a recent large-scale study of 53 fourth- to eighth-grade classrooms, my colleagues and I found that in classrooms where this talk was more common, students' CALS grew more quickly (Phillips Galloway & McClain, 2020). This was true both for students designated as English-proficient and for English learners, with both groups demonstrating the fastest growth in classrooms where language levels were heterogeneous. In other words, talk is a primary driver of language growth in middle childhood, and more so in settings where students bring varying levels of ALs.

We have long known from the literature in early child language development that talk—as a forum for learning language and for learning about language—is a powerful driver of language growth. Classrooms, however, become quieter and quieter with each year of schooling. The research above suggests that developing students' skills in ALs is a matter of creating opportunities for talk, which can serve as a forum for noticing how language works and for practicing less familiar ALs.

Academic Vocabulary in the Content Areas

Dianna Townsend, University of Nevada, Reno

Mr. Mendocino's sixth-grade social studies students are sitting in table groups. There are books, articles, and photographs related to the concepts of community and identity scattered across their tables. Drawing from both the National Council for the Social Studies (2013) College, Career, and Civic Life (C3) Framework and the newly revised standards for social studies in the state of Nevada (Nevada Department of Education, 2018), Mr. Mendocino is helping his students work toward the following two standards as they begin their year together, studying early world civilizations:

- SS.6-8.EWC.14. Describe the factors that shape identity—including institutions, religion, language, social class, geography, culture, and society in ancient civilizations.
- SS.6-8.EWC.25. Compare and contrast government structures, processes, and laws within and across early civilizations.

The students are reviewing local newspaper articles, photos of area events and festivals, maps of local neighborhoods, lists of local businesses and organizations, and other artifacts representing the different communities of which many students are members. Mr. Mendocino has asked the students to create a list of all of the communities—as small as their immediate families and as large as entire regions or cultures—to which they feel they belong. Next, he will have students explore how those communities have contributed to their identities. Using Community/Identity maps (i.e., graphic organizers with Venn diagrams), students are charting their thinking about their identities and the communities to which they belong. Following this work, the students will explore the definitions of *community* and *identity* in Figure 2.3, which come from Vocabulary.com (*www.vocabulary.com*). Mr. Mendocino prefers this online dictionary tool because of its student-friendly and often humorous definitions, as well as the many examples of word usage in authentic sources that it includes.

Mr. Mendocino has chosen not to start with these definitions, because he wants students to recognize the multifaceted nature of these words. He wants them to be able to apply a deep understanding of *community* and *identity* to the multiple cultures, geographic regions, and civilizations they will be studying. So he begins by sending them into their own worlds first, in order to personalize and explore what *community* and *identity* mean in their own lives. The definitions come next, and both the deep personalization and the definitions will serve as anchors as they move forward in their unit of study.

Marzano (2004) asserted, and Mr. Mendocino would likely agree, that students' background knowledge is represented by their vocabulary knowledge. This is also the case for academic vocabulary and the background knowledge students need for learning and problem solving in the disciplines. Deep and enduring knowledge of concepts is often the anchor and organizer for disciplinary knowledge more broadly (National Academies of Sciences, Engineering, and Medicine, 2018). If we want to

Community:	**Identity:**
If a number of people consider themselves one group based on location, work, religion, nationality, or even activity, they can be called a community. If you like to play online games, you are active in the gamer *community*.	Your identity is what makes you "you." If you are having "an *identity* crisis," then I guess you can't figure out who you are. Good luck with that.
The original meaning of Latin *communitatem* "a sense of fellowship" shifted to mean "a specific group of people with a common interest" during the Middle Ages. The modern English word *community* has both of these meanings available. Street festivals or school fairs can help to develop a sense of community in schools or neighborhoods. If you start a campaign to clean up the community, you want to make the area you live in more attractive.	The noun *identity* can also refer to a name or persona. Criminals tend to use false identities so they won't get caught. If you falsely identify someone, it is a case of "mistaken *identity*." The word *identity* doesn't have to be used for a single person either. People refer to "corporate *identity*" when talking about what makes a company unique.

FIGURE 2.3. Definitions of *community* and *identity* from Vocabulary.com.

support students with learning in the academic disciplines, we need to be intentional and strategic in how we help students build that deep and enduring word knowledge.

Decades of vocabulary research have given us guiding principles for how to do just this (Beck, McKeown, & Kucan, 2013; Graves, August, & Mancilla-Martinez, 2013). If we want *all* of our students, with their varied language and cultural backgrounds, to develop deep conceptual knowledge in the disciplines, we need to provide effective academic vocabulary instruction. This includes providing students with multiple exposures to words in multiple contexts, opportunities to practice and personalize word meanings, and independent word-learning strategies. And these approaches are particularly important for the challenges of academic vocabulary.

What Makes Academic Vocabulary *Academic?*

Academic vocabulary words are typically abstract, or technical, or both. They are generally not high-frequency words in fiction texts or in spoken language, but they appear with regularity in written academic and informational texts. As noted in Chapter 1 of this book, academic vocabulary is often conceptualized in two main categories: *general academic* words and *domain-specific* words. These categories are not hard and fast, but they constitute a useful framework for thinking about the kinds of words we want students to learn. Domain-specific words are often the conceptual and technical anchors for learning in the disciplines—words like *mitosis* and *democracy*. General academic words are those high-utility words that appear frequently in academic language in all content areas—words like *establish* and *process*. The line between the two types of words can easily be blurred, however. Words like *force, function, conjecture,* and *area* are *polysemous* (pə•li´•sə•məs); that is, they have multiple meanings. Polysemous words often have specific, technical meanings in one domain and more general, adaptable meanings for other domains.

Furthermore, some of the concepts that we target for deep and enduring knowledge, like the terms *identity* and *community* in the opening vignette, are essential for historical thinking while also used in other domains. So, rather than focusing too much on categorizing words as general academic or domain-specific, it may be more useful to think about targeting words that support the disciplinary objective and then to explore how those words play out in other academic and nonacademic contexts.

Academic Vocabulary in the Content Areas

Following are brief explanations of what characterizes academic vocabulary in the four primary content areas. Most important in the following descriptions is that academic vocabulary does not exist in a vacuum. Rather, it is embedded in the linguistic features and discourse patterns of each discipline (Snow & Uccelli, 2009). The primary implication of this is that we need to attend simultaneously to important vocabulary words *and* to how and why they are used in a given context.

In the domain of **English/language arts** (ELA), many words worthy of instructional time do not fit neatly into the general academic and domain-specific categories. ELA will certainly include general academic words like *analyze* and *function,* as well as domain-specific words like *metaphor* and *iambic pentameter.* However, at least one more category of words is essential to studying literature, poetry, and drama, and that is *literary vocabulary* (Baumann & Graves, 2010). To do the work of ELA, which includes things like analyzing tone, characters, and author's purpose, students need to build ownership of the descriptive and literary words an author uses to convey nuanced stories and messages. In Pam Muñoz Ryan's (2000) book *Esperanza Rising,* the Ortega family owned and ran a large ranch in Aguascalientes, Mexico, in 1930. Early in the novel, in the chapter "Las Uvas," Muñoz Ryan describes how the main character and only child of the Ortegas, Esperanza, was feeling when her father was late to come home after a day working with the cattle. She was waiting in the garden for him, and he had never previously given her reason to worry. While she was waiting, she picked a red flower, and "pricked her finger on a vicious thorn." She immediately concluded that the prick was an omen of bad luck, and she tried to brush away the feeling, but it lingered while she waited for her father.

There are many candidates for vocabulary learning in the excerpt from *Esperanza Rising* that tell this part of the story. Literary vocabulary like *vicious, pearls, horizon,* and *uneasiness* appear and lend a great deal of meaning to the passage and to the tone it creates. Other words from the passage, like *automatically, dismissed,* and *cautiously,* could be targeted because they are important in the passage, while also having utility in other domains (i.e., as general academic vocabulary). Finally, a teacher may choose to focus on an ELA domain-specific academic word from the passage, like *premonition,* and connect it to words that are not in the passage, like *omen* and *symbol,* as well as to the literary move of *foreshadowing.*

Mathematics also has a unique set of academic language demands for students (Schleppegrell, 2007). Math vocabulary usage requires precision, because symbols, numbers, and words have to map onto each other exactly. For example, consider the fifth-grade math problem in Figure 2.4. Along with the question, students need to attend to a diagram, whole numbers, and fractions. They need to know that "which number" refers to the mixed number options at the bottom of the problem. They also need to know that "the one shown" refers to a number that is represented by the diagram. Finally, they need to know that the diagram has multiple components, but that all of the components together represent one number. While students would not typically be challenged by words like *which, number, one,* and *shown,* when those words map onto abstract representations of quantity in an abstract diagram, they present an entirely new level of challenge. An additional challenge with math words is their polysemous nature. In other words, many math vocabulary words have multiple meanings: technical, domain-specific meanings in math, and more general meanings that apply to other domains (Zwiers, 2014). Consider, for example, the math meanings and the additional meanings of words like *plane, point, area,* and *variable.*

In the domain of **science,** students are often challenged by large quantities of technical terms, most of which are organized into hierarchies and other classification systems (Brown, Ryoo, & Rodriguez, 2010). To situate science research findings in the previously established knowledge of a topic, writers rely on precise, concise, and technical language in science (Fang, 2012). A by-product of this approach to conveying information is density; in other words, conceptual information is tightly packed

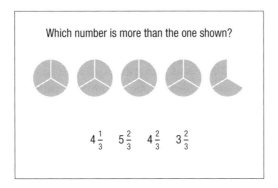

FIGURE 2.4. Fifth-grade math problem.

into each word, phrase, and sentence. Consider the vocabulary from one paragraph from a National Geographic Society (2019a) article (adapted to sixth-grade level through the website Newsela): *physical, chemical, atoms, molecules, oxygen, dense,* and *hydrogen.* These domain-specific words are used in conjunction with a number of general academic words, including *present, substance, undergo, exists, properties, constant,* and *naturally.* These words all appear in a passage that is only 94 words long, resulting in a high density of both language and ideas.

Finally, in **social studies**, academic vocabulary poses two specific challenges. First, students need to apply abstract ideas like *conflict* and *progress* to multiple eras, events, and historical figures. Second, historical study inevitably includes a close look at causality, and the language used to demonstrate cause and effect can be quite nuanced and implicit (Fang, 2012). For example, in another National Geographic Society (2019b) article adapted to sixth-grade level by Newsela, the authors explain causes of the American Revolutionary War. However, rather than use the explicit terms *cause* and *effect,* the authors use more implicit causal phrases such as *brought about* and *it was rooted in.* In addition, the article employs many domain-specific and general academic words, including *transportation, communication, economic, social, political, American Revolution,* and *infrastructure.* However, the significance of these concepts could potentially be lost without attention to the causal language.

Learning Academic Vocabulary

What do these intensive vocabulary demands suggest about vocabulary instruction? First, notice that the heading of this subsection is "*Learning* Academic Vocabulary," as opposed to "*Teaching* Academic Vocabulary." An emphasis on learning words rather than teaching words pushes us to ask, "What opportunities to learn and practice do my students need to learn these words?" Instead of focusing on "covering words" for our students, we need to focus on creating opportunities to practice and personalize word meanings. Practicing with words encourages productive vocabulary knowledge (Webb, 2005). And productive vocabulary knowledge is the depth of knowledge we need to understand words in nuanced and contextualized ways in the disciplines, as well as to generate those words in appropriate ways in speaking and writing.

Along with engaging explicit instruction, we need to put students in charge of *using* the words (Townsend, 2015). They need opportunities to read, write, and discuss the words that will give them the most leverage in disciplinary learning. And to meet the needs of *all* students, they need opportunities to personalize their word knowledge, making connections to the language, community, and cultural resources they bring to the classroom. Mr. Mendocino's approach encourages both this practice and personalization, via the following steps:

1. Students generate existing background knowledge on targeted academic vocabulary.
2. Teachers offer engaging, explicit instruction to begin deepening word knowledge as it relates to the content area, text, and other in- and out-of-school contexts.
3. Using teacher-created prompts and activities, students practice with and personalize word meanings, bridging their existing background knowledge with new knowledge.

In sum, academic vocabulary words that are worth learning are worthy of multiple opportunities for practice and personalizing. And exploring how and why those words are used in disciplinary texts and contexts will connect students' developing concept knowledge to the broader discourse patterns in disciplines, supporting their reading, writing, speaking, and listening in the content areas.

Vocabulary Instruction and Multimedia for Students with Disabilities: Providence or Pitfall?

Michael J. Kennedy, University of Virginia

At the hypothetical intersection of content that only contestants on *Jeopardy!* need to know and "I can't believe how much I have to teach" resides content-area vocabulary. In other words, the amount of vocabulary that students need to learn is rivaled only by the technical and complex nature of many terms within the curriculum. Teachers could spend all day every day teaching little more than vocabulary and still not get through it all. It is within this omnipresent yet obtuse issue that the purpose for this chapter arises: If vocabulary teaching and learning constitute such a challenge for typically developing students, what must the challenge be for students with disabilities?

It is true that some words are harder for students to learn than others, given frequency of use in daily life (or lack thereof) and characteristics of the words. However, most students are typically successful, if exposed to a steady diet of teachers using evidence-based practices (e.g., explicit instruction of specific terms, word-learning strategies) and if given multiple opportunities to learn and use the terms in various contexts (Graves, 2006). Many students also learn new vocabulary by reading texts assigned by teachers, or by reading for pleasure at home. Nonetheless, even when the best available evidence-based practices and appropriate opportunities to use the term in various contexts are provided, some students remain unsuccessful. Overall, students with disabilities are significantly hindered by the volume and complexity of vocabulary present within many upper-elementary and secondary-level content courses (Elleman, Lindo, Morphy, & Compton, 2009).

Students with Disabilities and Vocabulary Learning

Students with disabilities—defined here as students with individualized education programs (IEPs) who receive special education services, but do so primarily within the general education classroom (e.g., students with learning disabilities, autism spectrum disorder, behavioral disorders, ADHD, or communication disorders)—often need instruction and other interventions that are more intensive than the approaches to learning vocabulary discussed in the other portions of this volume. This is not to say that those practices are not effective, but these students often need something more. General educators therefore have a critical role to play in supporting students with IEPs in their classrooms. *Intensive intervention* is a process containing a continuum of specialized supports delivered by a special educator or other specialist (e.g., use of standardized curriculum for instruction, ongoing progress monitoring, diagnostic testing, team-based and data-driven decision making) that are far more intensive and individualized than what can be reasonably expected to occur within the general education classroom (Fuchs, Fuchs, & Vaughn, 2014). For content related to intensive intervention, please visit the National Center on Intensive Intervention website (*www.intensiveintervention.org*).

Mismatch of Student Needs and Prevailing Pedagogies

Although some students with IEPs have access to individualized, intensive interventions in a one-on-one or very-small-group setting (e.g., Tier 3), they usually receive core instruction within the general education classroom. This is particularly true for students as they make the transition from the upper elementary to middle school grades (National Center for Education Statistics, 2019). Thus, their first exposure to content-area vocabulary is typically provided by their general education teachers, who may or may not use evidence-based practices at the dosage and intensity needed to support learning outcomes for these students (Kennedy, Deshler, & Lloyd, 2015). A special educator (and other specialists) is responsible for augmenting instruction occurring within a general education classroom. However, the classroom teacher can do much to support vocabulary instruction. Yet numerous observational studies report general educators as having questionable implementation of practices known to improve literacy outcomes for upper elementary students with disabilities (Ciullo, Ely, McKenna, Alves, & Kennedy, 2019; Klingner, Urbach, Golos, Brownell, & Menon, 2010). Instead, observers in the aforementioned studies documented some teachers using ineffective practices, such as providing vocabulary instruction by having students copy the definitions off a board or overhead projector. Though this is a questionable practice for all students, most students are able to complete the task of copying the notes. Nonetheless, without discussion or elaboration, the exercise is not likely to be successful for all students.

Reasons why students with disabilities struggle are numerous, but they often include the number of terms to learn (Ebbers & Denton, 2008), the pacing and structure of instruction (Berkeley, Mastropieri, & Scruggs, 2011), and within-student issues related to cognitive functionality (Johnson, Humphrey, Mellard, Woods, & Swanson, 2010). An example of the last reason is auditory processing capacity. When instruction is orally driven, teachers expect students to listen to what they are saying and learn the content. However, this creates a mismatch between pedagogy and student learning capacity, as many students with disabilities have working memory processes that function imperfectly, compared to those of typically developing learners. In other words, students with an auditory processing disorder or other disorder affecting cognition may have severe difficulty taking active cognitive action (e.g., making fast connections between working memory processes and schemas in long-term memory) when they only have one, orally driven chance to hear new content. Each of these issues, either independently or in combination with others, can result in significant inability to learn new vocabulary terms. While teachers do not have control over the amount of content in the curriculum (which affects the number of new terms to learn), they can make individual decisions about chunking information and using various modes of instruction.

The purpose of this section of this chapter is to highlight effective vocabulary practices for students with disabilities that can be deployed to help expedite and ensure the students' success. Included in the discussion is how multimedia approaches can be levers in improving vocabulary teaching and student learning. Technology is often thought of as a panacea to help promote engagement within vocabulary learning, but empirical research evidence to support that belief is usually limited (at best) or altogether absent. Therefore, a key thesis of this section is for practitioners and other school leaders to be thoughtful about the extent to which instruction, including new technologies, is appropriate for supporting students' individualized vocabulary-learning needs.

Explicit Instruction for Vocabulary Terms

Many researchers consider explicit instruction to be the backbone of effective vocabulary instruction for all students (Archer & Hughes, 2011; Bryant, Goodwin, Bryant, & Higgins, 2003; Jitendra, Edwards, Sacks, & Jacobson, 2004). Explicit instruction consists of clear and repeated teacher explanations of content, including student-friendly definitions and use of relevant examples; multiple opportunities for students to respond, along with matching feedback; teacher modeling while thinking aloud; use of guided practice; and overseeing independent use of content or practices by students, while providing feedback (Hughes, Morris, Therrien, & Benson, 2017). The *model, lead, practice/test* approach, sometimes called "I do, we do, you do," is key within explicit instruction. Meaningful repetition (not so-called "drill and kill"), with authentic opportunities for students to respond to teacher prompts, is essential. This can include a series of questions at various levels of difficulty intended to confirm student learning of the new term. An example of a deep or probing question might be "Why is photosynthesis critical for human life on Earth?" The answer requires the definition of photosynthesis, but also capacity to apply that knowledge. This is more complex than a student's parroting back the answer to "What is photosynthesis?" Explicit instruction also emphasizes teacher-provided cues to orient students to pay attention to key information, the breaking of meaty topics into manageable chunks, and instruction that follows a logical sequence (Archer & Hughes, 2011).

When teaching vocabulary within an explicit framework, the effective teacher provides (1) a review of background knowledge and confirms understanding of that background knowledge; (2) a student-friendly definition (i.e., free from other terms that potentially need to be defined); and (3) a range of examples (and when appropriate, non-examples) with a confirmation of student understanding for each. The effective teacher might also (when appropriate) select from a menu of practices, including teaching morphological parts of terms, highlighting semantic relationships among related terms, providing a demonstration, and engaging students in a discussion (Bryant et al., 2003; Jitendra et al., , 2004). Each practice within this explicit framework is repeated (individually or in combination) as needed, because students with disabilities often need more than 10 unique and meaningful exposures to a term before mastering the content. A library of multimedia vignettes that provides guidance and demonstrations of these practices is available at *https://vimeo.com/channels/1466441*. It is highly unlikely that a student with a disability such as a specific learning disability (e.g., dyslexia), autism spectrum disorder, intellectual disability, or a communication disorder will successfully learn new and complex vocabulary without sustained instruction of this sort.

Tension between Need for Best Practice and Limited Instructional Time

The amount of time it takes to provide explicit instruction as described above is substantial. As such, it may bump up against both teacher knowledge and readiness to implement explicit instruction with fidelity (Dingle, Brownell, Leko, Boardman, & Haager, 2011), and pressures related to pacing guides and other variables within the curriculum (Kennedy, Rodgers, Romig, Mathews, & Peeples, 2018). These concerns are valid: Teachers could easily spend literally hours per day explicitly teaching vocabulary, given the volume of terms within content-area courses; obviously, this is not a realistic possibility. The tension between the need to move quickly and the learning needs of students with disabilities often comes to a head with regard to vocabulary. Teachers often find themselves in the paradoxical situation of needing students to learn and understand key vocabulary, but not having the time or pedagogical skill needed to ensure mastery.

While learning and achievement within upper elementary and middle school courses requires more than just vocabulary, success without strong vocabulary in place is unlikely. This is one reason why intensive intervention is so important: It enables special educators and other specialists to provide (1) standardized instruction using evidence-based practices (which include principles of explicit instruction); (2) frequent progress monitoring; and (3) nimble decisions for needed instructional changes, based on input from a team of professionals armed with the best available data (Lindström, Gesel, & Lemons, 2019). General educators play an important role in this process, as they likely spend the most time with these students. A special educator working within an intensive intervention framework can provide the explicit instruction described above in the amounts needed to help support students' needs; however, this too takes substantial time, so schools need to make hard decisions about how resources will be allocated. For example, students who require Tier 3 intensive intervention are likely to need word-level reading instruction in addition to their vocabulary needs. In sum, the field has solid knowledge regarding what works to support these students' vocabulary-learning needs, but many schools struggle or fail to find a way to ensure that those practices are implemented with fidelity.

Generative Word-Learning Strategies

One solution offered by researchers to combat this issue is to teach students *generative word-learning strategies* to help them develop skills and strategies to unlock the meanings of unknown words on their own. Generative word-learning strategies focus on teaching students to understand the meaning of morphemes within terms—a strategy that plays a prominent role in this text—and to use that knowledge to figure out, or at least make a good guess at, what a term means (Harris, Shumaker, & Deshler, 2011). For example, a student who learns the meaning of the prefix *bio-* can potentially understand a substantial number of terms that have something to do with "life." However, teachers still need to take significant time to explicitly teach students the meanings of these morphological parts, and provide meaningful opportunities for practice and deliver feedback.

While there are other evidence-based practices for teaching vocabulary to students with disabilities (see Bryant et al., 2003; Jitendra et al., 2004; Kuder, 2017), providing explicit instruction and generative word-learning strategies remain two of the most essential practices. Some researchers and practitioners have turned to multimedia as a potential solution to help general and special educators provide a higher dosage of evidence-based vocabulary instruction to students with disabilities. However, as previously noted, caution is needed. Important questions remain regarding the extent to which the specially designed instruction called for within students' IEPs can be provided by an app or other technology tool not specifically designed for those students (Thomas, Peeples, Kennedy, & Decker, 2019). A brief introduction to some multimedia options for supporting vocabulary instruction to this population is provided next.

Multimedia-Based Vocabulary Instruction for Students with Disabilities: What Works?

Multimedia approaches are everywhere in today's schools. Teachers use technology in presentations, to collect and house assignments and content, and as a tool that students can access independently to learn new content. When teaching students with disabilities and others who struggle, teachers must ensure that whatever instruction is provided meets the standard of being specially designed, as called for in the students' IEPs. Few technology-based products meet this standard, particularly in the domain of vocabulary instruction.

Content Acquisition Podcasts and Underlying Theory

For as prominent an issue as vocabulary learning is for students with disabilities, and for as long as multimedia has been a viable packaging and delivery mechanism within education, there is surprisingly little by way of empirical evidence in this space (Boyle & Kennedy, 2019). One multimedia approach with multiple empirical research articles backing its use is that of *content acquisition podcasts* (CAPs; Kennedy et al., 2015; Kennedy, Thomas, Meyer, Alves, & Lloyd, 2014). CAPs are short multimedia vignettes that combine principles of explicit instruction and Mayer's (2008) cognitive theory of multimedia learning (CTML) to deliver focused instruction for one vocabulary term at a time.[1] CAPs constitute an approach to marrying evidence-based instructional and design principles that practitioners should consider for use with students with disabilities (and all students).

Implications of Cognitive Functionality for Learning

In brief, Mayer's (2008) theory takes into account that learners have limited working memory resources at any given time, which can easily lead to a lack of remembering new information such as vocabulary terms. Working memory resources are resilient and can snap back quickly from being overwhelmed; in schools, however, cognitive overload is a setback for students, and often causes the students to miss key information if given only one chance to learn (Feldon, 2007). In other words, if teachers present vocabulary instruction in a way that results in cognitive overload, and do not take time to evaluate whether students have learned the term, they may erroneously assume that the students have learned it and move on. Because cognitive overload is often invisible, teachers can easily miss when students have become lost. In addition, teachers themselves are subject to cognitive overload. An overloaded teacher is unlikely to remember to scan the room and evaluate student learning, or to use evidence-based practices with fidelity (Feldon, 2007).

Off-the-Rack Technology

Besides the potential for cognitive overload, students with disabilities often have imperfect or impaired cognitive processing capacity, which is a further barrier to learning. As a result, it is extremely easy for students with disabilities to have their limited cognitive functioning capabilities overwhelmed (Kennedy & Wexler, 2013). Many applications of technology cause cognitive overload for students, given their fast pace, assumed background knowledge, inclusion of jargon and other unknown terms, and lack of specific evidence-based practices.

Two examples of this are the videos on photosynthesis from the Khan Academy[2] and from BrainPOP.[3] The Khan Academy and BrainPOP are well-known and often-used sources for supplemental learning tools in schools. Many students can and do learn from these tools. However, these videos are not necessarily intended for use with students with disabilities. But, since teachers use them in this way, a word of caution is warranted. Both videos are fast-paced, assume significant background knowledge, and use multiple terms that a student who is struggling would be unlikely to know. The results may be cognitive overload and a lack of learning. This is especially true if a teacher has assigned students to watch these videos in class or independently, without any immediate assessment of their understanding or support for learning.

Comparison to CAPs

CAPs are different from BrainPOP and Khan Academy videos in that they are intended for students with disabilities, and they embed evidence-based practices for teaching vocabulary. In each CAP,

---

[1] A sample CAP can be seen at *http://qmediaplayer.com/show.htm?1000*.
[2] Kahn Academy video: *www.khanacademy.org/science/biology/photosynthesis-in-plants/introduction-to-stages-of-photosynthesis/v/photosynthesis*.
[3] BrainPOP video: *www.brainpop.com/science/cellularlifeandgenetics/photosynthesis*.

there is an explicit instructional sequence: review of critical background knowledge, student-friendly definition, example, non-example (when appropriate), a breakdown of morphological word parts (when appropriate), comparison with similar terms, and a repeat of the definition. The vignettes contain clear images; some specific on-screen text to highlight essential information (like the definition); and narration that is deliberate in both pacing and word choice. No extraneous or other potentially distracting information is included. Students can watch these vignettes in class, or independently, as many times as needed until they master the content. Use of CAPs also reinforces teachers' use of the embedded evidence-based practices (Peeples et al., 2019).

Making Good Choices

Decision makers in schools who are considering adopting technology to support vocabulary learning and other academic needs must weigh the empirical evidence supporting the use of this technology. In instances where such evidence is not yet available, careful study of the tools' theoretical underpinnings and instructional design features should occur. For example, even without the two published studies documenting the success of students who were learning with CAPs, an evaluation of these tools reveals the use of explicit instruction, as well as Mayer's (2008) validated design principles. A similar look at a Khan Academy video would not result in the same conclusion. BrainPOP videos do adhere to many of Mayer's design principles, but are not explicit in nature when it comes to teaching vocabulary. Again, neither sample video is trying to do what CAPs are made to do, but teachers rely on them in the same way, regardless of students' learning needs. This criticism is thus needed and valid.

When decision makers are applying the standard of empirical evidence to vocabulary instruction, it is critical for them to evaluate the extent to which evidence-based practices are present within the multimedia. If the videos incorporate explicit instruction, use rich imagery, have repetition, promote understandings of terms from multiple perspectives, provide opportunities to answer questions or write, or have other features such as cognitive anchors (specific connections made to content or objects students already know), they may be an appropriate match for students' needs.

Conclusion

Explicit instruction is the foundation of effective vocabulary instruction for students with disabilities (Archer & Hughes, 2011; Kennedy et al., 2015). Whether the explicit instruction is teacher-provided, or intersects with a multimedia packaging and delivery system, these principles (e.g., lots of opportunities to respond with matching feedback; teacher modeling; use of examples and images; and opportunities for students to practice independently through reading, writing, and sharing ideas with teachers and peers) give students their best chance to learn voluminous and complex terms. Embedding these practices within multimedia such as CAPs sets students up to learn new terms, but it serves the additional purpose of helping teachers see examples of implementation with fidelity, which can transfer into their teaching repertoires (Peeples et al., 2019).

Build Vocabulary Storage and Knowledge with Definition Work and Semantic Reasoning Lessons

Beth Lawrence, InferCabulary

Over the past 25 years as a speech–language pathologist, I have specialized in working with students who struggle with language and literacy. In recent years, my work has significantly emphasized vocabulary instruction. This emphasis began when an eighth-grade student was unable to demonstrate deep understanding of words, despite my best efforts at using state-of-the-art instruction methods. In searching for something that would work for this one student, I stumbled onto an approach that my colleague Deena Seifert and I would later name *semantic reasoning*.

In this contribution, I explain the rationale and process for using vocabulary interventions that develop knowledge of semantic relationships and semantic reasoning ability. Each approach aims to help students build their knowledge of and capacity to remember vocabulary, but in different ways.

Developing Knowledge of Semantic Relationships: Definition Template and Category Circles

What happens if older students lack well-developed neural networks for vocabulary, due to language or learning disabilities or to impoverished language environments? Among other things, they are far less likely to verbally formulate accurate definitions for common items (e.g., "A table is a kind of furniture that you put objects on. It has legs and a flat top") than their peers (Dockrell & Messer, 2004; Marinellie & Johnson, 2002; McGregor, Oleson, Bahnsen, & Duff, 2013). I have found working on oral and written definitions to be one of the most effective strategies not only for improving expressive language skills, but for improving depth of understanding of words, and shoring up foundational semantic relationship skills.

When I ask the students I work with (mostly bright, college-bound upper elementary and middle school students with language and/or learning differences) to define *table*, they tend to respond along the lines of "It's wood. You eat on it," or "It's a thing you have in your house." These types of responses are more similar to those of typically developing children under the age of 5, who are not including relational/superordinate information (Marinellie & Johnson 2002; Dockrell & Messer, 2004). Typically, older students have strong vocabulary "networks" in their minds, such as *banana–yellow–monkey–pie–crescent-shaped-fruit*. Each new encounter or context such a student has with *banana* (verbally, experientially, or from reading) is added to the network, thereby deepening the student's understanding of that word. When students "store words" within categories, they are more likely to retrieve the word *banana* easily in conversation, or *fruit* as the category label. Category labels are very important for word storage, and are important for quickly conveying meaning in speech or writing.

Students who provide vague definitions tend to exhibit word retrieval deficits, and/or to have difficulty learning and associating new words with already known words. Because their vocabulary foundation is not well structured, it becomes increasingly difficult for them to add and organize the new, sophisticated, nuanced words they encounter in the upper grades.

I work on the following definition activity with students of all ages, because I have observed that it powerfully improves students' word retrieval abilities and their structures for future vocabulary learning. In order to help improve students' foundational semantic skills (e.g., categorization skills and recognition of semantic features, such as function, parts, and attributes), I use the following process:

1. Project or provide handouts of the template in Figure 2.5.
2. Address each of the following aspects systematically:
   a. ***The complex concept of the category label.*** First, ask students to retrieve the category label for *table*—vague labels such as *thing* and *stuff* are not permitted! Similar to the orderly storage of items in a dresser or on shelves, category labels quickly orient the listener. If the student says "thing," the listener has millions of options to consider; however, if the student begins the definition with "a kind of furniture," the options are narrowed down to about 15 possible items. Because it is likely that at least some of our students will struggle with retrieving category labels to support them, draw a large circle on the board. Words

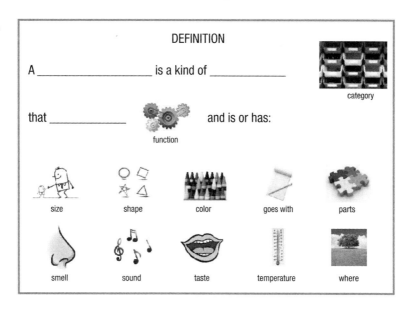

FIGURE 2.5. Definition template. Copyright © 2017 InferCabulary. Reproduced with permission.

and/or images that share a common thread can be grouped together, either fitting into or being excluded from the circle. In the example of *table*, if a student has called it a "thing" or otherwise struggled to retrieve the category, ask the student to draw a picture of a table inside the circle. Then prompt with "What are some other things that are sort of like a table?" Besides cues, the student might add drawings of a chair, bed, dresser, or the like. In my experience, with this support, it is very likely that the student will retrieve the category label *furniture*. If the student really does not know the category label, you can provide it and spend more time fleshing out this category.

b. *Function.* Once the category label has been retrieved or reviewed, the next step in the definition is to ask students how this item, *table,* differs from all the other items in the circle/category by eliciting its function. Many of my students need support with this. Again, visuals can be very helpful. You might use an image of a cogwheel associated with the written word *function* and/or a hand gesture to show movement, paired with the phrase, "What does it do?" After your students share the function, write that into the definition template. The definition for *table* is now "a kind of furniture that you put objects on."

c. *Traits.* In order to complete the definition, encourage students to think about what the item is made of/what parts it has, and add these aspects to the final part of the definition.

I have found that this activity, done two to three times per week, serves to shore up some foundational weaknesses in students' semantic relationship skills, enabling me to focus more effectively on instruction of more complex words.

Developing Semantic Reasoning Ability

As students move into upper elementary and middle school, they become increasingly responsible for learning less common, more nuanced, and conceptual vocabulary (Nagy, 2005; Nippold, 2002). There are many research-supported, state-of-the-art vocabulary instruction methods (Baumann, Kame'enui, & Ash, 2003; Beck et al., 2013; Ganske, this volume) that I've effectively used to help many students over the years. To these excellent techniques, I have added one more approach to my work with many students. In a 2019 TEDx talk,[4] I explained that one of my eighth-grade students struggled to learn nuanced word meanings even with morphology, multisensory instruction, and student-friendly definitions. She had avoided reading throughout elementary and middle school. As a result, she was not encountering multiple contexts of words like *prominent* and *prudent* over those years. Because she was not encountering these words by reading, my student had at best only a shallow understanding of these words, which in turn had a significant negative impact on her reading comprehension.

When I considered that this student had strong nonverbal reasoning skills but poor language skills, it struck me that there might be a better way for her to learn nuanced word meanings. Instead of using language to introduce her to a word (i.e., with a definition), she might be more interested (and successful) if I taught her word meanings with a visual approach that would enable her to use her critical thinking strengths to infer the definition for herself.

Soon after beginning to use this new approach, my student demonstrated significantly improved word learning (i.e., increased scores on vocabulary tests, qualitatively improved reading comprehension, and appropriate use of words in new contexts both orally and in writing). I was encouraged to share this approach with others at regional and national conferences. Because teachers found creating these lessons very useful but time-consuming, I partnered with Deena Seifert, another speech–language pathologist, and created a K–12 technology application that has semantic reasoning at its core. It is called InferCabulary (*https://infercabulary.com*). In the program, words are listed by grade level and category type, and (as appropriate) are associated with literature titles, such as *Abuela, Holes, Hatchet, To Kill a Mockingbird,* and *Romeo and Juliet.* Below I highlight the K–12 web-based application; however, teachers can create their own lessons by using PowerPoint or Google Slides, and simply following the InferCabulary format.[5]

Semantic Reasoning Lessons Using InferCabulary

InferCabulary was designed with a mountain-climbing themed gamification: Students climb higher and higher, and conquer mountains, as they learn more vocabulary and earn climbing gear. The screenshots provided here show the Basecamp (learning) aspect of game play that is embedded in InferCabulary. The following lesson emphasizes more sophisticated words from the popular book *Tale of Despereaux,* by Kate DiCamillo (2003). The process works like this:

1. **Choose the words.** When teaching a new construct or approach, you may find it helpful to model the thought process aloud for students (Baumann, Jones, & Seifert-Kessell, 1993). Before students arrive in class, login to InferCabulary (*https://infercabulary.com*; a free demo is included), and search the "Book List" for *Tale of Despereaux.* A total of 120 words are currently associated with this text. Choose a nuanced word such as *burden, ornate, inexplicable, egregious,* or *deliberate.*

2. **Present the words.** Display on a whiteboard or overhead projector the six Basecamp images for this word, as shown in Figure 2.6. Note that the definition is *not* visible.

3. **Introduce the approach.** Once students arrive in the classroom, give an explanation like this one: "Typically programs will tell us just the meanings of words. With InferCabulary [or with the semantic reasoning approach, if teacher-created lessons are being used], we need to figure out the meanings for ourselves by inferring how all the images go together. Sometimes just the images will be

---

[4] Available at *www.youtube.com/watch?v=WVZkHFXPKo8.*

[5] For more detailed information, please refer to *https://infercabulary.com/wp-content/uploads/2016/11/infercabulary-pd-2018-pdf. pdf,* or to an education website that walks users through each step of preparing a semantic reasoning lesson (*https://edu.workbencheducation.com/cwists/cwistings/24203/19492*).

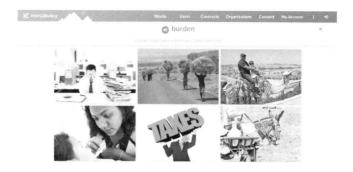

FIGURE 2.6. Basecamp screenshot for the word *burden* from InferCabulary.com. Copyright © 2019 InferCabulary. Reproduced with permission.

enough; at other times, the captions will support our thinking, and guide us to a deeper understanding of how this word could be used."

4. ***Speculate about the images.*** After the introduction to InferCabulary, read aloud the word *burden*, or click the audio button. Beginning in the upper left corner (see Figure 2.6), share aloud your thoughts about key features you see in that image. To encourage students to search deeply for common threads among images (which is the goal), it can be helpful to intentionally over-focus on a specific aspect of the first picture or two, and verbalize incorrect assumptions; then you can correct these misidentifications with later pictures. This process will lay the expectation for active engagement, and for a continual process whereby new context clues can lead to the expansion or retraction of an initial assumption. For example, starting in the upper left corner, you might reflect, "*Burden* might mean being stressed out at your desk. But wait, that can't be right: These people [point to the second image] are carrying huge piles of straw on their heads. The man in the first picture has a big pile of work on his desk. Maybe *burden* means 'a big pile'? No, that can't be right because this third picture shows people riding on a camel, so *burden* doesn't have to do with just a pile. Carrying all that does look kind of heavy for that poor camel. Maybe *burden* just means 'a lot of something'?" Continue sharing your internal thoughts with students with images in the second row. "Hmm. I'm not sure how a mom who looks worried about her sick child fits in here. We'll have to listen to the caption on that one." Point to the fifth picture, saying something like "Ugh, he looks stressed out over having a lot of taxes." Demonstrate your "aha moment" at finding the common thread with something like this: "Aha, maybe *burden* has to do with having to carry a lot and it feels heavy to the one carrying it. Yep. That donkey sure has a lot to carry."

5. ***Verify and refine thinking with the captions.*** After demonstrating your thoughts based on viewing just the images, click the pictures one at a time to reveal their captions, as seen in Figure 2.7. As you read aloud each caption, emphasize the key words or phrases, and confirm your assumption aloud for students. For example, for the upper left example, say something like, "Yep, a TON of work." For the second image, repeat the phrase "a LOT of hay." For the third item, emphasize "an ENORMOUS AMOUNT OF WEIGHT."

At this point, it would be appropriate to demonstrate your "aha moment" by saying, "I think I was right!" Because the fourth image of the mom and sick child has been tricky, it would be appropriate to say something like "Ah, I get that picture now—the mom is SO WORRIED about her sick daughter that it feels like a big weight to her emotionally. Yep, that makes sense." Continue with the remaining items, emphasizing the key phrases "HUGE EMOTIONAL STRESS" and "a LOT on his back."

6. ***Synthesize a definition.*** Wrap up this aspect of your think-aloud by saying, "Before I click on

FIGURE 2.7. Basecamp screenshot with captions for the word *burden* from InferCabulary.com. Copyright © 2019 InferCabulary. Reproduced with permission.

the definition they have, I am going to infer the definition for myself, using some of the words and phrases from the captions. I think *burden* means a big or heavy physical or emotional weight someone has to carry."

7. **Confirm with the actual definition.** Finally, reveal the definition and confirm that the inference is correct.

Engaging Students

Ensuring that students understand and become familiar with the semantic reasoning approach is essential before they engage independently with InferCabulary (or teacher-created semantic reasoning lessons). The next part of the process is effective for large- or small-group instruction, and can be modified for one-to-one work. Here is the process:

1. **Present a new word to check for transfer of learning.** Invite students to try to infer the meaning of the word *inexplicable,* which can be found on the InferCabulary website, in the Word List, or by searching for *Tale of Despereaux,* as seen in Figure 2.8.

2. **Speculate about the images.** Invite students to share their thinking, one picture at a time,

FIGURE 2.8. Basecamp screenshot for the word *inexplicable* from InferCabulary.com. Copyright © 2019 InferCabulary. Reproduced with permission.

making sure that they add the concept of the new image to the prior images so that they can eventually determine the common thread. With semantic reasoning instruction, it is easy to ask students higher-order questions such as "Why do you think that?" and "What do those have in common?" during this process.

3. ***Verify and confirm thinking with the captions.*** Once students believe they have an idea of the meaning (call on them one student at a time, or in small groups), the next step is to click on one picture at a time, asking students to say (and/or write down) the key words or phrases in each caption (see Figure 2.9).

4. ***Synthesize a definition.*** Finally, ask one student to define the word *inexplicable*, or have a student discuss this with a partner. Peer conversation can be a powerful method for students to learn more deeply (Murphy, Wilkinson, Soter, Hennessey, & Alexander, 2009).

As an extension activity, have students discuss and provide two additional examples of something *inexplicable*. They might also practice using the word in a sentence. There are additional activity types embedded in InferCabulary that students can play to reinforce understanding, such as Climb mode (similar to the *Test of Semantic Reasoning*; Lawrence & Seifert, 2016) and synonym–antonym activities.

Independent Work

Once students demonstrate the skills necessary to infer meaning through using the semantic reasoning approach, they can work independently. Some classrooms opt to have InferCabulary as a station that students rotate through for 15–30 minutes apiece, to work toward standards-based vocabulary goals. Following is an example of such a goal—Common Core State Standard.ELA-Literacy.CCRA.L.6:

> Acquire and use accurately a range of general academic and domain-specific words and phrases sufficient for reading, writing, speaking, and listening at the college and career readiness level; demonstrate independence in gathering vocabulary knowledge when encountering an unknown term important to comprehension or expression. (National Governors Association Center for Best Practices & Council of Chief State School Officers, 2010)

Because InferCabulary has significant differentiation capabilities, students within a group can be assigned to any grade level, and/or words can be assigned by chapters in specific books or by category types, depending on an instructor's goals. Teachers who work with students learning English may find

FIGURE 2.9. Basecamp screenshot with captions for the word *inexplicable* from InferCabulary.com. Copyright © 2019 InferCabulary. Reproduced with permission.

the visual nature of this approach to be particularly helpful, although additional support may be necessary. When creating their own lessons, teachers might differentiate by reading groups.

Conclusion

For students who have not fully developed a systematic way to keep words organized in their minds, one of my favorite activities includes category/function/components work within a definition framework. For students who enter school with low vocabulary, and do not become avid readers or listen to audiobooks, semantic work is essential. I suggest that in addition to using many state-of-the-art instruction techniques that emphasize word interrelationships and morphology, teachers learn to create semantic reasoning activities and/or explore InferCabulary to help deepen students' understanding of word meanings.

Monster, PI: Morphology Assessment to Guide Instruction

Amanda P. Goodwin, Vanderbilt University,
with Yaacov Petscher, Florida State University; Dan Reynolds, John Carroll University;
Tess Lantos, Vanderbilt University; Katie Hughes, Florida State University;
and Sara Jones, Vanderbilt University

Throughout this book, there has been quite a bit of focus on *morphology*, or the way in which the language system conveys meaning by combining units of meaning like root words, suffixes, and prefixes. These units are combined in particular ways (*beehive*, not *hivebee*) to express different meanings (*distaste* vs. *tasty*) and fit into certain syntactic structures (e.g., grammatical roles: *tasteful, taste, tasty, taster*). Putting these units together in correct ways often involves shifts in sound, spelling, grammatical role, and meaning (e.g., *know, knowledge; benefit, beneficial*), which can present challenges to students learning to read and write. For example, young spellers may spell *magician* as *magition*, because they do not distinguish the suffixes *tion* and *ian*, which sound alike but have different meanings (Nunes & Bryant, 2006).

Morphological knowledge is important and links to spelling, reading, vocabulary, and even writing (see Nagy, Carlisle, & Goodwin, 2014, for an overview). Students who have morphological knowledge can often figure out the spellings, pronunciations, and meanings of unfamiliar words such as *nationalistic*, through analysis of the morphemic units and their composite meanings (Anglin, 1993; Nagy & Anderson, 1984). As Nunes and Bryant (2006, p. 157) suggest, "Some of the most important correspondences between spoken and written language are at the level of the morpheme. . . . The system of morphemes, therefore, is a powerful resource for those learning literacy."

In this brief contribution, we consider how to assess morphological knowledge in a way that provides deeper understandings and instructional insights. We take work suggesting that different aspects of morphological knowledge are important to literacy (Goodwin, Petscher, Carlisle, & Mitchell, 2017) one step further, in an effort to identify assessable and teachable morphological skills. Importantly, we have found that by assessing the four morphological skills described below, we were able to explain more than half the variance in standardized reading comprehension for a sample of students in grades 5–8, and that some of the skills were uniquely related to reading comprehension even after we accounted for decoding and other language skills such as vocabulary and syntax. In other words, these morphological skills are foundational to reading comprehension for upper elementary and middle school students. Therefore, knowing how our students are doing in these areas is important to informing our instruction.

Monster, PI

Some figures have suggested that students in today's schools spend more than a month in standardized testing. But although the standardized tests assess performance on outcomes like reading comprehension or skills within reading comprehension (such as main ideas or inferencing), they do not assess underlying skills that students use to get to the outcome (such as morphological knowledge, which has been shown to be important).

With that said, we didn't want to create just another test. We created a gamified, computer-adaptive measure, because reviews like that of Mitchell and Savill-Smith (2004) have highlighted the many positive outcomes of games, such as increases in motivation and self-esteem. Based on the gaming literature, we created a game, Monster, PI, where students take on the role of a detective who must hunt for clues to catch a monster who is wreaking havoc on various scenes in a city. The students solve puzzles, which earn them clues to the monster's identity; they ultimately must identify and catch the monster to "win" the game. Throughout the experience, the players also get to play 30-second "mini-games" as brain breaks.

We focused on middle school students because research indicates that knowledge of words, and of the units of meaning that make up words, is particularly critical for middle school readers (Beck & McKeown, 1991; Biemiller, 2001; Nagy & Anderson, 1984; Nagy & Scott, 2000). We have fully developed the assessment for middle school students, but pilot testing with third and fourth graders has also shown promise. Although it is possible that variations exist for such students, our overall work indicates that these instructional guidelines can be applicable for both upper elementary and middle school students, and important for their teachers to consider. Below, we report on results from working with 3,000 middle schoolers (fifth through eighth graders) across 3 years of development. We describe the four morphological skills that Monster, PI, develops, and we share links to instruction. For instructional articles showing more ways to apply the assessment data, see Goodwin and Perkins (2015), Goodwin, Cho, and Nichols (2016), and Goodwin, Lipsky, and Ahn (2012). You can also visit our website (*www.worddetectives.com*) for more information about Monster, PI, including access and links to instruction.

Development of the Assessment

The development of Monster, PI involved a rigorous process, because morphological knowledge is a complex construct consisting of multiple skills. Across 3 years, we piloted 15 morphological measures and 491 items, assessing a wide range of skills and tasks that we thought might be applicable for determining the morphological skills that students use to support literacy. Some measures and items worked better than others; ultimately, we used seven measures and 181 items delivered via computer-adaptive testing, so that students take the sample of items most closely related to their performance (Mitchell, Truckenmiller, & Petscher, 2015). Student ratings of the assessment suggested that they liked the gamification, with over 97% rating it at 3 stars or higher (out of 5), more than 75% rating it at 4 stars or higher, and 35% rating it at 5 stars. We note that the larger Monster, PI system assesses morphological, vocabulary, and syntactical knowledge, but we focus here on morphological knowledge because it helps the ideas about morphology within this book come to life.

Morphological Skills

Our results emphasize that *morphological knowledge is multidimensional:* Why students get items right or wrong is due in part to the structure of a task, but also due to their knowledge of each skill (described below) and their overall general morphological abilities. The morphological skills assessed by Monster,

PI, are these: (1) Students can identify units of meaning; (2) students can use suffixes to gain syntactic information; (3) students can use morphology for meaning; and (4) students can read and spell morphologically complex words. Skill 1 focuses on students' being aware of morphemes in general, and Skills 2–4 focus on different properties of morphemes (i.e., Skill 2 = syntactic, Skill 3 = semantic, Skill 4 = orthographic and phonological information conveyed by morphemes).

Skill 1: Students Can Identify Units of Meaning

We used two measures to assess whether students could identify units of meaning, in terms of both breaking words down and connecting them to larger words. We used a task titled Odd Man Out, where students are given sets of three words and must identify the word that does not belong in each set. For example, in the set *estimate*, *classmate*, and *roommate*, the morpheme *mate* in *classmate* and *roommate* represents the meaning of "a person." *Estimate* is the odd man out; it is the example where the morphemes do not overlap in terms of meaning. This task forces students to think about how written language conveys meaning. Our second measure, which we call Meaning Puzzles, asks students to identify the word part that is most helpful in determining the meaning of each word, which in this case can be a morpheme or a morphologically related word contained in the larger word. Here, students need to look beyond overlap in spelling to figure out the link to meaning. For example, *accusatory* has spelling overlap with *accurate*, *accuse*, *cushion*, and *custom*, but only *accuse* overlaps in terms of meaning. Hence students who know they can use *accuse* to figure out *accusatory*, rather than using *accurate*, are more likely to figure out the word's meaning and apply that meaning to their literacy endeavors. It is important to note that although we developed other tasks to identify units of meaning in words, these tasks worked best.

In terms of instruction, this skill highlights that we need to help our students think about morphological overlap between words. We need to constantly challenge students to think about how a word's form and sound convey links to other words in the same morphological family. For example, thinking about the relationship of *astronomy* to *astronaut*, and then about the units like *astr* = *star*, will build a strong foundation of understanding how units of meaning can be put together to convey meaning or even broken down to figure out meaning. We have observed instructional work where students eagerly look up word origins to find overlap; create word webs to identify morphological word families; and find "imposters," or tricky spellings that look like morphemes but are not (see Goodwin & Perkins, 2015, for examples).

Skill 2: Students Can Use Suffixes for Syntactic Information

While we tend to think about the semantic roles of morphemes, morphemes also play an important role in conveying syntactic information. In other words, knowing how to adapt or interpret the form of *detect* to fit the phrase "the *detection* of evidence" is important for helping students deal with the complex syntactical structures involved in texts, particularly structures related to academic language. Two measures assess this skill. The Real Word Suffix tasks give students a sentence like "The countries benefited _____ from their membership in the European Union." Students need to identify the correct form of the missing word, given four options (*financial*, *financially*, *finance*, *financier*). This measure requires students to think about the information the suffix is conveying within a morphologically complex word. Similarly, our Making It Fit task asks students to complete a sentence with the appropriate derivation of a word. For example, students are given the statement "Amphibians are [create] that live on both land and sea." They have to adjust the root word *create* to contain the correct suffix for the context; hence *creatures*. Again, we attempted multiple measures to assess this skill, including a non-word suffix task, but ultimately these two tasks worked best.

In terms of instruction, this skill highlights the ability to use the syntactic information in a suffix as another clue to a word's meaning within a larger phrase. Here, we have seen instruction that provides many different phrases and then asks students to adjust the form of the word to fit the phrases. We have also seen students encouraged to play with words like this in their own writing, which draws attention to the syntactical role of the suffixes. One key here is that this is one of many strategies students can use to figure out the meaning of unknown words within phrases (Goodwin & Perkins, 2015). So if students read complex texts and show confusion, teachers may draw attention to the syntactic role of suffixes as a way to scaffold meaning making.

Skill 3: Students Can Use Morphology for Meaning

The third skill is perhaps the one that most often comes to mind when we think about uses of morphological knowledge in supporting literacy: the ability to use the semantic information in morphemes to figure out meanings of related words. Students complete a task titled Word Detectives, where they read sentences and then use units of meaning to figure out the meaning of the morphologically complex word. For example, students read, "The experiment required materials to be equidistant. The materials are a) equal in size and weight; b) spaced out evenly from each other; c) from far-away locations; d) ordered spatially." Students have to identify the two units *equi* and *distant,* and connect those to the meanings provided. The skill represented here is what Anglin (1993) would call *word solving,* which our research team has built upon and described further in Pacheco and Goodwin (2013).

In terms of instruction, this skill highlights the importance of getting students to use units of meaning to figure out the meaning of an unfamiliar word. We have seen students reading texts and marking unknown words with flags, then writing those words on sticky notes so that they (alone or with a partner) can box units like root words that they know. They can then synthesize the meanings of the separate units to estimate a meaning and then reread the text with that meaning to determine whether their hypothesis makes sense. See Goodwin and Perkins (2015) for more examples.

Skill 4: Students Can Read and Spell Morphologically Complex Words

The final skill identified from our work is the ability to read and spell morphologically complex words. This skill connects to the orthographic and phonological information conveyed via morphemes. For example, knowing the spelling of the word *know* can help a student to spell *knowledge* (not *nolidj*). Similarly, knowing how to read *finance* can support reading *financially*. Much work has shown these relationships (see Goodwin, Gilbert, & Cho, 2013), and the reason is that students' experience of building and applying knowledge of these patterns in reading and spelling builds higher-quality lexical representations, which they are able to use in their literacy endeavors (Goodwin, Gilbert, Cho, & Kearns, 2014). Our two measures ask students to spell a morphologically complex word they hear, and also to choose between three pronunciations of a morphologically complex word they see.

Instructionally, this indicates the importance of highlighting the overlap among morphological patterns, spelling, and phonological patterns. In other words, if students don't know how to spell a word, they may support sounding out the spelling with consideration of the units of meaning being conveyed by that word. Similarly, if students are faced with an unknown word, they may be able to find a part of the word that they know how to read and use that unit to support reading of the larger word.

Conclusion

So why does it matter that we now have this assessment that teachers can use to identify their students' morphological strengths and weaknesses related to these four morphological skills? First, we think that considering morphological knowledge as more than a single skill is important in highlighting why study after study shows the important role of morphological knowledge in literacy outcomes. Second, we think that these skills provide us with an instructional view and plan. As teachers, we can attune our students to the multiple roles of morphemes by drawing their attention to the different ways morphemes convey semantic, syntactic, orthographic, and phonological information. In doing this, we can give students the key to the code of print, which they can then use to support their literacy endeavors.

Acknowledgments

The research reported here was supported by the Institute of Education Sciences, U.S. Department of Education, through Grant No. R305A150199 to Vanderbilt University. The opinions expressed are our own and do not represent views of the Institute or the U.S. Department of Education.

Teacher to Teacher

Tips from Teachers for Teachers

3

Kristin Capel

Fifth-Grade Teacher, Solon Schools, Ohio

Kristin began using word study as a third-grade teacher. In her work with older students, she maintains students' interest by varying her approach. Here are some of her ideas.

The Looping Game and Getting Started

Before I begin small-group instruction based on informal spelling inventory results, I establish routines and expectations for each of the sorting activities I will be using within the classroom by engaging students in whole-class sorts. I focus on a feature that is problematic for all students and required by Ohio state standards—for example, homophones. Even if students are usually pretty fluent spellers, this is one feature on which they often falter. At the beginning of the year, I use one-syllable homophones to review patterns from the within word pattern stage. One of the activities I use is a looping game. I prepare a set of note cards; on one side I record a homophone, and on the other a sentence that reveals the meaning of another homophone. I continue the process, making sure to begin the second card with the word that matches the meaning on the first card. For the example shown, the second card would begin with *knight*. The meaning on the back of this card would match the word on the third card, and so on. The final card includes the meaning for the first word (in the example, *isle*). Every student is given one of these cards. Player 1's card might look like this:

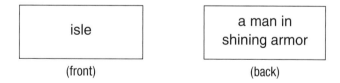

(front)   (back)

The game begins with Player 1 saying, "Who has *a man in shining armor?*" Player 2, the person with the corresponding word, replies, "I have *knight, k-n-i-g-h-t*," and then asks about the definition on the back, as, for example, "Who has *7 days make up a . . . ?*" If completed correctly, the loop will end with the last player saying the definition for Player 1's word, as "Who has *another name for an island?*" and Player 1 responding with "I have *isle, i-s-l-e.*" The students love this activity. It encourages listening and gets them to focus on the meaning and spelling of homophones. It could easily be used with other concepts as well.

3-S Activity

Once I begin meeting with word study groups, I do a few things to make management easier. We typically work with a set of words for a 2-week interval, due to scheduling issues. Although I meet with groups initially to guide students through the new sort and to help them identify generalizations about the patterns that will assist their spelling, for ease of scheduling I plan notebook activities for follow-up practice. This allows me to keep a check on students' progress and any difficulties they may have. Because many of the students have been engaged in word study since kindergarten, I have found that they need some fresh approaches to the follow-up practice—activities that offer a twist to just re-sorting their words. I have also found that in fifth grade, my students' success rate comes more from multiple opportunities to write the words in some type of format than from manipulating the word cards. I still give students the option of physically sorting the cards, but I hold them accountable for completing written word sorts in their word study notebooks. The day I introduce a sort, I follow up by asking students to return to their seats and complete what I call the 3-S Activity, in which they Say the words, Spell the words, and Sort the words. First, they look at their word and say it. Then they spell the word by either whispering or spelling it in their heads. Finally, they write the word in their journals in the columns in which they belong. After completing the written sort, they write down the gist of that sort. What did they learn that would help them to spell other words with the same pattern?

Home Communication Activity

Another routine notebook assignment is the Home Communication Activity. Parents in our district are very involved and really want to know what we are working on. To keep them informed about each cycle of words, students write notes to their parents that include a sampling of six words from their current sort. They explain the gist of the sort to their parents, and also provide a sampling of a few brainstormed non-sort words that fit the pattern. The communication goes home, and parents sign and return it to verify their receipt of it.

Cloze Sentences

Sometimes I also ask students to write sentences for their words, but they do them as cloze sentences. I show them how to do this with repeated modeling. Once words are learned, the students create a word bank with 5–10 of their words; then they create sentences for some of the words, blanking out the spelling word and making sure that their sentences meet a critical requirement: The sentence has to be one of description. It can't be vague so that just about any word could complete it, as, for example, *It is* _____ *(cold)*. They have to really describe *cold,* so that someone else is able to know what word would fit in the blank. This is really difficult for them at first, but it helps them to become more aware of meaning, which is useful for their later studies of more advanced words. When there's time, students can trade papers and fill in the answers to each other's sentences.

Writing Definitions

I suggest using this activity only occasionally, but I do find it useful, because our achievement tests require students to choose the correct word and its meaning from a list of possibilities. In their notebooks, students write a sentence for one of their words and then turn to the dictionary to see if they can pick out the meaning that matches the way they used the word. Once they find it, they rewrite the definition in their own words below the sentence, using five or fewer words.

Jennifer Herrick

Fifth-Grade Teacher, North Brunswick Township Schools, New Jersey

As a veteran teacher, Jennifer knows that motivation is a key to older students' learning. She offers suggestions for keeping students engaged in their word studies and for furthering their vocabulary development.

Weekend Word Warriors

To keep students learning out of school as well as in, I invite them to listen and look for interesting words over the weekend. The words may be new to them, fun to say, annoying, confusing, or fascinating for some other reason. On Monday mornings, we take a few minutes to talk about the words students heard over the weekend. Sometimes we dissect a word and break it down into spelling and/or meaning units. We also try to guess the meaning, spell the word, or talk about the experience that brought the word to attention. Then we add it to our "Words We Found" list that is displayed in the classroom.

Be the Computer

For this activity, I distribute a paragraph containing intentionally misspelled words and grammatical errors. I then ask students to "Be the Computer" by underlining misspellings in red and grammar, capitalization, or punctuation mistakes in blue, just as most computer word-processing programs do. (Colored pencils work well.) Students gain editing practice, and follow-up discussion provides an avenue for reviewing some of the issues raised as errors.

Sorting Variation

Practice sorting is an important component of a word study routine, because it helps students' recall of the patterns to become automatic. To vary the sorting practice, I provide each student with a laminated blank word card template on card stock paper, or with a small whiteboard. You can create your own template or photocopy one (see, e.g., the one in Appendix E). I allow students to use a dry-erase

---

Name: _____   Date: _____

YOU ARE THE COMPUTER

You're going to do the job of a computer. It is your job to show where the mistakes are in this paragraph below. Place a **blue** line under any words or phrases that have grammar mistakes. Place a **red** line under any spelling errors. Then go through and correct all the mistakes.

My dogs name is doodle. he isnt a very frendly dog. Whenever I take him for walk, he likes too bark at other dog. Sometime it annoying. once we saw a cat and He chased it up a tree Were taking him to school to learn how to behave

marker to sort their words on the blank template. When there are more categories than columns for the words, I have them use the lower part of a column as a separate category, suggest that they turn the paper sideways into a horizontal position, or distribute another page. Students find this activity a fun substitute for paper and pencil.

$1 Word Box

I use this activity to reinforce new vocabulary. Begin by photocopying a dollar bill manipulative or a reproducible. On the back, write a really interesting, long, or unusual word. You'll need enough words to fill a small box or manila envelope. Choose words to which students have previously been exposed (e.g., from a science textbook or other content area [see Appendices B–D], Weekend Word Warrior game, or current events). Once you have enough, invite students to pick a word out of the container without looking, as part of a whole-group activity. If they're able to use it correctly in a sentence, they earn $1 and get to keep the "bill." The bills can be saved, and when a certain goal is achieved they can be "spent" for something special, such as extra computer or library time.

Marianne Larson

Fifth-Grade Teacher, Warren Township Public Schools, New Jersey

Marianne taught an earlier grade (second) before moving to fifth-grade teaching 3 years ago. With this move, Marianne found not only that she needed to learn more advanced spelling , but that she also had to create a learning environment appropriate for older students. In the process, Marianne added several new activities to her routine to challenge and engage her students. Her description of a favorite follows.

Flap Books

To encourage vocabulary development as well as spelling knowledge, one of the writing activities I use with students is a foldable flap book, such as the one shown. To make a flap book, students begin with a piece of paper at least 8.5 × 11 inches and follow these directions:

- Fold the paper lengthwise (vertically). The result will resemble a skinny book.
- Fold this long rectangle in half by bringing the top down to meet the bottom.
- Repeat the previous step two more times, until you have made four folds. You should end up with a small rectangle, much wider than it is high.
- Unfold the paper until you are back to where you were after the first fold. The "cover" of the skinny book should now show creases across it that create eight rectangles.
- Cut the creases on the "cover" of the book, but only on the cover, making eight flaps. You should be able to lift the flap and see the inside of the back cover underneath.

There are many ways a flap book can be used at this point, including for science, social studies, and math. For word study, I have the students pick eight words that they feel they need to explore more in terms of definition and usage. They write one word on each flap of the cover. On the back side of the flap, they write a definition for the word, and on the rectangle underneath the flap, they write a sentence using the word according to their recorded definition. (See the accompanying figure.)

	barren
	brighten
	poison
	falcon
	rotten
	sharpen
	wooden
A large ocean fish that can be eaten	<u>Salmon</u> is the best ocean fish for eating.

Colleen Vay and Erin Greco

Sixth-Grade Teachers, West Irondequoit Community School District, New York

Colleen's and Erin's sixth-grade middle school students are eager to learn about the more sophisticated aspects of English spelling, so they set up routines and resources in the beginning of the year that will facilitate this process. They discuss a key ingredient for success—the word study journal.

Introducing the Journal

Students use a word study journal or notebook as a reference, a place of reflection, and an instructional tool throughout the year. The journal is on the students' supply list and comes in with each student on the first day of school. It is a 100-page spiral notebook, not a composition book. We help the students to set up their journals in two parts: a reference section (the last 20 pages) and an introduction/work section (the first 80 pages). For homework the first week of school, students are asked to number the pages for future reference. The first page is an explanation of word study. The class discusses the whole meaning of word study. At the end, students reflect in their journals on the personal implications of this type of study and set a goal for the upcoming year.

Reflection: A Critical Element

We again ask students to write a reflection after we have gathered information about their spelling knowledge through an informal spelling assessment, such as the DSA. They reflect on what they have previously learned about words, their patterns, and exceptions. As time goes on, students continue to reflect in their journals, sharing their thinking about the features we are studying, any generalizations they develop about how the features work (see the sampling of student reflections included at the end of this vignette), and ideas about new vocabulary. We have found the reflection piece to be very powerful in students' retention of the features. They not only reflect in a written form, but also are given a chance to discuss their reflections with others in their group. The word study lessons are very meaningful to students, as they talk about their progress, experiment with words in their writing, and develop understanding of the written words that they are reading.

The Reference Section

The last 20 pages of the journal are used to describe activities from professional resources. We provide students with half-page copies of directions for the activities; they add these to each page in this section of their journals and use the other half-page to practice the activity for future reference. Also, the different types of sorts are defined, and examples are given. When students are assigned to do homework, there is less confusion than there was before notebooks were used, and parents are able to assist if needed. For example, word hunts are a frequent form of homework: Students are hunting for words either in their current reading or in their own writing. When word hunting, students date the page in their journal, write down the feature being studied, and record the title of the literature work they are using. They organize the feature words they find by category, document how the word is used, and note the meaning of the word, as shown in the sample template here. We model this together as a whole class first, and then give students the opportunity to try it individually. At the end of the activity, the students all reflect on what they learned about that feature. With the pages numbered, students in the same group can find their place very quickly, instead of fumbling through the whole notebook.

WORD HUNT TEMPLATE

Feature: _____   Date: _____

Title of Literature: _____

Feature word	Part of speech	Definition

Reflection—What have you learned about this feature from this reading?

Monitoring Student Progress

Teachers can monitor student progress very easily by collecting the journals, which not only include all of their work but also a record of their thinking. Assessments are completed in the journal, so students can monitor their own progress and go back to features for clarification. The journal helps students manage their own learning, creates a tool they can use in the future, documents a year's worth of progress, and informs our teaching so that we can differentiate lessons based on what the students need.

Final Thoughts

The word study journal has provided us with a consistent routine for students to work within. While a teacher is working with a small group on a specific feature, individual students can be working independently, completing a word sort, documenting features in a word hunt, or reflecting with a partner about the current feature and word meanings. For upper elementary teachers, time is an important consideration when it comes to word study. How can we fit it into our daily instruction? By having a consistent routine, placing reference materials in the students' hands, and involving students in the process, we have made word study a strong part of our curriculum. The best part about all of this is that students see the connection between their effort and their success. They get it!

A Sampling of Student Reflections

4/06 I keep misspelling words that end with ion. I am still confusion tion, sion, and ion. There are so many words in this feature. Tonight I am going to look at the newspaper for homework and see what I can find. I hope it helps me with this.

11/06 Today's word hunt was easy for me. I found a lot of homophones in Tuck Everlasting. Then I went to my reading journal to hunt for homophones. I am writing them wrong. I used there instead of their 5 times. In my group discussion today, I am going to ask my partners if they are doing the same thing? Mrs. Vay says she sees this all the time in our papers. I will be more aware the next time I am writing homophones to use the correct one.

10/06 Short and long vowel sounds are easy when we are discussing them with Mrs. Vay. Sometimes I forget to put the e on the end of the word. That makes a big mistake. It changes the meaning of the word I want to write.

Tiffany Worden

Middle School Teacher, Montgomery Township School District, New Jersey

As a middle school language arts teacher who knows the importance of motivation, Tiffany works hard to pique students' interest in language. In her experience, there is no better way to accomplish this than to launch word study with idioms and follow up with homophones. Once she has aroused the interest of her students, she moves on to explorations of Greek and Latin roots in order to develop their vocabulary and spelling knowledge.

Idioms

I begin by asking students to brainstorm familiar expressions to activate their prior knowledge of idioms. As students list common phrases such as *raining cats and dogs, under the weather,* and *couch potato,* they are eager to understand what they mean and how they came to be. I explain that each word—or, in this case, phrase—in our language has a story behind it, an etymology that tells about its origin and how it developed through the centuries. I send partners off to our idiom dictionaries, such as the *Scholastic Dictionary of Idioms* by Marvin Terban (1996), to become familiar with some idioms and their etymologies (see the Idiom Scavenger Hunt on the facing page). The room is lively as students make connections and excitedly read the stories behind these everyday phrases. For the next week during our word study time, students use the idiom dictionaries to research an additional three to five idioms they find interesting. At the end of the week, students synthesize and share their knowledge through a small project of their choosing. They might:

- Write a journal entry from an idiom's perspective.
- Write a poem or story.
- Compose a song or rap about idioms.
- Create a small crossword puzzle using idioms.
- Develop a PowerPoint presentation.
- Illustrate an idiom.
- Create a poster with the word, etymology, and an illustration displayed (see example).
- Prepare a short skit about an idiom.

I encourage students to come up with their own ideas and to confer with me about them. Students share their final idiom project through a *gallery walk* (Rutherford, 2002). In a gallery walk, students leave their projects on their desks and walk around the room, learning about new idioms from their classmates' projects.

BAKERS DOZEN

THIRTEEN

In 1266, England made a rule that bakers had to give a certain amount of goods to the customers, so in order to meet the amount, bakers would give one extra to a dozen.

DOZEN

IDIOM SCAVENGER HUNT

Directions: Working with a partner at your table, use an idiom dictionary to find the meaning and story behind the following idioms.

I'll give you the definition; you find the idiom:

1. Sometimes we describe a person who spends lots of time watching television as a _____
   _____.

2. Manuel, from Gary Soto's short story "La Bamba," loves the attention he gets from the talent show.
   He loves to be in the _____.

3. An idiom we use to say "Have a good night's rest" is _____
   _____.

I'll give you the story behind the expression; you find the idiom:

1. In thirteenth-century England, bakers began including 13 baked goods instead of 12. We call this a
   _____.

2. When there was a storm at sea, sailors would go below deck. They were under the _____
   _____.

I'll give you the idiom; you find its meaning and the story behind it:

Idiom	What does it mean today?	What is the story behind this idiom?
Let the cat out of the bag		
Once in a blue moon		

It is important for students to understand how the idioms they have researched and integrated into projects relate to their reading and writing. We talk about how recognizing idioms as expressions and not literal sayings makes it easier to comprehend texts. I also explain how idioms are mostly used in speech. Writers usually choose to omit idioms from formal writing. We discuss times when writers may use idioms, such as within dialogue to develop a character. This new knowledge helps students to make choices about using idioms in their own writing.

Homophones

As in idiom study, homophones ignite students' enthusiasm for words. Before creating the following homophone activities, I review my students' writing and select three to four sets of homophones that students will benefit from studying. After introducing homophones and briefly reviewing the meanings of each set of words, I have the students interact with the homophones at learning stations over the course of several days. They:

- Use computers to explore homophone-related websites.
- Work with a partner to match homophones to sentences. The sentences are written on colorful strips of paper called *sentence strips*. In each sentence, a homophone is omitted; students must choose the word card that matches and insert it into the sentence, explaining their thinking to each other.
- Illustrate the meanings of homophone pairs, act out the meanings, or use the pair in a sentence.
- Scan their books, searching for homophone examples. When students find their one or two, for example, they record the sentence on a note card and post it on our bulletin board.

It is important for students to use their new knowledge of homophones in authentic writing activities, so I add the homophone sets to peer-editing sheets and to the editing section of our rubrics. This encourages students to look for these homophones as they edit their papers and carefully consider whether the words are being used correctly.

Root Study

When we study word roots as a means for developing vocabulary, I choose two roots to study together, with approximately six spelling words that contain either root. I want the roots and spelling words to be ones that students will use in authentic reading and writing tasks. The best way I have to ensure this is to connect our root study to the content-area classes. For example, my students study astronomy in science. Over the course of that science unit, students read and write many words containing the roots *astr* ("star") and *geo* ("earth"). Therefore, during this time, we study *astr* and *geo* in language arts class, and the words I choose include *astronomy, astronaut,* and *astronomical unit,* as well as *geocentric* from science and *geography* and *geometry* from social studies and math.

I introduce the words with a word web. I draw a circle with the root in the middle, and students brainstorm any words branching from that root. This task activates students' prior knowledge of words containing the root, and they enjoy deducing the root's meaning from our word web. Over the course of the week, students complete various activities to build their vocabulary and spelling skills and to make connections to their reading. For each set of words, I create a packet with directions for the various activities. Activities may include sorting the words, illustrating the roots, identifying each spelling word's root by circling it, searching for additional words with the roots, unscrambling spellings, alphabetizing the words, and completing a crossword puzzle (a free crossword puzzle maker can be found at *www.puzzle-maker.com*).

Mary Lou Cebula

Retired Principal, Warren Township Public Schools, New Jersey

When I was a principal, the birth of a differentiated spelling program in my school began the way educational leaders envision, but rarely witness—with the teachers. The school year was ending. Teachers were packing up their classrooms and planning summer vacations. Everyone, that is, except my third-grade teachers. They were standing at my office door with a proposal. When the teachers entered my office and asked to speak to me, I thought it must be serious for them to come together. I was outnumbered, but respected them and their dedication to their students.

They described their frustration with the traditional one-size-fits-all approach to spelling and its inability to meet students' needs. After describing the problem, they suggested a solution—differentiated word study. The teachers had researched other ways of teaching spelling, read professional books on the topic, and visited teachers from another district that implemented word study. They proposed to pilot the approach the following year and expressed a willingness to prepare for the venture over the summer. Fascinated by their enthusiasm and intrigued by the possibilities for students' learning, I agreed to their request. At the end of the next school year, when we discussed the project, the teachers asked to continue word study and expressed an interest in the possibility of expanding its implementation to fourth grade, so that their students could continue to benefit from the approach.

After receiving permission from the superintendent of schools to continue the word study pilot program, I asked teachers in second and fourth grades to pilot word study with their students. An interesting development occurred: By the middle of the school year, all the second-grade teachers were experimenting with word study, meeting with the third-grade teachers, and observing them implementing word study; but in fourth grade, the pilot was less successful. I knew more support was needed for the staff, so I provided professional development for all second- through fourth-grade teachers, including time to observe colleagues, professional books, and the opportunity to take a 1-hour graduate summer course. The six of us who took the class came away not only with ideas for implementing word study, but also with the knowledge that word study is not just about spelling, but about our language and the importance of vocabulary development. Over the summer, we developed word sorts to share with other staff members.

With the support and encouragement of the teachers who had piloted word study, we began the school year with a plan for full implementation of word study in second through fifth grades. The third-grade team, a second-grade teacher who had attended the summer word study course, and I designed 10 one-hour training sessions for our staff members and any other teachers in the district who were interested. Twenty-five teachers volunteered to attend the after-school classes. Word study had started with a group of interested classroom teachers, but quickly gained everyone's attention. As an administrator, I could hardly contain how proud I felt that the staff was committed to practices that required more time and effort than their previous one-size-fits-all approach. The needs of their students and the positive results they saw in the students' daily writing were the driving forces.

Over time, we continued to provide support for word study. Teachers still observed each other on a regular basis; a word study refresher class was held in the fall for interested staff members; new teachers received training at the beginning of the school year; new word sorts were created as needed; and teachers met together to share students' DSA results and to provide information, so that next year's teachers could continue the flow of instruction at the children's levels. Grade-level teachers met at the beginning of the year to discuss assessments and determine spelling groups. The lines of communication moved at and across grades.

How did parents react to this sudden shift from a traditional spelling list to a word sort? Once again, communication played a major role in making word study accepted. We invited parents to attend an information session on word study. Two teachers (grades 5 and 3) and I had prepared a PowerPoint presentation for district administrators. We revised this for parents, tracing the how, what, and why of word study. We included pictures of their children engaged in word sort activities and teachers conducting a word walk. Parents were able to see the program in action and develop a better understanding of the benefits of word study. Except for an occasional parent questioning the current small-group placement of his or her child, the program has been warmly received and supported.

Word study became an integral component of our balanced literacy program in kindergarten through grade 5. Several teachers in the middle school attended the training sessions offered in the district and began experimenting with word study in their classrooms. As a result of its positive effects, this type of word study eventually spread throughout the district, where it is still used today.

The teachers deserve all the credit for introducing word study and displaying the leadership that brought the program to our school district. My role was to learn all I could about word study and to provide the resources and encouragement to help the implementation succeed. As I traveled around the school and wandered into the classrooms, I witnessed students talking and interacting with words with an enthusiasm and knowledge I never observed with our former approach. It was a wonderful sight to behold.

Part Three

Word Study Instructional Activities

4 Word Study for Syllable Juncture Spellers

Syllable juncture spellers are likely to be upper elementary or middle school students who are well on their way to becoming proficient readers. They know how to spell many words, and most have solid understandings of how basic consonant and vowel patterns work in single-syllable words. At the syllable juncture stage (also known as the syllables and affixes stage), students learn to negotiate the patterns and structures of polysyllabic words. As they closely examine the longer words that characterize this stage, several new spelling issues surface. Not only must they learn to apply their knowledge of consonant and vowel patterns to the context of polysyllabic words and learn a few new patterns in the process, but they must also acquire a working knowledge of other aspects of spelling, particularly the doubling principle and syllable stress or accent. *To double or not to double,* that is the question—at least for many syllable juncture spellers. Doubling in the middle of words is one cause for deliberation (*His shirt was in tatters* [not *taters*] *after going through the thorn bushes*); the other is doubling before an inflected ending (*I am starring* [not *staring*] *in the movie*). Students must also grapple with syllable stress. In longer words, one syllable is usually accented or stressed, whereas another is unstressed. Sound provides a clue to spelling stressed syllables. Because it does not do so when a syllable is unstressed, these syllables are more challenging to spell. At this stage, vocabulary knowledge also becomes increasingly important for students, as they face understanding the many sophisticated words they encounter in their upper-grade reading materials and the need to respond to such material in writing. As noted in Chapter 1, the study of prefixes and suffixes and how they affix to other word parts, known as *morphology,* is a critical component of upper-level word study—one that receives considerable attention at this stage and even more at the next, and that builds on the foundational concept of joining meaning units, as illustrated through compound words

All of the sorts that follow can be used with the SAIL components (survey, analyze, interpret, and link) discussed in Chapter 1 to deepen students' learning and engagement, whether or not SAIL is explicitly mentioned in the "Considerations" sections. Likewise, academic vocabulary can (and should) be integrated into the teacher and student talk.

Introducing Compound Words

Many students will already be familiar with the concept of a compound word as two words put together to form a new word. (Compounds are introduced in the "Additional Sorts" section of *Word Sorts and More, Second Edition* [Ganske, 2018].) A brief study of compounds has been chosen to introduce the syllable juncture stage for several reasons. This stage focuses on words of more than one syllable and on the patterns of consonants and vowels within and across those syllables. Not only do the separate words in compounds clearly reveal the syllables, but they also enable students to see that although there are more letters in the words, many of the patterns are familiar. For example, the sort that follows includes numerous previously studied patterns, including several blends and digraphs, all five short vowels, several long-vowel patterns, numerous r-controlled patterns, and some abstract vowels. Finally, in addition to expanding students' pattern knowledge, the word studies at this stage begin to develop their awareness of meaning connections, which will form the heart of word study at the derivational constancy stage, and meaning is the essence of compound words. Note that 10 additional compound sorts, including 2 that focus on hyphenated compounds, are included in the "Additional Sorts" section of this chapter. Most may be used at any time during syllable juncture studies; those dealing with hyphenated compounds should be reserved for the latter part of this stage. The compound sorts might serve as a break from other word studies, as well as an alternative when schedules are not routine or when the class has a substitute teacher.

SORT 1. Introducing Compound Words

Sorting by Pattern/Meaning

book	back	ear	hair	way
bookmark	**backpack**	**earplug**	**haircut**	**doorway**
bookshelf	backbone	earache	hairbrush	driveway
bookworm	backfire	eardrum	hairline	freeway
cookbook	background	earring	hairpin	halfway
	backtrack	earshot		hallway
				stairway

Considerations: Ask students to examine and sort their words into groups. Discuss the results and their rationales for grouping certain words together. One of the outcomes will likely be a sort similar to the answer key above. Turn their attention to it and discuss the word meanings, being sure to encourage connections with the two smaller words that make up the compound. For example, an ache in your ear is an *earache*; the line formed by the growth of hair on your head is your *hairline*; and so forth. This is an opportune time to discuss the polysemous or multiple-meaning nature of any words, as in the phrase *a hairline crack*, or fracture in a bone. The meaning connection for *earshot* is less obvious than for most of the words; it refers to the range in which you can hear a sound unaided (if you are *out of earshot*, you are too far away to hear it). Ask students to speculate on the meaning connection to *shot* and to share their thinking. Perhaps the range was originally determined by a gunshot. With *earring*, draw students' attention to the double *r*, and remind them of the importance of thinking carefully about the words that make up a compound when spelling; spellings that may not "look right" can be correct because the spelling maintains meaning, as in *bookkeeper*. Finally, point out the various familiar patterns within the syllables and the ease with which syllables can be identified in compound words.

Talking Points

- Compound words are made up of two or more smaller words that affect the word's meaning.
- It is important to remember that meaning is the key to spelling compounds, because double letters that may not look right can occur where the syllables (words) come together, as in *earring*.

Integrating Idioms: "Mom said I don't have to give in to my sister, but I have to **meet her halfway**." (A compromise. If instead of making someone come to you, you walked half the distance to that person, you would be showing a willingness to reach out to her and consider her point of view.)

Did You Know? **Book** developed from *boc,* an Old English word for "writing tablet." *Beech* shares the same ancestry, probably because early inscriptions were made on tablets made from this wood. *Library* also derives from a word meaning "book"; however, because its roots are Latin, the spelling *liber* is not the same. Libraries have existed for a long time. Books in the first known library, which existed more than 4,000 years ago in Babylonia, were clay tablets rather than wood. The first public library in the United States opened in Boston in the mid-1600s. The world's largest library began as a library for the Congress of the United States and eventually became a national library. The Library of Congress is located in Washington, D.C. Its original 1801 collection included 740 volumes and 3 maps. Today the library has over 65 acres of floor space and about 838 miles of bookshelves! It includes about 24½ million books and 5½ million maps (as well as music, photographs, manuscripts, and other media)—more than 168 million items in all and covering 470 languages! The smallest book is about the size of the period at the end of this sentence; the largest about 5 × 7 feet! How did the collection become so big? According to law, two copies of every book that is copyrighted must be given to the library, including this one. It is truly a bookworm's paradise! Do you have a classroom, school, or home library? If so, what is it like?

Introducing Compound Words

book	back	ear	hair	way

bookmark	backpack	earplug
haircut	doorway	hairpin
stairway	backfire	earring
earshot	halfway	bookshelf
background	cookbook	hallway
earache	driveway	backtrack
bookworm	hairbrush	eardrum
hairline	backbone	freeway

Inflectional Endings

Sometimes people are unsure just what an *inflectional ending* is. The phrase refers to "a suffix that expresses plurality or possession when added to a noun, tense when added to a verb, and comparison when added to an adjective and some adverbs" (Harris & Hodges, 1995, p. 116). This section examines three of these issues: adding *-ing* or *-ed* to base words, forming plurals, and creating comparative adjectives. The greatest attention is given to adding *-ed* or *-ing* to base words where no change, *e*-drop, or doubling is required.

Adding *-ed* and *-ing* with No Change, *e*-Drop, and Doubling *(DSA Feature K)*

The sorts in the first part of this section address *-ed* and *-ing* inflected endings. Knowing how to correctly add these suffixes is critical for students, considering that more than one out of every three words with a suffix ends in *-ed* or *-ing* (Blevins, 2001). How the past tense and participle are formed depends on the base or root word. For example, we (1) add *-ed* or *-ing* to words that end in a VVC pattern—namely, ones that end with a single consonant preceded by two vowels, as in *mailed* and *peeking*; (2) drop the final *-e* of words with a VC*e* pattern, then add *-ed* or *-ing*, as in *taped* and *shaking*; and (3) double the final consonant and then add *-ed* or *-ing* to words with a VC pattern—namely, words that end with a single consonant and include a single vowel, as in *dotted* and *pinning*. A few words alter the spelling instead of adding an ending (e.g., *sleep/slept* and *say/said*) or follow other considerations for adding an inflectional ending (see Sort 2). Because base words are the building blocks for inflections, it is important that students know how to spell them. This is easily verified through discussion or by asking students to underline or record the spelling of the base words on their word cards. Following is a collection of sorts to teach this feature; choose those that seem most appropriate for your students' needs.

What Is Known: Vowel patterns in single-syllable words; *Word Sorts and More, Second Edition* (Ganske, 2018), has introduced students to the *e*-drop principle used when adding *-ed*. This principle is reviewed here.

What Is New: Learning to form inflections with *-ed* and *-ing*, especially those involving doubling of the final consonant.

SORT 2. Adding *-ing* to Words with No Change and *e*-Drop

Sorting by Pattern		
No Change		*e*-Drop
VCC	VVC	VC*e*
asking	**mailing**	**shaking**
blinking	cleaning	chasing
fishing	keeping	living
guessing	floating	making
jumping	shouting	riding
limping	snooping	saving
smelling	speaking	smiling
		using
		voting
		writing

Considerations: Explain to students that for this sort they will be exploring various ways of adding *-ing*. Discuss any unfamiliar meanings. Begin the exploration by asking students to underline or record the name of the base word on each card. Then ask them to consider possible groupings for the words by examining patterns that may reveal how the *-ing* ending was added. Students may need prompting to subdivide the no-change list. Also, some students may regard *living* as an oddball because it does not have a long-vowel sound. Remind them that the focus is on pattern rather than sound. Once the activity is completed, invite students to explain how the three categories are alike and how they are different. Some words with two vowels also end with two consonants; inflections for these are formed by just adding the ending, as in *coaching, touched,* and *pointing.* The same is true for words that end in VV, such as *chewing, played, snowing, seeing,* and so forth.

Talking Points

- Drop the final *-e* of a base word before adding *-ing,* as in *smiling.*
- Simply add *-ing* to one-syllable words that include a team of vowels or that end in two or more consonants, as in *cleaning* and *fishing.*

Integrating Idioms: "Ignore my sister if she comes dancing in here; she just got a new haircut, and she'll be **fishing for a compliment.**" (Hoping someone will say something nice. Just as a person who goes fishing tries various approaches to catch a fish, the sister will probably act or talk in certain ways to attract attention to her haircut.)

Did You Know? When we think of someone **snooping** around, we usually think of a detective or perhaps a thief. However, the original Dutch root of the word, *snoepen,* had more to do with our own habits of raiding the cookie jar or breaking a diet by secretly indulging in an ice cream cone; the Dutch word meant to "eat snacks and sweets on the sly."

SORT 3. Adding *-ed* to Words with No Change and *e*-Drop

Sorting by Pattern (and thinking about meaning—the base word)

No Change		*e*-Drop	
VCC	VVC	VC*e*	Oddball
lifted	**gained**	**liked**	**?**
combed	aimed	choked	knew
dressed	braided	named	popped
marked	healed	placed	slept
pulled	leaned	raced	
pushed	pouted	waved	
stacked		wiped	

Considerations: The same considerations described for adding *-ing* apply to adding *-ed.* A process similar to the one used for the previous sort may be used here. Note that this sort includes three oddballs; two of them are irregular past-tense verbs. As part of the discussion, ask students to brainstorm other words with irregular past tense (e.g., *blow/blew, drive/drove, eat/ate, feel/felt, grow/grew, keep/kept, make/made, meet/met, read/read, ride/rode, shake/shook, speak/spoke, strike/struck, take/took, write/wrote*). The third oddball provides students with a glimpse of yet another way to form the past tense—namely, by doubling the final consonant before adding *-ed.* As an extension, students might determine the past-tense form of each of the following words; several are irregular: *feel/felt, read/read, get/got, quit* (may be *quit* or *quitted*), *run/ran,* and *sit/sat.*

Talking Points

- As with *-ing,* just add *-ed* to one-syllable words that include a team of vowels or that end in two or more consonants, as in *aimed* and *pushed.*
- Drop the final *-e* of a base word; then add *-ed.* It may seem as though *-d* can just be added to words with a final *-e,* but *d* is just a letter; what's needed is the meaning unit for past tense, and that is *-ed.*
- Some words form the past tense in irregular ways, as in *knew* and *slept.*

Integrating Idioms: "Last night was my parents' wedding anniversary, and Mom was **dressed to the nines.**" (Dressed very well. In Olympic events in which judges rate contestants on their performance, if the ratings for a person's dress were straight 9's on a 10-point scale, that would be very high.)

Did You Know? The sulky expression of a ***pout*** stems from a word meaning to "swell up" or "inflate," perhaps because a pouting person's face resembles that of someone blowing out air. Some believe it may also relate to a Flemish word for "frog." These creatures puff out their throat area before making their traditional croaking sound. Either way, the look is less than complimentary and well worth avoiding. Interestingly, some pigeons are called "pouters," after their habit of puffing up their breasts as part of their mating ritual.

SORT 4. Adding *-ing* to Words with No Change, *e*-Drop, and Double

Sorting by Pattern		
No Change	*e*-Drop	Double
VCC or VVC	VC*e*	VC
meeting	**hoping**	**hopping**
climbing	hiking	begging
feeling	joking	getting
looking	piling	quitting
missing	taking	rubbing
reading	wading	running
standing		sitting
thinking		skipping
waiting		sobbing

Considerations: As students look over their words (the meanings of *wading* and *sobbing* may need to be discussed), they may notice that several contain double consonants, as does the oddball *popped* in Sort 3. Introduce the sort with the level of structure needed. (1) *Considerable:* Ask students to underline or write the name of the base word on each card and then sort the words under the appropriate header according to how the ending was added. Model and guide as needed. (2) *Some:* Provide the inflectional ending key words, and ask students to categorize accordingly. (3) *None:* Ask students to complete an open sort. Discuss the results. English includes numerous words that end with double consonants, especially with final *f, l, s,* and *z;* such words provide an opportunity to caution students to sort words with double consonants thoughtfully, because they do not always signal an added letter, such as *missing* in this sort. Students may notice that words in the doubling column all have short vowels; if they do

not, call their attention to the difference in the vowel sound of *hoping*, which relies on a single conso‑
nant, and *hopping*, which includes double consonants. It is important for students to understand that
in English double consonants signal a short‑vowel sound. To reinforce formation of inflected endings
with no change, *e*-drop, and double, see discussion of the Reach the Peak game in Chapter 7 of *Word
Journeys, Second Edition* (Ganske, 2014). Teaching students the 1‑1‑1 Check (a helpful mnemonic also
explained in Chapter 7 of Ganske, 2014) can make it easier for them to determine when and when not
to double the final consonant of single‑syllable words.

As an added challenge to this sort, write *putting* on the board, point to it, and ask students to
identify the base word and to name its past tense. Their responses may be *put* and *put*, or *put* and
putted. The former is correct; the latter is not. Point out that that the base of *putted* is *putt* (as in a
golf stroke). Although *put* and *putt* have different past tense spellings, their *ing* forms are both spelled
putting, which are pronounced differently. Note that there are numerous words of this type, called
homographs, that are spelled the same but pronounced differently—*read/read, bow/bow, desert/desert,
record/record, present/present*, and so forth. They present special challenges during reading and require
careful use of context clues to determine the appropriate pronunciation. Issues related to their spelling
are explored later at this stage.

Talking Points

- If a one‑syllable word includes one vowel and ends in one consonant (VC), double the final conso‑
  nant before adding ‑*ing*; this keeps the vowel sound short—*hopping*, not *hoping*.

Integrating Idioms: "Why are you **running around like a chicken with its head cut off?**" (Acting
frantic and disorganized. Amazing though it may seem, when a chicken is slaughtered, it will some‑
times wander around headless before dying.)

Did You Know? When we thank someone, we put a lot of **thinking** or thought into it. Perhaps it's not
surprising, then, that the words *think* and *thank* share the same ancestry. When someone asks you to
put on your thinking cap, this means to take time to consider the matter. The expression may come from
the fact that in the 1600s professional men such as scholars, clergymen, and jurists who were thought
to be intelligent, thinking men wore tight‑fitting caps. Judges, also, wore a "considering cap" before
determining a sentence.

SORT 5. Adding -*ed* to Words with No Change, *e*-Drop, and Double

Sorting by Pattern		
No Change	*e*-Drop	Double
VCC or VVC	VC*e*	VC
fooled	**traded**	**hugged**
crossed	baked	bragged
joined	blamed	grabbed
melted	closed	hummed
needed	faced	patted
slumped	filed	ripped
spilled	taped	slammed
treated		tapped
		zipped

Considerations: Check for students' understanding of the word meanings. As with Sort 4, this set of words may be introduced as an open sort or a closed sort with just the headers as guides. If the latter approach is used, remind students to consider the base word carefully when categorizing the words. Though *crossed* and *spilled* may resemble the "double" words, if we remove one of the final consonants what remains is not a word—*cros* and *spil*. Including a word or two of this type helps to encourage students to consider meaning in their decision making, rather than relying solely on visual cues. As with *hopped* and *hoped* in the previous sort, *taped* and *tapped* provide opportunity to discuss the effect of a doubled consonant on the vowel sound. Students might consider how words in the VCe category would be pronounced if they were written with double consonants or how words in the VC category would be read with just a single consonant. To review sounds of the *-ed* ending, extend the sort by asking students to recategorize the words according to /d/, /t/, and /id/ as follows:

Sorting by Sound

/d/	/t/	/id/
blamed	baked	melted
bragged	crossed	needed
closed	faced	patted
filed	ripped	traded
fooled	slumped	treated
grabbed	taped	
hugged	tapped	
hummed	zipped	
joined		
slammed		
spilled		

Talking Points

- Add *-ed* to a single-syllable base word in the same way as *-ing*: If the word has one vowel and ends in one consonant (VC), maintain the short-vowel sound by doubling the final consonant before adding *-ed*, as in *tapped*.

Integrating Idioms: "I know you lost your homework paper, but there's no point in **crying over spilled milk**." (Regretting something you can't change. If you've tipped over a glass of milk on the table, crying about it isn't going to help. Instead, take action: Clean up the mess and pour a new glass.)

Did You Know? We have early metalsmiths to thank for the word *fool,* which derives from a Latin word meaning "bellows" or "windbag." Rather than blowing on the fire to heat it up so he could temper his metal, a smith would use a bellows, a kind of hand-operated apparatus, to increase the draft. When a person went around talking nonsense as though he were knowledgeable, he reminded people of the bellows, a windbag full of hot empty air. Court jesters sometimes played the part of a fool in order to mimic people of the ruling class. *Foolscap,* a large-sized paper (13″ × 16″) used for writing or printing, got its name from the watermark of a jester's cap found on the paper. (A *watermark*—see Sort 53—is a design impressed on certain kinds of paper when it is made; it becomes visible when held to the light.)

SORT 6. Adding *-ed* to *r*-Controlled Words with No Change, *e*-Drop, and Double

Sorting by Pattern

No Change	e-Drop	Double
started	**scared**	**scarred**
burped	dared	barred
cheered	fired	blurred
harmed	scored	marred
learned	shared	slurred
parted	snored	starred
purred	stared	stirred
soared	stored	
squirmed		

Considerations: This sort provides an opportunity to review *r*-controlled vowels while reinforcing spelling with the *-ed* ending. As with the other sorts in this section, knowledge of the base word is important. This is particularly apparent in *scared* and *scarred*, *stared* and *starred*, and *purred*. The two pairs of words are often misspelled and misread by students, and the last word is likely to be missorted by students who are relying primarily on visual cues rather than on what the base word actually is. Be sure to discuss the meanings of unfamiliar words. You may want to ask students to sort the words by the rime pattern of the base word (the vowel and what follows) as an introduction to the sort or as an extension. The results follow:

Sorting by Pattern

VC	VCC	VVC	VCe
barred	burped	cheered	dared
blurred	harmed	learned	fired
marred	parted	soared	scared
scarred	purred		scored
slurred	squirmed		shared
starred	started		snored
stirred			stared
			stored

The placement of *squirmed* may prompt discussion from students who regard the *u* as part of the vowel pattern. Remind them that the vowel pattern is not *ui*, but that the *u* partners with *q*, as in *quick, quiet, squirt, squint,* and so forth.

Talking Points

- Words with *r*-controlled vowels follow the same principles as other words when *-ed* is added.
- Drop the final *-e* of VC*e* words; just add *-ed* if the word ends in a VVC or VCC pattern; and double the final consonant of words with V*r* to maintain the vowel sound: *He scarred his arm*, not *scared his arm*.

Integrating Idioms: "**I started with a clean slate,** but I'm already in trouble." (Nothing was held against this person when he or she started. The origin of this idiom is unknown. You might ask students to speculate on its origin.)

Did You Know? Perhaps you've gotten a **scar** before by burning yourself. It's likely that many people did in ancient Greece, when open fires provided warmth and means for cooking food. The word stems from the Greek word *eskhara,* meaning "hearth" (the floor of a fireplace). As the word came to be used by the Romans and later the French, it took on the related but slightly different meaning of "scab caused by burning"; its meaning was altered again by the time we got it to indicate the mark left on the skin after a wound has healed. What might the word mean in another few hundred years?

SORT 7. Adding *-ed* and *-ing* to Words with No Change, *e*-Drop, and Double

Sorting by Pattern

No Change	*e*-Drop	Double
greeted	**graded**	**planning**
bending	guided	batted
blushing	lined	fanning
boiled	owed	jogged
groaned	poking	letting
packed	rated	rotted
peeled	shaped	tipped
screamed		tugging
walking		

Considerations: Review the meanings of any unfamiliar words. Be sure to check students' understanding of the base-word spelling. If students find the inclusion of both *-ed* and *-ing* words confusing, ask them to begin by sorting the words into two categories, *-ing* and *-ed,* and then re-sort the words by pattern as in Sort 6. This sort, as well as Sorts 4–5, may be introduced or extended by asking students to categorize the words according to vowel sound and/or pattern, as shown next. Students should notice that all of the short-vowel words have two consonants before the inflectional ending, either as a result of doubling or because the base word ends in two of them. By contrast, a single consonant precedes the ending of long-vowel words.

Talking Points

- When we are adding either *-ed* or *-ing* to a one-syllable word, it's important to think about the base word. Drop the final *-e* of VCe words before adding the ending; if the word ends in a VVC or VCC pattern, just add the ending; and double the final consonant of VC words, as in *shaped, screamed, blushing,* and *tipped.*

Sorting by Vowel Sound

Short	Long	Other
batted	graded	boiled
bending	greeted	walking
blushing	groaned	
fanning	guided	
jogged	lined	
letting	owed	
packed	peeled	
planning	poking	
rotted	rated	
tipped	screamed	
tugging	shaped	

Sorting by Pattern

VC	VCC	VVC	VCe
batted	bending	boiled	graded
fanning	blushing	greeted	guided
jogged	packed	groaned	lined
letting	walking	peeled	owed
planning		screamed	poking
rotted			rated
tipped			shaped
tugging			

Integrating Idioms: "**Keep your eyes peeled;** we don't want to miss them." (Keep a sharp lookout. When something is peeled, the outer covering is removed so that nothing is in the way of getting at whatever is underneath—an orange, a potato, and so forth. In other words, if you *keep your eyes peeled*, there's nothing to prevent you from seeing well.)

Did You Know? The *l-i-n* spelling connection between **line** and *lint*, *lingerie*, and *linoleum* is obvious, but a meaning connection among the words may seem surprising. The origin of *line* goes back to ancient times and to *linum*, the Latin word for "flax," a plant used to make a kind of cloth called *linen*. Cloth making was important, so other words stemmed from *linum*, including *lint*, bits of linen left on the loom; *lingerie*, which was made from linen; and even *linoleum* (though much later, in 1860), which was originally canvas coated with a preparation made from linseed oil, the oil of flax seeds. Many words and expressions relate to *line*, including *lineage*, *linear*, *airline*, *ocean liner*, *draw the line*, *fall in line*, *toe the line*, *out of line*, *bottom line*, *end of the line*, *hold the line*, *sign on the dotted line*, *line of thought*, and so forth.

No Change		*e*-**Drop**
asking	mailing	shaking
cleaning	voting	snooping
living	riding	fishing
guessing	keeping	making
floating	writing	smelling
shouting	blinking	chasing
limping	using	jumping
smiling	speaking	saving

No Change		***e*-Drop**
lifted	gained	liked
waved	slept	aimed
healed	pulled	wiped
dressed	placed	leaned
choked	pouted	combed
pushed	raced	popped
named	marked	knew
stacked	braided	**?**

SORT 4   Adding *-ing* to Words with No Change, *e*-Drop, and Double

No Change	***e*-Drop**	**Double**
meeting	hoping	hopping
sitting	thinking	piling
hiking	begging	standing
waiting	taking	running
quitting	feeling	getting
reading	skipping	looking
wading	climbing	sobbing
missing	rubbing	joking

No Change	*e*-Drop	Double
fooled	traded	hugged
treated	zipped	filed
slammed	joined	spilled
needed	tapped	blamed
taped	closed	bragged
grabbed	crossed	patted
faced	hummed	slumped
melted	ripped	baked

From *Mindful of Words, Second Edition,* by Kathy Ganske. Copyright © 2021 The Guilford Press. Permission to photocopy this form is granted to purchasers of this book for personal use or use with students (see copyright page for details). Enlarge 135% to fill letter-size paper, 175% for 11″ × 17″ paper.

No Change	*e*-Drop	Double
started	scared	scarred
shared	parted	snored
harmed	blurred	stared
scored	dared	cheered
stirred	learned	marred
starred	slurred	soared
purred	burped	stored
fired	barred	squirmed

Adding *-ed* and *-ing* to Words
with No Change, *e*-Drop, and Double

No Change	*e*-Drop	Double
greeted	graded	planning
shaped	letting	groaned
packed	guided	rated
poking	bending	jogged
walking	rotted	peeled
blushing	batted	owed
tipped	boiled	tugging
screamed	lined	fanning

Plurals

In the following sorts, students increase their understanding of how to form plurals. This is an important concept, as more than 30% of words with a suffix are plurals (Blevins, 2001). You may need to explain to students that plurals are formed with nouns to express *more than one*. Plurals can be formed by adding *-s* (*socks*) or *-es* (*churches*) or through spelling changes, such as changing *-y* to *i* and then adding *-es* (*fly/flies*), changing *f* to *v* and then adding *-es* or *-s* (*half/halves* and *life/lives*), or changing vowels (*foot/feet*). There are also a few unusual formations, such as adding *-en* (*ox/oxen*) or using the same word for both the singular and plural forms (*deer, moose, sheep*), as well as words that have more than one correct form (*gases* or *gasses*, *zeros* or *zeroes*, and *dwarfs* or *dwarves*). Despite the variation, understanding a few key principles about plural formation will enable students to correctly change the number of most nouns. Developing a spelling awareness that helps them to realize when they are unsure of the formation and need to check it out with an expert or the dictionary will help them to tackle the rest.

What Is Known: Spelling of the base words, and likely the simple plural formation of adding *-s*.

What Is New: Forming plurals by adding *-es* and through spelling changes.

SORT 8. Plurals with *-s* and *-es*

Sorting by Pattern				
Base + *-s*	Base + *-es*			
	-ch	*-sh*	*-s*	*-x*
pieces	**inches**	**wishes**	**classes**	**foxes**
bridges	branches	brushes	guesses	indexes*
chances	crutches	dashes	losses	sixes
sevens	peaches	dishes	passes	taxes
sponges	stitches			
voices	watches			

*Also spelled *indices*.

Considerations: Whether or not *-es* is used to form the plural of a noun is determined by the final consonant(s) of the base word; *-ch*, *-sh*, *-s*, and *-x* (and *-z*, as in *quizzes*) require *-es*. For most words that end in other consonants or final *-e*, you just add *-s*. Although students likely will be familiar with the word meanings, remind them that the words they are working with are all nouns. Many of the words in this sort can also function as present-tense verbs; however, because plurals are the focus, it is important for students to consider the noun-related meanings.

Talking Points

- *Plural* means "more than one."
- To form the plural, add *-s* to words that end in *-e*; add *-es* to words that end in *-ch, -sh, -s, -x,* or *-z*.

Integrating Idioms: "Everyone in the class **was at sixes and sevens** after having a substitute for two weeks." (Confused and disorderly. Six is an even number and seven is an odd number, so to be at sixes and sevens is to be out of harmony.)

"His dad told him if he dropped out of school, he'd be **burning his bridges behind him.**" (Making a decision he can't reverse. The reference is to historical and literary figure Gaius Julius Caesar, who burned bridges behind his army at the start of a civil war, making it impossible to turn back.)

Did You Know? Although your experiences with **taxes** may be limited to paying a little extra for an item when you purchase it, there are many kinds of taxes—property tax, inheritance tax, sales tax, income tax, and so forth. In fact, it was a tax called the *stamp tax* that was a stimulus for the Revolutionary War. That taxes are significant to people is evident in the expression that "there is nothing as certain as death and taxes." Though people have an aversion to taxes, the word actually comes from the Latin root for "to touch," *tangere.* Why touch? People used to pay a certain percentage on everything they owned that could be touched—in other words, their property. The origin of *task* is also related to tax; if you couldn't pay your taxes in goods, you might work off the debt by completing some sort of task.

Index is also related to "touch." Many people use their index finger to flip through the indexes of reference books, touching each page as they go. This second finger was called *towcher,* meaning "toucher" in Middle English, because it was so often used to touch objects. Today's name of *index* for a part of some books stems from our common use of this finger for pointing.

SORT 9. More Plurals

Sorting by Pattern

-y + -s	-y → i + -es	-f(e) → -ves	Oddballs
turkeys	**cities**	**lives**	**?**
alleys	armies	knives	deer
holidays	babies	leaves	geese
journeys	bodies	shelves	mice
monkeys	copies	thieves	women
valleys	duties	wolves	
	ladies		

Considerations: This sort builds on the previous sort by extending plural formation to words that require a change of spelling. Although the sort contains numerous one-syllable words, several new spelling issues are explored, making the sort more complex than it may initially seem. Because knowledge of the base word is once again very important, you may want to introduce the sort by checking students' understanding of the base words. Ask them to record the base word for each of the plurals underneath the word on the card. Discuss the spellings or misspellings and any unfamiliar words; then ask the students to look for different ways in which the plural is formed. Guide them to discover the categories listed for the sort, and discuss the results. Explain to students that words sometimes have more than one acceptable spelling for the plural form, as in *hoofs* and *hooves.*

When determining what to do about words that end in *-y,* students will need to consider the letter that precedes the *-y.* If the letter is a consonant, the change to *i* should be made; if the letter is a vowel, an *-s* is all that is needed, as in *alleys* and *turkeys.* Because spelling such words can be confusing, most dictionaries include the plural spelling as part of the word's entry, whether or not a spelling change is needed. You might invite students to brainstorm or hunt for other nouns that end in *-ey* (or other vowel *-y* words) and verify the spelling of their plurals with a dictionary. Generated examples might include *chimneys, donkeys, galleys, jerseys, jockeys, monkeys, surveys, trolleys.* Both *moneys* and *monies* are correct for the word *money,* but the former is more commonly used. How can you tell which spelling is more common? Dictionaries typically list the most common form of a word first when there are several possibilities. You may also wonder why there are two spellings. Perhaps this is because the change-*y*-to-*i* principle was mistakenly applied so often by writers that the alternative spelling became common, so lexicographers—those who write dictionaries—decided to accept it. When talking about the change-*y*-to-*i* category, you might point out to students that this principle or rule applies to adding many other suffixes. These changes are described in later studies. When discussing the oddball words, ask students to explain why they placed the words in this category. They should note that *deer* is both the plural and singular form of the word (as is *sheep*), and that the other words involve spelling changes. You might ask students to try to generate other examples of unusual plurals (such as *oxen, children, mice*).

Talking Points

- Change the *-y* to an *i* and add *-es* to form the plural of words that end in consonant *-y*; just add *-s* to form the plural of words that end in vowel *-y*, as in *copies* and *monkeys*.
- Words with final *-f* or *-fe* often change to *v* or *ve* before *-s* is added to make the plural, as in *wolf/wolves*.
- Some words have irregular plural forms, and some words use the same spelling for both plural and singular forms, as in *woman/women* and *deer/deer*.
- When in doubt about the spelling of a plural, consult a dictionary.

Integrating Idioms: "Upon her return to the classroom, the teacher shook her head and said, 'I guess **when the cat's away, the mice will play.**'" (Cause mischief when not watched. Mice must be very cautious when a cat is watching their mouse hole, but they can put down their guard when the cat is away.)

Did You Know? You may know that Benjamin Franklin once suggested the **turkey** for consideration as our national bird. But did you ever wonder why this bird, which is native to the New World, is called a *turkey?* After all, Turkey is a country of southwest Asia and southeast Europe, situated between the Mediterranean and Black Seas, and far from the New World. As *The Merriam-Webster New Book of Word Histories* (1991) tells the story, the bird was first domesticated by Indian tribes in Mexico and Central America. It was later exported by the Spanish conquerors and first introduced to the Mediterranean region in the early 1500s. It was immediately confused with a bird long found in the area and known by various names: *guinea fowl* or *guinea cock,* because it had originally come from the country of Guinea on the African west coast, and *turkey-cock,* because Europeans imported the bird from an area they called Turkey, which was much larger then than the country of Turkey today. At that time Turkey was considered exotic, so something out of the ordinary was often assumed to have come from there. A well-known botanist of the time even attached the name *turkey* to two New World plants. He cataloged maize as *Turkish corn* and pumpkins as *Turkish cucumbers.* It is not so surprising, then, that the New World fowl came to be associated with the Old World turkey-cock that it resembled.

SORT 8 Plurals with -s and -es

Base + -s		Base + -es
pieces	inches	wishes
classes	foxes	passes
crutches	dishes	sponges
guesses	bridges	dashes
sevens	taxes	branches
sixes	peaches	chances
indexes	brushes	losses
stitches	voices	watches

More Plurals

-y + -s	-y → i + -s	-f(e) → -ves
turkeys	cities	lives
mice	holidays	shelves
ladies	women	bodies
journeys	wolves	alleys
leaves	babies	geese
copies	armies	knives
monkeys	thieves	deer
valleys	duties	?

Comparisons

SORT 10. Adding -*er* and -*est* to Words with No Change, *e*-Drop, Double, and Change -*y* to *i*

Sorting by Pattern

No Change	*e*-Drop	Double	Change -*y* to *i*
cheaper	**bravest**	**bigger**	**driest**
brightest	closer	hottest	busiest
oddest	finest	sadder	easier
quicker	larger	slimmer	happier
smaller	ripest	thinnest	prettier
			silliest

What Is Known: Students know the concept of a base word and have had experience with the four category principles through their work with adding -*ed*, -*ing*, and plural endings. Also, students should be familiar with base-word spelling patterns in the first three categories. Although the polysyllabic base words in the final category are more challenging, most students at this stage will know how to spell them.

What Is New: Considering four options (no change, *e*-drop, double, and change -*y* to *i*) when adding an inflected ending, as well as working with comparatives and superlatives (-*er* and -*est*).

Considerations: This sort includes just 21 words in order to accommodate additional headers. Introduce students to comparisons by writing on the board *loud, louder,* and *loudest.* Explain that one of the ways we express differences when comparing two or more things is by adding -*er* or -*est* to the base word, as with the words on the board. Write *comparative* and *superlative* on the board; then say something such as this:

> "*Louder* is the comparative form, and *loudest* is the superlative form. The word *comparative* tells us we're comparing two things, and just as *super* means first-rate, *superlative* means 'superior to all others' and is used when we are comparing three or more things. Although we usually show comparison by attaching the -*er* or -*est* ending, as with *louder* and *loudest*, sometimes we add a word such as *more* or *most,* as we do with *more beautiful* or *most beautiful.* Could you imagine trying to say *beautifuller* or *beautifullest*?! Certain other words use different words to show comparison. This is the case with *good.* Here *better* and *best* are the comparing words, not *gooder* and *goodest* or even *more good* and *most good.* For the set of words we're working with, we'll just be using -*er* and -*est* comparisons."

Introduce the sort by asking students to classify the words according to whether they are comparative or superlative adjectives.

Sorting by Meaning/Pattern

Comparative	Superlative
bigger	bravest
cheaper	brightest
closer	busiest
easier	driest
happier	finest
larger	hottest
prettier	oddest
quicker	ripest
sadder	silliest
slimmer	thinnest
smaller	

As you go over the listing, ask students to say the other form of the adjective (*biggest* for *bigger*, *braver* for *bravest*, etc.). For a few of the words, you might ask students to brainstorm sentences that clearly show the word's comparative or superlative status (e.g., *I saw two pairs of shoes that I liked, but I bought the **cheaper** pair*, or *On moonless nights, Venus is often the **brightest** object in the night sky*).

Let students know that for this sort they will have a chance to use understandings they have gained from their recent work with *-ed* and *-ing* endings and plurals. Ask them to identify each base word and its spelling (you might ask them to write the base word at the bottom of the word card). Place the four headers and the key words in front of the students as category headers, and point out how the *-er* or *-est* ending was added to each: no change, *e*-drop, double, or change *-y* to *i*. Explain that they will be sorting the rest of the words in the same way, according to how the comparison is formed. If needed, model the placement of a few words before inviting their participation. Discuss the categories when the sorting is complete. As an extension or assessment, ask students to complete a chart for their words, similar to the one started here. Additional words could be added, if desired.

Base word	Comparative form	Superlative form
big	bigger	biggest
brave	braver	bravest

Talking Points

- Add *-er* to the base word when a comparison involves two things, and add *-est* when the comparison involves three or more things, as in *bigger brother* and *tallest girl in class*.
- Apply the *e*-drop, doubling, no-change, and change-*y*-to-*i* principles when adding *-er* or *-est* to base words, as in *finest, sadder, quicker, busiest*.

Integrating Idioms: "My mom is always telling me that **my eyes are bigger than my stomach.**" (I take more food than I can eat. When a meal or a particular food item looks good to eat, a person may take a lot of it, and then not be able to eat it all.)

Did You Know? The word **odd**(*est*) comes to us from Scandinavia, a region of northern Europe. In medieval times, the Old Norse word *oddi* was the name for triangle. The connection between *odd* and *triangle* stems from fact that a triangle can be thought to have a pair of angles at the bottom and an

Comparative		Superlative	
No Change	***e*-Drop**	**Double**	**Change -*y* to *i***
cheaper	bravest	bigger	
slimmer	larger	busiest	
ripest	happier	thinnest	
quicker	finest	easier	
sadder	silliest	smaller	
driest	brightest	hottest	
closer	prettier	oddest	

unpaired, or odd, one at the top. The same connection gives us *odd man,* an unpaired person in a game or the person who can cast a deciding vote, as well as other words and phrases. Odd numbers have no partner; an oddball stands out as though unpartnered; odd jobs are typically unrelated jobs; and if you are at odds with someone, you are certainly not working like partners.

Patterns across Syllables: Other Syllable Juncture Doubling
(DSA Feature L)

This section introduces students to two key syllable patterns—open and closed syllables. In the sorts that follow, four basic vowel and consonant patterns found across the juncture of syllables are described: VCV, as in *tiger* and *lemon;* VCCV with double consonants (also called a *doublet*), as in *hello;* VCCV with different consonants, as in *forget;* and VV, as in *diet.* Other sequences of letters, such as the three consonants in *athlete,* are introduced as variations of one of these four basic syllable patterns. As we will see, in these other sequences of letters, two of the letters act as a team (namely, as a consonant blend or digraph, or as a vowel digraph). This approach limits the number of patterns that students must otherwise consider as they form generalizations, and it encourages them to look for and use what they already know about patterns from the letter name and within word pattern stages. Let's look at a few examples.

Consider *athlete;* the basic across-syllable pattern is VCCV, represented by *a, th, l,* and the first *e.* The *th* is a digraph, and the letters work together as a team. In *reason,* the pattern is VCV: V (*ea*), C (*s*), V (*o*). What about *instead?* Which of the four basic across-syllable patterns is it, and what letters make up each element? It is a VCCV pattern, with V (*i*), C (*n*), C (*st,* a blend), and V (*ea,* a vowel team). Each team of letters acts as a unit, not as separate letters. Knowing how syllables are put together can aid students in spelling and reading polysyllabic words, especially when they also understand the key principles that govern the vowel sounds associated with open and closed syllables. *Open* syllables are those that end with a vowel rather than a consonant sound, and typically the vowel sound is long, as in *tiger, beaver,* and *diet. Closed* syllables are those that end with one or more consonants, as in *lemon, hello, forget, instead,* and even *trickster.*

What Is Known: Students who have completed sorts from *Word Sorts and More, Second Edition* (Ganske, 2018) may have been exposed to syllable structures as part of learning to recognize polysyllabic words (see Part I there). For other students, the concepts may be new. By this stage, all students should be familiar with long- and short-vowel patterns and with syllables.

What Is New: The concept of open and closed syllables, and the patterns across syllables that signal whether the vowel sound of the first syllable is long or short.

SORT 11. Open and Closed Syllables with VCV and VCCV (Doublet)

Sorting by Sound and Pattern

Open	Closed	
VCV	VCCV Doublet	Oddball
diner	**dinner**	?
crater	better	study
crazy	bottom	
duty	letter	
even	matter	
meter	penny	
music	ribbon	
paper	soccer	
ruler	summer	
student	supper	
super		
unit		

Considerations: Clarify any unfamiliar words. In particular, a discussion of the relationship among *diner, dinner,* and *supper* may be beneficial. Some students may not be familiar with *diner* as both "a small, inexpensive place to eat" and "one who dines." You might ask students whether they call their evening meal *dinner* or *supper.* Guide them to understand dinner as the main meal of the day, whether at midday or in the evening. The other light meal is usually called *lunch* or *supper,* depending on the time of day. Then introduce the sort by saying something such as this:

> "Although we've been working with multisyllabic words in our studies of *-ed, -ing,* plurals, and compounds, and thinking about the way they are spelled—especially where the ending joins the base word or, in the case of compounds, where the two base words come together—we're now ready to explore other ways syllables join. All of our words this time have two syllables." (After students have surveyed their words to check for unfamiliar words or meanings, and these have been discussed, continue with something like this:) "I want you to sort the words into two categories according to whether the vowel sound in the *first* syllable is long, as in *paper,* or short, as in *summer.*"

(Results will be the same as those shown in the sound and pattern sort, except that *study* will be placed in the "summer" category.) If necessary, model the process by categorizing a few words; then invite students to assist with those that remain. Once the sound sort is complete, ask students to analyze each category to ensure correct placement of the words and to look for pattern similarities. Students should notice the doubled versus single consonants. Guide with questions as needed, and discuss the ideas. If they do not recognize *study* as an oddball, point this out. Then move *diner* and *dinner* as key words to the top, and point out to students that in learning how syllables join, it is important to keep in mind consonant and vowel patterns, just as it was helpful to consider the pattern of the base word when adding *-ed* or *-ing.* Show students that all of the words under *diner* have a VCV pattern at the syllable juncture. (It will likely be worth the time to go through each word and point out the VCV pattern, or invite students to do so; do likewise with the VCCV doublet pattern.) As students interpret the sort, they should demonstrate or develop understanding that VCV patterns in the sort are associated with a long-vowel sound and the VCCV pattern with a short-vowel sound. You may need to point out that the syllable division in words with double consonants occurs between the two consonants. By closing off the first syllable with a consonant, we make the vowel sound short. Students should acquire understandings to aid them in reading and spelling words with VCV and VCCV across-syllable patterns. To link these understandings to reading or writing, ask them to read or write a sentence that contains multiple open-/closed-syllable words, such as *We saw that it was foggy the moment we stepped outside.* To bring closure to the lesson, guide students to the following concepts:

> "There are two strong principles that can be gleaned from today's lesson. The first relates to reading words: When double consonants occur at the juncture of two syllables, the first syllable will have a short-vowel sound, as with *dinner* and other words in our second category. The second principle deals with spelling: When trying to spell words with a long-vowel sound like *diner* and the others in our first category, follow the vowel with one consonant rather than two. You can see what happens if you mistakenly include two consonants: Instead of writing, 'I did a *super* job on my project,' you'd end up with 'a *supper* job,' which makes no sense. Finally, as you can see from the word *study*, which has a short vowel but just one consonant following it, there's more to learn about joining syllables in longer words. Keep your eyes peeled as you read and write, and perhaps you'll pick up some clues to help us figure that out."

Open and closed syllables and patterns at syllable junctures are discussed further in Chapter 7 of *Word Journeys, Second Edition* (Ganske, 2014).

Talking Points

- An open syllable ends with a long-vowel sound; it has a VCV pattern across the syllables, as in *diner*; the syllable divides after the first vowel.
- A closed syllable has a short-vowel sound and ends with a consonant; it has a VCCV pattern across syllables, sometimes with double consonants, as in *dinner.* The syllable divides between the consonants.
- Being able to divide words into syllables provides readers and writers with more manageable chunks for decoding and spelling words.

Integrating Idioms: "I know you said you got a good deal on this skateboard, but buying it is just being **penny-wise and pound-foolish;** there is nothing wrong with the one you have." (Saving a little by spending a lot. *Pound* here refers to money, not weight. Just as the dollar is the basic monetary unit in the United States, in the United Kingdom the basic unit is called the *pound* or *pound sterling.* The idiom points out how unwise it is to think you've done well if you saved a little but spent a lot to do so.)

Did You Know? Perhaps you've heard someone talk about their dislike of the **dog days of summer,** usually referring to the hot months of July and August. People sometimes mistakenly relate the expression to the fact that during the really hot months dogs tend to do little more than lie around. Instead, the phrase comes to us by way of a star in the constellation *Canis Major,* or "Greater Dog." The ancients called this second brightest of stars (our own sun being the brightest) *Sirius,* meaning "scorching or burning," because they associated its appearance with the dry, hot days of summer.

How did **soccer,** a game known most commonly in the world as *football,* get its name? Rules of the game were first written down in 1863 in England under the name of *association football* in order to avoid confusion with other types of football, such as rugby football. The longer name of *association football* was soon shortened to **soccer.**

SORT 12. Open and Closed Syllables with VCV and VCCV (Doublet or Different)

Sorting by Sound and Pattern

Open	Closed		Oddball
VCV	VCCV Doublet	VCCV Different	
open	**funny**	**contest**	**?**
bacon	dizzy	insect	limit
focus	follow	history	
human	pattern	number	
rotate	pretty	problem	
tulip	spelling	sandwich	
	traffic	sister	
	yellow	winter	

Considerations: This sort expands understanding of the VCCV across-syllable pattern to include different, as well as like, consonants. After surveying and reviewing any unfamiliar words, invite students to try categorizing the words based on work from the previous sort and from what they anticipate to be the focus of this lesson. When they are finished, ask them to analyze the categories to be sure each word belongs there, and then pair up and share their rationales for placing certain words together and to interpret the categories (namely, discuss what they can learn from the words that will enable them to be better readers and writers). Discuss the results as a group, including the oddball. If students do not suggest the VCCV pattern with different consonants as one of the categories, demonstrate and discuss this possibility. To link students back to contextual reading or writing, generate a sentence, such as *For their trip to the cabin, the family packed a basin, venom remover, and tablets for the water in case it was toxic,* and ask students to read or write it, applying what they know about syllable structure.

Talking Points

- The consonants in a closed VCCV pattern across syllables can be the same or different, as in *contest* and *funny.* Divide into syllables between the consonants.

Integrating Idioms: "I've got to show Mom and Dad my report card first, before they see my brother's; his will be **a tough act to follow.**" (Hard to compete with or show to be as good. In a performance, if the person or group before you performs really well, it's difficult to be the one who follows, because the audience may think your act is not as good and will be disappointed.)

Did You Know? Sandwich is a word with special beginnings because it originated from a person's name, or actually his title. John Montagu was the fourth Earl of Sandwich, an area in southeast England, during the 18th century. He was a hard-core gambler who reportedly sometimes gambled around the clock (24 hours straight). Instead of stopping the game for a meal, he asked that cold beef be brought to him between slices of bread, so that he could continue playing, and voilá, the sandwich was born. Words such as *sandwich,* which originate from the name of a person (or place), are called *eponyms.*

Although **tulip** is not an eponym, its origin is also interesting. You might think the word originally meant how it sounds—"two lips"; however, it was actually borrowed from a Turkish word for muslin or gauze, *tulbent. Turban* has its beginnings in the same word. In fact, the tulip was given its name because the fully opened flower was thought to resemble a turban.

SORT 13. Open and Closed Syllables with VCV, VCCV (Doublet or Different), and VV

Sorting by Pattern

Open	Closed		Open
VCV	VCCV Doublet	VCCV Different	VV
famous	**slipper**	**pencil**	**poet**
clover	happen	chapter	create
cocoa	million	expert	cruel
humid	muffin	member	dial
pupil	sudden	publish	giant
		sentence	lion
		until	quiet

Considerations: This sort introduces students to a new across-syllable pattern: VV. As you work through the lesson, remember to integrate academic vocabulary and to apply the basic components of SAIL—survey, analyze, interpret, and link. Discuss any unfamiliar words and expand students' understanding of the double meanings of words such as *sentence* (a "grammatical unit" and a "term of punishment") and *pupil* (a "student" and the "opening in the center of an eye"). Begin by asking students to sort the words into two groups by sound: open syllables and closed syllables (long vowels and short vowels). Then they can subdivide each list by pattern. The end results are shown in the Sort 13 answer key. Once the categories are complete, discuss the results. Although there are few two-syllable words with the VV pattern, it appears much more often in three- and four-syllable words, so it is an important pattern for students to be aware of. Caution them when sorting words with two vowels to pay heed to their sound. The vowels sometimes cross syllable boundaries, as in this sort, so that the sound of each is heard; at other times, the vowels work as a team, as in *reason*. Because this sort can be completed just by looking at the patterns, you may want to provide students with opportunities to sort the words without looking at these, so that they also attend to sound.

Talking Points

- Two vowels together are not always a team; sometimes the vowels are situated across syllable boundaries, creating a VV pattern but with the syllable division between them, as in *poet*.

Integrating Idioms: "Hey, what are you thinking about? **You're a million miles away.**" (Distracted or daydreaming. If you were literally a million miles away, you would have no idea of what other people were doing.)

Did You Know? **Pupil** provides an opportunity for students to discover that certain words are entered in the dictionary more than once. Looking up *pupil* will reveal two separate entries, designated with a superscript 1 or 2: pu•pil[1] and pu•pil[2]. Students may wonder why all of the meanings are not listed under one entry. Ask them to speculate before explaining that different entries for a word mean that each meaning has its own origin or story. For example, *pupil*, meaning "student," stems from a word that means "boy," whereas the *pupil* of an eye was borrowed from a word meaning "little doll" because of the miniature image reflected in a pupil. Students might search in the dictionary for other common words with multiple meanings and multiple histories.

Just how tall does someone have to be to be considered a *giant?* To a toddler, most parents are giants. According to a Wikipedia entry, 7 feet 5 inches tall has been used as a benchmark for giant size. The tallest person in history, or at least the tallest one whose height has been confirmed, was a man from Illinois who grew to nearly 9 feet! You might invite students to brainstorm a list of well-known giants from literature (such as Roald Dahl's BFG—Big Friendly Giant; Hagrid from the *Harry Potter* series; Rumblebuffin from C. S. Lewis's *The Lion, the Witch and the Wardrobe*; the giant of *Jack and the Beanstalk* fame; Paul Bunyan; Polyphemus, the Cyclops in Homer's *The Odyssey*; and the Bible's Goliath).

SORT 14. Open and Closed Syllables with VCV and VCCV (Doublet or Different)

Sorting by Sound and Pattern

Open	Closed		Oddballs
VCV	VCCV Doublet	VCCV Different	Consonant and vowel teams
lazy	**classic**	**basket**	**?**
humor	comma	absent	apple
recent	gallon	distant	athlete
silent	inning	napkin	constant
	ladder	picnic	control
	mammal		hundred
	tennis		program
			reason

Considerations: Up to this point, the V or C elements in VCCV and VCV structures have represented single letters. However, as discussed in the introduction to this section, consonant blends and digraphs and vowel digraphs sometimes occur at the syllable juncture. If individual letters are used to examine across-syllable patterns, students will need to think about an increasing number of patterns. To help them keep in mind the basic patterns that occur across syllables, and to limit the number of patterns they must consider, words with digraphs and blends at the juncture of syllables are highlighted as oddballs in this sort. In subsequent sorts, words of this type are categorized as VCV, as VCCV doublet or different, or as VV, with the vowel or consonant team regarded as a unit, V or C.

Begin by going over any unfamiliar words. Explain to students that the sort includes several oddballs for which they should be watchful. Provide the headers; then ask them to sort their words according to the categories they have studied—VCV and VCCV doublet and different—and to place words in the ? category that do not seem to fit. Their ultimate aim should be to discover characteristics that result in words' being classified as oddballs. Suggest that students work in dyads or triads, and ask that they share their results with another team when they are finished. Once everyone is finished, discuss the results. Then ask students to identify any consonant or vowel teams and try to determine which syllable structure is the best match for each oddball. The following chart illustrates the thinking that may result (VCCV doublet and VCCV different have been combined into one column):

	V	**C**	**V**			**V**	**C**	**C**	**V**	
pr	O	GR	A	m		A	P	P	LE	
r	EA	S	O	n		A	TH	L	E	te
					h	U	N	DR	E	d

V	C	V		V	C	C	V
				c	O	N	TR	O	l
				c	O	N	ST	A	nt

During the discussion, clarify the pattern in *apple,* which is considered VCCV doublet. Although students may have thought of *pl* as a consonant team, sound does not support this; instead, *l* and *e* together make the vowel sound /əl/, as they do in many words—for example, *buckle, people, candle,* and *title.* The first syllable in *apple* consists of *ap,* and the final syllable is *ple,* or *Cle.* Remind students that awareness of vowel and consonant teams can help with reading unfamiliar words. It is important for students to learn to approach words flexibly. If applying one pattern does not lead to a correct pronunciation during reading, have them try another. For example, *h-u-m-o-r* is a VCV pattern with an open syllable, but if *t-o-p-i-c* were approached in the same manner, the pronunciation would be tō•pĭc, instead of the actual pronunciation of *topic,* which has a VCV pattern but with a closed syllable. This pattern is discussed in the next sort.

Suggest that students be alert for other words with blends and digraphs at the syllable juncture, and explain that in the future, words of this type will be included in one of the basic categories: VCV, VCCV doublet or different, or VV. Ask students who are up to an extra challenge or even a super-duper challenge to try to determine the syllable pattern for one or both of the following words (be sure they understand what the words mean as well; you will almost certainly have to explain the meaning and perhaps the pronunciation for the super-duper challenge):

Challenge: *gypsy* (V = *y*, C = *p*, C = *s*, V = *y*) closed syllable

Super-Duper Challenge: *queuing* [pronounced /Q + ing/] (VV) open syllable

A *queue* means "a long line of waiting people or cars"; it also refers to a long braid. We might say *People are queuing up for the movie.* No letter divisions are listed for *queuing,* because just which letters should be considered part of the vowel pattern (V) is debatable; ask students to provide a rationale for their decisions.

Talking Points

- Sometimes consonants that occur at the juncture of syllables form a team; careful consideration is needed to decide where to divide the syllables, as in *program, control,* and *athlete.* Teams can also consist of vowels, as in *rea/son,* not *re/ason.*
- When dividing words with three or more consonants at the juncture, look for consonant blends and digraphs that often work together in words, such as *th* and *dr.*

Integrating Idioms: "The teacher said our group's work on the project seems to be **without any rhyme or reason.** She asked if we would get it done on time." (No real purpose or direction. A *rhyme* typically has a pattern or other organization, and *reason* is a motive for acting; without these two, it's unlikely much is being accomplished.)

Did You Know? What do *mop, map,* and **napkin** have in common? *Mop* was borrowed from the Latin word *mappa,* meaning cloth. In 1496 a similar word, *mappe,* designated a bundle of yarn or cloth used to clean or spread pitch on a ship's planking to keep water out. *Map* has a similar background because early *mappa mundi,* "maps of the world," were made of cloth to last for long sea journeys. *Napkin* comes from the same word with a later adding of *-kin* to mean "little cloth." These "little cloths," even when paper, sometimes serve varied purposes: Popular author J. K. Rowling began the *Harry Potter* series in a café, writing on a paper napkin.

Literature Link

Truss, L. (2006). *Eats, shoots and leaves: Why commas really do make a difference*. New York: G. P. Putnam's Sons. This picture book, with its cartoon drawings, highlights what happens to meaning when commas are misplaced or omitted. Entertaining for all ages.

SORT 15. Open and Closed Syllables with VCV (Long or Short) and VCCV (Doublet or Different)

Sorting by Sound and Pattern			
Open	Closed		
VCV Long	VCCV Doublet	VCCV Different	VCV Short
moment	**attic**	**enjoy**	**planet**
climate	rabbit	elbow	clever
freedom	tunnel	enter	comet
local	village	garden	rapid
sequel		mustard	second
		picture	solid
		orbit	travel
			value

Considerations: Again, apply the SAIL framework as you guide students through the following: Survey and discuss any unfamiliar words; then introduce the sort by asking students to categorize the words according to open and closed syllables. This will result in one very long list (closed) and a short list (open). Next, analyze the categories; discuss pattern differences in the closed-syllable column; and, as a group, subdivide the list into the VCCV doublet, VCCV different, and VCV short categories. As the categories are formed, add the corresponding header. *Freedom* is considered a VCV long pattern here, with a vowel team (*ee*) for the first vowel. In *sequel,* the *u* works with the *q* as a team, creating a VCV long pattern. Discuss and interpret the results, and ask students to tell what they learned. They will likely mention something about the confusing nature of the VCV pattern: It can lead to either a long- or a short-vowel sound. Caution students when they are reading and writing such words. Remind them that if the syllable ends in a long-vowel sound, the consonant that follows will not be doubled when they write the word. However, if the syllable is closed and the vowel sound short, there may or may not be doubled consonants at the juncture—for example, *rabbit/habit, buddy/study,* and *bobbin/robin*. Words with closed syllables require caution in spelling. In reading words with a VCV pattern, it is best to consider the syllable open and the vowel sound long, and then try identifying it. If that approach does not produce a recognizable word, the syllable should be considered closed, and a short-vowel sound applied. Explain that it is not as difficult as it may seem, just something that wise spellers and readers keep a lookout for. Generate a short sentence to link learning to reading or writing, such as *In the crater they found a meteorite that had once been part of a comet before the fragments plummeted and crashed into the surface of the planet.*

Talking Points

- Although VCV usually signals an open syllable, sometimes this is the pattern of a closed syllable, as in the difference between *moment* and *comet*.
- Read words with a VCV pattern as an open syllable first; if this does not produce a known word, try closing the syllable and reading again.
- When writing, if you hear a long vowel, make sure you don't have a double consonant following it, as in *local*, not *loccal*.

Integrating Idioms: "Sorry I wasn't home for your call; I went shopping **on the spur of the moment.**" (All of a sudden. We typically think of spurs as short spikes attached to the heel of a rider's boot and used to goad or urge a horse to move more quickly. In this expression, a particular moment is serving as a spur and causing the speaker to suddenly, and without prior planning, decide to go to the mall.)

Did You Know? The ancients observed several heavenly bodies that changed their positions relative to each other and to stars that seemed fixed in their positions (the sun and moon; and Mercury, Venus, Mars, Jupiter, and Saturn, thought to revolve about the Earth). The Greeks referred to these bodies as *planetai*, or "wanderers." The word was borrowed by the Romans, the French, and later the English and eventually became ***planets.***

Garden stems from a Latin word for "fenced or walled area." Then as now, intruders, whether four-legged or two-legged, were cause for concern to anyone trying to grow plants, so enclosures provided a deterrent. The words *guard* and *kindergarten* are related to *garden*. The latter word is made up of *kinder*, the German word for "children," and *garten*, which means "garden." The word dates back to 1840, 3 years after Friedrich Fröbel started the first kindergarten as a place in which children could be cultivated and bloom.

SORT 11
Open and Closed Syllables with VCV and VCCV (Doublet)

Open	Closed	VCV	VCCV Doublet
diner	dinner		unit
paper	summer		soccer
student	letter		crater
matter	study		better
duty	ribbon		meter
penny	ruler		even
music	bottom		crazy
super	supper		?

Open and Closed Syllables
with VCV and VCCV (Doublet or Different)

VCV	VCCV Doublet	VCCV Different
open	funny	contest
limit	history	dizzy
follow	bacon	pattern
human	sandwich	pretty
number	winter	focus
rotate	spelling	problem
sister	tulip	yellow
traffic	insect	?

Open and Closed Syllables
with VCV, VCCV (Doublet or Different), and VV

VCV	VCCV Doublet	VCCV Different	VV
famous	slipper		pencil
poet	quiet		million
dial	sentence		publish
expert	clover		happen
humid	sudden		until
giant	lion		cocoa
member	cruel		chapter
muffin	pupil		create

Open and Closed Syllables
with VCV and VCCV (Doublet or Different)

VCV	VCCV **Doublet**	VCCV **Different**
lazy	classic	basket
picnic	control	napkin
apple	inning	tennis
recent	absent	constant
program	mammal	athlete
comma	hundred	humor
reason	gallon	ladder
silent	distant	?

SORT 15

Open and Closed Syllables
with VCV (Long or Short) and VCCV (Doublet or Different)

VCV **Long**	VCCV **Doublet**	VCCV **Different**	VCCV **Short**
moment	attic		enjoy
planet	second		tunnel
mustard	value		climate
local	elbow		travel
garden	rapid		freedom
clever	rabbit		picture
village	solid		sequel
orbit	enter		comet

Vowel Patterns in Stressed Syllables

Long-Vowel Patterns in Stressed Syllables *(DSA Feature M)*

This section is the first of several to focus on vowel patterns in stressed syllables. Here, long vowels are targeted, with short vowels used as a contrasting sound. Later sections deal with *r*-controlled and abstract vowels. Identifying which syllable is stressed or accented can be difficult for students, so you might be wondering, "Why study them?" Typically, vowel patterns in stressed syllables are easier to spell than those in unstressed syllables, because sound provides a clue to the pattern. By identifying the vowel sound, students are able to apply much of their pattern knowledge from previous stages to spell longer words. In contrast, the schwa vowel sound /ə/ of unstressed syllables, which will be studied later at this stage, is less predictable: All five vowels and several vowel combinations can produce the sound. Recognizing stressed and unstressed syllables, and realizing which part of a word is the more difficult, can alert students to focus their mental energy on the tricky part as they learn to spell the word. Work with stressed syllables can also encourage students to approach unfamiliar words in their reading with flexibility. If pronouncing a word one way does not lead to a known word, shifting the stress to another syllable and trying an alternative pronunciation may. Finally, work with stressed syllables provides an opportunity to help students learn to navigate unfamiliar aspects of the dictionary.

Introduce students to the concept of syllable stress by taking a step back. In advance of the lesson, on the board or a transparency, record the following words and their dictionary entries, which also show syllable division and pronunciation. Cover up the entry word and pronunciation so that these aspects of the words can be revealed one word at a time. Then ask students to clap and count the number of syllables in the words, as in *pencil* (2), *principal* (3), *computer* (3), *gym* (1), and *dictionary* (4).

pencil	**pen•cil**	(pĕn´səl)
principal	**prin•ci•pal**	(prĭn´sə-pəl)
computer	**com•put•er**	(kəm-pyōō´tər)
gym	**gym**	(jĭm)
dictionary	**dic•tion•ar•y**	(dĭk´shə-nĕr´ē)

Next, say something such as this:

TEACHER: When words have more than one syllable, one of the syllables is usually stressed or said with a little more emphasis, as in *pencil*. (*Points to the word.*) A dictionary often identifies the stressed syllable by placing an apostrophe-like mark called an *accent* [´] after the stressed syllable in the word's pronunciation, as we see here. (*Uncovers the entry word and pronunciation for* pencil *to demonstrate.*) The bolded word is the *entry word*. Entry words are usually bolded so you can easily find the word you're searching for; the pronunciation is the part in parentheses. From what you see, which syllable of *pencil* is stressed?

STUDENT: It's the first syllable, the *pen* part; see, here is the accent mark. (*Points.*)

TEACHER: That's right. Here, the syllable that is stressed is the first syllable. (*Points to bolded word and underlines the first syllable.*) Notice that the entry word separates the syllables with a little dot, but it doesn't show us which of the syllables is stressed, and it doesn't show us how to pronounce the word, either. We might think that the first syllable is pronounced like the writing tool, since it's spelled the same, but look at the second syllable in the entry word. (*Points to* cil.) If you came upon *c-i-l* as a new word in your reading, you would probably pronounce it like the last syllable in *windowsill*, with a short-*i* sound. But do we pronounce the letters in *p-e-n-c-i-l* as *pensill*?

STUDENT: No way! That sounds silly.

TEACHER: That's right. It sounds funny to our ears, because when we say *pencil*, the second syllable isn't stressed at all; in fact, we say that it is *unstressed*. When a syllable is unstressed, the vowel changes from its usual long or short sound to the schwa sound of "uh." You can always tell when a syllable has this sound, because a dictionary represents it with this special upside-down, backward *e* that we see in the second syllable of *pencil*. (*Points*.) The schwa tells us to pronounce the word as *pensull,* not *pensill*. We're going to begin our study of syllable stress by exploring vowel patterns and sounds in the stressed syllables of words, but eventually we'll come back to the schwa, because it can be tricky to spell and is the cause of many spelling errors. [Students may notice other schwa vowels during the lesson. You may wish to comment on these but maintain focus on the stressed syllables at this time.] Okay, let's think about the other words we used for counting syllables and see if we can pick out the stressed syllable. What about *principal*; which syllable do you think is stressed?

STUDENT: It's the first one again, just like *pencil*.

TEACHER: (*Uncovers the entry word and pronunciation*.) That's right; when we say *principal,* we stress the first syllable—*prin*. (*Underlines this portion of the word*.)

STUDENT: Is it always the first syllable?

TEACHER: What do you think?

STUDENT: No, because look at *computer*. Who says, "Can I work on the **com**puter?"

TEACHER: Good thinking. So which syllable do we stress in *computer?*

STUDENTS: (*Repeat the word to themselves*.) The second part.

TEACHER: Yes, we stress the second syllable in *computer*. (*Uncovers the information for* computer, *then models by saying the word and slightly emphasizing the second syllable*—com**pu**ter; *underlines this part of the word*.) [Note: Dictionary entry words divide words into syllables according to meaning units, whereas the pronunciation of the word is divided according to sound. Thus, the *t* in the entry word *computer* is included with the second syllable of the entry word, because it is part of a meaning unit, the word root—*put*. It is not included in the second syllable of the pronunciation, because this is not how we say the word. There is no need to call students' attention to this distinction unless they notice the difference.]

TEACHER: All right, what about *gym?*

STUDENTS: You're trying to trick us. That word has just one syllable; you said at the beginning that stress has to do with words that have *more* than one syllable.

TEACHER: (*Uncovers the information for* gym.) Excellent thinking and remembering! That's right. When a word has just one syllable, we don't have to consider stress at all. Okay, let's think about the last word, *dictionary;* then we'll check to see what the stress or accent mark for this word looks like in the dictionary. Let's clap and say *dictionary* again: *dic-tion-ar-y*. This is a long word; who will give it a try?

STUDENT 1: I think it's the first syllable.

STUDENT 2: I think it's the third one.

TEACHER: Good job, both of you! Sometimes words with several syllables, like this one, can have more than one stressed syllable. Although a word like *dictionary* may have more than one stressed syllable, one of the stressed syllables is said with greater emphasis than the other. It is the *primary stress,* and the other syllable is the *secondary stress*. [Younger or less capable students may be confused by the additional terms. If so, disregard this portion of the discussion.] Which syllable in *dictionary* is given the main or primary stress?

STUDENT 2: (*Repeats the word.*) It's the first syllable, but the third one gets the other stress.

TEACHER: (*Uncovers the entry word and pronunciation for* dictionary.) That's right; very good observation! Notice that the accent for the syllable that is said with the most emphasis is shown with a heavier line than the less stressed syllable. In some dictionaries, the accented syllable is boldfaced rather than indicated by the special mark.

At this point, students may be guided to find some of the lesson words, or other polysyllabic words, in the dictionary. Keep the activity engaging by making it a game: Invite each student to suggest one or more polysyllabic words to classmates to guess the stress, and then check the accuracy of their responses with a dictionary. Note that dictionaries sometimes vary slightly in how they record a word's pronunciation. The pronunciations provided in this section are from *The American Heritage College Dictionary* (2020). Also, bear in mind that dialect may cause a student to pronounce a word differently from what is shown in a dictionary entry.

Depending on the needs and interests of the group, you might engage students in the States Stress Break included in Sort 63 in this chapter before moving on to the sorts that follow. Initially, use the States Stress Break word cards just to reinforce students' ability to identify the stressed syllable in the words. At the end of the syllable juncture stage, after students have studied the various vowel patterns, students may revisit the words with the expectation of learning to spell the names of the states. For further information on working with syllable stress at the syllable juncture stage, see *Word Journeys, Second Edition* (Ganske, 2014).

The following series of seven sorts focuses on long-vowel patterns in stressed syllables. First students identify the syllable that is stressed (first or second), and then they compare and contrast long- and short-vowel patterns in the stressed syllable. Some students may have a difficult time considering both long- and short-vowel words. If so, eliminate the short-vowel words, or tell students to focus only on long-vowel stressed syllables and to categorize all other words as oddballs.

What Is Known: (Sorts 16–22) Students should be confident in their use of long- and short-vowel patterns in single-syllable words; a few specific patterns may be new to them. They should also be familiar with stress and syllables. Though they are not likely to be confident in identifying the stressed syllable in a word, they should know that it can occur in different syllables.

What Is New: (Sorts 16–22) Examining vowel patterns in stressed syllables will be new. Also, because students were just introduced to the open-syllable long-vowel pattern earlier in this book, it is still relatively new to them; a few other patterns may also be new. For example, the long-*e* pattern *eCe* (*compete*) and *y* as a short-vowel pattern (*symbol*) may be new.

SORT 16. Long and Short *a* in Stressed Syllables

Sorting by Syllable Stress

1st Stress	2nd Stress	Oddball
bracelet	**afraid**	**?**
April	amaze	[none]
basement	complain	
basic	contain	
chocolate	erase	
crayon	escape	
daily	explain	
fable	obey	
later	perhaps	
nation	remain	
raisin		
rather		
Saturday		
shadow		

Considerations: Introduce the sort in a manner similar to the following, and integrate relevant academic vocabulary into the talk:

Survey

1. Read through the template of words, and discuss any that might be unfamiliar (perhaps *fable* and *nation*).

2. Ask students if they noticed anything about the words. They should have detected that nearly all of the words have a long-*a* sound. If they do not mention that a few of the words have the short-*a* sound, bring this to their attention.

3. Put out the headers *1st Stress* and *2nd Stress* with their respective key words (*bracelet* and *afraid*) and the card used for oddballs (?), though the words can be sorted without it.

4. Say "bracelet," and slightly emphasize the first syllable: **bracelet**. Explain that *bracelet* has been placed in the first category because the first syllable is stressed. Follow a similar process with *afraid* to highlight its placement in the 2nd Stress category.

5. Explain to students that with their help, you will be sorting the remaining words under the appropriate 1st Stress or 2nd Stress category. Choose a short-vowel word to model another example. Invite students to attempt the next word. (Sometimes it can be helpful to read the words aloud without showing them to students. This takes away any visual distraction and allows full concentration to be on the sound. Be sure to pronounce the words with natural emphasis.)

Analyze

6. When all of the words have been sorted, guide students to analyze the word placements: Read down the column of 1st Stress words; slightly accentuate the stressed syllable. Ask students if they can hear the accent or stress on the first syllable. If anyone has difficulty, ask the group to reread the column with you. Identify the vowel sound in the stressed first syllable of each word and discuss. Point

out that because long vowels often occur in stressed syllables, hearing a long-vowel sound can help to identify which syllable is stressed. Ask the students to consider whether all the words fit the category.

7. Repeat the process with the other column. Discuss the results, drawing students' attention to the difference in stress from the first category. Identify the vowel sound in each stressed syllable. Point out that with the exception of *chocolate,* all of the words have either a long- or a short-*a* vowel sound in the stressed syllable.

8. *Saturday,* with its long- and short-*a* sounds, may give rise to special debate; although the third syllable, *day,* receives some stress, the primary stress is on the first syllable. Because dialect may influence the pronunciation of this and other words, avoid being overly concerned about correctness; instead, allow for individual differences by suggesting the oddball category as a way to resolve such questions.

Interpret

9. Ask students what their take-away from the sort is for reading and writing. If they don't mention the following, be sure to bring it up, as well as any of the other Talking Points that follow. Explain to students that vowel patterns in stressed syllables tend to be easier to spell because the sound provides a clue—as, for example, the *aCe* pattern in *basement,* which is stressed, compared with the same pattern in *chocolate,* which is not.

Link

10. Generate a sentence with two or three words with the features targeted in the sort; then ask students to write it or show them the sentence and ask them to read it.

Sorting by Sound and Pattern

Short *a*	*aCe*	*ai*	Open *a*	Oddball
shadow	**bracelet**	**afraid**	**fable**	**?**
perhaps	amaze	complain	April	chocolate
rather	basement	contain	basic	daily
Saturday	erase	(daily)	crayon	obey
	escape	explain	(daily)	
		raisin	later	
		remain	nation	

After completing the sound sort with stressed syllables for Sort 16, or at a later time, ask students to suggest other ways to categorize the words. Likely someone will suggest sorting by pattern. The results would be the same as shown in the sound and pattern sort above, except that the short-*a* and open-*a* categories would be combined. If no one mentions it, suggest that students try sorting by pattern and vowel sound, as shown. The group session would go something like this (a similar process can be used for Sorts 17–22):

1. Put out *shadow, bracelet, afraid,* and *fable* as key words; add the question mark for oddballs. Highlight or underline the vowel pattern in each stressed syllable. If someone suggests that the two categories represented by *shadow* and *fable* should be combined, since they both have the *a* pattern, say something such as this:

"That is one way the words could be looked at, because both *shadow* and *fable* do have *a*'s, but because we want to think about sound as well as pattern, we're going to keep them separate. Listen: The *a* makes a short sound in *shadow* and a long sound in *fable*. Because the vowel sound ends the syllable in *fable*, it makes a long sound; it's like the other open-syllable words we studied earlier. It is kind of confusing, because the vowel is tucked between two consonants, just as it is in *shadow*. Patterns like these that look alike on the surface can cause problems during reading, too. Obviously, we'll need to be careful about our placement of words with the *a* pattern."

2. Ask students to help you sort the words into their appropriate categories.

3. *Chocolate* is an oddball; although it has the *aCe* pattern, the pattern does not make a long *a* sound. *Obey* is also an oddball; it has a long-*a* sound, but there is no *ey* category. *Daily* is an oddball because it has both open-*a* and *ai* patterns. Allow students to place the word in any of the three pattern categories.

4. Review the categories for the appropriate sound and pattern; discuss the results and add the category headers. As part of the discussion, you might temporarily move an open-*a* word or two to the short-*a* category and ask students how the word(s) would be pronounced. You might also ask them how *s-h-a-d-o-w* would be pronounced if it had an open *a*. Invite students to brainstorm other long-*a* patterns in stressed syllables, as, for example, *ay* in *decay* or *mayor*. Explain that in the future they will be examining other vowel patterns in stressed syllables.

Talking Points

- Vowel patterns in stressed syllables tend to be easier to spell.
- A particular vowel pattern may be stressed in the first syllable of one word (*bracelet*), in the second syllable of another (*escape*), and not at all in some other word (*chocolate*).
- Three common long-*a* patterns found in stressed syllables are *aCe*, *ai*, and open *a*, as in *amaze*, *contain*, and *later*.

Integrating Idioms: "Are you sure, **beyond a shadow of a doubt,** that he took your paper?" (Completely. If the only doubt you had could be compared to a shadow, there would be little substance to it; taking the matter a step further and saying "*beyond* a shadow of a doubt" suggests no possibility of a doubt.)

Did You Know? **Saturday,** like the other days of the week, gets its name from a celestial body—the sun, moon, or planets. *Saturday* was originally called *Saturn's Day* (the Latin expression would have been *Dies Saturni*) and was named after the Roman god of agriculture. In ancient times, each year a 7-day period of high-spirited and carefree celebration called *Saturnalia* was held in his honor. The way that many people still like to enjoy themselves on a Saturday evening is a good reminder of Saturn's connection to this day.

The rest of the days, in order, translated from the Latin as *Sun's Day, Moon's Day, Mars's Day, Mercury's Day, Jupiter's* or *Jove's Day,* and *Venus's Day.* The relationship of the sun and moon to the names of our days of the week is obvious, but what about the other days that were named after planets? How did *Tuesday* evolve from *Mars's Day,* and so on? The days named after planets were names of gods, as *Saturday* for Saturn. However, because Old English (the ancestor of modern-day English) was a Germanic language, when the names of the days of the week were borrowed into early English, writers not only translated the Latin words but also substituted similar German or Norse gods for the names of four of the Roman gods. So instead of *Mars's Day,* it was *Tiu's Day* ("Tuesday"). Tiu, like Mars, was a god of war. *Mercury's Day* became *Woden's Day* ("Wednesday"). Mercury was quick, well spoken, and known for his general skill, and Woden as the supreme god would have been recognized for similar traits. *Jupiter's Day* became *Thurin's* or *Thor's Day* ("Thursday"). Jupiter was the supreme Roman god, and Thor, a son of Woden, was the most popular god. He was known as the "thunder god" because whenever he traveled across the sky in his chariot, the sound of the wheels made thunder. *Venus's Day* became *Frigga's Day* ("Friday"). Both Venus and Frigga, the wife of Woden, were goddesses of love and beauty. So why was *Saturn's Day* not replaced? Apparently the Germanic people had no similar god to substitute, so they just translated the Roman god's name. A table comparing current English spelling to that of the ancient Latin and Old English follows. Contemporary French and Spanish spellings are also included. These were also derived from the Latin but without the substitution of different gods, so the names of the Roman gods are more discernible in their spellings. The weekend days, with their religious significance, were altered in the French and Spanish forms to words related to *Sabbath* and to a phrase meaning "Lord's Day."

English	Latin	Old English	French	Spanish
Sunday	*Dies Solis*	*Sunnandaeg*	*dimanche*	*domingo*
Monday	*Dies Lunae*	*Monandaeg*	*lundi*	*lunes*
Tuesday	*Dies Martis*	*Tiwesdaeg*	*mardi*	*martes*
Wednesday	*Dies Mercurii*	*Wodnesdaeg*	*mercredi*	*miércoles*
Thursday	*Dies Jovis*	*Thunresdaaeg*	*jeudi*	*jueves*
Friday	*Dies Veneris*	*Frigedaeg*	*vendredi*	*viernes*
Saturday	*Dies Saturni*	*Saeternesdaeg*	*samedi*	*sábado*

(Note: The word Saturday is included in this sort; for the other days of the week, see: Sunday, Sort 54; Monday, Tuesday, and Thursday, Sort 22; Wednesday, Sort 17; and Friday, Sort 19.)

Literature Links

D'Aulaire, I., & D'Aulaire, E. P. (1967). *D'Aulaires' book of Norse myths*. New York: Doubleday.
D'Aulaire, I., & D'Aulaire, E. P. (1992). *D'Aulaires' book of Greek myths*. New York: Delacorte Books for Young Readers.
Vinge, J. P. (1999). *The Random House book of Greek myths*. New York: Random House for Young Readers.

SORT 17. Long and Short *e* in Stressed Syllables

Sorting by Syllable Stress		
1st Stress	2nd Stress	Oddball
fever	**delete**	**?**
deeply	asleep	[none]
effort	between	
either	complete	
evening	degrees	
female	expect	
ketchup	extreme	
legal	idea	
never	indeed	
people	succeed	
secret	supreme	
Wednesday	trapeze	

Sorting by Sound and Pattern

Short *e*	*ee*	*eCe*	Open *e*	Oddball
effort	**asleep**	**delete**	**fever**	**?**
expect	between	complete	female	either
ketchup	deeply	evening	idea	people
never	degrees	extreme	legal	
Wednesday	indeed	supreme	secret	
	succeed	trapeze		

Considerations: As in previous sorts, apply the elements of SAIL to the structure of your lesson, and be sure to integrate academic vocabulary into the talk. VCe is a new pattern for *e*, as the pattern seldom occurs in one-syllable words. Also, as a point of information, although *Wednesday* looks as though it has three syllables due to its three separate vowels, it has only two. Discuss meanings as needed, but check for understanding of *trapeze* and the multiple meanings of *degrees* (university-related, temperature, and others). The same basic process described for introducing Sort 16 may be used here. When you are discussing the results, there is no oddball for the syllable stress sort, unless students pronounce *either* with a long *i*. *People* and *either* are oddballs in the sound and pattern sort. Although each has a long-*e* sound in the stressed syllable, their long-*e* patterns are not included in the sort. Students may be able think of other long-*e* patterns. Also, some students may suggest that *delete* has an open syllable as well as *eCe*. Remind them that the vowel pattern needs to be in the stressed syllable. Say the word with them, slightly emphasizing the second syllable. If they continue to pronounce it with a long-*e* sound in each syllable, suggest that they place the word as an oddball.

Talking Points

- Three long-*e* vowel patterns often found in stressed syllables are *ee*, *eCe*, and open *e*, as in *between*, *delete*, and *fever*.
- Although very few one-syllable words have *eCe*, this pattern is found in the second syllable of numerous polysyllabic words.
- Because various patterns can represent the same sound in a stressed syllable, when trying to spell one, if you're not sure which is the right one, check a dictionary or ask an expert.

Integrating Idioms: "I'd like to create a model of the White House for my project, but I know **it'll never fly** with Ms. Papier, because she said it had to be a report." (It will never be approved. The project won't get the go-ahead from Ms. Papier, just as airplanes sometimes don't get clearance to take off.)

Did You Know? **Ketchup** is also called *catchup* and *catsup*. Although all three variations are in use today, *ketchup* has been around the longest; it came into use in 1711. The word is thought to have been borrowed from a Malay word (*kechap*) for a sauce that contained fish brine and sauces, but no tomatoes. During the 1700s and 1800s, *ketchup* referred to any sauce that had vinegar as a base. The other ingredients were anything that was available—walnuts, mushrooms, and so forth. What might you add to the vinegar if you were going to make this type of ketchup?

Fever derives from the Latin word *febris*—a connection still apparent in several "$100 words," including *febrile*, which means "feverish," *febrifuge*, a medication used to reduce a fever, and *febrifacient*, which means "fever-producing." With 98.6°F considered normal body temperature, just what temperature is considered a *fever*, "an abnormally high body temperature"? A temperature greater than 100°F is indicative of a fever, and one greater than 104°F should receive immediate medical attention. Two well-known diseases characterized by high fevers are *scarlet fever*, caused by bacteria, and *yellow fever*, a tropical disease caused by a mosquito-transmitted virus.

SORT 18. More Long and Short *e* in Stressed Syllables

Sorting by Syllable Stress

1st Stress	2nd Stress	Oddball
season	**believe**	**?**
breakfast	achieve	[none]
diet	agreed	
eastern	beneath	
healthy	instead	
heavy	proceed	
jealous	relief	
meaning	repeat	
needle	retrieve	
ready		
science		
seedling		
sweater		
weather		
western		

Sorting by Sound and Pattern

Short *ea*	*ee*	Long *ea*	*ie*	Oddball
ready	**agreed**	**season**	**believe**	**?**
breakfast	needle	beneath	achieve	diet
healthy	proceed	eastern	relief	science
heavy	seedling	meaning	retrieve	western
instead		repeat		
jealous				
sweater				
weather				

Considerations: This sort expands on Sort 17 in two ways. It reviews two additional long-*e* patterns—*ea* and *ie*—and it includes numerous short-*e* words spelled with *ea*. Before introducing the sort, discuss any unfamiliar words (perhaps *relieve* and *seedling*). This is also a good time to make students aware of meaning connections that may help them to spell some short-*e* words: *breakfast = break + fast*; *healthy = heal*; *heavy* is related to *heave*. You might call students' attention to the final *-e* in *believe, achieve,* and *retrieve,* and explain that it is not part of the long-vowel pattern but instead closes off the *v*, which does not end English words. Prompt students to be on the alert for words that may be tricky. Introduce the sound and pattern sort in a manner similar to that described for Sort 16, using the SAIL structure. Discuss the results when complete, being sure to talk about the oddballs *diet, science,* and *western*. The first two sound incorrect due to the syllable division occurring between the *i* and *e* (VV structure), and the third has a short-*e* pattern that does not fit the categories.

Talking Points

- Two more ways to spell long *e* in a stressed syllable are *ea* and *ie*, as in *repeat* and *relief*.
- In a stressed syllable, the *ea* pattern can produce either a long- or a short-*e* sound, as in *season* and *ready*.
- Sometimes *ie* works as a team, as in *relief*, and sometimes the letters are in separate syllables, as in *diet*.
- A related word can sometimes help to determine a vowel spelling, as in *heal* for *healthy*.
- The sound of /v/ at the end of a word is spelled *ve*, as in *achieve*.

Integrating Idioms: "She's **under the weather** today, so we're supposed to go on to school without her." (Slightly ill. If you were out walking in stormy weather and it was sleeting, snowing, or hailing, you would not be feeling well and would want to get out of it. The same is true of airlines; to avoid being under weather and in turbulence, they fly *above* the weather, so you can have a positive experience.)

Did You Know? Achievers are sometimes those who have made their way to the head of the class or of an organization. **Achieve** comes from an Old French phrase, *à chef*, meaning "at an end," or from the Latin word for "to bring to a head," *accapare* (for a discussion of related words, see Chapter 5, Sort 40). Those who achieve typically have the help of other fine "heads" or "chiefs"—teachers, parents or guardians, and other mentors.

On a chilly or cold day, we put on a **sweater** to keep warm, so why call the garment a *sweater*? In the early 1800s, heavy blankets were put around the bodies of racehorses to make them perspire heavily during training. Not surprisingly, the blankets were called *sweaters*. By the late 1850s, the word referred to flannel underclothing that athletes wore to work off weight. A generation later, the word took on a new meaning in the realm of sports: It referred to woolen vests and pullovers worn by rowers and other athletes. This connection led to the word's current meaning. Will this meaning last? If not, what might be the next reference for *sweater*?

SORT 19. Long and Short *i* in Stressed Syllables

	Sorting by Syllable Stress	
1st Stress	2nd Stress	Oddball
minus	**excite**	**?**
building	behind	[none]
crisis	beside	
differ	decide	
figure	describe	
Friday	despite	
frighten	extinct	
highway	polite	
justice	tonight	
kitchen		
library		
lightning		
pilot		
spider		
window		

Sorting by Sound and Pattern

Short *i*	*iCe*	*igh*	Open *i*	Oddball
figure	**excite**	**lightning**	**minus**	**?**
differ	beside	frighten	crisis	behind
extinct	decide	highway	Friday	building
kitchen	describe	tonight	library	justice
window	despite		pilot	
	polite		spider	

Considerations: Discuss word meanings as needed; then introduce the sort in a manner similar to Sort 16. After each activity, discuss the category characteristics. Ask students why *justice, behind,* and *building* are oddballs in the second sort. (In *justice,* the stressed syllable has a short *u,* and the *iCe* pattern does not make a long sound. *Behind* has a long *i,* but there is no category for its *iCC* pattern. The short-*i* pattern in *building* is *ui.*) In case students wonder about the peculiar short-*i* spelling in *building,* which also occurs in the related words *built, builder,* and *build,* how we came to have this unusual spelling is unknown. One hypothesis is that it is a combination of two earlier spellings—*bilden* and *bolden.* Before the session ends, remind students that when they are reading words with an *iCV* pattern, as in *minus* and *figure,* it is important to pay careful attention to the context and to read flexibly, because the vowel sound can be either long (open) or short (closed). Again, if applying one sound to the pattern does not produce a known word, they should try another.

Talking Points

- Three common ways to spell long *i* in polysyllabic words are *iCe, igh,* and open *i,* as in *decide, frighten,* and *minus.*
- As with *aCe,* as in *chocolate, iCe* does not always make a long sound; the sound depends on whether or not the syllable is stressed—*excite* versus *justice.*

Integrating Idioms: "Mr. Marino just gave us that hard quiz yesterday. Hopefully he won't give us another today, because I didn't read the new chapter last night. I know they say that **lightning never strikes twice in the same place,** but I'm not sure that includes Mr. Marino." (It is really unlikely that the same problem will happen again. Just as lightning doesn't follow the same path twice, so, too, it is extremely unlikely that Mr. Marino will provide his class with another sudden quiz.)

Did You Know? Although we think of a *window* as transparent, hidden in the origins of this word is a wonderful metaphor. Scandinavians who invaded and settled in England sometime during the early Middle Ages (before 1200) are the source of this word. There is no record of the exact word they gave us, but it was related to *vindauga,* an Old Icelandic word for "window," a compound of *vindr* (wind) and *auga* (eye). Besides being poetic, the metaphor of "wind eye" for *window* suggests an openness that would have characterized windows of the time, as there would have been no glass. Scandinavians (Norse) and Old English poets loved to use this type of figurative language, known as *kenning,* where they replaced a single noun with a compound. Other examples are "whale road" for *sea* and "storm of swords" for *battle.* Can you think of other examples of kenning, or perhaps create one yourself? (For a discussion of *library* and its origins, see Sort 1.)

SORT 20. More Long and Short *i* in Stressed Syllables

Sorting by Syllable Stress

1st Stress	2nd Stress	Oddball
finish	**advice**	**?**
crystal	apply	[no words]
hyphen	arrive	
island	divide	
listen	good-bye	
mystery	July	
ninety	provide	
rhythm	reply	
river	supply	
symbol	surprise	
symptom	survive	
system		
visit		

Sorting by Sound and Pattern

Short *i*	Short *y*	*iCe*	Long *y*	Oddball
finish	**symbol**	**advice**	**July**	**?**
listen	crystal	arrive	apply	good-bye
river	mystery	divide	hyphen	island
visit	rhythm	ninety	reply	
	symptom	provide	supply	
	system	surprise		
		survive		

Considerations: Discuss words that may be somewhat unfamiliar—perhaps *symptom, system,* and *hyphen.* You might also point out that there are several acceptable ways to spell *good-bye*, including *goodbye* and *good-by.* The use of *y* as a short vowel is a new feature, although students may be familiar with its use in words such as *gym* and *myth.* They may wonder how it is that *rhythm* has more than one syllable but just one vowel. Invite their speculations. The inclusion of words with both short- and long-vowel sounds for the *y* spelling adds further challenge to this sort. Introduce the words with as much support as necessary; discuss the results. The first sort has no oddballs unless the dialect of students leads to some. In the sound and pattern sort, there are two oddballs to discuss. *Island* has a long-vowel sound in the stressed syllable, but its VCCV pattern suggests a short-*i* sound. *Good-bye* has a long-*i* sound in the stressed syllable, but the pattern is *ye* (as also in *dye*). You might close the group session by asking students to suggest tricky aspects of some of the words that will require careful attention when spelling. Although responses will vary, suggestions may include the silent letters in *listen* and *island*; the unstressed *o* or *e* in *symbol, symptom,* and *system*; and the silent *e* in *ninety.*

Talking Points

- The letter y sometimes acts as a vowel; its sound can be long or short, as in *system* and *hyphen*; when y occurs at the end of a syllable it creates an open syllable and has a long-vowel sound, as in *supply*.
- As with *ea*, caution is needed when reading words with y; in addition to its consonant sound and long- and short-*i* possibilities, it can also make a long-*e* sound, as in *city*. Context clues and flexibility will help to ensure a correct word identification.

Integrating Idioms: "I know the movie was good, but you saw it three times last week. Didn't you **get it out of your system** yet?" (Have enough of it. Sometimes systems, like engines, get matter in them that prevents them from working normally. The person in the sentence example seems to be obsessing on a movie, doesn't want to move ahead to something new, and may not be attending to other tasks that need to be completed.)

Did You Know? Good-bye (or whichever spelling you prefer) is a contraction of the phrase "God be with ye [you]." Just as there are several ways to spell the word today, there are numerous earlier forms of the expression, including *God be wy you, god b'w'y, godbwye, god buy' ye,* and *good-b'wy.* Over time the word *God* was replaced with *good,* as it was in the phrase *good day.* The change may have come about because people lost sight of the original meaning of the phrase, or because of confusion between *god* (meaning "good") and God.

July takes its name from Julius Caesar, the famous Roman general and statesman mentioned in "Integrating Idioms" for Sort 8, who was born during this month. Just how it is that *Julius* has a first-syllable stress and *July* a stress on the second syllable is unknown. The first syllable of July was commonly stressed into the mid-1700s and continues to be heard today in much of the southern part of the United States.

SORT 21. Long and Short *o* in Stressed Syllables

Sorting by Syllable Stress

1st Stress	2nd Stress	Oddball
ocean	**compose**	**?**
bony	alone	[none]
bowling	approach	
clothing	below	
common	forgot	
honest	improve	
lonely	remote	
modern	suppose	
movement	unknown	
notebook		
notice		
owner		
product		
robot		
total		

Sorting by Sound and Pattern

Short *o*	*oCe*	*ow*	Open *o*	Oddball
honest	**compose**	**below**	**ocean**	**?**
common	alone	bowling	bony	approach
forgot	lonely	owner	clothing	improve
modern	notebook	unknown	notice	movement
product	remote		robot	
	suppose		total	

Considerations: Discuss any unfamiliar words. If *remote* is discussed, ask students to consider a common meaning connection among the following uses of the word: dinosaurs as creatures of the *remote* past, a *remote*-controlled car, and a *remote* chance of going to a movie. They should come up with something like "distant" or "far removed in time, space, possibility." Begin the sort in a way similar to that described for Sort 16, integrating the elements of SAIL. Discuss the results. How are categories alike or different? *Improve* and *movement* are oddballs in the sound and pattern sort. Despite their VC*e* pattern in the stressed syllable, they have no long-*o* pattern. By contrast, *approach* has a long *o* with a second-syllable stress, but *oa* is not a targeted feature. You might ask students if they can think of any other pattern from their studies of patterns in single-syllable words that can make the long *o* sound. Numerous words have *oCC*, as in *almost, enroll, hostess, molten,* and *soldier.*

Talking Points

- Common long-*o* patterns in accented syllables include *oCe, ow,* and open *o* as in *alone, below, robot. Oa* and *oCC* are two more long-*o* patterns.
- Flexibility is needed in reading words with long-*o* patterns; what looks like long *o* may not be, as in *remote* versus *improve,* and *robot* versus *modern.* Similarly, what looks like short *o* may actually be long *o,* as in *adopt* versus *almost.*

Integrating Idioms: "I've saved up fifty dollars, but that's just a **drop in the ocean** of what I'll need to buy the bike." (A very small amount. Imagine how many drops there must be in the ocean—or in a bucket of water, for that matter, as the idiom sometimes is worded *drop in the bucket*—and you'll have an idea of how incredibly much farther this person has to go to save enough for the bike.)

Did You Know? As discussed in earlier "Did You Know?" sections, many words in our language have been borrowed from other languages. For example, the days of the week were named after various gods; others, such as *sandwich,* get their name from a person or place. Still others come about because someone created a word that became popular and was accepted as part of our language. This was the case with **robot**. In 1921 a new play was performed that featured mechanical men who revolt and threaten to take over the world. The robots eventually become human and save the world. This was the first time the word had been used to describe mechanical men. The word caught on quickly, and its meaning was extended to include people who seem to have no feelings and who respond in a mechanical way. There has long been a synonym for robot—*automaton* (ô•tŏm•ə•tən). This word has been part of our language since the early 1600s and came from a phrase that meant "self-acting." Estimates are that there are now tens of thousands of robots in use in the United States. Though they may look nothing like a human, they are machines that are programmed to move parts, materials, tools, and so forth to complete tasks. When a person creates a word that catches on, as when the playwright wrote about robots, we say he *coined* the word. You might invite students to read or hear the delightful children's novel *Frindle* by Andrew Clements (1996). The story tells how a fifth grader went about coining a new word for "pen." Students may also enjoy brainstorming or writing about new words they would like to coin.

SORT 22. Long and Short *u* in Stressed Syllables

Sorting by Syllable Stress

1st Stress	2nd Stress	Oddball
tuna	**perfume**	**?**
beauty	amuse	Thursday
future	balloon	
hungry	cartoon	
Monday	cocoon	
pumpkin	computer	
punish	erupt	
toothache	excuse	
truly	include	
Tuesday	pollute	
uncle	reduce	
	shampoo	

Sorting by Sound and Pattern

Short *u*	*uCe*	*oo*	Open *u*	Oddball
pumpkin	**perfume**	**cartoon**	**tuna**	**?**
erupt	amuse	balloon	computer	beauty
hungry	excuse	cocoon	future	Monday
punish	include	shampoo	truly	Thursday
uncle	pollute	toothache		Tuesday
	reduce			

Considerations: Discuss any unfamiliar words. For *uncle*, check to see that students understand that this is the brother of their father or mother; for *excuse*, ask students for two ways to pronounce the word and to explain what each word means: final-consonant sound of /z/ when the word is a verb, and /s/ when it·is a noun. (See "Additional Sorts" for a homograph activity with words that have multiple pronunciations.) Because vowels other than *u* can produce the long-*u* sound, you might introduce this sort by reading the words aloud to see what students notice about the vowel sounds. Then engage them in the syllable stress and sound and pattern sorts as described in Sort 16. Discuss the results; in both sorts *Thursday* is an oddball, because its vowel is neither long nor short. The other three oddballs in the sound and pattern sort all have appropriate sounds (short *u* in *Monday* and long *u* in *beauty* and *Tuesday*), but have patterns with no categories. The multiple ways of representing long *u* present a spelling challenge. Ask students if they notice anything about the words that might provide a clue to their spelling. Accept any reasonable and justified response. Be sure to link new learning to students' reading or writing. (For a discussion of the origin of *Thursday*, see Sort 16.)

Talking Points

- Three patterns that produce the long-*u* sound are *uCe, oo,* and open *u,* as in *amuse, cartoon,* and *future.*
- As with the other long-vowel patterns studied, care and flexibility are needed in reading words with a VCV pattern with *u,* because it can be long or short, as in *tuna* or *punish.*

Integrating Idioms: "We tried asking for an extension on our project, but that idea went over **like a lead balloon.**" (Failed. Balloons are usually filled with helium or air, so they are very lightweight and easily float up in the air. Lead is a soft and heavy metallic element. A lead balloon would go nowhere.)

Did You Know? **Pumpkin** comes to us from a Greek word, *pepon,* meaning "cooked by the sun." Unlike some vegetables in the garden that can be eaten "green," this squash is inedible until it has been "baked" on the vine out in the sun for a long enough time. Pumpkins originated in the Americas and were a mainstay of the Pilgrims.

    Uncle derives from *avunculus,* a Latin word for "mother's brother." Although today we regard an uncle as the brother of either parent, there is one uncle that is shared by every American—*Uncle Sam.* The United States is often personified as a tall, thin man with a flowing white beard, wearing red-and-white-striped trousers, a blue coat with tails, and a tall hat banded with stars. This well-known image of Uncle Sam was created at the time of the American Civil War by a British cartoonist named Sir John Tenniel, famous for his illustrations of *Alice in Wonderland* and *Through the Looking Glass.* Tenniel portrayed the United States as an awkward, unsophisticated person—striped pants, big heavy shoes, and a straw hat—and modeled the figure after Abraham Lincoln, who was president at the time. Despite the figure's unattractiveness, it caught on with Americans and was soon refined by an American cartoonist into the image we know today. Origin of the name *Uncle Sam* is less certain. The most likely story seems to be that *Uncle Sam* stems from a humorous interpretation of the letters "U.S." printed on casks of meat provided to army men during the War of 1812. The supplier was Samuel Wilson, who was locally known as "Uncle Sam," because meat labeled *U.S.* was said to have come from "**U**ncle **S**am." In 1961 Congress made Sam Wilson the official namesake of Uncle Sam.

SORT 16 Long and Short *a* in Stressed Syllables

Short *a*	*aCe*	*ai*	Open *a*
1st Stress	**2nd Stress**		**?**
shadow	bracelet		afraid
fable	complain		escape
contain	obey		crayon
basement	Saturday		daily
raisin	erase		amaze
chocolate	nation		explain
remain	April		later
basic	rather		perhaps

Long and Short *e* in Stressed Syllables

Short *e*	*ee*	*eCe*	Open *e*
1st Stress	**2nd Stress**		**?**
effort	asleep		delete
fever	idea		supreme
indeed	secret		people
either	deeply		evening
extreme	female		legal
complete	succeed		trapeze
degrees	between		Wednesday
ketchup	never		expect

SORT 18 More Long and Short *e* in Stressed Syllables

Short *ea*	*ee*	Long *ea*	*ie*
1st Stress		**2nd Stress**	**?**
ready	agreed		season
believe	sweater		diet
meaning	seedling		heavy
instead	beneath		science
weather	relief		breakfast
repeat	jealous		eastern
needle	achieve		retrieve
western	healthy		proceed

Long and Short *i* in Stressed Syllables

Short *i*	iCe	igh	Open *i*
1st Stress	**2nd Stress**		**?**
figure	excite		lightning
minus	polite		justice
describe	decide		pilot
behind	frighten		crisis
tonight	library		highway
spider	beside		building
despite	Friday		differ
kitchen	window		extinct

More Long and Short *i* in Stressed Syllables

Short *i*	Short *y*	*iCe*	Long *y*
1st Stress	**2nd Stress**		**?**
finish	symbol		advice
July	survive		mystery
hyphen	system		arrive
ninety	surprise		supply
island	good-bye		provide
reply	apply		symptom
crystal	divide		rhythm
visit	listen		river

SORT 21 Long and Short *o* in Stressed Syllables

Short *o*	oCe	ow	Open *o*
1st Stress	**2nd Stress**		**?**
honest	compose		below
ocean	approach		clothing
notebook	remote		unknown
robot	lonely		notice
bowling	total		movement
suppose	alone		bony
improve	owner		product
modern	common		forgot

Long and Short *u* in Stressed Syllables

Short *u*	uCe	oo	Open *u*
1st Stress	**2nd Stress**		**?**
pumpkin	perfume		cartoon
tuna	toothache		Monday
excuse	Thursday		pollute
cocoon	amuse		computer
include	future		shampoo
Tuesday	beauty		reduce
truly	balloon		hungry
uncle	punish		erupt

r-Controlled Vowel Patterns in Stressed Syllables   *(DSA Feature N)*

The following five sorts review the sounds and patterns of *r*-controlled vowels, but in the context of stressed syllables in polysyllabic words. There are still multiple patterns that produce the same sound, making *r*-controlled vowels challenging to spell, though perhaps less so than they are when the patterns occur in unstressed syllables. To introduce each of the sorts in this section, ask students to work with partners to determine categories for the words, making sure that the categories are mutually exclusive (namely, defined in ways that prevent words from being classified in more than one category, unless they are ultimately placed as oddballs). After discussing their results, if sound and pattern were not used as the bases for their sorting, ask students to re-sort their words by sound and pattern, using the indicated key words as guides to the categories. Discuss the results, add the header cards, and encourage students to share insights for spelling words with *r*-controlled vowels. Extend their thinking through a discussion of the talking points.

What Is Known: Students are familiar with most of the *r*-controlled patterns from studies of one-syllable words at the within word pattern stage. They are aware that several patterns can represent a particular *r*-controlled sound. They also know what stressed syllables are and can identify the accented syllable in longer words.

What Is New: Examining *r*-controlled patterns in the stressed syllables of polysyllabic words is new. Also, students are likely to lack experience with several of the patterns, including *ere*, *orr*, and *arr*.

SORT 23. *r*-Controlled Vowels with V*re* Patterns in Stressed Syllables

Sorting by Sound and Pattern

are	*ere*	*ire*	*ore*	*ure*	Oddball
barely	**sincere**	**admire**	**before**	**surely**	**?**
aware	adhere	desire	boredom	endure	failure
beware	merely	entire	explore	secure	terrible
compare	severe	fireman			therefore
		inspire			
		retire			

Considerations: Discuss words with meanings that may be unfamiliar, such as *adhere, merely, endure,* and *secure.* Except for the two oddballs, the words in this sort can easily be classified by either sound or pattern, because multiple patterns for the same sound have not been included as separate categories. This aspect of the sort should make this set of words easier to spell. The oddballs *terrible* and *therefore* provide a glimpse of the multiple patterns that can produce the same sound. *Failure* is an oddball because the first syllable is stressed, not *ure.*

Talking Points

- Words with the V*re* pattern have a long-vowel pattern with an *r*-influenced or -controlled vowel, as in *explore* compared with *explode.*
- There are often multiple ways to spell a particular *r*-controlled vowel, as in *barely, terrible,* and *therefore.*

Integrating Idioms: "We nearly **died of boredom** before the movie was over." (Suffered from lack of stimulation. Though it is unlikely anyone ever died from being bored, boredom can be excruciating.)

Did You Know? If someone has ever **inspired** you, you probably felt energized and invigorated; it's no wonder, as the word literally means "to blow or breathe into," although it was likely that thoughts or feelings were inhaled rather than air. Other related words include *aspire, conspire, perspire,* and *transpire.* Word families, such as the *spir* family, are a primary focus of the next chapter of this book.

When we think of *sincere,* we think of someone or something that is "genuine," "true," or "pure." Although most experts believe that *sincere* stems from the Latin word for "clean" or "pure," there is an old story that lends a bit more color to the word's roots. According to it, the word's origin goes back to the days of the famous Italian sculptor, painter, architect, and poet Michelangelo, who lived from 1475 to 1564. Sculptors of his time often used marble blocks to carve out their sculptures. The marble sometimes had imperfections. Roman quarrymen would often rub wax on the marble to hide such flaws from the eyes of prospective purchasers. To stop the deceptive practice, the Roman government dictated that all marble had to be *sine cera,* which means "without wax." In time, the phrase was applied more generally to mean "without deception."

SORT 24. *r*-Controlled *o* in Stressed Syllables

Sorting by Sound and Pattern

or	*ore*	*orr*	Oddball
order	**ignore**	**sorry**	**?**
afford	adore	borrow	resource
corner	ashore	horror	worry
forty	foreman	sorrow	worthless
forward	restore	tomorrow	
inform		torrent	
northern			
report			
stories			

Considerations: Discuss the meanings of any unfamiliar words. Possibilities include *afford, forward* (compare with *foreword*), *foreman, restore,* and *torrent.* Except for two of the oddball words, whose vowel patterns are influenced by *w,* there is no sound contrast in this sort. The importance here is for students to bear in mind that there may be several different ways to spell a particular *r*-controlled sound, and to develop spelling awareness so that if they are not sure of a spelling, they will know that they need to take action and look it up in a dictionary or check with an expert.

Talking Points

- *r*-controlled vowels with long- and short-*o* patterns produce the same sound, /ôr/, as do the *or, ore, orr,* and *our* patterns of this sort, as in *order, ignore, sorry,* and *resource.*
- The letter *w* nearly always influences the sound of *or,* as in *worry* and *worthless.*

Integrating Idioms: "To **make a long story short,** my homework was thrown out with the trash this morning." (Summarize the main points or get to the main idea of a happening. Writers often delete extraneous matter when they revise a story, thereby shortening it up to the essentials.)

Did You Know? As bothersome as it can be to **worry** about something, the word has a far more gentle meaning now than it once had when it meant "to kill by violence." Over the centuries, the word evolved from its harsh Old English meaning to the softened meaning of "to harass or distress" to the commonly used meaning of today, "to feel troubled or uneasy."

SORT 25. *r*-Controlled *a* in Stressed Syllables

Sorting by Sound and Pattern

ar	*are*	*air*	*arr*	Oddball
party	**declare**	**repair**	**carry**	**?**
barber	barefoot	dairy	arrow	parents
farther	prepare	despair	carrots	toward
harvest	rarely	fairly	narrow	
market		prairie	sparrow	
partner				
scarlet				

Considerations: Discuss any words that may be unfamiliar to some students, such as *harvest, scarlet, declare, dairy, despair,* and *prairie.* (The last is discussed in the "Did You Know?" section for this sort.) Clarification should also be given for the meaning of *farther. Farther,* in this sort, and *further,* in the next, have often been used interchangeably. However, according to a rule noted in the third edition of *The American Heritage Dictionary of the English Language* (1996), the use of *farther* should be limited to "physical distance" and *further* used for "advancement along a nonphysical dimension." This sort explores the long and short sounds of *r*-controlled vowels with *a.* Although *ar* usually has the sound heard in *art,* it can also sound like a long *r*-influenced pattern, as in the oddball word *parents.* There are several ways to spell the long-*a* sound influenced by *r,* including *are, air,* and *arr* (categories in this sort), and *er* and *err* (*merit* and *cherry*). Students may notice the influence of the *w* in *toward* on the *ar* vowel pattern. If they do not, call their attention to this, and encourage them to brainstorm other words with a *war* spelling (e.g., *award, awkward, warning,* and *warrant*).

Talking Points

- The /är/ sound is usually spelled *ar,* as in *party;* and similarly, the *ar* pattern in a word is usually pronounced as in *art.*
- There are several ways to spell the /âr/ sound; some common spellings include *are, air,* and *arr,* as in *prepare, fairly,* and *carry.*
- A preceding *w* usually causes *ar* to sound like /ôr/ as in *award* or /ər/ as in *awkward.*

Integrating Idioms: "Mom said that my brother and I have to **carry our own weight** now that Dad's in the hospital." (Do our share. If you literally carried your own weight, you would be no worry or trouble for anyone else.)

Did You Know? Much of the U.S. Midwest (this usually includes Illinois, Indiana, Iowa, Kansas, Michigan, Minnesota, Missouri, Nebraska, Ohio, and Wisconsin) was once covered by tall grasses. The French were the first to come to the lands that we now know as Iowa, Illinois, and Indiana and some of the adjoining areas. What they saw were vast expanses of grasses, growing 5–9 feet tall and crowded with insects, creatures of various sorts, and flowers, but not a tree in sight—so they called it *prairie,* the French word for "meadow." In time some of the plants and animals took on the "prairie" descriptor, as in *prairie dog, prairie chicken* (a type of grouse), *prairie beans,* and so forth. In the 1700s, when settlers headed west across the prairies, they traveled in covered wagons known as *prairie schooners,* because of their resemblance to ships sailing through the grasses. Today both Illinois and North Dakota bear the nickname *Prairie State,* but only tiny remnants of the tall grass prairie remain; the rest has been converted into farmland by burning and draining.

SORT 26. *r*-Controlled /ûr/ in Stressed Syllables

Sorting by Sound and Pattern			
er	*ir*	*ur*	Oddball
person	**dirty**	**during**	**?**
determine	birdhouse	disturb	hurry
nervous	chirping	furnish	series
perfect	thirsty	further	spirit
prefer	thirty	jury	
thermos		purple	
verdict		purpose	
		sturdy	

Considerations: Discuss any words that may be unfamiliar, such as *thermos, verdict, sturdy,* and *series.* Also, use of the word *further* should be reviewed (see Sort 25). As in Sort 24, this sort includes no sound contrast except for two of the oddball words (*series* and *spirit*). All of the other words include the /ûr/ sound but with various spellings—*er, ir,* and *ur* (and *urr* in the oddball word *hurry*). Just as with one-syllable words, words with /ûr/ in the stressed syllable are difficult to spell. Sound provides no help in determining the correct pattern. Students need to realize this and exert caution when spelling such words if they are uncertain of the pattern.

Talking Points

- In stressed syllables, the /ûr/ sound is usually spelled with *er, ir,* or *ur*; similarly, *er, ir,* and *ur* are typically pronounced as /ûr/ in unfamiliar words, as in *person, dirty,* and *further.*
- Because of the spelling variations, when in doubt about how to spell the /ûr/ sound, consult a dictionary or an expert.

Integrating Idioms: "She **gave me a dirty look** when I asked for a pencil." (Frowned or looked angry. Something dirty is usually unpleasant, as a dirty look would be.)

Did You Know? The word **person** comes from the Latin *persona,* a word that originally meant "mask," as in an actor's mask. Over time the word came to be associated with the real character or role of the character and eventually with the actual person, an individual. Although we sometimes use the word *persons* as the plural of *person*, when a group of persons is the reference, the more commonly used word is *people*, as in *Today more than 7,600,000,000 people live on earth* [over a billion more people than when the first edition of this book came out], *of which nearly 330,000,000 live in the United States.* (For a minute-by-minute counting of the persons of either the world or the United States, go to the U.S. Census Bureau's U.S. and World Population Clock website at *www.census.gov/popclock*.)

SORT 27. *r*-Controlled *e* in Stressed Syllables

Sorting by Sound and Pattern

er (Short)	*ear* (Short)	*ear* (Long)	Oddball
sternly	**early**	**nearby**	**?**
alert	earning	appear	career
hermit	earthquake	clearing	pioneer
merchant	learner	dreary	
observe	rehearse	spearmint	
reserve		teardrop	
sermon		weary	
service		yearbook	

Considerations: Discuss any words that may be unfamiliar, such as *hermit, merchant, dreary,* and *pioneer* (the last is discussed in the "Did You Know?" section). This sort introduces *ear* as an /ûr/ pattern for review and contrasts it both with the same sound (spelled *er*) and with the same pattern, *ear* but with the sound heard in *dreary*. When students are trying to read unknown words with an *ear* spelling, the sound is more likely to be the long *r*-controlled sound (*dreary*); however, if applying that sound does not lead to a known word, the alternative sound of /ûr/ should be used. A mnemonic might be of help in remembering the spelling of *rehearse:* When actors re*hear*se, they *hear* lines said again and again. Ask students to brainstorm known spellings pronounced as /îr/ (e.g., *ere*, previously introduced, and *ear* and *eer* from this sort).

Talking Points

- The *ear* pattern can be pronounced with a short-vowel as well as a long-vowel *r*-influenced sound, as in *earning* versus *clearing*.
- There are different ways to spell /îr/, including the common *ear, ere,* and *eer*.

Integrating Idioms: "I'm turning in my paper on Friday, even though it's not due until Tuesday. You know . . . **the early bird catches the worm.**" (Being ahead of schedule can benefit you. In the heat of the sun, worms are typically underground, but early morning will often find them on the surface, making it easy for an early-rising bird to enjoy a good meal.)

Did You Know? The notion of **pioneers** as settlers of the wilderness is very different from the original meaning of the word, which related to the military. These pioneers prepared the way for the armies that followed by clearing paths and building roads. In the early 1800s, when a writer applied the term to describe those who were venturing into new territory, settling there, and paving the way for others, the word became popular. *Pioneer* now often refers to someone who is the first to discover or explore, as in *space pioneers* or *pioneers of medicine*.

r-Controlled Vowels with V*re* Patterns in Stressed Syllables

are	*ere*	*ire*	*ore*	*ure*

barely	sincere	admire
before	surely	explore
severe	retire	beware
failure	therefore	fireman
inspire	aware	secure
merely	endure	terrible
entire	desire	boredom
compare	adhere	?

or	*ore*	*orr*
order	ignore	sorry
horror	restore	sorrow
resource	worry	torrent
borrow	ashore	inform
report	northern	foreman
forty	worthless	corner
tomorrow	forward	adore
afford	stories	?

r-Controlled *a* in Stressed Syllables

ar	*are*	*air*	*arr*
party	declare		repair
carry	fairly		toward
sparrow	rarely		farther
market	carrots		barefoot
prairie	barber		dairy
prepare	narrow		partner
harvest	parents		arrow
despair	scarlet		?

er	*ir*	*ur*
person	dirty	during
further	purple	thirty
perfect	chirping	nervous
jury	series	disturb
determine	birdhouse	hurry
purpose	spirit	prefer
thermos	furnish	thirsty
sturdy	verdict	?

r-Controlled *e* in Stressed Syllables

er	*ear* (Short)	*ear* (Long)
sternly	early	nearby
yearbook	appear	observe
sermon	pioneer	earthquake
earning	spearmint	reserve
weary	hermit	clearing
rehearse	teardrop	service
alert	dreary	learner
career	merchant	?

Abstract Vowel Patterns in Stressed Syllables

Abstract vowels are neither long nor short nor *r*-controlled. The following two sorts review abstract vowels in the context of longer words. As with *r*-controlled vowels, introduce the sorts by asking students to pair up to sort the words into categories. Remind them to examine the characteristics of each category carefully so they can describe them. Students have now had much experience with sorting by sound and pattern, so many may arrive at the same categories as those listed. If they do not, after discussing their results, suggest that students re-sort the words by sound and pattern, using the key words as a guide.

What Is Known: Students have worked with all of the abstract vowel patterns at the within word pattern stage. They have also examined patterns in stressed syllables.

What Is New: Examining abstract vowels in polysyllabic words is new; also, the sound of *ou* as in *trouble* may be new.

SORT 28. Abstract Vowels with *o* in Stressed Syllables

Sorting by Sound and Pattern				
oi /oi/	*oy* /oi/	*ou* /ou/	*ow* /ou/	*ou* /ŭ/
avoid	**loyal**	**county**	**power**	**trouble**
appoint	annoy	announce	allow	country
moisture	destroy	counter	brownie	enough
poison	employ	doubtful	coward	southern
		thousand	shower	
		without	towel	

Considerations: Discuss any unfamiliar words; *county* and *loyal* may benefit from clarification. This sort reviews the *oi* and *oy* spellings of /oi/ and the *ou* and *ow* spellings of /ou/, and presents another pronunciation for the *ou* spelling. Students have previously worked with *ow* as a long-*o* spelling (see Sort 21). By now, given the key words and instructions to sort by sound and pattern, students should be able to categorize the words without other preliminary sorting. However, if needed, ask students to begin with a sound or pattern sort. Either will result in a combining of some of the categories shown in Sort 28. Then they can re-sort with attention to aural and visual cues. Discuss the results, including talking points. There are many additional sounds for *ou*, as in *though*, *through*, and *thought*; encourage students to find such oddballs during a word hunt.

Talking Points

- *Oi* and *oy* are used to spell the /oi/ sound; *oy* is usually used at the end of a syllable, as in *employ* and *loyal*.
- *Ou* and *ow* are used to spell the /ou/ sound; *ow* is usually used at the end of a syllable, as in *power* and *allow*.
- *Ou* and *ow* can be pronounced in multiple ways; when reading words with these spellings, if one sound doesn't lead to a known word, try another.

Integrating Idioms: "I might as well **throw in the towel;** I'm never going to finish this by tomorrow." (Give up and admit defeat. This expression stems from boxing, in which a fighter used to concede defeat by throwing the towel with which he wiped his face into the boxing ring. The expression "throw in the sponge" means the same thing.)

Did You Know? The **brownie** is all-American, though there is disagreement regarding its origins. According to one story, in a careless moment a cook forgot to add baking powder, a rising agent, to the batter in a chocolate cake recipe. According to another, the brownie was invented in 1892 at a Chicago hotel. Box lunches were being prepared for an exposition, and the brownie seemed like a good way for ladies to be able to enjoy a cake-like dessert and keep their hands clean. Though the brownie originated in America, it is now found in many parts of the world. Which of the origin stories do you agree with? Can you imagine another possibility?

SORT 29. Abstract Vowels with *a* in Stressed Syllables

Sorting by Sound and Pattern

au	*aw*	*al*	Oddball
author	**awful**	**almost**	**?**
applaud	awesome	already	all right
August	awkward	also	laughter
daughter	drawback	although	
exhausted	flawless	altogether	
faucet	lawyer	always	
laundry			
naughty			
sausage			

Considerations: Discuss any unfamiliar words, such as *drawback* and, for some students, *sausage*. All three patterns in this sort produce a similar sound. Spelling can be aided by realizing that *aw* is usually used at the end of a syllable (*flawless*), and that when /l/ immediately follows the /ô/ sound, the spelling is likely *al* (*always*). Although *all right* sounds as though it is one word, standard English dictates that it be spelled as separate words.

Talking Points

• There are multiple ways of spelling the /ô/ sound, including *au*, *aw*, and *al*, as in *laundry, awful,* and *also. Aw* is usually used at the end of a syllable.

Integrating Idioms:

"I thought I'd **split my sides with laughter** when I first heard Jon Sciezska's [1992] *The Stinky Cheese Man* read out loud." (Laugh so hard that your skin would burst. Other, expressions about *laughter* from *www.spellzone.com* include *a barrel* or *a bundle of laughs, laughing stock, die laughing, laugh your head off, split your sides with laughter, laugh all the way to the bank, no laughing matter,* and *have the last laugh*. Invite students to brainstorm or create some other expressions with *laughter*, and to consider the meanings of quotes such as those that follow from *www.laughteronlineuniversity.com:* "Always laugh when you can. It is cheap medicine" (Lord Byron), "Earth laughs in flowers" (Ralph Waldo Emerson), "A smile is a curve that sets everything straight" (Phyllis Diller).

Did You Know? The meaning of **naughty,** like *worry* (see Sort 24), has softened over time. In the 1400s it was used to describe a very bad or wicked person. A century or so later it had the sense of "inferior quality," as in *naughty olives* that would likely have to be thrown away. Today the word is most often applied to children and their minor mischievous offenses.

SORT 28   Abstract Vowels with *o* in Stressed Syllables

oi /oi/	*oy* /oi/	*ou* /ou/	*ow* /ou/	*ou* /ŭ/
avoid	loyal			county
power	trouble			thousand
employ	southern			doubtful
appoint	allow			annoy
enough	counter			coward
destroy	towel			moisture
brownie	announce			country
poison	without			shower

Abstract Vowels with *a* in Stressed Syllables

au	*aw*	*al*
author	awful	almost
flawless	sausage	laundry
applaud	already	all right
although	August	awkward
naughty	drawback	always
also	altogether	exhausted
daughter	laughter	awesome
lawyer	faucet	?

Unstressed Syllables

(DSA Feature O)

Sorts in the previous three sections have dealt with vowel patterns in stressed syllables. In this section (Sorts 30–35), we explore unstressed syllables and the schwa vowel sound, /ə/. In all but the last sort, the unstressed syllable is the final syllable. The schwa sound of an unstressed syllable (pronounced as "uh") is difficult to spell because so many different patterns can represent it, and sound is of no help, as the bolded letters in the following examples show: *again, fasten, fossil, button, focus, mountain, curious.* Sometimes meaning can provide a clue to the correct spelling; for example, comparative adjectives end in *-er* (*higher, dimmer*) rather than *-ar* or *-or.* Sometimes the letters surrounding the schwa sound can be of help; for instance, if the final syllable of *cancel* was spelled with an *-le*, the second *c* would lose its soft sound /s/. As students explore the patterns in this section and search for more examples of the patterns through word hunts, they also will learn the helpful strategy of *best guess*; some patterns, such as *-le* for final /əl/, are far more common than others, and knowing which ones are makes it possible to guess at the spelling when there are no other options. Nonetheless, it is particularly important for students to realize that when they are learning to spell words with the schwa, that portion of the word is likely to require careful attention so the pattern can be memorized. When confronted with writing the schwa of an unfamiliar word, wise spellers check in a dictionary or ask an expert to confirm the correct spelling. For further tips on teaching and learning with unstressed syllables, see Chapter 7 of *Word Journeys, Second Edition* (Ganske, 2014).

What Is Known: Students are familiar with identifying the accented syllable in words. Several of the patterns in this section, especially those in Sorts 30–33, have been examined as long- or short-vowel patterns at the within word pattern stage.

What Is New: Although students have been exposed to the schwa at the beginning of the section on "Long-Vowel Patterns in Stressed Syllables," work with unstressed syllables and the schwa is new.

SORT 30. Unstressed Final Syllables with Long-*a* Patterns

Sorting by Sound and Pattern

-ace	*-age*	*-ain*	Oddball
surface	**manage**	**certain**	**?**
furnace	bandage	bargain	engage
menace	cabbage	curtain	obtain
necklace	courage	fountain	practice
palace	damage	mountain	
	garbage	villain	
	luggage		
	message		
	package		

Considerations: Before distributing the templates of words to the students, you might introduce the study of unstressed syllables by dictating a short spelling quiz with *obtain, certain, explain, villain, curtain, complain, bargain,* and *fountain.* If you wish, include or substitute some of the following words, being sure to include words with long vowels, as well as a schwa: *engage, garbage, teenage, bandage,* *disgrace, furnace, fireplace, palace.* When discussing the results, ask students what made some of the words more difficult to spell than others. If they do not mention that the same spelling pattern can be used to spell different sounds, draw their attention to this. Ask them how this might be explained (the sound in the stressed syllable provides a clue to the spelling pattern, whereas in an unstressed syllable you cannot tell which pattern to use). Place the headers on the table or overhead, and distribute the templates of words. Ask students to cut apart the word cards and sort them by the vowel patterns shown on the headers. When they are finished, draw students' attention to the first-syllable stress in each of the key words (*surface, **man**age,* and *certain*). Remind them of the work they have done with stressed syllables. Then point to the second syllable and explain that now they are ready to turn their attention to the unstressed syllable, which, as they have likely discovered from the quiz, is more difficult to spell because of the schwa vowel sound. Tell students that for this sort and for most of the others that they will study related to unstressed syllables, the second syllable will be the one that is unstressed. Ask them to review their categories to find any words that have the appropriate pattern but a different sound. These should be moved to the oddball category. Discuss the results, including the oddballs *engage* and *obtain,* both of which have a stressed final syllable, and *practice,* which does have an unstressed final syllable but a different spelling pattern. Talk about the meanings of any unfamiliar words, perhaps *villain* and *menace.* Before ending the session, remind students to pay attention to how an unstressed syllable is spelled in order to remember it.

Talking Points

- Vowel patterns in unstressed syllables are difficult to spell, because there are many patterns for the schwa sound.
- When reading an unfamiliar word, if applying a long-vowel sound to a known long-vowel pattern does not lead to a recognizable word, try shifting the stress to another syllable and reading the pattern with a schwa sound. *Villain,* for example might be misread as /vīl•lān/; by shifting the stress to the first syllable, the correct word can be detected, /**vīl**•lən/.

Integrating Idioms: "I know I wore your shirt without asking you, but don't **make a mountain out of a molehill.**" (Exaggerate a small problem. When moles burrow underground, their tunnels barely raise the ground above; to call the slight upheaval a *mountain* would be a gross exaggeration.)

Did You Know? A *palace* is typically associated with royalty and as a residence is impressively large and luxurious. The palaces of fairy tales are often situated on a hill or other prominent place, away from the ordinary people. The word is derived from Palatine Hill in Rome, where people of power and wealth had their homes beginning around 330 B.C., including the emperors Augustus, Tiberius, and Nero. The Latin word for this hill, *Palatium,* eventually evolved into *palace* and came to be associated with any expensive and splendid house.

SORT 31. Unstressed Final Syllables with /ən/

Sorting by Meaning (Parts of Speech)

Verbs	Nouns	Oddball
darken	**dozen**	**?**
awaken	button	urban
fasten	cabin	
loosen	chicken	
sharpen	cotton	
strengthen	cousin	
tighten	dragon	
	eleven	
	lemon	
	margin	
	method	
	pardon	
	robin	
	siren	
	slogan	
	woman	

Sorting by Pattern and Meaning

Verbs	Nouns					(Adjective)
-en	*-an*	*-en*	*-in*	*-on*		Oddball
darken	**slogan**	**dozen**	**cabin**	**lemon**		**?**
awaken	woman	chicken	cousin	apron		urban
fasten		eleven	margin	button		
loosen		siren	robin	cotton		
sharpen				dragon		
strengthen				pardon		
tighten						

Considerations: Discuss any unfamiliar words, such as *pardon, margin, urban,* and *slogan.* Students may need an example of the last word; say, for instance, "Sometimes runners and joggers use the following slogan: *Motion is lotion.*" Talk about the meaning of the phrase, and ask students to think of slogans they have heard in advertising or politics. Introduce this set of words as a two-category meaning sort: verbs and nouns. Discuss the results. Many will recognize *urban* as an adjective and therefore an oddball; they will also likely notice that all of the verbs end in *-en.* Then ask students to re-sort the words by meaning and pattern. This type of combined sort will be new to them, so after putting out the key words and headers, model the sorting with a think-aloud if necessary. Discuss the results. As students collect and examine other words with the same patterns through word hunts, encourage them to be on the lookout for patterns that occur frequently. This will help them to develop a best-guess strategy for final /ən/.

Talking Points

- There are many ways to spell the unstressed final syllable /ən/; meaning can be of help. For example, verbs tend to be spelled *-en,* as in *sharpen* and *darken.*

Integrating Idioms: "Whenever I say that I'm going to buy a new skateboard if my essay wins the contest, Mom tells me I shouldn't **count my chickens before they hatch.**" (Plan on something until you're certain it will happen. According to *The American Heritage Dictionary of Idioms* [Ammer, 1997], this expression stems from one of Aesop's fables, in which a milkmaid dreams about getting rich from some chickens she hopes to buy with the milk that she is carrying in a pail on her head. She tosses her head as she dreams of wealth, spilling the milk.)

Did You Know? Our decimal system shows much consistency with its counting, as in *twenty-one, twenty-two, twenty-three . . . ninety-seven, ninety-eight, ninety-nine.* Though we do not say "tenty-three, tenty-four," a similar consistency exists in the tens through application of the "ten"-related suffix *teen,* as in *thirteen, fourteen . . . eighteen, nineteen.* But what about **eleven** and **twelve?** Unlike the teens, these two numbers derived from Old English words that were made up of the roots for "one" (or "two" in the case of *twelve*) and "left over." So *eleven* literally means "one left over" or "one past ten," and *twelve* means "two left over" or "two past ten."

SORT 32. Unstressed Final Syllables with /ər/

Sorting by Meaning

People Nouns	Other Nouns
brother	**finger**
doctor	answer
father	collar
grocer	cover
mayor	dollar
mother	drawer
neighbor	error
sailor	favor
soldier	harbor
swimmer	honor
traitor	litter
	mirror
	sugar

Sorting by Pattern and Meaning

People Nouns		Other Nouns		
-er	*-or*	*-er*	*-or*	*-ar*
brother	**doctor**	**finger**	**favor**	**sugar**
father	mayor	answer	error	collar
grocer	neighbor	cover	harbor	dollar
mother	sailor	drawer	honor	
soldier	traitor	litter	mirror	
swimmer				

Considerations: This is the first of two sorts related to the unstressed final syllable /ər/. During their within word pattern studies and earlier work at the syllable juncture stage, students have explored the confusing aspects of the *r*-controlled /ûr/ sound, which can be spelled with *-er* (*her*), *-ir* (*first*), and *-ur* (*fur*). Spellings of the /ər/ sound in unstressed final syllables are equally confusing but involve different patterns: *-er*, *-ar*, and *-or*. Start by discussing any words that may be unfamiliar, such as *traitor*, as well as words with multiple meanings, such as *litter* ("trash," "a cat box," and a "type of framework for carrying a person"). Introduce the sort by asking students to categorize the words by meaning: *People Nouns* and *Other Nouns*. Point out to students that although several of the words in this sort can function as verbs—for example, *answer* and *honor*—their use as nouns is the focus here. Students who are ready for a greater challenge may be asked to determine categories through open sorting or with only the help of key words. Discuss the results, and then ask students to re-sort the words by meaning and pattern, as shown above. Ask students to speculate on the best-guess pattern or patterns for final /ər/. After they have collected more words through word hunts, check to see whether they need to change their hypothesis. They should conclude that *-er* is most commonly used. As with other sorts, apply the SAIL structure to the lesson, and integrate academic vocabulary into the talk.

Talking Points

- Final /ər/ can be spelled several ways; the most common is *-er*, as in *swimmer* and *cover*.

Integrating Idioms: "Don't worry about my sister; I can always **twist her around my little finger.**" (Easily influence her. A person's pinkie is very small, so it would take very little to wrap something around it.)

Did You Know? **Dollar** has its origin in Jachymov, a small town in central Europe. In the 1500s the town was known by its German name—Sankt Joachimsthal—and was the namesake for coins called *joachimstaler*, which were minted with silver from a nearby mine. The name of the coin was shortened in German to just *taler* and was borrowed into English as *daler*, a word that referred to various similar coins. Thomas Jefferson proposed that the "dollar" be adopted as the U.S. unit of currency, and in 1785 this was formalized by the Continental Congress.

SORT 33. More Unstressed Final Syllables with /ər/

Sorting by Meaning (Parts of Speech)

Nouns (People)	Adjectives
farmer	**younger**
actor	fewer
beggar	hotter
burglar	polar
editor	regular
governor	similar
miser	smarter
plumber	smoother
sculptor	solar
settler	stellar
shopper	
sponsor	
visitor	
voter	

Sorting by Pattern and Meaning

Nouns (People)		Adjectives		
_-er_	_-or_	_-er_	_-ar_	Oddball
farmer	**actor**	**younger**	**solar**	**?**
miser	editor	fewer	polar	beggar
plumber	governor	hotter	pop-	burglar
settler	sculptor	smarter	ular	
shopper	sponsor	smoother	reg-	
voter	visitor		ular	
			simi-	
			lar	
			stel-	
			lar	

Considerations: Discuss any unfamiliar words—perhaps _miser, sponsor,_ and _stellar._ This sort extends work from the previous sort with final /ər/ through the inclusion of adjectives. Ask students to sort the words into meaning categories based on part of speech, as shown. Discuss what the students notice about the two categories. Ask them to re-sort the words by meaning and pattern, and then have each student share results with a partner, being sure to talk about their observations and any helpful generalizations for spelling. Discuss their ideas, and clarify and elaborate as needed. If an idea is suggested that seems questionable but is plausible, say something such as "I can see why you think that. As we gather more words, let's keep a close lookout for words that will support or disprove your idea." Some likely generalizations follow.

Talking Points

- Nouns related to people usually end in *-er* or *-or* (such as *farmer* and *governor*).
- Adjectives that compare end in *-er*, as in *hotter* and *smarter*; *-ar* is often used for other adjectives (*polar* and *similar*).

Integrating Idioms: "We're holding elections next week at school to see how our voter results compare with the rest of the country, and I still can't decide whether to **vote a straight ticket or a split ticket.**" (Vote for only candidates of one party or divide the votes between the two parties. The meaning of *ticket* as the "listing of candidates on a ballot" probably stems from mid-1500 when the word referred to a public notice.)

"My friend loaned me this hat to wear for the parade, since I forgot mine. I hate it, but **beggars can't be choosers.**" (You can't criticize what you get for free. If you are really in need of a certain item and someone gives it to you, you're in no position to find fault with it.)

Did You Know? **Plumber** evolved from *plumbum,* the Latin word for "lead." As far back as Roman times, many pipes used to carry water in a building were made of lead. This lead structure came to be called *plumbing,* and the person who dealt with its maintenance and installation a *plumber.* The root of *plumbum* (*plon*) made its way into English as the name for a lead weight attached to a line and dropped to determine a straight vertical line on a flat surface, such as a wall, or in water to determine depth. Use of such a *plumb line* to measure depth or verticality eventually led to the figurative meaning "to examine closely or in depth," as in *The detective stayed up late and plumbed the many available clues, looking for a common link to solve the mystery.*

SORT 34. Unstressed Final Syllables with /chər/ and /zhər/

Sorting by Sound and Pattern

-cher /chər/	*-ture* /chər/	*-sure* /zhər/	Oddball
pitcher	**nature**	**measure**	**?**
catcher	capture	leisure	danger
rancher	creature	pleasure	injure
stretcher	culture	treasure	
teacher	feature		
	furniture		
	gesture		
	mixture		
	pasture		
	posture		
	texture		
	torture		

Considerations: Discuss the meanings of any words that may be unfamiliar or need clarifying—perhaps *culture, gesture, leisure,* and in some areas *pasture.* Although the words in this sort all have similar-sounding final syllables, there are slight variations that, when coupled with meaning, can provide clues to the different spellings. To illustrate the help that sound and meaning clues can provide, introduce the sort as a teacher-guided listening sort. Explain to students that after you model the placement of a few of the words, you will read the rest of the words aloud while they determine their placement without looking at the spelling. Ask them to think carefully about the sound of the final syllable and any meaning connections that may be of help. Model the placement of one or more words in each category by saying the word carefully but naturally, and then placing the word under the appropriate key word (do not stack the cards; students should be able to see the spellings once their placement is decided). Continue to read aloud others of the words; as students begin to catch on, ask them to point to the category they think is correct. Lay the card down and verify whether the word fits or not before reading the next word. Save the oddballs until the latter part of the sort to avoid confusion. If students have difficulty distinguishing between the two /chər/ patterns, think aloud to reveal that -er is used with base words that end in /ch/. Talk about the results. Students' observations should raise generalizations similar to those listed next; if not, make them aware of them.

Talking Points

- In words that end with /zhər/, the final syllable is spelled -sure, as in *treasure*.
- Many words end in /chər/; if the word includes a base word that ends in /ch/, the ending is -er, as in *rancher* and *catcher*; if not, the ending is -ture, as in *creature* and *nature*.

Integrating Idioms: "This old computer needs to be **put out to pasture**." (Retired from use. This expression comes from the traditional practice of keeping farm animals that were too old to work, especially horses, in a pasture.)

Did You Know? What do **treasure** and a *thesaurus* have in common? Both relate to storing: the one is "stored wealth" in the form of valuables, such as money or jewels, and the other is a "storehouse of synonyms." Both words evolved from the Greek word *thesauros,* meaning "something stored up or laid away." Although it is currently regarded as a book of synonyms, *thesaurus* initially carried the meaning of a "monetary treasury."

SORT 35. Unstressed Final Syllables with /əl/

Sorting by Sound and Pattern

-le	-al	-el	Oddball
angle	**rural**	**angel**	**?**
bottle	equal	cancel	canal
couple	final	channel	fossil
little	normal	level	
middle	plural	model	
pickle		nickel	
simple		novel	
wrinkle		vowel	

Considerations: This sort introduces students to final /əl/, which, like other unstressed-syllable patterns examined in this section, can be represented in several ways—here as -le, -el, -al, and -il. The sort highlights the very common -le pattern and reviews the structure of syllables. If students need greater awareness of how confusing it can be to spell unstressed syllables, you might dictate a few of the words to them before distributing the word cards and discuss the results of their spelling. Before introducing the sort, go over any words students do not know, perhaps *rural* and *canal*. Ask if they can think of a recently studied word that is an opposite, or *antonym*, of *rural* (*urban*; see Sort 31).

After discussing unfamiliar vocabulary, ask students to pair up and, with their partners, determine the sort categories (the category headers should be reserved for later). Remind them to carefully define the categories so that a word matches just one category; otherwise, it should be placed as an oddball, or the categories should be redefined. A sound-and-pattern sort, such as depicted in the Sort 35 answer key, may result; if not, after discussing the students' results, ask them to re-sort the words according to the pattern and sound of the unstressed syllable. Discuss the new results, including the two oddballs and add the category headers. Contrary to the other *-al* words, the *-al* in *canal* is stressed and therefore not a schwa vowel. *Fossil* includes a schwa but has a pattern that is not represented as a category. Ask students to share any generalizations they notice. Use the "Talking Points" below to expand on their ideas. As an extension during this session or at a later time, review the structure of syllables, being sure to highlight V*le*. As students work with the patterns and word hunt for additional examples, invite them to see whether they can determine which is the most frequently occurring pattern.

The *-le* pattern, which appears in many words, wins the frequency competition for /əl/ and is truly the best guess. So many words include this pattern that it is considered one of the six basic syllable patterns (the others have previously been studied: closed, open, VC*e*, vowel team, and *r*-controlled). When you are identifying a syllable with *-le*, as in the word *syllable*, the consonant preceding the *-le* is considered part of the syllable. (See also Sort 14.) In the case of *syllable*, the final syllable is *-ble*, and the *l* is part of the vowel pattern, *le*, rather than part of a *bl* blend. So where do words with final *-le* fit when the structure of the word is being examined? You may remember that there are several across-syllable patterns. These include VCCV, in which the consonants may be either doublets or different, as in *manner* and *basket*; VCV open, as in *paper*; VCV closed, as in *robin*; and VV, as in *create*. When syllable structures that include the *-le* syllable pattern are discussed in this book, the *-le* pattern is designated by a superscript *le* immediately following the V designation. For example, in this sort the structure for the word *little* is VCCV*le* Doublet. The V*le* reveals that the second vowel pattern is *-le*. The structure of *simple* is also VCCV*le* but not a doublet. *Able* has a VCV*le* open structure. Though not included in this sort, *triple* is an example of a VCV*le* closed structure. You might ask students to determine the structure of the other *-le* words included in this sort or of those they find when word hunting. You might also check to be sure they realize that whereas *angle* is VCCV*le*, *angel* is VCCV.

Talking Points

- The /əl/ in unstressed syllables can be spelled in several ways (*-al*, *-il*, *-el*, *-le*), but the most common or best guess for spelling this sound is *-le*, as in *simple*.
- When examining the structure of syllables with final *-le*, the preceding consonant is part of the syllable, and *-le* acts as a vowel unit, as in *simple*, of which the structure is VCCV*le*.
- Surrounding letters in the word can help to determine the spelling of final /əl/. For example, if the *-el* ending is used with *angle*, the word becomes *angel*, because the *e* softens the hard *g* from /g/ to /j/. *Circle* would become *circel* /sûr•səl/, with the hard final *-c* altered to the soft sound of /s/. (For more on hard and soft *c* and *g*, see Sort 37.)

Integrating Idioms:
"My brother's **in a real pickle;** he has a party planned for Friday night, but just got grounded for failing his math test today." (In a difficult situation or predicament. The phrase may stem from a Dutch use of the word *pickle* in the phrase *sit in the pickle*. As sticky as pickling brine or solution can be, you would certainly be in a troublesome situation if you sat in it!)

Did You Know? Browse through any grocery store, and you are likely to find a large assortment of pickles: dill, sweet, sour, with garlic, from midget- to giant-sized, sliced or whole. Stories of the word's origins also vary. One story identifies *pickle* as an eponym, a word that is derived from the name of a person, such as the previously described *sandwich* (see Sort 12). As the story goes, the process of pickling started in the 1300s with a Dutchman by the name of Willem Beukelz (**Boi•**kĕlz). The English really liked Beukelz's idea, but when they talked about it, they pronounced his name so that it sounded like "pickles," and the word caught on (Terban, 1988). Another source suggests that *pickle* was likely borrowed into English from the Dutch word *pekel*, meaning a "solution for preserving and flavoring food." When *pickle* was first recorded around 1400, it had a different meaning from the one we think of today. It was a type of spicy gravy that was served with fowl and meat. In time it took on more of the Dutch meaning, referring to the brine or to foods such as cucumbers preserved in the brine (*The American Heritage Dictionary of the English Language*, 1996).

SORT 36. Unstressed Initial Syllables

Sorting by Sound and Pattern

a	*e*	*o*	Oddball
alarm	**select**	**consume**	**?**
against	demand	collect	college
another	depend	command	comment
attend	develop	pronounce	serious
banana	result	protect	
canoe			
garage			
marine			
patrol			
salute			

Considerations: (*Note:* For the introduction to this sort, you will need five or six blank note cards for every pair of students, and one set of header cards.) In the final sort of this section, attention is shifted to unstressed syllables in the initial position of the word. The focus is not on particular sound-alike patterns, as in the previous sorts, but simply on developing understanding that the infamous schwa can occur in another part of the word and that, because it can be spelled by any of the vowels, it requires careful attention. Differences in dialect are likely to cause some students to question whether certain words really have a schwa sound in the first syllable, as in *demand* (/də•mănd/), which they may pronounce with a stressed first syllable, /dē•mănd/, or with a reduced stress, /dē•mănd/. Be sensitive to such differences. Unanimous agreement is not important; what is important is that students become aware of the schwa in the beginning syllable of words, and that they realize they need to remember its spelling. As a change of pace, before distributing the template of words, hand out five or six blank word cards to pairs or trios of students and send them on a scavenger hunt. Each team will need to find or brainstorm words with a schwa sound ("uh") in the first syllable. Remind them that the "uh" cannot be in a stressed syllable, because then the vowel would be short *u*, as in *drummer*. Advise them to record one word per card. When everyone is finished collecting, bring the group together. Ask each group to read aloud their words; discuss word meanings as needed, and encourage the listeners to attend to which syllable is stressed. Eliminate any inappropriate words. Then place each of the five header cards (*a, e, i, o, u*) in front of the students and, going around the group, ask students to sort their cards according to the schwa pattern (e.g., *fatigue* would be placed under *a* and *severe* under *e*). Continue until all of the cards have been categorized. Discuss the results and any spelling insights. Students will likely collect schwa examples for each of the vowels; if they do not, draw from the following list to illustrate: *marine, patrol, select, severe, divide, divorce, cocoon, polite, support,* and *supply*. After the scavenger hunt, or at a later time, ask students to sort the words on their templates according to the stressed syllable—first or second. This will result in a list of only three words for first-syllable stress (the oddballs shown in the Sort 36 answer key) and placement of all the other words in the second-syllable-stress category. Then turn their attention to the lengthy list of unstressed-first-syllable words. Ask them to re-sort the words in this category according to the schwa pattern: *a, e, i, o, u*. The results should look similar to the Sort 36 key; note that the *i* and *u* categories will be empty. Discuss why *college, comment,* and *serious* are oddballs (the first syllable is stressed; also, *comment* has no unstressed syllable).

Talking Points

- The schwa sometimes occurs in the first syllables of words; it is just as difficult to spell in the initial position as in the final, because it can be represented by any of the five vowels.
- Notice how the schwa is spelled in an unstressed syllable so you can remember it.

Integrating Idioms: "I go **bananas** every time I hear her sing!" (Become very excited and enthusiastic; go crazy—a slang expression. This is a good time to discuss what is meant by *slang*. Slang refers to words and phrases that are coined and used for effect; they are usually short-lived and used mainly in casual and playful speech. Carl Sandburg [1878–1967], a well-known American poet, once shared these thoughts about slang: "Slang is the language that rolls up its sleeves, spits on its hands, and goes to work." What do you think he meant by these words? Can you think of other slang expressions? If you are not sure about a phrase, check the dictionary to see if it indicates *slang* in the entry.)

Did You Know? The first *canoes* were made by Native Americans. Columbus first saw the *canoa*, as the native people of Haiti referred to their boats, on a trip to the West Indies. These early canoes were made by hollowing out entire large trees with a sharp stone. Although paddling such a big boat may seem challenging, some of these early canoes had space for as many as 40 paddlers! Over the centuries, canoes have been used widely for travel and have been made of readily available or desirable materials. For example, birch bark was lighter than a whole tree, and therefore a birch bark canoe could be carried between rivers or lakes if portage was necessary; buffalo hide was plentiful on the plains, where trees were rare. Today, besides wood, canoes are made of plastic, fiberglass, and aluminum. Regardless of the material, they continue to be streamlined so they can be maneuvered in very shallow or narrow waters.

Unstressed Final Syllables with Long-*a* Patterns

-ace	*-age*	*-ain*
surface	manage	certain
luggage	practice	fountain
furnace	villain	courage
mountain	message	bargain
garbage	obtain	necklace
curtain	bandage	engage
cabbage	menace	package
palace	damage	?

Unstressed Final Syllables with /ən/

-en	-an	-en	-in	-on
Verbs		**Nouns**		**?**
darken		slogan		dozen
cabin		lemon		tighten
woman		robin		siren
button		cousin		fasten
eleven		sharpen		dragon
cotton		awaken		chicken
loosen		pardon		urban
margin		method		strengthen

SORT 32 Unstressed Final Syllables with /ər/

-er	-or (People)	-er	-or (Other)	-ar
People Nouns		**Other Nouns**		
brother	doctor	finger		
favor	sugar	traitor		
honor	answer	father		
mother	error	swimmer		
mayor	soldier	harbor		
cover	litter	collar		
mirror	grocer	neighbor		
dollar	drawer	sailor		

More Unstressed Final Syllables with /ər/

-er (Nouns)	-or	-er (Adjectives)	-ar
Nouns	**Adjectives**		**?**
farmer	actor		younger
solar	polar		governor
smarter	regular		shopper
voter	editor		stellar
fewer	miser		sponsor
settler	similar		smoother
sculptor	burglar		visitor
beggar	plumber		hotter

Unstressed Final Syllables with /chər/ and /zhər/

-cher /chər/	**-ture** /chər/	**-sure** /zhər/
pitcher	nature	measure
pasture	torture	teacher
capture	treasure	culture
danger	catcher	leisure
feature	injure	mixture
pleasure	posture	rancher
stretcher	texture	furniture
gesture	creature	?

Unstressed Final Syllables with /əl/

-le	*-al*	*-el*
angle	rural	angel
vowel	fossil	novel
cancel	wrinkle	final
pickle	nickel	bottle
equal	couple	channel
little	canal	simple
level	model	plural
normal	middle	**?**

a	e	i	o	u

alarm	select	consume
salute	command	serious
another	demand	collect
develop	college	attend
canoe	marine	depend
comment	pronounce	garage
protect	result	banana
patrol	against	?

Consonant Extensions

The five sorts in this section extend and review patterns with *complex consonants* (see *Word Journeys, Second Edition* [Ganske, 2014] or *Word Sorts and More, Second Edition* [Ganske, 2018]). Hard and soft *c* and *g* and final *k* are revisited in the context of polysyllabic words. New sounds for the *ch* digraph are explored, and *ph* is introduced as a digraph. Use of *gu(e)* and *qu(e)* are also examined. In anticipation of the Chapter 5 word studies, the final investigation looks at environments in which *i* helps to form consonant sounds, as in *ci, si, ti,* and *i(on)*.

What Is Known: Although each sort in this section targets different letters or patterns, students will likely have previously studied either the sound or the pattern in one-syllable words at the within word pattern stage. Known concepts relevant to the sorts that follow include hard and soft *c* and *g*; final /k/ spelled *-ck, -ke,* and *-k*; /sh/ spelled *sh*; /qw/ spelled *qu*; and /f/ spelled *f*.

What Is New: The context of polysyllabic words is new for all of the patterns. Also, there are several new spellings for known sounds and some new sounds for known spelling patterns, as /k/ can also be spelled with *c* (*topic*), *ch* (*chorus*), and *-que* (*unique*); final /g/ in longer words tends to be spelled *-gue* (*fatigue*); /f/ tends to be spelled with *ph* in polysyllabic words (*trophy*); *i* sometimes sounds like /y/ (*onion*); and in certain word environments /sh/ is spelled with *ch, ci, si,* or *ti*.

SORT 37. Consonant Extensions with Hard and Soft *c* and *g*

Sorting by Sound and Pattern

Hard *c*	Hard *g*	Soft *c*	Soft *g*
custom	**guilty**	**center**	**gentle**
camera	gadget	cement	general
coffee	goalie	census	genius
compass	gossip	cereal	genuine
cookie		circle	gigantic
correct		circus	gymnast
		citizen	
		cycle	

Considerations: (Note that the sort contains several three-syllable words.) Because the same principles guide the use of hard and soft *c* and *g*, the two principles can be taught together. After discussing any unfamiliar words, ask students what they notice about the words. They should mention that all of the words begin with either *c* or *g*. Their comments may reveal much greater understanding, such as that when the letter has a hard sound, /k/ or /g/, it is followed by *a, o,* or *u,* and when it is soft, the following letter is *e, i,* or *y*. If their responses show this type of depth, ask them to sort the words in a manner that demonstrates how *c* and *g* work, such as shown here, or with the letters combined so that there is one "hard" column and one "soft" column. If students demonstrate more limited knowledge of the feature, explain that both *c* and *g* can produce more than one sound. Then ask them to sort the words by their initial consonant sound. This will result in four categories. Point to the columns with hard *c* and *g*, and explain that in these words the sound of the beginning *c* or *g* is hard. Then point out the two columns of words that begin with soft *c* and *g*. Ask students to pair up and examine the words, to try to discover what makes the *c* and *g* hard sometimes and soft others. Prompt students who need hints to look at the second letter in each word. Discuss and clarify their findings. As part of the discussion, invite students to identify and explain the sounds of *g* and *c* in other positions of some of the words (*cycle, circle, circus, gadget,* and *gigantic*).

Although the principles or rules that govern spellings with hard and soft *c* and *g* are powerful ones that work with most words, there are "rule breakers"—for instance, *cello* and *façade, giggle, geyser,* and *margarine*. Students may be able to think of other exceptions or search for them during word hunts. The etymology section of dictionary word entries can provide insights as to why they are oddballs. *Façade,* for example, is a French borrowing; the small diacritical mark beneath the *c* (called a *cedilla*) tells us that the *c* will have a soft sound, despite the following *a*. Dictionaries and computer programs often represent the word in English with its French spelling, using the cedilla to point out the word's unusual soft *c* sound. The same mark is often used in *garçon,* another French borrowing.

Talking Points

- When followed by *a, o,* or *u, c* and *g* usually make a hard sound (/k/ and /g/), as in *camera, cookie, custom, gadget, gossip,* and *guilty*.
- When followed by *e, i,* or *y, c* and *g* usually make a soft sound (/s/ and /j/), as in *center, circle, cycle, gentle, gigantic,* and *gymnast*.

Integrating Idioms: "Our game was rained out for the third straight day; I guess **that's the way the cookie crumbles.**" (Just what you have to expect sometimes. Seldom can you bite into or eat a cookie whole without bits and pieces falling off; so, too, in life things do not always go smoothly.)

Did You Know? We have the Dutch to thank for **cookie,** which we probably borrowed from their word for "little cake"—*koekje*. The Dutch were not the first to make cookies; the first cookie-like cakes probably came from Persia, which was one of the first places in the world to grow sugar. Many countries have their own names for these little delicacies; for example, in England they are called *biscuits,* in Germany they are *keks,* in Italy they are *biscotti,* and in Spain they are *galletas*. Do you know any other names?

SORT 38. Consonant Extensions with Final /k/

Sorting by Pattern

-ck	*-ke*	*-k*	*-c*	Oddball
shamrock	**cupcake**	**chipmunk**	**topic**	**?**
attack	keepsake	crosswalk	arctic	antique
cowlick	rebuke	remark	elastic	
hammock	turnpike		fabric	
limerick			metric	
padlock			mimic	
			panic	
			plastic	
			specific	

Considerations: Although *-ck, -ke,* and *-k* are typical spellings for final /k/ in one-syllable words, students will discover as they work with the words in this sort and search for additional examples through word hunts that these patterns occur relatively infrequently in polysyllabic words. Probably the most common of the three is *-ck,* and even it tends to be limited to compound words. The *ck* pattern does occur frequently at the end of other syllables, as in *bicker, cackle, chuckle, freckle.* In polysyllabic words, the final /k/ is most often represented with *-c.* Many adjectives, such as the word *polysyllabic,* end in *-ic: angelic, classic, economic,* and so forth. Discuss any unfamiliar words (for some students, words such as *cowlick, rebuke,* and others may need clarifying or explaining). Then introduce the sort by spreading the words in front of the students or displaying them on an overhead. Ask them what they all have in common. If someone suggests that they all have two syllables (actually *limerick* has three, but certain dialects may cause it to be pronounced with two—/**lĭm**•rĭk/), ask "What else?" Once the focus is on the final /k/ sound, ask them to sort their word cards according to how this sound is spelled. Talk about the results, and encourage generalizations that will aid spelling. Brainstorming additional words or searching for more examples through word hunts may be necessary before this can be accomplished. *Antique* is introduced as an oddball in anticipation of Sort 40, which looks at final *-que.* As an extension, ask students to consider which words could have *-ed* added to them to form the past tense. How would the new word be spelled? Record their responses on the board. Discuss the results, which should include *attacked, rebuked, padlocked, remarked, mimicked,* and *panicked.* Some students are likely to misspell the last two. Ask them to hypothesize why *k* was added (to maintain the hard *c* sound).

Talking Points

- Final /k/ can be represented in many ways (*-ck, -k, -ke, -c,* or *-que*); however, in polysyllabic words, the most common form is *c,* which occurs in many adjectives as *-ic,* such as *classic.*

Integrating Idioms: "Last night my mom **pressed the panic button** and called 911. She thought my grandfather had had a heart attack, but it turned out he was just asleep." (Overreacted to the situation. According to one source [Ammer, 1997], some World War II bombers had bell-warning systems that enabled flight crews to bail out of the plane if it was badly hit; however, pilots sometimes overestimated the damage and pushed the signal unnecessarily. By 1950, use of the term had broadened to mean other types of overreaction.)

Did You Know? The word **panic** comes to us by way of a figure from ancient Greek mythology—Pan. Pan was the god of woods, fields, and flocks. He had the body and head of a human and the legs, ears, and horns of a goat; he lived and wandered about in mountains and valleys. He was fond of music and is often shown playing panpipes, an early instrument made of reeds of different lengths, which is played by blowing across the open ends. Greek gods, such as Pan, who dwelt in the forest were feared by those who had reason to pass through the forest at night; the darkness and loneliness of the woods ignited their fears and superstitions, and they attributed the cause to Pan. Consequently, any sudden overpowering terror came to be known as *panic.*

SORT 39. Consonant Extensions with *ch* and *ph*

Sorting by Sound and Pattern

ch			ph
/ch/	/k/	/sh/	/f/
chimney	**chorus**	**brochure**	**nephew**
attach	chaos	chaperone	alphabet
challenge	character	machine	elephant
mischief	echo	mustache	pamphlet
spinach	schedule	parachute	paragraph
	stomach		phrases
			physical
			trophy

Considerations: Talk about any unfamiliar words, such as *chaos*. You might ask students to look up *brochure* and *pamphlet* in a dictionary to determine whether they are synonyms or have somewhat different meanings. Review the meaning of *digraph*, and then explain to students that they will be examining the digraphs *ch* and *ph*. Ask them to sort their words by pattern and sound so that the results reveal the sound or sounds of each of the two patterns. The outcome will resemble the Sort 39 answer key. Discuss the results and any generalizations that students can draw about reading or spelling words with *ch* and *ph*. The latter is a relatively rare spelling for /f/ in common English words; it occurs more often in low-frequency words. A browsing of the *ph* section of the dictionary will quickly show this. Although *ch* makes various sounds, as in *echo*, *attach*, and *machine*, when students are reading words with *ch* their best guess is /ch/, which is the most common pronunciation for the pattern. If that does not produce a known word, students need to be flexible and apply the other sounds. More recent borrowings from the French have given us the /sh/ pronunciation, as in *chaperone*, and those from Latin and Greek the sound of hard *c*, as in *chorus*. Because the different pronunciations relate to time and place of borrowing rather than to meaning or surrounding letters, spelling can be a challenge.

Talking Points

- *Ch* can make several different sounds, including /ch/ as in *attach*, /k/ as in *echo*, and /sh/ as in *machine*; when you are learning to spell a word with one of the sounds, make note of the pattern to remember it.
- /ch/ is the most common pronunciation for *ch*, and therefore it is your best guess when trying to read an unfamiliar word with the pattern.
- *Ph*, as in *pamphlet*, is a common spelling for /f/, but appears mostly in low-frequency words.

Integrating Idioms: "Our neighborhood is having a **white elephant** sale this weekend, so people can get rid of their junk." (A useless or unwanted item. According to *The American Heritage Dictionary of Idioms* [Ammer, 1997], this custom started with the Siamese. An albino or white elephant was rare and considered sacred. Sometimes the king would give a white elephant to a subject he did not like; because the elephant was sacred, the person could not kill the animal, and eventually the cost of feeding the animal ruined the person.)

Did You Know? **Parachute** is borrowed from the French *para* (as in the light umbrella, *parasol*, which literally means "shield or protection from the sun") and *chute*, meaning "fall." The parachute indeed offers protection from a fall; its lightweight, umbrella-like structure creates resistance that slows down a fall. The word was coined in the 1780s and demonstrated by an early French balloonist named Blanchard, who attached a parachute to a basket, placed a dog inside, and dropped it from a balloon. A few years later, Blanchard's hot air balloon ruptured, and he had cause to safely use the device himself. Early parachutes were made of canvas; to increase strength and lightness, Blanchard began making them of folded silk. Despite the pioneering efforts of Blanchard and others in the 1700s, documents of the Middle Ages show that people were already experimenting with devices to protect them when falling from a height, and in the 1400s the famous Leonardo da Vinci drew a sketch of a parachute.

SORT 40. Consonant Extensions with *gu(e)* and *qu(e)*

Sorting by Sound and Pattern

gu	*-gue*	*qu*	*-que*	Oddball
penguin	**fatigue**	**question**	**unique**	**?**
extinguish	dialogue	frequent	critique	disguise
jaguar	league	liquid	opaque	guidance
language	prologue	quality	technique	mosquito
	vague	require		
		sequence		
		squirrel		

Considerations: Students may need to have the meanings of some words clarified—perhaps *extinguish, jaguar, league, prologue, vague, unique, critique,* or *opaque.* Spread the words out for students to review, and ask them what the words have in common. Most will notice that all of the words include either *gu* or *qu.* Next, gather the cards and place the key words *penguin* and *fatigue,* as well as the *?* card, in front of them. Say each word, emphasizing the portion with *g.* Then read aloud each of the remaining *gu* or *-gue* words (for the time being, skip over words with *qu*). Ask students which category the word should be placed in, but do not reveal the word until they have made their selection; then place it in the appropriate category. When complete, discuss possible generalizations to facilitate spelling. *Disguise* and *guidance* are oddballs because they do not have a /gw/ sound, as the *gu* words under *penguin* do. Proceed in the same manner with the *qu* and *-que* words, creating two new categories under the key words *question* and *unique.* Exceptions can be added to the oddball list already started. Talk about any observations and generate ideas to aid spelling. Add the headers as the spelling patterns are discussed. Point out to students that *mosquito* is an exception. The unusual pronunciation stems from the word's Spanish ancestry. As a follow-up, ask students to re-sort the words using all four key words to guide them. This approach may be used for the initial sort if students are able to handle the somewhat subtle distinctions in sound. In case students wonder, there are other words in which *u* sometimes produces a /w/ sound (as in *cuisine, Duane, suede, suave, suite, tuille*—the last of these is a piece of armor for covering the thigh). As in the /gw/ and /qw/ words in this sort, the *u* is preceded by a consonant and followed by another vowel.

Talking Points

- Sometimes *gu* is pronounced with a hard-*g* sound, /g/, as in *disguise,* and sometimes as /gw/, as in *language;* final *-gue* is usually pronounced as a hard *g,* as in *fatigue,* and is a common spelling for final /g/ in polysyllabic words.
- In English, *q* is followed by *u,* and *qu* is pronounced /kw/; final *-que* is pronounced /k/, as in *unique.*

Integrating Idioms: "The snowstorm was **a blessing in disguise:** Our flight was canceled, but the resort gave everyone two nights of free lodging, so we got to extend our vacation." (Something that seems like a misfortune turns out to be a lucky occurrence.)

Did You Know? **Language,** with its current spelling, was first recorded as the word for "talk" in the early 1300s. It evolved from the Latin word for "tongue," *lingua.* Estimates of just how many languages there are vary by the thousands, depending on the definition of *language.* If we define *language* as a "living language," or one that is used widely by a particular group of people, the estimate is 7,111 known living languages on the website Ethnologue: Languages of the World (*www.ethnologue.com/guides/how-many-languages*). So which language has the greatest number of native speakers? Mandarin Chinese, followed by English (which has the greatest number of both native and non-native speakers).

The origin of ***penguin*** is somewhat of a mystery and perhaps a case of mistaken identity. According to one story, the word originated in Wales, far away from any penguins. In Welsh, *pen* means "chief" or "head," and *gwyn* means "white," resulting in "white head." However, the heads of penguins are mainly black, so what is the explanation? In the late 1500s when explorers were traveling around the world, British sailors visited Newfoundland. The island was crowded with large gray and white flightless birds. Perhaps Welshmen were among the sailors, as both the island and the bird were named *pen gwyn.* Although the birds had large white spots on their heads, they were not white, so perhaps the island (and its flightless inhabitants) got its name because the sailors thought that all or part of the island resembled a white head. No one knows. Still later in the century, when English explorers traveled south of South America, they saw flightless birds that reminded them of the ones in Newfoundland. They called them *penguins,* though these birds were very different from those sighted in Newfoundland. Today we know the birds seen in Newfoundland by the name of *great auk,* a species that soon became extinct because the birds were easily caught.

SORT 41. Consonant Extensions with Vowel *i*

Sorting by Sound and Pattern

ci /sh/	*si* /sh/	*ti* /sh/	*i* /y/	Oddball
special	**mansion**	**motion**	**onion**	?
ancient	session	caption	billion	vision
conscience	tension	fiction	junior	
conscious		mention	opinion	
crucial		option	senior	
glacier		patient		
vicious		station		

Considerations: This sort introduces *i* as a consonant sound in particular contexts, as in *ancient,* in which it makes the /sh/ sound when combined with *c.* Several of the final-syllable patterns found here are the focus of sorts at the beginning of the next stage, in which one aim is to develop the understanding that words related in meaning also tend to be related in spelling (thus *disrupt/disruption,* not *disrupt/disrupsion*). Discuss any unfamiliar words; *conscience* and *conscious* may need clarifying, and perhaps *crucial, caption,* and *ancient.* More capable students may be able to complete the sound and pattern sort, independently or with partners, with minimal guidance, using the headers and key words as guides. Others may benefit from more teacher direction and modeling. In either case, go over the key words and headers, emphasizing the targeted portion of the word: /sh/ for *ci; si, ti,* and /y/ for *i.* Remind students to consider both pattern and sound as they sort. When completed, discuss the results.

Talking Points

- /sh/ in an unstressed final syllable is often spelled *ci, si,* or *ti,* as in *glacier, tension,* and *caption.*
- In unstressed final syllables, *i* sometimes sounds like a *y,* /y/, as in *onion* and *senior.*

Integrating Idioms: "When I stay with my grandmother, she often asks me how my day went and says that **a clean conscience** makes a good pillow." (Feeling free of guilt makes it easy to sleep. Benjamin Franklin's proverb "A quiet conscience sleeps in thunder" from *Poor Richard's Almanack* has a similar meaning.)

Did You Know? Anyone who has ever had to make a **crucial** decision has been at a crossroads of having to decide between one option or the other. *Crucial* stems from the Latin word *crux,* meaning "cross." In the 1500s, *crux* referred to a guidepost marking directions for a division in the road. A person can encounter many such crossing points—in his or her studies, in a relationship, in deciding how to spend time, and so forth—at which the decision made is a very important one.

The words **onion** and *one* share more than the first two letters of their spellings. *Onion* actually stems from the Latin word for "oneness" or "union"—*unio.* So what is the meaning connection, you might wonder? The vegetable is made up of many layers that are *united* at the bottom. It is this same layering connotation that led Romans to call pearls by the same name, *unio.*

Consonant Extensions with Hard and Soft *c* and *g*

Hard *c*	Hard *g*	Soft *c*	Soft *g*
custom	guilty	center	
gentle	cement	compass	
gossip	gymnast	gadget	
gigantic	circle	coffee	
camera	genius	cycle	
goalie	circus	correct	
general	cookie	cereal	
citizen	genuine	census	

Consonant Extensions with Final /k/

-ck	-ke	-k	-c
shamrock	cupcake	chipmunk	
topic	antique	turnpike	
specific	fabric	limerick	
cowlick	hammock	arctic	
panic	elastic	attack	
crosswalk	keepsake	plastic	
metric	mimic	rebuke	
padlock	remark	**?**	

Consonant Extensions with *ch* and *ph*

ch /ch/	***ch*** /k/	***ch*** /sh/	***ph*** /f/
chimney	chorus		brochure
nephew	pamphlet		schedule
parachute	attach		alphabet
stomach	trophy		mischief
spinach	chaperone		paragraph
chaos	elephant		character
physical	challenge		machine
echo	mustache		phrases

Consonant Extensions with *gu(e)* and *qu(e)*

gu	-gue	qu	-que
penguin	fatigue	question	
unique	sequence	prologue	
opaque	league	quality	
jaguar	mosquito	extinguish	
technique	frequent	critique	
require	disguise	dialogue	
guidance	language	liquid	
vague	squirrel	?	

SORT 41

Consonant Extensions with Vowel *i*

ci /sh/	*si* /sh/	*ti* /sh/	*i* /y/
special	mansion		motion
onion	conscience		fiction
option	tension		crucial
glacier	vicious		billion
vision	patient		session
junior	conscious		mention
caption	senior		opinion
ancient	station		?

Prefixes and Suffixes

In this section, students explore some of the most common prefixes and suffixes and their affixation to base words. In Chapter 5 of this book, prefixes and suffixes are reexamined in the contexts of more sophisticated base words and word roots. Meaning lies at the heart of the word studies that follow. Students need to understand the meaning changes that prefixes and suffixes bring about, as well as to realize that readers and writers can use their knowledge of these common word parts to break longer words down into more manageable chunks for easier word identification, meaning making, or spelling. To help students understand that prefixes and suffixes add meaning (not just letters) to a word, careful attention has been given to including certain words to encourage students to think about this meaning connection. For example, consider *relish* and *unite* in Sort 42. Even though the words begin with *re-* and *un-*, if the letters are removed, what remains is not a base word. *Misspell* in Sort 43 serves a similar purpose. Sometimes adding a prefix to a base word results in a spelling that may not "look right," such as *reelect*. Students need to realize that meaning is a very powerful force in English spelling, especially when low-frequency words are involved. This concept is further emphasized in studies at the next stage.

What Is Known: It is assumed that students know what a base word is and understand the concept of suffixes through their previous studies of inflectional endings: *-ed, -ing, -s, -es, -er,* and *-est.*

What Is New: The concept of prefixes and suffixes as *affixes,* nonword parts that alter the meaning of a base word, may be new and should be explained. Although base words are used in the following sorts, let students know that sometimes prefixes and suffixes attach to word parts called *roots* that are not complete words. They will learn about these later.

SORT 42. Prefixes (*un-* and *re-*)

Sorting by Pattern and Meaning

un-	*re-*	Oddball
unwrap	**rebuild**	**?**
unable	recycle	relish
unclear	reelect	unite
uneven	remove	
unfair	reorder	
unhappy	replace	
unkind	reread	
unsure	return	
untied	review	
unusual	rewind	
	rewrite	

Considerations: Show students the words, and discuss any that are unfamiliar; encourage them to share ideas about what the categories may be. Then ask everyone to sort the words according to their thinking. When they are finished, talk about the categories. If students group *relish* and *unite* with the *re-* and *un-* categories, respectively, ask how the words in each column are alike and whether the words might be grouped another way besides words that begin with *un-* or *re-*. If necessary, suggest that they consider meaning. Students should note that (apart from the oddball category) the *un-* words all add "not" to the meaning of their base words, and that those with *re-* have been changed to mean "back" or "again." Explain that the *un-* and the *re-* in these words are *prefixes*. Before ending the session, invite the group to brainstorm more words with *un-* or *re-* beginnings and to identify whether and how the spellings affect the words' meanings. If a questionable word is put forward, suggest that the group consult a dictionary.

Talking Points

- A prefix is a meaningful word part that is sometimes added to the beginning of a word to alter its meaning. The prefixes *un-* and *re-* are very common; the former means "not," and the latter means "back" or "again."
- As with compound words, sometimes a correct but "doesn't-look-right" spelling can result when a prefix is added to a base word, as with *reelect*; writers need to remember that it is meaning that really matters.
- Some words, such as *relish* and *unite*, may look as though they have a prefix attached to a base word, but the meaning connection is lacking.

Integrating Idioms: "Hey, guys, we all agree we could have chosen a better topic, but don't you think we're **past the point of no return?**" (Too far into the project to decide on another one. If you had just enough fuel to get to a destination, once you're past the halfway point, you have to keep going; you don't have enough to make the trip back.)

Did You Know? We often reread text to increase our understanding, especially if it's difficult. **Read** comes from the Old English word *raedan*, meaning to "advise" or "interpret something difficult that is written." Although many words in English share a common ancestry with words from other Western European languages, this is not the case with the verb *to read*. Italian, French, German, and other language versions stem from the Latin word *legere*. Although *read* did not develop from this word, *legend* and *legible* did. The ancestry of **write** also differs; it stems from an Old English word *writan*, which in turn came from a root meaning "to cut, scratch." It is likely that early writing on parchment involved much scratching with the quill pen. Other Western European languages drew on the Latin word *scribere*, for "to write." Although English did not borrow *to write* from this word, others of our words do stem from it. What do you think they might be? (*Scribe* and *scribble*, for example; for others, see Sort 38 in Chapter 5.)

SORT 43. Prefixes (*dis-, fore-, mis-*)

Sorting by Pattern and Meaning

dis-	*fore-*	*mis-*	Oddball
dislike	**forehead**	**mistrust**	**?**
disagree	forecast	misjudge	foreign
discomfort	foreground	mismatch	forest
discover	foremost	misplace	
dishonest	foresight	misprint	
disobey	forewarn	misspell	
disorder		mistake	
distrust			

Considerations: This set of words introduces students to three more prefixes: *dis-* ("opposite of"), *fore-* ("before, in front of"), and *mis-* ("to do something wrongly"). First, ask students to sort the words according to their prefixes. Then discuss the word meanings by applying the meaning of the prefix to the base word—for instance, "If you *dislike* something or someone, it's the opposite of liking them; you don't like them." In some cases, the connection may be more implied than direct, as, for example, with *forecast.* You might ask students to hypothesize on what is being cast or thrown before. Students should realize that *f-o-r-e* in *forest* and *foreign* are just letters and not meaning units, as evident in the absence of a base word. Ask them if they can think of any other words that could have been included in the sort. If a word such as *distance* is mentioned, let students know that although *dis-* is a prefix in the word, *tance* is not a base word but a word root.

Talking Points

- *Dis-, mis-,* and *fore-* are all prefixes. *Dis-* means "opposite of," *fore-* means "before" or "in front of," and *mis-* means "to do something wrongly."
- Two good reminders that words can look as though they have a prefix, but do not have the meaning associated with a combined prefix and base word, are *forest* and *foreign.*

Integrating Idioms: "Last night when my brother was helping me with my math homework, he became frustrated and said that I **couldn't see the forest for the trees.**" (Let details get in the way of seeing how to solve the problems. You can get so bogged down with details [all the trees] of a situation that you actually lose sight of the big picture.)

Did You Know? **Foreign** and **forest** share ancestral beginnings; both come from Latin words for "outside"—*foris* and *foras.* In ancient times, anyone who lived outside and away from the town gates was considered *foreign.* Today we typically associate the word with "outside of a person's native country." The *g* in *foreign,* which gives many spellers difficulty, was added later and is thought to be the result of confusion with the spelling of either *reign* or *sovereign.* The word *forest* originally had no connection to trees. In medieval times, it meant a protected area in which royalty kept deer and other game for hunting and sport.

    Spell, as in **misspell,** developed from Middle English *spellen,* to "read letter by letter," which in turn came from an Old French word, *espeller. Spell* itself was probably first recorded over 600 years ago. The concept of a *spelling bee,* in which everyone's hope is not to *misspell,* came about during the first half of the 1800s and the phrase itself within a few decades. The meaning of *spell* as "a charm or trance" derives from an Old English word for "discourse" or "story." Whether referring to a "trance" or to "correct writing," the root of both words is *spel. Spel* comes from a large family of languages that includes most of Europe and parts of Asia. We can still see the root today in *gospel,* which literally means "good tidings" or "discourse." (For a list of common misspellings, check-your-spelling quizzes, and other activities, go to Miss Spelling's Spelling Center at *www.alphadictionary.com/articles/misspelling.html.*)

SORT 44. Prefixes (*in-, in-, non-, pre-*)

Sorting by Pattern and Meaning

in-	*in-*	*non-*	*pre-*	Oddball
Indent	**inactive**	**nonstop**	**prepay**	**?**
income	incomplete	nonfat	precaution	pretzel
indoors	incorrect	nonfiction	preheat	
inflamed	indirect	nonsense	prejudge	
input		nonsmoking	preschool	
insight			preteen	
			preview	

Considerations: With this set of words, students learn about three more prefixes: *in-, non-,* and *pre-*. *Non-* means "not," and *pre-* means "before." Because *in-* can mean "in/into" as well as "not," the two meanings are treated as separate categories, so actually students will be working with four categories besides oddballs. *In-* is a common prefix, especially in lower-frequency words, in which it is often attached to a root rather than to a base word; it is revisited at the next stage. Ask students to sort their words according to prefix, and then to carefully consider meaning in order to subdivide the list of *in-* words. Next, initiate a discussion of the words; encourage students to make meaning connections between the prefixes and base words. By now students should readily recognize a word such as *pretzel* as an oddball, included to make sure they are thinking.

Talking Points

- *In-, fore-,* and *non-* are three more prefixes. *Non-* means "not," *fore-* means "before" or "in front of," and *in-* can mean "in/into" but also "not."
- Because prefixes can have multiple meanings, and more than one prefix can carry the same meaning, it's important to interpret and use them correctly. For example, *inactive* means "not active" rather than something that is actually "in action," and a room in which smoking is prohibited is a *nonsmoking* room, not an *insmoking* room.

Integrating Idioms: "You should have exercised precaution instead of **throwing caution to the wind.**" (Being very careless. If you throw something to the wind, you're likely to lose it, because it will blow away and you won't be able to find it. It would be a very careless act.)

Did You Know? **Pretzel** has an interesting history or story behind it. The pretzel as we know it was likely first introduced in the United States during the 1800s by German immigrants, who originally called it the *brezel*. It had been enjoyed in German countries as a food item for several centuries before that, and its origins are even older. The knot-shaped pretzel probably goes back to medieval Latin and to a story that suggests that a monk first created the shape to symbolize arms folded in prayer. The word derives from *bracchiatus*, meaning "having branches," which in turn comes from a word for "branch" or "arm." Estimates of the average annual per-person consumption of pretzels range from 2 pounds per year to 20 pounds. What might account for the large range (size of pretzel and person, where one lives, taste, etc.)?

SORT 45. Suffixes (-*ful*, -*less*, -*ly*, -*ness*)

Sorting by Pattern and Meaning

-*ful*	-*less*	-*ly*	-*ness*
careful	**careless**	**loudly**	**illness**
cheerful	breathless	finally	darkness
colorful	helpless	friendly	coolness
painful	homeless	really	openness
peaceful	priceless	safely	stillness
thoughtful		smoothly	weakness
useful			

Considerations: This word study builds on previous suffix work with inflectional endings (-*ed*, -*ing*, -*er*, -*est*, -*s*, -*es*). The new suffixes are -*ful*, meaning "full of"; -*less*, meaning "without"; -*ness*, meaning "state of being"; and -*ly*, meaning "in a particular manner." Unlike earlier studies, which have dealt with suffixes that begin with a vowel and require dropping the final -*e* or doubling the final consonant of the base word, here the suffix begins with a consonant and requires no change. This is an important concept for students to gain from their work. Inclusion of the words *peaceful, useful, homeless, priceless,* and *safely* illustrate this principle. Base words that end with the same consonant with which the suffix begins (*finally, really, openness*) help students to realize that double consonants can occur for reasons other than application of the doubling principle, and that though they may not look right, meaning dictates their inclusion. Ask students to sort their words by suffix, or guide them through the sort with modeling as needed. Discuss word meanings in light of the suffix and base-word meanings. As part of the discussion, you might write *chilly* on the board or overhead and ask students to consider where it would be categorized. They should reason that it would be an oddball, because if they take away the base word *chill*, all that would remain is -*y*, a suffix but not one currently being examined. If you wish, extend the sort with a review of parts of speech by asking students to categorize the words according to adjective, adverb, and noun, as follows:

Sorting by Meaning

Noun	*Adjective*	*Adverb*
coolness	breathless	finally
darkness	careful	(friendly)
illness	careless	loudly
openness	cheerful	really
stillness	colorful	safely
weakness	(friendly)	smoothly
	helpless	
	homeless	
	painful	
	peaceful	
	priceless	
	thoughtful	
	useful	

Talking Points

- A *suffix* is a meaningful word part attached to the end of a base word to alter its meaning; knowing the meaning of suffixes can help you better understand words. The suffix *-ful* means "full of," *-less* means "without," *-ness* means "a state of being," and *-ly* means "in a certain way."
- Unlike previously studied suffixes, which begin with a vowel and usually require dropping a final *-e* or doubling a final consonant (such as *-ing*, *-ed*, and *-es*), suffixes that begin with a consonant do not require a change.

Integrating Idioms: "Dad says not to **hold my breath** on going to the movies Friday night." (Count on it. If you tried to hold your breath until something that was unlikely to occur happened, you would end up breathless.)

Did You Know? The adjective form of **coolness,** *cool,* has evolved with numerous meanings. Its original temperature-related meaning dates to well before the 1400s, when the word was spelled *col.* During Shakespeare's time (the 1500s), the idea of coolness was applied to less than enthusiastic feelings expressed about people, events, and so forth, as "He was pretty cool to my idea of turning in my project late." It was applied to money in the sense of a lot, "a cool million," during the 1700s. In the 1900s, a new type of music called jazz was described as "cool," and people began to use the word to express the ideas of "good," "excellent," or "great" (the "coolest"). What other meanings might be added to the word in years to come?

War is a time of conflict; peace is the opposite, a state of harmony with an absence of hostility. When there is peace, there tend to be fairness, respect, and kindness. Both concepts have spawned scores of books, including at least one that features both words in its title (Tolstoy's *War and Peace*), and have given rise to numerous related words and phrases: *warlike, warlord, warrior, warplane, warship, wartime,* and *war chest*; and **peaceful,** *peaceable, peacekeeper, peacemaker, peacenik, peacetime, Peace Corps, peace officer, peace offering, peace pipe, peace sign,* and others. The *Nobel Peace Prize* is awarded annually to individuals considered to have done the best job in promoting world peace. *Peace,* which was first recorded in the mid-1300s, was borrowed from Old French (*pais*), which came from the Latin words *pax* and *pac,* meaning "tranquility" and "absence of war." *Pacific Ocean* and *pacifier* also derive from the latter root (for further discussion of this root, see Chapter 5, Sort 48). What might the meaning connection be (*calm*)? The word *war* stems from a root meaning "mixed up" or "confused" (*liverwurst,* which is a type of sausage made up of a meat mixture, shares the same root and the meaning connection of "mixed up").

SORT 46. Adding Suffix -*y* to Words with No Change, *e*-Drop, and Double

Sorting by Pattern (and thinking about meaning—the base word)

No Change	*e*-Drop	Double	Oddball
grouchy	**shady**	**sunny**	**?**
bossy	breezy	baggy	angrily
curly	crumbly	foggy	many
lengthy	drizzly	furry	
silvery	greasy	skinny	
squeaky	juicy	starry	
	noisy		
	scary		
	tasty		

Considerations: With their knowledge of base words and the no-change, *e*-drop, and doubling principles, many students will be able to approach this set of words as an open sort. Others will likely be able to categorize the words with minimal support; provide the headers and key words, and possibly model one or two words. Go over any unfamiliar words at the onset, and follow up the sorting with a discussion of the categories and oddball words and a review of the base words. You might ask students to record the base word at the bottom of each of the cards; for the oddballs, *many* is the base word rather than *man*, and *angrily* includes the suffix *-ly* affixed to *angry*. In addition to becoming aware of the different ways to add *-y*, students should recognize that adding the letter changes the part of speech; in most cases, the change is from noun to adjective. (Students may notice that some of the words, such as *taste*, *scare*, *crumble*, and *drizzle*, can or do function as verbs.) Nouns are not the only parts of speech that can become adjectives; though this is unusual, even a conjunction can: *if* → *iffy*. Invite students to choose nouns to change into adjectives by adding *-y*: *flowery*, *thorny*, *tinny*, and so forth. Students may enjoy learning that adjectives can also become nouns (but often ending in *-ie*), as in *soft* → *softy/softie*, *pink* → *pinky/pinkie*, *good* → *goody/goodie*, *brown* → *brownie*, *old* → *oldie*, *quick* → *quickie*, *sweet* → *sweetie*. Their usage is usually informal.

Talking Points

- Adjectives ending in *-y* can be formed from many nouns by following the *e*-drop, doubling, and no-change principles for *-ed* and *-ing*: Drop the final *-e* before adding *-y*; double the final consonant and then add *-y*, if the noun ends in a VC pattern; and just add *-y* if the word includes a team of vowels or ends in more than one consonant.

Integrating Idioms: "I've only got a few minutes to **shoot the breeze**." (Chat; engage in idle conversation. Even on a breezy day, to take aim at the gusts would not be a very productive use of time.)

Did You Know? Have you ever been in a situation in which you became sick of a noise? *Noise*, from which we get **noisy**, has long been associated with sickness. The word stems from *nausea*, a word that usually conjures up images of being sick and ready to vomit. *Nausea* derives from the Greek root for "ship," *naus*, and is related to other sea words—*naval* and *nautical* (see also Chapter 5, Sort 36). Being on a ship often made people sick, and this in turn would lead to lots of crying out and complaints, giving rise to the word *noise*.

Literature Link

Heller, R. (1989). *Many luscious lollipops: A book about adjectives.* New York: Grosset & Dunlap. Colorful, informative, and full of an exciting array of adjectives.

SORT 47. Putting It All Together: Prefixes and Suffixes with Base Words

Sorting by Meaning

Prefix Only	Suffix Only	Prefix and Suffix	Suffix and Suffix	Prefix, Suffix, and Suffix
redirect	**wonderful**	**disrespectful**	**noisiest**	**unknowingly**
disqualify	beautiful	indebted	annoyingly	reassuringly
research	frequently	misleading	carelessness	unexpectedly
uncommon	happiness	unfriendly	fuzziness	
	heavily		playfulness	
	usually		usefulness	
	worried			

Considerations: This sort encourages students to pull together their understandings about prefixes and suffixes. You might introduce the sort and talk about word meanings by analyzing the words with students in a manner similar to the following, being sure to keep the focus on the gist of the meaning rather than exact wording.

dis ("the opposite of") + *respect* ("think highly of, regard") + *ful* ("full of") = "lacking in regard for someone"

As you talk about each word, you might ask students to underline prefixes in one color and suffixes in another. Categorize each word after it is discussed according to the additions: *prefix only, suffix only; prefix and suffix; suffix and suffix; or prefix, suffix, and suffix.* Encourage students to collect and record more words throughout the week. Ask them to try to identify other category combinations besides those used in this sort and suggest that they create a listing, including the meaning, of the various prefixes and suffixes they come across.

Integrating Idioms: "She's a star and looks great, but I met her last summer, and she may be beautiful, but her **beauty is only skin deep.**" (Superficial, on the surface. Once you get beyond a person's outward appearance and get to know the individual, you can find that the person acts in a way that is not so appealing.)

Did You Know? **Indebted** means "obligated to" or "in debt to" some other person. The tricky-to-spell silent letter *b* in *debt* was not always there. Its early spelling of *dette* (the end of the 13th century) was borrowed from an Old French word, *dete*; neither word included the letter *b*. However, a couple of hundred years later, scholars added the *b* to both the French and English words to show that the word originally came from the Latin word *debitum*. The *b* was never pronounced and has been eliminated from the French, but is maintained in English. Can you think of other words with silent letters? Might they have a similar story? How could you find out?

Prefixes (*un-* and *re-*)

un-		*re-*
unwrap	rebuild	untied
rewrite	relish	unclear
return	unite	replace
unfair	rewind	unkind
remove	unsure	review
unhappy	reread	reorder
unable	recycle	unusual
reelect	uneven	?

SORT 43 Prefixes (*dis-*, *fore-*, *mis-*)

dis-	fore-	mis-
dislike	forehead	mistrust
forest	forewarn	distrust
discover	misjudge	foresight
foreground	disorder	misprint
misplace	foremost	discomfort
disobey	misspell	mistake
forecast	mismatch	dishonest
disagree	foreign	?

SORT 44 Prefixes (*in-*, *in-*, *non-*, *pre-*)

in-	*in-*	*non-*	*pre-*
indent	inactive		nonstop
prepay	incomplete		preteen
insight	preview		incorrect
nonfat	indirect		nonsense
preheat	indoors		pretzel
income	precaution		inflamed
nonfiction	input		prejudge
preschool	nonsmoking		?

SORT 45 Suffixes (-*ful*, -*less*, -*ly*, -*ness*)

-ful	**-less**	**-ly**	**-ness**

careful	careless	loudly
illness	cheerful	homeless
darkness	safely	colorful
thoughtful	finally	coolness
really	weakness	painful
helpless	smoothly	breathless
peaceful	stillness	friendly
priceless	useful	openness

**Adding Suffix -y to Words
with No Change, e-Drop, and Double**

No Change	e-Drop	Double
grouchy	shady	sunny
angrily	skinny	tasty
squeaky	greasy	scary
many	foggy	crumbly
curly	drizzly	breezy
juicy	starry	lengthy
furry	bossy	baggy
silvery	noisy	?

SORT 47

Putting It All Together:
Prefixes and Suffixes with Base Words

Prefix	Suffix	Prefix & Suffix	Suffix & Suffix	Prefix, Suffix, & Suffix
redirect		wonderful		disrespectful
noisiest		unknowingly		worried
misleading		usefulness		usually
frequently		disqualify		playfulness
unexpectedly		fuzziness		indebted
annoyingly		happiness		research
beautiful		unfriendly		uncommon
carelessness		heavily		reassuringly

Additional Sorts

The sorts in this section address multisyllabic homophones and less common single-syllable homophones, homographs, and other compounds. For the studies of homophones (same sound, different spelling) and homographs (same spelling, different sound), game-like activities are used to encourage repeated reinforcement of spelling–meaning or pronunciation–meaning connections. Ten additional sorts focusing on compound words, including hyphenated compounds, are also included. They may be used as typical word sorts, or they may be introduced and then placed at a learning station.

Homophones

What Is Known: By the end of the syllable juncture stage, students have examined the structures within and across syllables; vowel patterns in both stressed and unstressed syllables; consonant patterns; and various meaning units, including compound words, prefixes, and suffixes. They have been exposed to a few *homophones* (sound-alike words with different meanings) in earlier sorts and have likely dealt with single-syllable homophones at the within word pattern stage. Homophones used in previous sorts are asterisked.

What Is New: In homophones of more than one syllable, the spelling variation can occur in either a stressed or unstressed syllable, as in *morning/mourning* or *council/counsel*. Several homophones used in the following sorts are likely to have unfamiliar meanings.

SORT 48. Additional Sorts: Homophones Set 1

	Sorting by Sound	
1st Syllable Stressed	2nd Syllable Stressed	Single-Syllable Trios (no stress)
boarder/border	**allowed*/aloud**	**cent/scent/sent**
berry/bury	ascent/assent	flew/flu/flue
ceiling/sealing		rain/reign/rein
choral/coral		vain/vane/vein
colonel/kernel		
desert/dessert		
fairy/ferry		
marry/merry		
morning/mourning		
weather*/whether		

SORT 49. Additional Sorts: Homophones Set 2

Sorting by Sound		
1st Syllable Unstressed	2nd Syllable Unstressed	Single-Syllable Trios (no stress)
accept/except	**title/tidal**	**seas/seize/sees**
affect/effect	council/counsel	frees/freeze/frieze
	currant/current	peak/peek/pique
	dual/duel	raise/rays/raze
	hangar/hanger	
	lessen/lesson	
	manner/manor	
	miner/minor	
	muscle/mussel	
	patience/patients*	

SORT 50. Additional Sorts: Homophones Set 3

Sorting by Sound		
Two-Syllable Pairs	Three-Syllable Pairs	Two-Syllable Trios
cellar/seller	**addition/edition**	**pedal/peddle/petal**
bazaar/bizarre	capital/capitol	carat/caret/carrot*
borough/burrow	cereal*/serial	medal/meddle/metal
cymbals/symbols*	complement/compliment	palate/palette/pallet
profit/prophet	principal/principle	
roomer/rumor	stationary/stationery	

Note. In Set 3, *mettle*, meaning "courage, spirit," could also be included with the *medal* group of homophones, and *burro*, a "small donkey," could be added to make a trio with *borough* and *burrow*.

Considerations: *Homophones* (sound-alike words with different meanings), sometimes called *homonyms,* are sources of numerous spelling confusions, largely because the spelling of one homophone is confused with the meaning of another. Because meaning plays such a critical role in correctly spelling homophones, the primary aim of the homophone studies that follow is to clarify and develop the vocabulary of students as a means for helping them learn to spell the words. The categories serve to assist students as they talk about the words and, in some cases, to focus their attention on the part of the word with the spelling variation. Several single-syllable homophones of lower frequency are included in Set 1. A different format is used for the cards in these sorts to accommodate reinforcement through Homophone Rummy, a game that will enable students to become familiar with the word meanings and spellings and encourage repeated practice. Begin by reviewing what a homophone is. Then ask the students to make pairs or trios of the various homophones in order to discuss their meanings. Elaborate or clarify as needed, and suggest a dictionary to settle any disputes. Next, invite students to help group the words. (See answer keys for possibilities.) Discuss the results. For follow-up practice, make sets of the cards available for Homophone Rummy; each set will accommodate three or four players. One more person may be designated as a "judge" to determine whether or not a response is correct. A reproducible answer key with sentence examples is provided as Appendix F. Although the 108 words included in this section have been divided into three sets, words from one set can be mixed with another after students have studied the words. If desired, more common single-syllable homophones can be mixed in for review (see *Word Sorts and More, Second Edition* [Ganske, 2018]), or they can be used as a separate set for students at the within word pattern stage. Directions for the activity follow.

Homophone Rummy

Scramble the cards and distribute them one at a time to each of the players until everyone has six cards. Place the remaining cards face down in a draw pile. Turn over the top card and place it next to the pile. Before turn taking begins, players identify any pairs or trios of homophones they may have, place them on the table, and provide a definition for each of the words or use the words in sentences. If the meanings are correct, the cards remain on the table; if not, the player must pick them up again. Turn taking then begins.

Player 1 has the choice of taking the top card from the draw pile or selecting the face-up card next to it. If the latter decision is made, the card must be playable; that is, it must complete a pair (or trio) in the player's hand. Player 1 lays any newly formed pairs (or trios) on the table and demonstrates understanding of the words, as described. Player 1 then discards by placing an unwanted card face up next to the already started line of discards; if that card has been picked up and used, the card is laid in its place to begin a new line of discards. Play then passes to Player 2, who has several options: (1) to draw from the draw pile; (2) to pick up the last card from the discard line, if it is playable; or (3) to select one of the other cards in the discard line, as long as it is playable. In this last instance, the player must also pick up all of the cards that follow the one chosen, even if they are not playable. Rotations of play continue either until someone runs out of cards (one way to end the game) or until no one can play any more cards (another way to end it). The decision about how to end the game should be determined at the onset of the game. In either case, the winner is the person who played the most cards. Note that trios of words may be played all at once by a single player, or the third card may be played by the same or another player at a later time, as long as the two related words have already been played. In either case, the player must demonstrate an understanding of the word's meaning.

Talking Points

- *Homophones* are words that sound alike but have different meanings, such as *marry* and *merry*; they are sometimes called *homonyms*. Because homophones are the cause of many spelling errors, caution is needed in spelling this type of word.

Integrating Idioms: "It doesn't work to **bury your head in the sand;** you need to face up to the matter. If you don't start completing the work, you're not going to pass the class." (Ignore a problem or sign of danger. This expression stems from the mistaken belief that because ostriches cannot fly, they burrow in the sand in order to hide. Actually, ostriches, like other fowl, take in sand or gravel to help digest their food.)

Did You Know? **Muscle** and **mussel** not only sound alike, but also have a common ancestry. Both words derive from the Latin word *musculus,* which means "little mouse." What, you might wonder, does a mouse have to do with bodily tissues that help our bodies to move or with a sea creature? If you ever watched someone with a well-developed arm muscle flex it, you will get a hint. As the muscle moves, it resembles a small mouse, with the tendons serving as the tail. The meaning connection of *mussel* is less clear. It may also relate to "mouse," as the basic outline of a mussel in its shell is similar to that of a mouse, or the connection may relate to "muscle." After all, in its shell a mollusk appears to be not much more than a muscle. Although it may seem like a tall tale to think that both *muscle* and *mussel* are named after a small rodent, it is interesting to note that the two words are also related in Greek: The Greek word *mys* came to mean both "mouse" and "mussel."

boarder	allowed	fairy	whether
boarder	allowed	fairy	whether
weather	dessert	merry	ferry
weather	dessert	merry	ferry
desert	marry	aloud	border
desert	marry	aloud	border

morning	sealing	colonel	berry
morning	sealing	colonel	berry

assent	ceiling	bury	ascent
assent	ceiling	bury	ascent

coral	choral	kernel	mourning
coral	choral	kernel	mourning

cent	vane	reign	flu
cent	**vane**	**reign**	**flu**
flue	sent	vein	rain
flue	**sent**	**vein**	**rain**
rein	flew	vain	scent
rein	**flew**	**vain**	**scent**

accept	title	mussel	lessen
accept	title	mussel	lessen
miner	effect	lesson	minor
miner	effect	lesson	minor
except	muscle	affect	tidal
except	muscle	affect	tidal

manner	current	patients	hanger
manner	current	patients	hanger

duel	counsel	hangar	dual
duel	counsel	hangar	dual

council	patience	currant	manor
council	patience	currant	manor

seas	raze	frees	rays
seas	**raze**	**frees**	**rays**
frieze	peak	raise	pique
frieze	**peak**	**raise**	**pique**
seize	peek	freeze	sees
seize	**peek**	**freeze**	**sees**

cellar	addition	cereal	roomer
cellar	**addition**	**cereal**	**roomer**
cymbals	serial	symbols	capitol
cymbals	**serial**	**symbols**	**capitol**
capital	rumor	edition	seller
capital	**rumor**	**edition**	**seller**

profit	principal	borough	complement
profit	principal	borough	complement
stationery	burrow	bazaar	stationary
stationery	burrow	bazaar	stationary
bizarre	compliment	principle	prophet
bizarre	compliment	principle	prophet

pedal	carrot	medal	palate
pedal	**carrot**	**medal**	**palate**
caret	peddle	pallet	metal
caret	**peddle**	**pallet**	**metal**
palette	meddle	carat	petal
palette	**meddle**	**carat**	**petal**

Homographs

This section includes two sorts to increase students' understanding of *homographs,* words that have the same spelling but are pronounced differently and have different meanings. A sort may be used to introduce the words, but for follow-up practice, games such as Concentration or Export/Import, described later, are recommended. These will encourage repeated practice and add enjoyment to the study. Shifting the stress to come up with an alternative pronunciation will help students to become more flexible in their approach to reading homographs and other unfamiliar words encountered in text. For the games, a second template is included with sentence examples for the homographs. This template is formatted so that after the word card template and the sentence template are cut out, the two can be photocopied back-to-back for the Import/Export game.

What Is Known: Students have likely encountered homographs in their reading and spelling (e.g., *read*), but may not know the term for the concept. They should have a working knowledge of the patterns involved and should be able to identify the stressed syllable. A few of the words have previously been studied (see asterisked words).

What Is New: Understanding that stress in a homograph relates to part of speech.

SORT 51. Additional Sorts: Homographs Set 1

Sorting by Sound and Meaning		
1st Stress	2nd Stress	Oddball
Nouns	Verbs	?
address	ad**dress**	
conflict	con**flict**	
desert*	de**sert***	
minute*		mi**nute** (adjective)*
object	ob**ject**	
permit	per**mit**	
present	pre**sent**	
produce	pro**duce**	
project	pro**ject**	
rebel	re**bel**	
record	re**cord**	
refuse	re**fuse**	

SORT 52. Additional Sorts: Homographs Set 2

Sorting by Sound and Meaning		
1st Stress	2nd Stress	Oddball
Nouns	Verbs	?
conduct	con**duct**	lead /lēd/ (n., v.)
contract	con**tract**	lead /lĕd/* (n., adj.)
increase	in**crease**	
insert	in**sert**	
insult	in**sult**	
reject	re**ject**	
row /rou/	row /rō/	
subject	sub**ject**	
survey	sur**vey**	
tear /tîr/	tear /târ/	
wound /woond/	wound /wound/	

Considerations: Because the spellings of homographs do not differ, Sorts 51–52 may be combined (24 different spellings will result), or they may be used separately. All of the words in Sort 51 have two syllables; Sort 52 includes both single-syllable and polysyllabic words. The stressed syllable is the source of pronunciation differences in polysyllabic homographs; this syllable is in boldface (in their work, students can underline or circle the stressed syllable). For other homographs, the pronunciation is recorded underneath the word. Before distributing the templates of words, begin by writing the following sentences on the board or overhead projector:

> The doctors and nurse showed a lot of **patience** toward their **patients**.

> If we **record** the conversation, we'll both have a **record** of the interview.

Ask students to read each of the sentences and then pair up to talk about their observations. After a minute or two, ask them to tell what they noticed. They should realize that the first sentence contains a pair of homophones, and that the second sentence includes two words that are spelled the same but sound different and have different meanings. Point out that just as we call the first pair *homophones* (write the word after the sentence) because they have the "same sound," so we call the second pair *homographs* (write this word also) because they have the "same writing" or spelling. Explain to students that most of the homographs they will be working with have two syllables, like those in the sentence. Because differences in pronunciation and meaning for these words relate to differences in stress, the stressed syllable is in boldface on their word cards. Refer back to *record* and *record,* and ask students which syllable is stressed in each; underline it. Lay down the category header cards *Noun, Verb,* and *?,* and, beginning with the two words from the sentence, ask students to say the words, discuss their meanings, and determine their categories. When the sorting is complete, encourage students to share talking points with a partner. *Minute,* with a second-syllable stress, is an adjective and therefore an oddball; *lead* is also an oddball. When pronounced with a short vowel, it can be either a noun (*The lead in my pencil broke*) or an adjective (*The book said he died of lead poisoning*). As part of the discussion, you might remind students that the past-tense verb is *led,* not *lead.*

To reinforce pronunciation–meaning connections with the homographs in this sort, as previously noted, a second page of sentence examples with the homographs is included for the games of Concentration and Import/Export, described next.

Concentration

Students will likely have experience with this activity, though they may know it as Memory. For this homograph variation, they will need one complete set of word cards and sentence cards (namely, pages 1 and 2 of Sorts 51 or 52, except for the cards labeled *Noun, Verb, ?, Import,* and *Export,* which are not needed in this game). Photocopy the set of homographs on one color of paper and the sentences on another color. Scramble the cards from each template. Place the homographs face down in a 6 × 4 array; next to this array, make another 6 × 4 array, using the sentence cards. Player 1 begins by turning over one word from each array and reading aloud the word and sentence. If the two cards make a match (correct pronunciation and meaning), they are set aside, and Player 2 takes a turn. If the two cards do not make a match, the cards are returned to the array face down, and Player 2 takes a turn. Back-and-forth turn taking continues until all of the cards in the arrays have been used. The winner is the person with the most cards. A dictionary or expert can be used to settle disputes.

Import/Export

This game is a variation of the OH NO! game included in *Word Sorts and More, Second Edition* (Ganske, 2018). It will be more challenging if words from both sorts, 51 and 52, are used. This will make a total of 48 words. Every pair or trio of students in the group will need a set of playing cards with each word photocopied on one side of a card and the sentence on the other, as described at the onset of this section. Students should bear in mind that the sentences are merely examples to aid in verifying responses. Although the *Noun, Verb,* and *?* cards will not be used in the game, the two cards (or four if both sets are used) labeled *Import* and *Export* will be used. Nothing should be printed on the back side of these cards. Determine playing order for the game; then place the cards in scrambled order, word side up, as a stack on the table. If an *Import* or *Export* card chances to be on top, hide it randomly in the middle of the pile. The object of this game is to accumulate the most cards (one point is awarded for each card, plus a bonus point for each pair of homographs). To begin the game, Player 1 takes the top card from the pile, reads the word, and provides a definition or sentence for the word. Correct use of the word is verified by reviewing the sentence on the back of the card. If correct, Player 1 keeps the card, starting a points pile of cards. If incorrect, the card is returned to the bottom of the stack, word-side up. (Sentences on the cards are just examples; if in doubt about the correctness of a response, consult a dictionary or expert.) Player 2 then takes a turn and follows the same process. If Player 2 (or any other player) draws an *Import* card, Player 2 earns the right to "import" or select a card from each of the other players' accumulated cards to add to his or her own collection of cards. As long as Player 2 can pronounce the word and provide a correct meaning for it, Player 2 may keep the card. Otherwise, the card is returned to the bottom of the draw pile. Players who have not accumulated cards are passed over in the importing process. A similar but opposite procedure is followed when an *Export* card is drawn. In this case, the player must give each of the other players an accumulated card to add to their collections. When exporting cards, if the player does not have enough cards for each of the other players, the player distributes the card(s) in a clockwise manner until they are used up. In order to keep an exported card, the receiving player must correctly identify the word and its meaning. Otherwise, it is returned to the bottom of the card pile. Turn taking continues in like manner until all of the cards have been correctly identified. *Import* and *Export* cards are set aside after being drawn; they are not reused and do not count in the final scoring. The game ends when there are no more cards to be drawn; cards and pairs of homographs are counted and totaled to determine the winner.

Integrating Idioms: "First I couldn't find my homework; then I missed the bus because of looking for it; and then to **add insult to injury,** I got in trouble for coming to class late." (To worsen an already bad situation. If you were suffering from an injury and someone came along and insulted you about something, it would just make the situation worse.)

Did You Know? When you survey something or distribute a survey to people to find out their views on a matter, you are taking a very close look at whatever it is. So it is not surprising that *survey* stems from a Latin word, meaning "super look." When you survey your words as part of SAIL, you are taking a "super look" to see which ones you may not know, and another "super look" to decide which category is the best choice for a card.

Although the origins of *row* /rō/ as a line of people or objects, or as an action for forwarding a boat, are known and directly relate to the meaning, the origin of *row* /rou/ as a noisy disturbance is unknown. What do you think the story of this word might be?

Noun	Verb	?
address	ad**dress**	**min**ute
min**ute**	ob**ject**	**des**ert
produce	**con**flict	re**cord**
re**fuse**	de**sert**	**ob**ject
pro**duce**	**ref**use	pre**sent**
record	con**flict**	**proj**ect
per**mit**	pro**ject**	**reb**el
present	re**bel**	**per**mit

Export	**Import**	
I'll be with you in just a **minute.**	Please help me to **address** these envelopes.	What is the **address** of the company?
The **desert** is a hot, dry place.	I **object** to walking all the way home.	There was a **minute** particle of dirt in her eye.
Will you help me to **record** a song?	They must resolve the **conflict** between the two countries.	The corner market always has lots of fresh **produce.**
We need to move that **object** off the table.	I am surprised he was willing to **desert** his friend.	I **refuse** to clean up my brother's room.
They will **present** the trophy during halftime.	Trash collection is tomorrow, so I took the **refuse** out.	They're going to **produce** a movie here next year.
I've finished the **project,** and it's not due until next week.	The play and game schedules **conflict.**	She broke the **record** for running the quarter mile.
My little sister's a **rebel;** she never does what you ask.	Can you **project** your pictures onto the screen?	She'll **permit** me to use her calculator for the project.
You need a **permit** before you can drive the car.	If we have peas one more time for dinner, I'm going to **rebel.**	I have never seen such a big and beautiful **present.**

Additional Sorts: Homographs Set 2 *(p. 1 of 2)*

Noun	Verb	?
wound /woond/	**con**duct	in**crease**
in**sert**	row /rō/	**sub**ject
sur**vey**	**re**ject	tear /tîr/
tear /târ/	con**tract**	**in**sert
in**sult**	row /rou/	con**duct**
lead /lĕd/	sub**ject**	**in**sult
increase	wound /wound/	**con**tract
survey	re**ject**	lead /lēd/

Import	Export	
We need to **increase** environmental awareness.	The child's **conduct** was unacceptable.	The nurse came to bandage the man's **wound.**
My favorite **subject** is science.	Stand in the front **row** so you can see them **row** past.	Please **insert** these flyers into the newspapers.
A **tear** fell from her eye as she listened to the sad story.	I don't want the shirt; it's a **reject.**	We had to **survey** the class about their favorite books.
That store always has an **insert** in the Sunday paper.	Muscles **contract** in the cold.	Be careful when you turn the pages so you don't **tear** them.
Some metals **conduct** electricity better than others.	There was quite a **row** at the bus stop today.	Mom says if you **insult** people they won't be your friends.
After the **insult** the clerk apologized.	Why **subject** us to the torture of memorizing dates?	The **lead** of my pencil broke, *or* This is a **lead** pipe.
They signed a **contract** when they bought the house.	She **wound** the string into a ball.	Scientists say there is an **increase** in volcanic activity.
He will **lead** the group this time.	If you **reject** the invitation, you may not be asked again.	The telephone **survey** was about shopping interests.

More Compound Words

Each of the 10 sorts that follow is themed; in other words, the categories all relate to a particular topic. For instance, in the Space sort, each of the compounds includes one of the following words as part of the compound: *sun, moon, star,* or *sky.* The sorts may be introduced as open sorts, with an aim that students determine a theme that unifies the categories. It is not necessary for students to work formally with each of the compound sorts. Select those that seem most appropriate for particular content areas or for the students' needs, or use them as a break from other features being studied or to simplify planning when you need to be absent. You might also include some of the sorts in station activities after briefly discussing the meaning connections. If word hunts are incorporated as part of the study of compounds, allow students to search for other compound words, and then group their findings into categories of their own choosing. Searching for the particular categories included in each of the following sorts may be too limiting and may lead to a frustrating experience for students. You might also ask students to illustrate the individual words in found compounds and then invite peers to try to guess the entire word.

What Is Known: For the following compound-word sorts, students should be quite confident in their use of letter name and within word pattern features. Depending on when the sorts are used, they may also know features at the syllable juncture stage.

What Is New: The sorts in this section review compound words as two words put together to make a new word, while providing opportunities to expand vocabulary and consider the meaning of words and their word parts. The final two sorts, with hyphenated compounds, will likely be the most challenging for students.

SORT 53. Compounds with Substance Words

Sorting by Meaning			
air	*fire*	*land*	*water*
airplane	**fireplace**	**landmark**	**waterfall**
airborne	firearm	landfill	watercolor
aircraft	firecracker	landlady	waterlog
airline	firefly	landlord	watermark
airport	fireproof	landmass	watermelon
	fireworks	landscape	waterproof
		landslide	

Considerations: Be sure to discuss word meanings, as several of the words may be unfamiliar to some students—in particular, *airborne* (*borne* is the past participle of *to bear,* meaning "to carry"), *firearm, landfill, landmass,* and *landscape.* Ask students to explain the relationship of the two words to the compound as a whole. Students may brainstorm compounds with word parts similar in meaning to those used in the sort, such as *earth* and *sea,* as in *earthquake, earthworm, seashell, seacoast, seafood, seaport, seashore,* and *seasick.*

Talking Points

• Compound words are two words put together to make a new word. Thinking about the meanings of each of the smaller words can help to determine the meaning of the compound.

Integrating Idioms: "The candidate **won by a landslide.**" (Won by a lot of votes. Sometimes in a real landslide, the whole side of a mountain comes sliding down.)

Did You Know? The first **watermark** was made in 1282 in Bologna, Italy. This impression is made by pressing a metal stamp or a wire design on a roller against freshly made paper before most of the water has been removed. Watermarked paper serves a variety of purposes: It discourages counterfeiting, identifies a product, and makes stationery and other paper more impressive by showing an institution's logo or seal. Does your school office use watermarked paper?

When we think of the word **landscape,** we are likely to think of an expansive natural scene that we can take in all at once (or perhaps of the horizontal paper placement for printing, as opposed to the vertical placement known as *portrait*). However, the word, which was first recorded in 1598, began as a term in the art world. Dutch painters of the time were perfecting a genre of painting known as *landscape,* which the English considered to mean "a picture showing scenery on land." (To show students examples of 16th-century Dutch landscapes, such as those by the Bruegels, try an art-related website like *www.en.gallerix.ru,* or search online for a virtual museum tour.) Over 30 years passed before the English used the word *landscape* to describe a scene in the world around them. Today we have other related terms, such as *cityscape* and *landscape architect.* What do you think these terms mean? Some years ago I wrote a poem about the difficulty writers sometimes experience in thinking what to write—situations where "words must be squeezed drop by drop from an idea-dry mindscape." What did I mean by that, and how could you use *-scape* to make a new compound?

SORT 54. Compounds with Space Words

Sorting by Meaning

sun	*moon*	*star*	*sky*
sunburn	**moonbeam**	**starfish**	**skyline**
sunbathe	moonlight	starboard	skydive
Sunday	moonrise	starburst	skyrocket
sundial	moonscape	stargazing	skyscraper
sundown	moonwalk	starlit	skywriting
sunflower			
sunglasses			
sunlight			
sunstroke			

Considerations: This sort contains several words whose meanings may be unfamiliar to some students: *sundial, sunstroke, moonrise, moonscape, starboard, starburst, skyline, skydive,* and *skywriting.* Thinking about the meanings of similar words, such as *moonscape–landscape* and *skywriting–handwriting,* or illustrating such words can help students with the vocabulary. (For an illustration of skywriting, see the work of Gritch the Witch in Margie Palatini's [1995] delightful tale *Piggie Pie!* The book contains numerous compound words as well.) After investigating the meaning of *starburst,* students might create their own with pastels or colored pencils. Students may benefit from a review of the e-drop principle that is at work in *stargaz(e)ing* and *skywrit(e)ing*. While discussing the various *moon* words, invite students to ponder the meanings of *earthlight* or *earthshine* and *earthrise*. The meanings are similar to their *moon* counterparts but with a different perspective. *Earthrise* refers to the rising of the earth above the moon's horizon, and *earthlight* to the sunlight reflected from the earth's surface that lights up part of the moon.

Talking Points

- Knowledge of a known compound word can often be used to understand an unfamiliar one, as in *landscape* for *moonscape* or *handwriting* for *skywriting*.

Integrating Idioms: "We haven't had extra recess time **in a month of Sundays**." (A very long time. Suppose there are 30 days in a month; a month of Sundays would be 30 weeks, or about 7½ months!)

Did You Know? The word **skyscraper** was first used in the late 1800s to describe a tall ornament on the top of a building, rather than the building itself. In more recent times, *skyscraper* has come to mean a "very tall building." But just how tall does a building have to be to be called a *skyscraper*? It is really a matter of perspective: After all, is our idea of a very tall building the same as that of our grandparents and great-grandparents? Over time greater and greater heights have earned the distinction of *skyscraper*. In 1873 the tallest building was 142 feet high and had 6 floors. By 1890, the tallest building included 15 stories. Though staggering for its time, the building was soon dwarfed in 1913 by the Woolworth Building in New York City, which had 60 stories. The well-known Empire State Building in New York became the tallest building in 1931, with 102 stories and a height of 1,250 feet, plus its spire. It remained the tallest building for some 40 years, when it was surpassed by the 1,454-foot, 110-floor Willis (formerly Sears) Tower in Chicago. One World Trade Center, built in 2014 in New York City, is now the tallest building in the United States (North American and the Western Hemisphere), but even with its 104 stories and 1,775-foot height, it ranks seventh in the world. Taller buildings are found in the Republic of Korea, China, Saudi Arabia, and the United Arab Emirates. The tallest building (2,717 feet), which has been the tallest since 2010, is the Burj Khalifa in Dubai. According to the online World Atlas (*www.worldatlas.com/articles/10-tallest-buildings-in-the-world.html*), this building has "30,000 residences spread out over 19 residential towers, an artificial lake, nine hotels, and a shopping mall"! It was designed by the same architects as the Willis Tower and One World Trade Center. Will even taller buildings be constructed? If so, what will the limiting factors be?

Skywriting, first recognized as a word in 1923, was developed by an English aviator in 1922. Skywriting creates words by releasing visible vapor from an airplane. How long the image lasts depends on the wind, but it typically disappears within a few minutes. Skywriting usually consists of one or two words used as an advertisement or other message, such as the warning "Surrender, Dorothy" written by the Wicked Witch of the West in the 1939 movie version of *The Wizard of Oz*. A more advanced form of skywriting called *skytyping* relies on a fleet of five to seven specially equipped planes that electronically type out a message composed of little dots, similar to a dot-matrix printer. Messages created this way can be 15 miles long, seen for 40 miles, and last up to about 30 minutes. Although some people may be fascinated by skywriting and skytyping, others regard these media as types of pollution. What are your thoughts about it?

SORT 55. Compounds with Opposite Words

		Sorting by Meaning		
work	*play*	*day*	*night*	Oddball
workshop	**playground**	**daylight**	**nightmare**	**?**
workbench	playbill	birthday	(fortnight)	(fortnight)
workbook	playhouse	daybreak	nightfall	(playwright)
workman	playroom	daydream	nightgown	
workout	(playwright)	daylily	nighttime	
workroom		daytime		
		today		

Considerations: Nighttime may present a spelling challenge for some students, who find that the double *t*'s "don't look right." This provides a great opportunity to emphasize that compound words are composed of two or more words, and that without the double *t*'s, this meaning element is lost. You will likely need to discuss the meaning of *fortnight* (a period of 2 weeks, or 14 days), which will probably be unfamiliar to students. Although the word looks as though it is connected to our word *fort*, it is really an altered spelling of the Old English word for "fourteen." Also, while discussing the meaning of *playhouse*, call students' attention to the word's meaning as "a theater" if they do not suggest it. This meaning also occurs in *playbill* (a theater program) and *playwright* (one who writes plays). Some students will likely be unfamiliar with the meaning of *bill* (a public notice) and *wright* (one who makes or repairs something, as in *shipwright* and *wheelwright*). They may not even consider *wright* a word and think it should be classified as an oddball; this is fine. Students might enjoy being *wordwrights* and coining other possible *wright* words. Note that the meaning of *smith* is similar to that of *wright* but usually refers to one who works with or makes things from metals, as in *blacksmith, goldsmith, locksmith, silversmith, tinsmith*. An exception, *wordsmith*, is often used to describe a person who is good at using words or is knowledgeable about them. Students are likely to become wordsmiths through their word studies. Some students may prefer to place *birthday* and *today* in the oddball category, because the targeted word part appears in the second syllable rather than the first.

Talking Points

- The spelling of a compound word may not "look right," but it is important to keep in mind the meaning connection, as in *nighttime*, not *nightime*.

Integrating Idioms: "After working on the project for a week, we could begin to **see daylight**." (See the end of the project approaching. If you were moving through a long tunnel, it would seem very dark until almost at the end.)

Did You Know? The common **daylily** has flowers that last only 1 day. Each plant gets many buds, so each day there are new flowers to see. There are about 60,000 different kinds of daylilies, in nearly every color but blue. Some daylilies are even scented. Although daylilies originated in Eurasia, they are very adaptable and are found in very cold, as well as very warm, climates. Another flower also has ties to the word *day*. Although the word *daisy* does not contain the *d-a-y* spelling, it does relate in meaning. The word comes from the Old English name, *daeges-eages*, meaning "day's eye," which is pronounced similarly to *daisy*. The meaning connection stems from the flower's tendency to close its petals at night and reopen during the day to reveal its round center.

SORT 56. Compounds with Around-the-Home Words

Sorting by Meaning

home	bed	bath	table	door
homemade	**bedtime**	**bathtub**	**tabletop**	**doorbell**
homebody	bedbugs	bathhouse	tablecloth	doorkeeper
homecoming	bedroll	bathrobe	tablespoon	doorknob
homeland	bedside	bathroom	tableware	doorstep
homesick	bedspread	bathwater		
homework				

Considerations: Discuss word meanings as needed. *Bathhouse*, like *nighttime* in the previous sort, provides an opportunity for students to see that even though a spelling may not look right, (in this case, because of the double *h*'s), meaning dictates that both letters be included.

Talking Points

• The word *bathhouse*, with its double consonants, is a good reminder that meaning dictates the spelling of compounds.

Integrating Idioms: "Hey, just because we know one idea doesn't work, let's not **throw the baby out with the bathwater.**" (Get rid of the good in the process of getting rid of something bad. What a loss it would be if, in throwing out the dirty bathwater, the baby was cast out also.)

Did You Know? Students might enjoy speculating on the meaning of the well-known phrase "Sleep tight and don't let the *bedbugs* bite." Although they are likely to realize that the intention is to sleep well, they may never have given consideration to the word *tight*. Before the days of bedsprings, mattresses were placed on ropes tightly stretched across the length of the bed. A saggy bed would not lead to good sleep; thus the wish to "sleep tight." As for bedbugs, no one back then or now wants those around for a restful night. Bedbugs are flat, reddish brown in color, and about ¼ inch long. They hide during the day and come out at night to feed on human blood.

SORT 57. Compounds with Position Words

Sorting by Meaning

down	up	over	out	under
download	**upset**	**overcoat**	**outdoors**	**underline**
downcast	upbeat	overcast	outbreak	underbrush
downpour	upcoming	overgrown	outcast	underground
downspout	upkeep	overheard	outgoing	understand
downstairs		overlook	(outrage)	
			outside	

Considerations: The words that form part of each of the compound words in this sort are found in many other words. You may wish to include or substitute other possibilities, such as *downfall, downhill, downstream, downtown, update, upend, uphold, uphill, upright, uproar, uproot, upscale, upside down, overbite, overflow, overhang, overload, oversleep, overthrow, outcome, outcry, outfield, outlaw, outline, underdog, understate,* or *underwear.* Note that the word *outrage* looks like a compound, but as its "Did You Know?" story relates, it really is not. Although no *?* card is included, students may choose to place it to the side after hearing its story. For this and other compound word studies, consider providing students with opportunities to write riddles using the compound in the question or the answer, such as this one:

Q: We know that sometimes it rains cats and dogs, but what do we call it when it rains ducks?

A: A downpour.

Talking Points

- Sometimes the meaning connection of a compound to its individual parts is unclear, as with *understand.* (*Under* used to mean "among" or "between"; perhaps if you stood among or between people, plants, animals, or objects, your on-the-spot vantage point would enable you to clearly grasp or *understand* the situation.)

Integrating Idioms: "If we're going to solve this problem, you've got to **think outside the box.**" (Consider atypical possibilities. A box is used to contain something; its insides are all the same and usually quite blank. Solving problems often requires considering various possibilities and thinking creatively.)

Did You Know? Although today we commonly associate **outrage** with *rage,* as though the word were formed by *out + rage,* the word is actually a borrowing from the French word *outré* (meaning "beyond") plus the Latin ending *-age.* To understand the meaning connection, consider that when something is an outrage, it is so bad that it is beyond our ability to think of its occurring, especially in this day and age.

SORT 58. Compounds with Weather Words

Sorting by Meaning

rain	*wind*	*snow*	*thunder*	Oddball
raindrop	**windburn**	**snowball**	**thunderbolt**	**?**
rainbow	windbreak	snowdrift	thundercloud	hailstone
raincoat	windfall	snowflake	thunderhead	
rainproof	windmill	snowmobile	thunderstorm	
rainstorm	windpipe	snowshoe		
	windshield	snowstorm		
	windstorm			

Considerations: Discuss the meanings of *windbreak, windfall, windpipe, snowshoe, thunderhead, hailstone,* and any other words that may be unfamiliar. For some of the words, using a picture may be the easiest way to build understanding of the word's meaning. When discussing *snowshoe,* you might ask students to consider why a particular rabbit found in the northern part of North America is called the *snowshoe rabbit.* An online search could be used to validate their thoughts. Students may suggest placing the *-storm* words in a separate category. If they do, ask them to consider the meaning connection to *brainstorm*.

Talking Points

- Sometimes the meaning of a compound is unclear from its parts because the meaning is figurative rather than literal, as in *windfall*. (If something fell from the wind, it would likely be sudden and unexpected; the connotation of a *windfall* as something of benefit was added later.)

Integrating Idioms: "I hope Mr. Eeger doesn't assign another book and paper today; I'm **snowed under** right now with projects." (Overwhelmed. Just as a snowstorm can deeply bury plants and objects [see "Did You Know?" below], work sometimes piles up, making people feel like they are buried.)

Did You Know? **Wind** is a word that we have had since the middle of the 700s, and it has the same spelling today that it had back then. When we think of ***thunder,*** we may not associate it with wind, but we usually do with a recent flash of lightning. Because light and sound travel at different speeds, the amount of time between the flash and the thunder depends on how far away the lightning occurred. If the lightning bolt is a mile away, it will be about 5 seconds before we hear the thunder. If it is 10 miles away, it will take nearly a minute. If it is more than 15, we will not even hear it. When lightning strikes nearby, the thunder is extremely loud.

Weather that extends beyond the norm often catches our attention; for instance, consider the wettest place on earth, a mountain in Hawaii, where for the past 20 years the average annual rainfall has been 460 inches! Or how about the greatest annual snowfall—a whopping 1,224.5 inches (102 feet!) recorded in Mount Ranier National Park, Washington, during 1971–1972 (*www.snowbrains. com*). Or the 318-miles-per-hour winds, the highest ever recorded by the U.S. Weather Service, that occurred during a 1999 tornado in Oklahoma. What other extreme weather situations are you aware of, especially where you live? A good source for more information on extreme weather (books, journals, and videos) is the National Geographic Society (*www.nationalgeographic.com*).

Literature Links

Barrett, J. (1978). *Cloudy with a chance of meatballs.* New York: Scholastic. The unusual weather in the town of Chewandswallow is sure to engage students across the grades in this longtime favorite picture book; or try the sequel, *Pickles to Pittsburgh* (1997).

Libbrecht, K. (2007). *The art of the snowflake: A photographic album.* St. Paul, MN: Voyageur Press. View pages and pages of incredible macrophotography that has captured snowflakes in color with all their beauty, detail, and uniqueness.

Martin, J. B. (1998). *Snowflake Bentley.* Boston: Houghton Mifflin. This Caldecott Medal-winning picture book describes the story of Wilson Bentley, a scientist who first photographed snowflakes.

SORT 59. Compounds with Food Words

Sorting by Meaning

corn	*bean*	*pea*	*butter*	*egg*
corncob	**beanbag**	**peanut**	**butterfly**	**eggshell**
cornflower	beanpole	peacock	butterball	eggbeater
cornhusk	beanstalk	peashooter	buttercup	egghead
cornmeal			butternut	eggnog
cornrows			butterscotch	eggplant
cornstalk				
cornstarch				
popcorn				

Considerations: When possible, use illustrations, photographs, or real objects to help explain word meanings; otherwise students may draw inaccurate conclusions. For example, students may mistakenly think of a wire whisk when considering what an eggbeater is. Also, ask the students to speculate on the meaning connections of such words as *cornrows, peacock, butterfly, egghead,* and *eggnog.* Students who wish to may consider *popcorn* an oddball word, because *corn* is at the end of the word. They may also wonder about *nog* as a word. *Nog,* a strong alcoholic beverage, was often added to the eggs, milk, and sugar mixture we think of as *eggnog.*

Talking Points

• Words that are found in numerous compounds sometimes appear at the beginning of the word and sometimes at the end, as in *cornmeal* and *popcorn.*

Integrating Idioms: "Before a test, I always **get butterflies** in my stomach." (Feel nervous. If you really had butterflies in your stomach fluttering around, they would give you a very uneasy feeling.)

Did You Know? Students may or may not have heard **corn** used to describe a horny hardening of the skin on a person's toe, but this meaning, which derives from a different source than the corn you eat, is related both to *unicorn* ("one horn") and to the cornucopia of Thanksgiving ("horn of plenty"). The edible *corn* comes from an Old English word meaning "grain" and often refers to the most common type of grain. In the United States the word refers to the eared grain—*Indian corn* or *maize.* In England it refers to wheat, in Scotland and Ireland it means oats, and in Germany *korn* refers to rye. Corn or maize comes from Central America and Mexico. The United States grows a lot of corn. How much is a lot? According to the National Corn Growers Association website (*www.worldofcorn.com*), in 2018 the United States produced 14.4 billion bushels of corn; considering that each bushel weighs about 56 pounds, this means that about 28,000,000 tons of corn are produced. According to the U.S. Department of Agriculture, about a third of the corn crop is used to feed livestock; another third is used to produce a type of biofuel, known as ethanol; and the rest is used for food, beverages, and other industry needs. Corn starch is also being used to create biodegradable products that normally would be made of plastic (bags, straws, etc.). What other products are made of corn? Why do you think there is an interest in producing ethanol? What might be the pros and cons? Is ethanol available at gas stations in your area?

The origins of **butterfly** are unclear, but the third edition of *The American Heritage Dictionary of the English Language* (1996) offers two colorful possibilities: (1) An early Dutch name for *butterfly* suggests that this flying creature may have been named after the color of its excrement, and (2) it was believed to be a mischievous witch transformed into a flying insect who liked to steal milk and butter. What do you think? For more information on butterflies, see one of the many books written on the topic, such as *Butterflies!* (Editors of *Time for Kids*, 2006), or *Amazing Butterflies and Moths* (Still, 1991), a book in the Eyewitness Junior series.

Literature Link

U'Ren, A. (2003). *Mary Smith*. New York: Farrar, Straus & Giroux. A picture book based on the life of Mary Smith, who lived in London in the early 20th century and who had an unusual way of waking people up before the days of reliable and affordable alarm clocks: a peashooter.

SORT 60. Compounds with Color Words

Sorting by Meaning

black	white	blue	green	red
blacktop	**whitecap**	**bluebird**	**greenhouse**	**redhead**
blackball	whiteout	bluebell	greenbelt	redwood
blackberry	whitewash	blueberry	greenhorn	
blackbird		bluegill	Greenland	
blackboard		bluegrass	greenroom	
blackmail		blueprint		
blackout				
blacksmith				

Considerations: Several words in this sort may be unfamiliar to students. Be sure to discuss the meanings thoroughly and in multiple ways. Pictures and artifacts may be of help in enabling students to comprehend the concepts. Depending on the geographic area, students may be more or less knowledgeable about a particular word. For example, students living in mountainous regions may have firsthand experience with a *whiteout,* and children in the urban northeast areas may understand *blackout.* Similarly, few students from Kentucky will likely need assistance with *bluegrass. Greenland,* the largest island in the world, can be located on a map; students might search to discover why it is named as it is. After all, nearly all of Greenland lies in the Arctic Circle. You might also play a game of Would You . . . ?, using some of the words. Provide students with clues such as these:

"Would you **whitewash** a blackboard; why or why not? Would you be more likely to find an environmentalist or an actor in a **greenroom?** Would you rather smell a **bluebell** or a **bluegill?** Would you find a **greenbelt** in a closet or outside a town?"

Talking Points

- Compounds' meanings can differ from those of the words that make them up, as in *greenroom* and *greenbelt.*

Integrating Idioms: Following are explanations of several common idioms with color-related words. The words are not in this sort, because they are compounded either through hyphenation or by writing the words separately:

"The thief was **caught red-handed** with the vase." (Caught in the act of doing something wrong, as though with the blood of a terrible deed still on the criminal's hands.) "His report card so impressed his parents that they gave him the **red-carpet treatment.**" (Treated him as very special. The phrase refers to the fact that a red carpet is sometimes unrolled for an important person to walk on.) "It says here in **black and white** that your journal is due every Tuesday." (Written down. The expression refers to black type on white newsprint or other paper.)

Did You Know? The word *blackmail* has nothing to do with the post office. In Scotland during the 1500s, farmers were treated unfairly. Besides working hard, they also had to deal with outlaws who forced them to pay a fee to have their land protected. If the fee was not paid, their crops were destroyed. The word *blackmail* comes from a Scottish word meaning *rent* or *tax,* and from the common association of dark or bad with the word *black,* as in *blackball.*

One story about the origin of *greenhorn* relates to a type of 17th- and 18th-century jewelry making. Certain decorative pieces were made from brown-colored animal horn and set in silver. The horn was impressed with a figure, often a head, and heated to complete the process. If temperatures too high were used, the horn turned green. Because apprentices were often the cause of this, the word came to refer to any inexperienced person.

Literature Links

Macaulay, D. (1990). *Black and white.* Boston: Houghton Mifflin. Four stories or one story? A cleverly written book that can be enjoyed on various levels.
O'Neill, M. (1989). *Hailstones and halibut bones.* New York: Doubleday. Twelve poems that reveal how various colors look, sound, feel, smell, and taste.

SORT 61. Hyphenated Compounds

Sorting by Meaning				
Body	Numbers	Sports	Heat/Cold	Oddball
hands-on	**first-class**	**all-star**	**warm-blooded**	**?**
dog-ear	fifty-fifty	out-of-bounds	freeze-dried	hot dog
empty-handed	forty-five	runner-up	ice-cold	ice cream
head-on	one-sided	time-out	red-hot	
left-handed	twenty-one			
right-handed	two-faced			
tongue-tied				

Considerations: Discuss the meanings of any unfamiliar words. When possible, demonstrate the meaning or have students act it out, especially words such as *dog-ear, tongue-tied,* and *two-faced.* You might ask students to illustrate the literal and figurative meanings of these particular words. Also, remind students that numbers are consistently hyphenated but that they need to beware of other words or phrases that sound like compounds, because compounds can be joined into one word, hyphenated, or even written as two separate words, such as *hot dog* and *ice cream.* What is more, one form of the word may be used one time and another the next time, depending on the context of the sentence and the meaning of the word. Also, a few words may be correctly spelled in several ways. For example, all of the following are correct:

I ate a hot dog for lunch.

I ate a hotdog for lunch.

My little brother likes to hot-dog on his skateboard.

What's your favorite kind of ice cream?

Shall we get an ice-cream cone before we leave?

Notice in the last sentence above that *ice cream* is acting like an adjective instead of a noun. When that is the case, the word or phrase is usually hyphenated, as in *She is in fifth grade* versus *A fifth-grade boy just moved into our neighborhood*. Writers sometimes create their own hyphenated compounds to add interest to a story, as Margie Palatini (see also Sort 54, "Considerations") has done in *Piggie Pie!* with the phrases *dragon-tongue pudding* and *still-smoking tootsies*. Such hyphenated compounds may consist of two tied-together words or a whole string, as in *never-to-be-completed homework*. You might invite students to try their hands at creating hyphenated compounds to describe one of the following nouns or a noun of their own choosing:

fence   *clothes*   *house*   *book*

Talking Points

• When two or more words describing a noun seem to work together, they should probably be hyphenated as a compound word.

Integrating Idioms: "You can't **be two-faced** and expect people to like you." (Be insincere. The person acts like two different people by saying one thing but acting in a different way.)

Did You Know? Americans are ice-cream lovers. According to the International Dairy Foods Association (*www.idfa.org/news-views/media-kits/ice-cream/ice-cream-sales-trends*) the average American eats more than 23 pounds (equal to about 23 pints) of ice cream per year! And vanilla and chocolate are our top two favorites. In 2017 the United States made about 1.4 billion gallons of ice cream and other frozen desserts. Can you guess which month the most was produced? Just consider how many cows it takes to supply the milk and cream for the population of a large city! The word was first recorded in 1744, but for more than 70 years before that, it was called *iced cream*, just like our *iced tea* and *iced coffee* of today. For all of our love of this tasty treat, its origins go back much farther than 17th-century England, to ancient Rome, China, and India.

SORT 62. Hyphenated Compounds with Repeated Elements

Sorting by Meaning

Noun	Verb	Adjective/Adverb
eager-beaver	**dilly-dally**	**itty-bitty**
bow-wow	(fiddle-faddle)	(harum-scarum)
fender-bender	(hurry-scurry)	helter-skelter
(fiddle-faddle)	(pitter-patter)	lovey-dovey
flip-flop	(shilly-shally)	pell-mell
fuddy-duddy	(teeter-totter)	rinky-dink
heebie-jeebies		(shilly-shally)
hocus-pocus		teeny-weeny
(hurry-scurry)		willy-nilly
nitty-gritty		wishy-washy
(pitter-patter)		
razzle-dazzle		
(shilly-shally)		
(teeter-totter)		

Note. Words that act as multiple parts of speech are shown in parentheses.

Considerations: Compound words are not always composed of two words, as in the previous sorts. Although some of the words in this set follow that pattern (*eager-beaver* and *flip-flop,* for instance), others do not. This sort includes many *reduplications*—words formed with doubled parts that differ in only a single element of the word, such as *flip-flop* and *wishy-washy.* (Meanings for all of the words in this sort are included at the end of this discussion.) Ability to spell the words may or may not be an aim of this sort; fostering appreciation for language, as well as building vocabulary, are goals. The sort can be used whenever you believe students are ready to handle it. The words may be categorized in ways other than by part of speech, if desired, such as changed part (e.g., vowel or consonant). Students might also classify the words as "can define," "have heard," and "unknown." The Would You . . . ? activity described in Sort 60 might also be used, as in this example:

> "If your family had a **fender-bender,** would you be more likely to go home in a taxi or in the family car? If your teacher is about to explain the **nitty-gritty** of tonight's math homework, would you likely listen carefully or think about a weekend trip? If you were promised a chance to see your favorite movie, which of the following would you do: **shilly-shally, dilly-dally,** or **hurry-scurry?** Would you be more likely to regard a new baby brother or sister or a grandparent as a **fuddy-duddy?** If a dog gave you the **heebie-jeebies,** would your reaction to it be **lovey-dovey** or **wishy-washy?**"

Word Meanings

Bow-wow, bark of a dog; *dilly-dally,* dawdle; *eager-beaver* (slang/informal), person who is very, or overly, industrious; *fender-bender* (informal), a car accident involving minor damage; *fiddle-faddle,* nonsense, to waste time; *flip-flop,* a flapping sound or (when used informally) a reversal; *fuddy-duddy,* old-fashioned; *harum-scarum,* lacking sense, in a reckless manner; *heebie-jeebies* (old slang), jitters; *helter-skelter,* in a hurried manner, confused; *hocus-pocus,* foolishness, trickery; *hurry-scurry,* hurrying and confusion;

itty-bitty, very small (also *itsy-bitsy*); *lovey-dovey* (informal), very affectionate; *nitty-gritty* (informal), details; *pell-mell,* in a reckless manner, headlong (also *pellmell*); *pitter-patter,* light tapping sound, to make such a sound; *razzle-dazzle* (informal), dazzling excitement; *rinky-dink* (slang), old-fashioned, shoddy; *shilly-shally,* indecision, vacillation; *teeny-weeny* (informal), tiny; also *teensy-weensy; teeter-totter,* seesaw; *willy-nilly,* whether it is wished for or not; *wishy-washy,* weak, indecisive.

Integrating Idioms: "My sister's a real **eager-beaver;** she's sure to help us get the project started." (Hard-working and enthusiastic. We often associate beavers with hard work, as they build dams and lodges and cut down trees in preparation for their construction projects.)

Did You Know? Teeter-totter: Depending on the region of the country, other terms may be used for this outdoor play equipment. *Teeter-totter* is common in the U.S. Midwest and West. *Seesaw* is also common. In New England, there are many possibilities, including *tilt, tilting board, dandle, dandle board, teeter,* and *teeterboard.* One term is not better than another; they are just different.

Literature Link

Clements, A. (1997). *Double trouble in Walla Walla.* Brookfield, CT: Millbrook Press. Words for this sort were chosen from Clements's delightful book.

States Stress Break

This sort may be used to provide students with practice in identifying stressed syllables before they begin the "Vowel Patterns in Stressed Syllables" studies (Sorts 16–29). Due to the many and varied spellings in the words, if they are used at that time, limit the focus to detecting the stressed syllable (the one said with greater emphasis). Toward the end of the syllable juncture stage, or even as part of studies at the next stage (derivational constancy), the words may be reviewed with the expectation that students learn their spellings. If the aim is to practice listening for the stressed syllable, use both of the States Stress Break pages. If spelling is an aim, provide opportunity for students to work with one page at a time.

To focus just on stress, lay out the headers and read the words aloud one at a time while students listen without seeing the words. Model and think aloud to classify a few of the words; be sure to slightly emphasize the syllable that is accented. Then invite student participation. For state names that consist of two words, determine the stress for the polysyllabic word. Discuss the results. The same approach may be used when spelling is also an aim. To encourage repeated practice, offer students several game-like options for working with the words. The cards could be used for Concentration (a "pair" would be any two words that share the same stressed syllable). They could also be used with a folder game; each time the stressed syllable of one of the words is correctly identified, the player advances along a path. The cards could also be formed into a draw pile, with two or three additional cards labeled *Stressed Out.* As students take turns drawing cards and identifying the accented syllable, they keep those they correctly identify and return to the bottom of the stack the ones they miss. A player who draws a *Stressed Out* card must return all accumulated cards to the bottom of the draw pile. For many states-related activities, maps, and printables, see edHelper.com's United States Theme Unit—50 States (*www.edhelper.com/geography/Fifty_States.htm*).

SORT 63. States Stress Break

Sorting by Sound			
Syllable 1	Syllable 2	Syllable 3	Oddball
Arkansas	**Alaska**	**Alabama**	**?**
Delaware	Connecticut	Arizona	(Louisiana*)
Florida	Hawaii	California	Maine
Georgia	Kentucky	Colorado	New York
Idaho	Missouri	Illinois	
Iowa	Montana	Indiana	
Kansas	Nebraska	(Louisiana*)	
Oregon	Nevada	Massachusetts	
Maryland	North Dakota	Minnesota	
Michigan	Ohio	Mississippi	
New Hampshire	South Dakota	North Carolina	
New Jersey	Vermont	Oklahoma	
New Mexico	Virginia	Pennsylvania	
Rhode Island	West Virginia	South Carolina	
(Tennessee)**	Wisconsin	(Tennessee)**	
Texas	Wyoming		
Utah			
Washington			

Note. For state names made up of two words, use the polysyllabic word to determine the stress.

Louisiana may be pronounced with either four or five syllables; in the former instance, the first two are combined, and the primary stress is then on the third syllable rather than the fourth.

**Tennessee* may be pronounced with either a first- or a third-syllable primary stress.

SORT 53 Compounds with Substance Words

air	fire	land	water

airplane	fireplace	landmark
waterfall	airline	waterproof
landmass	watercolor	firefly
waterlog	firearm	landslide
landlady	airborne	landscape
aircraft	landlord	fireworks
firecracker	watermark	airport
landfill	fireproof	watermelon

SORT 54 Compounds with Space Words

sun	moon	star	sky
sunburn	moonbeam		starfish
skyline	stargazing		sunlight
skyrocket	sunflower		starboard
sunglasses	moonrise		sunstroke
skyscraper	Sunday		skywriting
moonwalk	skydive		sundown
sundial	starlit		moonlight
moonscape	sunbathe		starburst

SORT 55 — Compounds with Opposite Words

work	play	day	night
workshop	playground		daylight
nightmare	daydream		birthday
playhouse	workbook		nighttime
daytime	playroom		workbench
workout	nightfall		playwright
nightgown	daylily		workman
fortnight	workroom		playbill
daybreak	today		?

Compounds with Around-the-Home Words

home	bed	bath	table	door

homemade	bedtime	bathtub
tabletop	doorbell	bedroll
tableware	bathroom	homebody
bedbugs	bathwater	doorkeeper
homecoming	doorstep	bathrobe
tablecloth	bedspread	homeland
doorknob	homework	tablespoon
homesick	bathhouse	bedside

SORT 57 Compounds with Position Words

down	up	over	out	under

download	upset	overcoat
outdoors	underline	outrage
underground	overlook	downcast
downstairs	outgoing	understand
overcast	downpour	overgrown
downspout	outbreak	upbeat
overheard	upkeep	outside
upcoming	outcast	underbrush

SORT 58   Compounds with Weather Words

rain	wind	snow	thunder
raindrop	windburn	snowball	
thunderbolt	snowstorm	rainproof	
windshield	thunderhead	windmill	
snowflake	hailstone	thunderstorm	
snowdrift	windfall	raincoat	
rainbow	thundercloud	windpipe	
snowshoe	windstorm	rainstorm	
windbreak	snowmobile	**?**	

Compounds with Food Words

corn	bean	pea	butter	egg

corncob	beanbag	peanut
butterfly	eggshell	butternut
cornrows	buttercup	beanstalk
peacock	cornhusk	egghead
eggplant	cornstalk	peashooter
cornflower	butterscotch	popcorn
eggnog	beanpole	butterball
cornstarch	eggbeater	cornmeal

Compounds with Color Words

black	white	blue	green	red

blacktop	whitecap	bluebird
greenhouse	redhead	bluegrass
greenhorn	whiteout	blackberry
blacksmith	greenroom	bluegill
bluebell	redwood	greenbelt
blackball	blueberry	blackmail
Greenland	blackboard	blueprint
blackbird	whitewash	blackout

SORT 61 Hyphenated Compounds

Body	Numbers	Sports	Heat/Cold
hands-on	first-class		all-star
warm-blooded	runner-up		two-faced
red-hot	twenty-one		left-handed
forty-five	dog-ear		freeze-dried
time-out	hot dog		tongue-tied
empty-handed	out-of-bounds		one-sided
ice cream	fifty-fifty		head-on
right-handed	ice-cold		?

SORT 62 Hyphenated Compounds with Repeated Elements

Noun	Verb	Adjective/ Adverb
eager-beaver	dilly-dally	itty-bitty
fiddle-faddle	helter-skelter	teeny-weeny
nitty-gritty	pitter-patter	hocus-pocus
pell-mell	fender-bender	harum-scarum
razzle-dazzle	shilly-shally	heebie-jeebies
flip-flop	lovey-dovey	hurry-scurry
willy-nilly	wishy-washy	teeter-totter
fuddy-duddy	bow-wow	rinky-dink

1st-Syllable Stress	2nd-Syllable Stress	3rd-Syllable Stress
?	Kansas	Alaska
Alabama	Louisiana	Florida
Missouri	Ohio	Kentucky
South Carolina	Colorado	Pennsylvania
Hawaii	Iowa	North Carolina
Delaware	Virginia	Georgia
California	New Jersey	New York
Maryland	Wyoming	Nevada

Arkansas	Vermont	Illinois
Minnesota	Washington	Michigan
Oklahoma	Idaho	North Dakota
New Hampshire	Arizona	Texas
Connecticut	Wisconsin	New Mexico
South Dakota	Indiana	Massachusetts
Montana	Mississippi	Utah
Maine	Oregon	West Virginia
Tennessee	Nebraska	Rhode Island

5 Word Study for Derivational Constancy Spellers

Students at the derivational constancy stage of spelling development (also known as the derivational relations stage) are likely to be proficient readers and to have considerable knowledge about spelling various one- and two-syllable words. They are also likely to be students in the upper elementary grades, middle school, or beyond. As students work with words at this stage, they gradually gain confidence in dealing with what appears on the surface to be an erratic spelling system, in which sounds of letters fluctuate from word to word (e.g., /k/ for the final -c in *critic*, but /s/ for the same c in *criticize*). Students come to realize that it is not what is on the surface that matters in spelling such words, but what lies underneath. For, though complex, the system governing the spelling of the lower-frequency words studied at this stage is stable and orderly at a deeper level—a level that preserves the meaning of derived or related words. Thus, though the sound of the letter c has shifted or alternated in the words *critic* and *criticize*, the spelling that carries the meaning is retained. This would not be the case if the words were spelled as they sound, as, for instance, *critic* and *critisize*. The same applies to many other words, such as *discuss/discussion*, not *discuss/discushon*, and *democratic/democracy*, not *demacratic/democracy*. The principle at work here—*words that are related in meaning also tend to be related in spelling, despite changes in sound* (Templeton, 1983)—is a powerful one and one that has importance for understanding vocabulary, as well as for spelling words. There are 58 sorts in this chapter; the first 25 examine spelling–meaning patterns, and the next 33 explore meaning relationships among families of words derived from Greek and Latin roots. (For additional information related to understanding and teaching the features associated with the first 25 sorts, see *Word Journeys, Second Edition*, Chapter 8 [Ganske, 2014].) Specific "Talking Points" sections are not included for the Greek and Latin roots section of this chapter. The understandings that students need to take away relate to associating specific roots with particular meanings, and to realizing that families of words can share the same root. This information is integrated into the answer key for each sort. Idioms are included for some, but not all, of the sorts at this stage. Expect students to continue to reflect on understandings they gain from each sort about how words work, and to discuss these understandings and/or record them in their word study notebooks. The components of SAIL—survey, analyze, interpret, and link—can easily be applied to the categorizations in this chapter, as can academic vocabulary. Be sure to provide students with the opportunity to link their new understandings to reading and/or writing of a sentence that includes the word features under study.

Revisiting Prefixes and Suffixes

This section includes seven sorts that extend and review knowledge of prefixes and suffixes. The issue of when and when not to double the final consonant of a base word is reexamined with polysyllabic base words; several new prefixes are introduced; and -y-to-i changes are revisited.

What Is Known: At the syllable juncture stage, students have worked with the principles of doubling, *e*-drop, and no change, using one-syllable words. They have also worked with various prefixes and suffixes and how they attach to base words, including suffixes involving -*y*-to-*i* changes.

What Is New: Affixing suffixes to polysyllabic base words is a new concept. Also, although some of the prefixes were introduced at the previous stage, others are new here.

SORT 1. *e*-Drop and No Change with -*ed* and -*ing*

Sorting by Pattern

e-Drop	No Change	-*y* to *i*	Oddball
becoming	**returning**	**hurried**	**?**
balanced	concerned	buried	carrying
continued	followed	emptied	studying
dividing	functioning	replied	
exciting	interesting		
imagined	published		
involved	surrounding		
measuring			
realized			
surprising			

Considerations: This sort reviews *e*-drop, no-change, and -*y*-to-*i* principles for adding inflected endings, and it extends the concepts to base words of more than one syllable. Begin by explaining to students that they will be examining how endings such as -*ed* and -*ing* are added to longer words in this and other sorts. Make clear that just as with one-syllable words, how the ending is attached depends on the spelling of the base word. As you discuss the meanings of any unfamiliar words, go over the base-word spelling for each of the words. Tell students to record the spelling somewhere on the card—for instance, *realized/realize*. Then ask students to work with partners to sort the words under the appropriate category headers. Remind them to consider the base word as they make their category decisions. Discuss the results. Students may have placed *carrying* and *studying* under the no-change category. This is fine, because no change is actually involved. However, they are placed as oddballs in the answer key because, contrary to the other base words ending in -*y*, the -*y* did not change to *i*. Prompt students to consider why this might be. They should come to realize that the principle for changing -*y* to *i* does not usually apply when adding -*ing* (e.g., *buried* and *emptied*, but *burying* and *emptying*). Though not evident from this sort, the same is true when adding -*ed* to words in which the final -*y* is part of the vowel pattern, as -*oy*, -*ay*, and -*ey* in *destroyed*, *displayed*, and *conveyed*.

Talking Points

- As with one-syllable words, drop the final -*e* of a polysyllabic word before adding -*ed* or -*ing*, as in *realized* and *measuring*.
- As with single-syllable words, change final -*y* to *i* before adding -*ed* unless the -*y* is part of a vowel pattern—for example, *carried* but *displayed*.
- Do not change the base word when adding -*ing* to words ending in -*y*, such as *carrying and conveying*.

Integrating Idioms: "I'm **following in my uncle's footsteps;** I plan to be an artist one day, too." (Be like someone else. If you literally walked in the footsteps of somebody else, you would do exactly the same things and be just like that person.)

Did You Know? Why is **bury** pronounced like *berry* instead of like *fury* and *jury*? The answer goes back to the early days of the English language (more than 1,000 years ago) and to the influence of dialect. The Old English form of *bury* was *byrgan*, which was pronounced as /**bür•yən**/. Sometime between the 1100s and 1400s, pronunciation of the *u* changed; however, due to dialect, the change varied from region to region of England. The spelling tended to remain consistent and reflected the pronunciation of people around London, which was the capital of England and therefore influential. People in that area pronounced *u* with the sound you hear in *foot*, which when put with *r* sounded like the *ur* in *burn*. However, the pronunciation that became the dominant one was from a different region; this mismatch of a spelling from one region but a pronunciation from another is why *bury* is different from *fury* and *jury*. *Busy* has a similar history. Regional dialects are common in the United States and often affect the pronunciation of words. Sometimes in different regions even different words are used for a particular concept, such as *pop–soda, bag–paper sack, green beans–string beans–snap beans, earthworm–angleworm, skillet–frying pan,* and so forth. Dialect differences are often noticeable on television shows or in movies. Have you noticed any differences in dialect?

SORT 2. Doubling and No Change with *-ed* and *-ing*

Sorting by Pattern and Sound

Double	No Change
permitted	**edited**
concurred	angered
conferred	benefiting
controlling	considered
equipped	entered
forgetting	exhibited
inferring	exited
occurred	gossiping
preferred	happened
regretted	inhabited
submitting	offering
	suffering
	visited

Considerations: Doubling is called for in single-syllable words when the word ends with a VC pattern, as in *tap/tapping*, not *tap/taping*; the doubled consonant preserves the short-vowel sound. With base words of more than one syllable, standards similar to the criteria for one vowel and one final consonant (VC pattern) apply. However, just the last syllable of the word is considered. An additional stress-related criterion must also be met, and this too applies to the final syllable. Thus, when the last syllable of a base word ends with a single vowel and consonant *and* is stressed, double the consonant before adding the ending. There are various ways to introduce the concept of doubling with polysyllabic base words. For an alternative to the one that follows, see *Word Journeys, Second Edition,* Chapter 8 (Ganske, 2014).

Start by telling students that they will be exploring the doubling principle with base words of more than one syllable. Review the process with a single-syllable word; then explain that doubling works a little differently with polysyllabic words, as they will learn. Go over the words together, and ask students to identify and underline each base word. Then prompt students to begin by categorizing the words according to doubled final consonant or no change. Discuss the results, which should be as shown in the Sort 2 answer key. Point to each of the base words, and note that they all end in VC, yet only some require doubling. Prompt students to examine the columns of words to try to figure out what else is involved in doubling besides a final-VC pattern. After a few moments, if no one mentions syllable stress, suggest that they underline the stressed syllable in each word. With guidance, they should notice that all of the words to be doubled have a stress on the final syllable of the base word. They may initially describe the words as having a stressed second syllable. If so, point out *considered,* *inhabited,* and *exhibited,* which do not have a doubled final consonant, although their stress is on the second syllable. After some discussion, ask students to agree on talking points to describe the doubling principle for polysyllabic words. Discuss their ideas and the following "Talking Points."

Talking Points

- When adding *-ed* or *-ing* to a polysyllabic word, if the final syllable ends in a VC pattern and the syllable is stressed, double the final consonant, as in *preferred,* but not in **suff**ering or cons**id**ered.

Integrating Idioms: "My mother reminded me not to **forget myself** at the wedding reception." (Forget my manners. It is important to consider your behavior or an embarrassing situation may result.)

Did You Know? It is likely no surprise that ***gossip*** is a word with a long history, as it seems probable that people have long been engaged in the practice. The word *godsibb* first appeared in the 11th century. It was formed of *sibb,* an Old English word meaning "kinship," and modern English *god.* The word *sibling* ("having one or more parents in common") is a descendant of *sibb.* *Godsibb* referred to someone who was spiritually related to another, such as godparents ("sponsors at a baptism"). Over time, the spelling evolved, first into *gossib* and then into *gossip.* The meaning also broadened to include close friends, as well as godparents. These people likely engaged in idle talk at times, perhaps even about the godchild or the child's parents. Soon the word came to mean "someone who engages in spreading bits of rumor," or the practice of doing so.

SORT 3. Doubling and No Change with Various Suffixes

Sorting by Pattern and Sound		
Double	No Change	Oddball
beginner	**piloted**	**?**
abhorrent	canceled	equipment
committee	conference	regretful
compelled	developing	
deferred	honored	
patrolling	limited	
propeller	orbiting	
referral	profited	
repellent	quarreled	
	reference	
	wandered	
	whispered	

Considerations: Explain to students that in this sort, they will be learning more about doubling when adding suffixes. Introduce the sort by going over any unfamiliar words and identifying each of the base words. Then, as with the previous sort, ask students to categorize the words under the header cards *Double* and *No Change*. Review the categories and discuss the results, which will be as shown in Sort 3, except that the two oddballs will be included under the no-change category. Then ask students to underline the stressed syllable in each word. Remind them of the previous sort in which the double words were stressed on the final syllable of the base word, whereas for other words, stress was on one of the other syllables. Ask if that is the case here. Move any words that do not fit this principle (*equipment* and *regretful*) under the *?* card. Then ask students to pair up to talk about why these words are oddballs. Discuss their ideas and the following "Talking Points," being sure to highlight the fact that doubling does not apply to adding suffixes that begin with a consonant. Some students may question the spelling of *canceled* or mention having seen the word spelled another way. *Cancelled* is the way the word is spelled in British English and is acceptable in American English, although the single *l* is more common. It may also be easier to remember considering the doubling principle: The final syllable is not stressed, so doubling is not expected. Students who live in snowy regions of the country may see both spellings in use; for instance, TV stations announcing school closings sometimes differ in which one they post. Other words ending in *-el* also have alternative spellings, as in *traveling/travelling, leveled/levelled, labeled/labelled,* and so forth. Unlike the doubling in *cancelled,* the double consonants of these words are rejected by computer spell checkers using American English.

Talking Points

- The final consonant of a polysyllabic base word is doubled if the suffix begins with a vowel and if the base word ends with a VC pattern that is stressed, as in *propeller* and *repellent,* but not *developing* and *equipment.*

Did You Know? **Repel** is made up of *re-,* meaning "back," and *pel,* meaning "to drive." If you are repelled by something, you literally are driven back from it. *Repellent,* which includes the same word parts, is often used to drive back mosquitoes. **Compel** is also part of the *pel* family of words. The *com-* in this word means "with," so *compel* means "with drive" or force. If you are compelled to do something, you are driven to do it. *Propeller* comes from the same root. The prefix *pro-* means "in front of," so to *propel* is "to drive in front of," which is just what the propeller of an airplane does; it drives the plane forward. *Compel, repel,* and *propel* have been part of the English language since the 1300s and 1400s. However, *repellent* as a substance for driving away insects is much more recent; it was first recorded in 1908. *Propellers,* referring to devices used on ships and flying machines, was first recorded during the early 1800s.

SORT 4. Suffixes with Final -*y* (-*ier, -iness, -ious, -ily, -ied*)

Sorting by Meaning				
-ier	*-iness*	*-ious*	*-ily*	*-ied*
heavier	**happiness**	**various**	**luckily**	**multiplied**
cloudier	business	envious	angrily	magnified
healthier	friendliness	furious	necessarily	occupied
livelier	loneliness	mysterious	ordinarily	qualified
	uneasiness	studious	readily	satisfied

Considerations: This sort, which reviews -*y*-to-*i* changes before suffixes, is fairly straightforward. Only the -*ous* suffix is new. To increase the level of challenge, omit the headers and invite students to sort the words according to the suffix. When they are finished, ask them to identify the base words; they might record the spellings on the word cards. Discuss the results and any unfamiliar words. You might point out that *busy* can also be added to -*ness* without a spelling change. Whereas *business* refers to "work," *busyness* refers to "a state of being busy," as in *My busyness kept me from attending the movie.* As you discuss the students' observations and the talking point, remind them that the principle for changing -*y* to *i* does not hold true when the suffix begins with *i* (see Sort 1 of this chapter).

Talking Points

- Usually final -*y* changes to *i* when a suffix is added, regardless of whether the suffix begins with a consonant or a vowel (except *i*), as in *lonely* → *loneliness* and *vary* → *various*, but *vary* → *varying*, not *variing*.

Integrating Idioms: "Wednesday night we won our first game in two years, but Thursday when the coach taught our government class, it was **business as usual**." (The routine was normal. Some students may have thought there should be some discussion about the game, as the coach was the teacher, but the class stayed on topic.)

Did You Know? **Multiply,** *multiplication, multiplicand,* and *multiplicity* are all related to *multiplex* ("a movie theater or other building with separate units"). Their meanings derive from *multi-,* which means "many," and *plex* or *plic,* which means "folds." Just as a blanket has many layers folded in, when you multiply, you increase or "fold in" a number multiple times. A multiplex theater has several theaters "folded" into one building. We can think of something that is *complicated* as being "with folds." When you *duplicate* something and make an identical copy, you have "two folds." Can you think of other words with the *plic* or *plex* pattern, in which the pattern is a root that means "fold"?

SORT 5. Prefixes (*un-, dis-, in-*)

Sorting by Meaning			
un-	*dis-*	*in-*	Oddball
uncertain	**disbelief**	**incapable**	**?**
unafraid	disapprove	inaccurate	indentured
unfamiliar	disclose	inadequate	
unimportant	discolor	indistinct	
unnatural	disconnect	infamous	
unsuccessful	discount	injustice	
	discourage	insecure	
	disease	insincere	

Considerations: This sort is straightforward. It reviews prefixes introduced at the syllable juncture stage. Students may not know the meaning of *indentured,* although it is often used in intermediate-grade social studies texts (see the "Did You Know?" story for this word). Review the meaning of each prefix: *Un-* and *dis-* both mean "not" or "the opposite of"; although *in-* can mean "in, into," here it means "not" in all of the words except *indentured.* As you go over the words, ask students to apply the prefix meaning to the word—for instance, *uncertain* means "not certain." Draw attention to the word *unnatural*, which has a double consonant due to affixation; the spelling may look strange, but the double consonants are needed to maintain meaning. At this time, you might distribute copies to students of Appendix G, "Understanding Prefixes." It can be attached to their word study notebooks for future reference.

Talking Points

- *Un-* and *dis-* are prefixes that mean "not" or "the opposite of"; *in-* can mean "in/into" as well as "not."
- When prefixes are added to words, double consonants can result, as in *unnatural*. Though they may look peculiar, they are needed for meaning.

Integrating Idioms: "I told my sister **in no uncertain terms** to stay out of my room." (Specifically and directly. If something is said very clearly, there can be no question as to what is meant by it; the statement emphasizes how serious the person saying it really is.)

Did You Know? In early America, people sometimes bound themselves to work for another person for a period of time (usually 7 years) in exchange for something, such as passage on a ship. The practice of indenturing servants was outlawed under the U.S. Constitution. **Indenture** refers to the document or contract of agreement. *Indent-* literally means "in tooth" in Latin. So why was the agreement given this name? The document was cut or torn in two with ragged or serrated edges, and each party received half. The toothed edges allowed the document to be put together to prove their agreement.

SORT 6. Prefixes (*mis-, en-, de-, anti-*)

Sorting by Meaning				
mis-	*en-*	*de-*	*anti-*	Oddball
misbehave	**enlarge**	**defrost**	**antisocial**	**?**
miscalculate	enable	decompose	anticrime	English
misfortune	encircle	dehumidify	antifreeze	envelope
mismanage	encourage	deodorant	antigravity	
mispro-	enrage	dethrone	antismoking	
nounce		devalue		

Considerations: Like the previous sort, this sort is straightforward and can be completed by students without teacher direction. However, there should be follow-up discussion. Unfamiliar words should be discussed, as should the meanings of the prefixes. Although *mis-* ("badly" or "wrongly") is a review for students, the other three prefixes are new. *En-* means "to put into" or "cause to"; its spelling sometimes alters to *em*, as in *empower*. *De-* has several meanings: "out," "off," "apart," and "away"; *anti-* means "against" or "opposing." If students miscategorize *envelope* with the *en-* words, ask them to identify the base word. Because there is none, it is considered an oddball in this sort. Then point out that *en-* does function as a prefix in the word. However, instead of attaching to a base word, it is affixed to a word root, something they will learn more about later on. *English* is an intact word; it has no prefix. Remind students that it is always capitalized, whether it refers to the language, to people, or to a course of study. Be sure each student has a copy of Appendix G, "Understanding Prefixes," as a reference.

Talking Points

- *Mis-, en-* (also *em-*), *de-*, and *anti-* are all prefixes; *mis-* means "wrongly," *en-* means "cause to," *de-* means "away," and *anti-* means "against."
- *English* is always capitalized.

Integrating Idioms: "Just **tell me in plain English** why you had to stay after school." (Simply, clearly, and straightforwardly. Sometimes excitement or concern can cause someone to ramble in a way that is unclear, or the person might be using technical language; in this case, you might say, "Just tell me in plain English what is wrong with my computer.")

Did You Know? English has sometimes been called a *living language,* because it is not static but ever-changing, just like other living things. Old words become obsolete and disappear from the language; new words and new meanings (*neologisms*) are added as they are coined or borrowed from other languages. It is difficult to determine just how many words there are in English because of the changes that take place and because different forms of words may not be counted the same way. For example, how many different words follow: *record, recording, recorded, records, accord,* and *discord?* These are decisions that lexicographers who compile dictionaries must make, as well as deciding what to do about scientific and technical terms; do you include some . . . or all?

English has changed considerably over the centuries. Old English (used from the middle of the 5th to the 12th centuries) is for the most part unreadable without benefit of a translation. The alphabet then was even somewhat different; it included letters we no longer use and did not include letters we do use. (To see what Old English is like, you might search online or ask at a library to borrow a copy of Seamus Heaney's [2000] bilingual translation of *Beowulf,* a poem written sometime between the 8th and 10th centuries. It shows Old English on one page and the modern translation on the facing page.) We have Old English to thank for many of our basic words, such as *the, and, in, is, I, wife, father, man, child, house,* and *work.* An invasion by the Normans in 1066 led to the borrowing of many French words. Sometimes the borrowing resulted in multiple words for the same concept. The Old English is usually identifiable as a shorter, simpler word, as in *come/arrive, eat/devour,* and *sight/vision.* It is interesting to note that animal names tend to come from the Old English, whereas the foods made from them derive from the French, as in *sheep/mutton, cow/beef,* and *pig/pork.* Why might this be? Since the Norman Conquest, words have been added to the English language from countries all over the world.

SORT 7. Prefixes (*inter-, mid-, sub-, super-*)

Sorting by Meaning				
inter-	*mid-*	*sub-*	*super-*	Oddball
interstate	**midnight**	**subway**	**supermarket**	**?**
interact	midair	subconscious	superman	interfere
interchange	midday	subheading	supernatural	
international	midpoint	sublease	superpower	
interview	midstream	subsoil	superstar	
	midsummer	substandard		

Considerations: As with the previous two sorts, this sort is straightforward, but all of the prefixes are new. After students have sorted the words, discuss the word meanings. Give them an opportunity to identify the meaning of each prefix before you tell them. Talking with partners may help them to generate ideas. Remind students that the meaning they identify must apply to all of the words in the category. Discuss their ideas and clarify as needed. *Inter-* means "between" or "within"; when you *interact* with someone, there is action going on between you. An *interchange* is "a change between roads"; it allows you to move from one to another. *International* activities are "between nations," and an *interview* is literally a "seeing between" (in other words, coming to understand a person or an issue). Although the prefix *inter-* is part of *interfere*, as with *envelope* in the previous sort, it is affixed to a root rather than to a base word. *Mid-* means "middle." Something in *midair* is in the "middle of the air"; *midpoint* is at "a point in the middle" of something, as in the *midpoint* of the semester or the *midpoint* of a line; *midstream* is in the "middle of the stream"; and *midsummer* is about "halfway through summer." *Sub-* usually means "below" or "under." A *subway* is a "way underground"; *subsoil* is "soil below the topsoil"; *subconscious* is "below the level of conscious thought"; *subheading* is "a heading below the main heading"; a *sublease* is a "lease under" in that the original renter, who still has a lease on the property, leases it to someone else; and *substandard* is "below standard" in quality. *Super-* means "above" or "over." In the words for this sort, it carries the connotation of exceeding the usual, as in *superstar*. As part of the discussion, draw students' attention to the double consonants in *midday*. You might also explain that another prefix, *intra-* (meaning "within"), is sometimes confused with *inter-*, as in *interstate* ("between or among states") *commerce is on the rise* versus *intrastate* ("within a state") *commerce is on the rise.*

Talking Points

- *Inter-* often means "between/among," *mid-* means "middle," *sub-* usually means "under," and *super* means "above/beyond."

Integrating Idioms: "Every time you tell a story, you **leave me hanging in midair**." (Stop without completing the story. Because humans spend their time on the ground except when assisted by artificial means such as an airplane or glider, to be left hanging in midair would be distressing.)

Did You Know? The story of **superman** begins with a German philosopher named Friedrich Nietzsche (**nē•chə**), who wrote about his concept of an ideal human, whom he called *Ubermensch. Ubermensch* was translated into English in 1895 as *Overman* and in 1896 as *Beyondman*. It was not until 1903 that the word was translated as *Superman* by playwright George Bernard Shaw. Superman as a man of extraordinary abilities and power was first recorded in 1925, and the nearly invincible superhero, capable of flying, was introduced to America through a comic strip in 1938. Then in 1943, Superwoman made her debut in *Action Comics.*

e-Drop and No Change with *-ed* and *-ing*

e-Drop	No Change	*-y* to *i*
becoming	returning	hurried
emptied	imagined	functioning
involved	buried	dividing
measuring	followed	published
studying	balanced	exciting
replied	surrounding	continued
surprising	concerned	carrying
realized	interesting	?

No Change		Double
edited	permitted	offering
forgetting	preferred	benefiting
suffering	equipped	considered
conferred	angered	occurred
gossiping	submitting	exited
regretted	concurred	exhibited
entered	inferring	happened
controlling	visited	inhabited

No Change	Double	
piloted	beginner	equipment
compelled	orbiting	repellent
honored	patrolling	canceled
regretful	propeller	reference
limited	conference	committee
profited	referral	developing
deferred	abhorrent	whispered
wandered	quarreled	?

SORT 4 Suffixes with Final -y (-ier, -iness, -ious, -ily, -ied)

-ier	*-iness*	*-ious*	*-ily*	*-ied*
heavier	happiness	various		
luckily	multiplied	readily		
furious	satisfied	friendliness		
cloudier	angrily	occupied		
envious	loneliness	healthier		
necessarily	studious	qualified		
magnified	livelier	mysterious		
business	ordinarily	uneasiness		

SORT 5 Prefixes (*un-*, *dis-*, *in-*)

un-	*dis-*	*in-*
uncertain	disbelief	incapable
indistinct	unfamiliar	disconnect
disclose	insincere	indentured
unsuccessful	disease	infamous
discourage	inaccurate	disapprove
insecure	unimportant	discount
discolor	injustice	unnatural
inadequate	unafraid	?

Prefixes (*mis-, en-, de-, anti-*)

mis-	en-	de-	anti-
misbehave	enlarge	defrost	
antisocial	English	enrage	
encircle	dehumidify	mispronounce	
misfortune	antifreeze	devalue	
encourage	miscalculate	envelope	
antismoking	dethrone	antigravity	
mismanage	anticrime	decompose	
deodorant	enable	?	

SORT 7 Prefixes (*inter-*, *mid-*, *sub-*, *super-*)

inter-	*mid-*	*sub-*	*super-*
interstate	midnight	subway	
supermarket	substandard	midstream	
midsummer	subsoil	midair	
superpower	interact	sublease	
international	superman	midpoint	
superstar	subconscious	interfere	
interchange	supernatural	midday	
subheading	interview	**?**	

Consonant Alternations

(DSA Features P and Q)

This section, which includes Sorts 8–12, examines the concept of *consonant alternations*. When suffixes are added to words, the sounds of certain consonants often change or alternate, though their spellings may remain intact; examples include the silent-to-sounded change that occurs from *sign* to *signal*, or the final-consonant sound change in *construct* when the suffix *-ion* is added, *construction*. Adding a suffix does not always mean a change, as we see in *constructive*. Sometimes when a suffix is added not only a change in sound but also a change in spelling occurs. Such changes tend to be predictable because they often occur in families of words, as in *admit/admission, commit/commission,* and *permit/permission*. Many related words involve a consonant alternation, and probably most common among them are words with the /shən/ ending. When spelling words with /shən/, writers must consider not only that the spelling may not correspond to the sound, but also that there are multiple ways to spell the ending, including *-tion, -sion,* and *-ian*. These and other issues are the focus of the sorts in this section.

What Is Known: Students should be familiar with many of the base words used in the sorts of this section. Also, they have worked with affixation of suffixes in this chapter and the previous chapter on syllable juncture spelling.

What Is New: The concept of consonant alternations is new, as is the principle that words related in meaning tend to be related in spelling despite changes in sound.

SORT 8. Silent and Sounded Consonants

Sorting by Sound	
Silent	Sounded
muscle	**muscular**
autumn	autumnal
bomb	bombard
column	columnist
design	designate
hasten	haste
moisten	moist
resign	resignation
sign	signature
soften	soft
solemn	solemnity
wrestle	wrest

Considerations: Although there are few words with sounded-to-silent alternations, their study can segue to the study of other alternations. Students will likely already know how to spell several of the silent-consonant words in this sort from their studies at the previous stage. Introduce the sort by placing *muscle* and *muscular* in front of the students. Inform them that the sort they will be working with is the first of many that will include pairs or families of words that are related in meaning, such as *muscle* and *muscular*. Sometimes they may know how to spell one of the words, but have difficulty spelling a related word. As they work with the pairs or families of words, they will learn ways to make the spelling easier. Ask them to talk about the easier and more difficult aspects of the words *muscle* and *muscular*. They will likely mention the silent *c*; if not, bring this to their attention by placing the appropriate header card above each word. Point out that because it is silent, spellers sometimes omit the *c* in *muscle* but not in *muscular*, where the sound of the *c* is a reminder that it needs to be included. Thinking of the *c* in *muscular* can be a reminder that a *c* is also needed in the related word *muscle*. Ask students to sort the remaining words according to whether the word has a silent consonant or just sounded consonants. Discuss the results and clarify the meanings of any unfamiliar words, such as *wrest*, which means "to take something forcibly by twisting," as in *We had to wrest the bone from the dog's mouth*. This same sense of "twisting" is apparent in a related word, *wrestle*. The meanings of *solemn* and *solemnity* as having to do with "serious" and "sober" may also need clarifying. Students may not perceive a relationship between *design* and *designate*, other than their shared spellings. Point out that both words literally have to do with "marking out." A design marks out an artistic work or the plan of a building, and when something is designated, it is marked out or selected for some purpose, as to *designate an area of sidewalk for repair* or *designate a person as the group leader*. Write the spelling–meaning principle on the board (see the first "Talking Point" below), and discuss it in relation to the sort. Ask students to record it in their notebooks. Note that due to the limited pool of words, word hunts are not appropriate for this sort.

Talking Points

- Words related in meaning tend to be related in spelling, despite differences in sound, as in *haste* and *hasten*.
- Sometimes thinking of a related word can help with spelling, as in *moist* for *moisten*.

Integrating Idioms: "We **can never move a muscle** in that class." (Must be very still. Because the heart is a muscle, the idea of not moving a muscle points to the extreme quiet that is expected.)

Did You Know? Could the silent *n* in **autumn** and the spelling difficulties associated with it be the reason we have two synonyms for this season, *fall* and *harvest*? More likely it is characteristics of the season that give these words their synonymous status with *autumn*. Autumn is the season when agricultural products are harvested and leaves fall. As long ago as 1545, the seasons were referred to as *spring time, sommer, fall of the leaf,* and *winter*. The expression was shortened to just *fall* more than 300 years ago, and today this word is commonly used in the United States.

SORT 9. Adding *-ion* to Base Words with No Spelling Change

Sorting by Sound and Pattern

-ct	*-ct + -ion*	*-ss*	*-ss + -ion*
direct	**direction**	**express**	**expression**
connect	connection	confess	confession
detect	detection	discuss	discussion
elect	election	impress	impression
infect	infection	possess	possession
predict	prediction		
react	reaction		

Considerations: Introduce the sort by showing students the template of words (without the headers) and asking them what they notice. After their work with silent and sounded consonants, they will likely mention that the sort comprises pairs of related words, and that many of the words end in *-ion*. Tell them that they will be learning to add the suffix *-ion* to words as part of this and later word studies. Ask them to partner the words by making two columns, one for the base word and one for the related word, as in *direct/direction*. When they are finished, ask students to examine the two lists to see whether they can be subdivided while keeping pairs of words together. If necessary, guide them to the four categories designated by the headers in Sort 9. Discuss their observations; students will likely notice that words in one category end in *-ct* and in another with *-ss*. They may not grasp the changes in sound that occur from the base word to the related form with *-ion* (the *t* in *direct* changes from /t/ to /sh/ in *direction,* and the final *-s* in *express* changes to /sh/ in *expression*). Draw their attention to this, using the key words as examples; underline the consonant alternation (*-ct* or *-ss*). Place the header cards above their appropriate categories. Explain to students that /shən/ can be confusing to spell, because *-tion, -sion,* and *-ian* are all appropriate for certain words. However, thinking about the base word can make the spelling obvious, because usually for words that end in *-ct* or *-ss,* you simply add *-ion.* There is no spelling change, just a change in sound. Before ending the lesson, discuss any unfamiliar word meanings. (Note that words with final *-ct* are somewhat less consistent than those with *-ss* in how *-ion* is added. For a few words, *-ation* is added, as in *expect/expectation.*)

Talking Points

• For most base words that end in *-ct* or *-ss,* just add *-ion,* as in *direction* or *expression.*

Integrating Idioms: "I heard him speak at an assembly, and he **made a real impression on me.**" (Had a lasting effect on the person. When something is pressed into a substance, it stays there for a long time, even permanently—e.g., the fossilized footprints of dinosaurs.)

Did You Know? Just as the final-consonant sound alters when the suffix *-ion* is added to *connect* (from /t/ to /sh/ to form **connection**), so, too, the story of *connection* is one involving changes—not of sound, but of spelling. Although the word evolved from the Latin word *conectere,* meaning "to bind together," its early spelling did not clearly reflect this heritage. In the late 1300s the word was spelled *conneccion,* and in the mid-1400s it was *connexioun.* The *-ction* spelling was not common, especially in America, until the 1700s, when other words (such as *direction* and *collection*), already spelled with final *-tion,* influenced its spelling.

    Many **discussions** live up to their dictionary definition of being "earnest conversations"; some may even become heated debates, in which one person attempts to shake up things by squashing the ideas of another through rational argument. Someone else may have it in mind to clear the air, shake out the tensions, and rescue the situation, objectively pointing out the merits and faulty logic of both parties. Considering this scenario, it may not be so surprising that *discussion* evolved from the Latin for "shaking apart" or "striking asunder," and that *squash* and *rescue* derive from the same "shaking"-related root.

SORT 10. Adding *-ion* and *-ian* to Base Words with No Spelling Change

Sorting by Sound and Pattern

-t	*-t* + *-ion*	*-ic*	*-ic* + *-ian*	Oddball
digest	**digestion**	**magic**	**magician**	**?***
adopt	adoption	clinic	clinician	present/presentation
assert	assertion	electric	electrician	
except	exception	music	musician	
invent	invention	optic	optician	
suggest	suggestion			

Considerations: Although no oddball card is included in this sort, there are exceptions. Students need to be guided by their examination of the words and categories to determine whether or not there is an exception, not be led by the presence of a *?* card. This sort builds on the previous one through an examination of words ending in other consonants plus *t* (designated as *-t* rather than *-ct*). It also introduces a new concept for words with /shən/—namely, that *-ian* rather than *-ion* is used to identify people. The use of *-ian* for people is true of many words, even words without /shən/: *librarian, guardian, Indian, custodian, Egyptian,* and *historian,* to name a few.

Begin the sort in a manner similar to the previous one, withholding the header cards until the categories have been discussed. If students are confounded by the absence of an oddball card as they sort, remind them that they can always set aside words that don't fit the categories. Students should again realize that there is no spelling change when the suffix is added, except in the case of *present/ presentation*. Discuss this pair of oddballs; numerous words that end in consonant *-t* do require *-ation,* such as *tempt/temptation, indent/indentation, protest/protestation*. Remind students that consonant alternations or changes can cause spellers confusion unless the base word is kept in mind. Go over unfamiliar word meanings before ending the sort. Be sure students have a clear understanding that *-ian* is used when the word refers to a person.

Talking Points

- For most base words that end in consonant *-t*, just add *-ion*, as in *digest/digestion*.
- For base words that end in *-ic*, add *-ian* to designate a person, as in *magician*.

Integrating Idioms: "I know I have to **face the music** for the broken window, but it's hard to take grounding *and* paying for it." (Accept the consequences of your actions. There is uncertainty as to the origins of this expression: Some believe it to relate to an actor facing the orchestra pit with a hostile audience behind it during a poor performance; others believe it refers to a formal and disgraceful dismissal from the military, which would be accompanied by music.)

Did You Know? **Music,** like the days of the week and many other words, has its origins in the world of the ancients and their beliefs. Music was an essential component of everyday life for the ancient Greeks. The word *music* originated from *Mousa,* which is Greek for *Muse*. The Muses were goddesses, and originally there were three of them. Over time, the myth expanded until there were nine Muses, each having purview or charge over a particular area of the arts or sciences, including various types of poetry, song, dance, drama, history, and astronomy. Ancient Greeks often called on them for inspiration. The Greek word *musike* referred to any of the areas presided over by the Muses. Music often evokes strong feelings. What do you think the following authors were trying to say about music?

"Music washes away from the soul the dust of everyday life."
—BERTHOLD AUERBACH

"Music expresses that which cannot be said and on which it is impossible
to be silent."
—VICTOR HUGO

SORT 11. Adding *-ion* to Base Words with *e*-Drop

Sorting by Sound and Pattern

-te	*e*-Drop + *-ion*	*-se*	*e*-Drop + *-ion*
educate	**education**	**confuse**	**confusion**
celebrate	celebration	averse	aversion
communicate	communication	immerse	immersion
cooperate	cooperation	precise	precision
evaporate	evaporation		
exaggerate	exaggeration		
illustrate	illustration		
pollute	pollution		

Considerations: Up to this point, /shən/ has been formed by simply adding *-ion* or *-ian* directly to the base word. In this sort, students must apply their understandings of final *-e* when adding *-ion*. As with other instances of *e*-dropping, the change is predictable, except in a few cases; for example, some *-se* words require the addition of *a*, as in *converse/conversation*. If discussing this with students, point out that without the *a* the result is *conversion*, an entirely different word.

Introduce the sort in a manner similar to that used with the two previous sorts. Discuss the results and talking points, as well as any unfamiliar meanings. Because many of the words in this sort (and in later sorts) involve a change in stress when *-ion* is added (*celebrate/celebration*), before ending the session or at a later time, ask the group to re-sort their words according to whether or not there is a stress change, as shown in the following sound sort. Discuss their observations.

Sorting by Sound: Stress Change

Stress Change	No Stress Change
celebrate/cele**bra**tion	a**verse**/a**ver**sion
com**mu**nicate/communi**ca**tion	con**fuse**/con**fu**sion
co**op**erate/coope**ra**tion	im**merse**/im**mer**sion
educate/edu**ca**tion	pol**lute**/pol**lu**tion
e**vap**orate/evapo**ra**tion	pre**cise**/pre**ci**sion
ex**ag**gerate/exagge**ra**tion	
illustrate/illus**tra**tion OR	
il**lus**trate/illus**tra**tion	

Talking Points

- Base words that end in *-te* or *-se* drop the final *-e* before the *-ion* suffix is added, as in *celebrate/celebration* and *confuse/confusion*.
- Sometimes adding a suffix changes the stress, as in **ed**ucate/edu**ca**tion.

Did You Know? **Pollution** can result from many different types of activity, such as agriculture, energy, industry, and transportation, and can affect air, soil, and water. Polluted areas are often considered "dirty," and indeed the words *pollute* and *pollution* derive from a Latin word meaning "to soil or defile." Although *pollute* as a word meaning "to dirty" or "to make foul" has been around since about the mid-1500s, its general use to describe dirtying of the atmosphere or environment is fairly recent, since 1954. Why do you suppose it took so long for this sense to come into use? Is pollution a problem in your area? If so, what, if anything, is being done about it?

SORT 12. Adding *-ion* to Base Words with Predictable Spelling Changes

Sorting by Sound and Pattern

-de → -sion	*-d → -sion*	*-mit → -mission*
conclude/conclusion	**extend/extension**	**admit/admission**
erode/erosion	comprehend/comprehension	omit/omission
explode/explosion	expand/expansion	permit/permission
invade/invasion	suspend/suspension	
persuade/persuasion		

Considerations: The last sort in this section goes well beyond simply dropping a final *-e* before adding *-ion*; here some letters are dropped and others are substituted. Although at first glance the changes may seem complex, they are predictable. The *-mit* category, in particular, involves a family of words—words that derive or stem from the Latin root *mit*, meaning "to send." As is evident from Sort 12, significant changes occur in words of this type when *-ion* is added, but the same changes are made to all words in the family. Examples of other word families that require multiple changes when *-ion* is added are *describe/description* and *prescribe/prescription*, *produce/production* and *reduce/reduction*, *receive/reception* and *deceive/deception*.

Introduce the sort by asking students to pair the base words with their derived forms. Then ask them to review the list and look for ways to subdivide it that will help them to understand how to add the *-ion* suffix. They may arrive at two categories: *-sion* and *-ssion*. If so, ask if the same type of change was used with all of the words. With guidance, they should arrive at the three groupings shown in the Sort 12 answer key. Discuss their observations and thoughts. Remind students again that considering the base word can help with the spelling of words ending in *-ion*. Also, point out that sometimes, as with the *-mit* family, thinking of another word in the family and how its *-ion* form is spelled can aid spelling of a different word in the family.

Talking Points

- Base words that end in *-de* or *-d* drop the letters and add *-sion*, as in *erode/erosion* and *expand/expansion*.
- Base words that end in *-mit* drop the *-t* and add *-ssion*, as in *omit/omission*.
- Although some spelling changes that occur when *-ion* is added are complex, they tend to be consistent across a whole family of words, and therefore predictable.

Did You Know? What possible connection could there be between animals such as beavers, gerbils, gophers, guinea pigs, hamsters, mice, muskrats, porcupines, rats, and squirrels and **erosion?** The animals listed are all *rodents,* mammals with upper and lower incisors that grow continuously. The word *rodent* shares a common ancestry with *erode.* Both derive from the Latin word for "to gnaw." Rodents must constantly gnaw in order to keep their ever-growing teeth from getting out of control, and erosion is a kind of "gnawing" or "eating away" of the earth's surface. It is not teeth that cause the wearing down, though; it is forces such as wind, moving water, gravity, and ice. Given enough time, these forces can erode just about anything (consider the Grand Canyon, or compare the heights of the older Appalachian Mountains and the younger Rocky Mountains).

Silent Consonant		Sounded Consonant
muscle	muscular	bombard
column	resign	haste
signature	autumn	wrest
bomb	solemn	resignation
moisten	design	soft
sign	hasten	columnist
autumnal	moist	designate
wrestle	soften	solemnity

SORT 9 Adding *-ion* to Base Words with No Spelling Change

-ct	*-ct + -ion*	*-ss*	*-ss + -ion*
direct	direction	express	
expression	infection	react	
impress	confession	detection	
reaction	possession	infect	
predict	connect	discussion	
election	possess	confess	
discuss	impression	detect	
connection	elect	prediction	

SORT 10 — Adding -*ion* and -*ian* to Base Words with No Spelling Change

-*t*	-*t* + -*ion*	-*ic*	-*ic* + -*ian*
digest	digestion		magic
magician	electric		invention
except	assertion		adopt
clinician	invent		musician
music	electrician		present
presentation	optic		suggestion
exception	assert		optician
suggest	adoption		clinic

SORT 11

Adding *-ion* to Base Words with *e*-Drop

-te	*e*-Drop + *-ion*	*-se*	*e*-Drop + *-ion*
educate	education	confuse	
confusion	averse	precision	
celebration	evaporation	cooperate	
exaggeration	pollute	communicate	
illustration	immerse	celebrate	
communication	pollution	cooperation	
precise	aversion	evaporate	
immersion	illustrate	exaggerate	

SORT 12
Adding *-ion* to Base Words with Predictable Spelling Changes

-de → -sion	*-d → -sion*	*-mit →* *-mission*
conclude	conclusion	extend
extension	admit	admission
comprehend	expansion	erode
persuade	omission	invasion
permit	explode	expand
erosion	persuasion	suspend
suspension	omit	permission
invade	comprehension	explosion

Vowel Alternations
(DSA Feature R)

This section introduces students to another type of alternation, *vowel alternations*. As with consonant changes, the sound of a vowel pattern shifts from the base word to a derived form. Changes in stress sometimes occur, as well. There are three types of vowel alternations: long to short, long to schwa, and short to schwa. Usually the base word has the more obvious spelling, and the derived form the more obscure, as in *deprive/deprivation*. However, sometimes it is the derived form that is pronounced in a way that makes the spelling pattern obvious, as in *vitality* versus *vital*. As with consonant alternations, vowel alternations sometimes also involve predictable spelling changes.

What Is Known: Students have thoroughly examined basic vowel patterns by the time they reach the derivational constancy stage, including the schwa. They have also worked with stressed syllables and with affixation of suffixes. At this point in time, they likely have the additional advantage of having worked with one type of alternations, those involving consonants.

What Is New: The concept of vowel alternations and the types of changes that can occur are new.

SORT 13. Long- to Short-Vowel Changes

Sorting by Sound	
Long	Short
cave	**cavity**
assume	assumption
athlete	athletic
crime	criminal
decide	decision
divide	division
humane	humanity
introduce	introduction
provide	provision
revise	revision
type	typical
volcano	volcanic

Considerations: This is a good time to observe the level of sophistication with which individual students approach the examination of words by asking them to complete an open sort (reserve the header words until the categories have been discussed). Do students begin by pairing the words, as that is how the last several sorts have been introduced? Or do they approach the words in some other manner? What do they do next? When they are finished sorting, ask for volunteers to share their results. Then, if no one has noticed the changes in vowel sound (which is likely), suggest that everyone pair up base words with their related forms in order to better examine the words. This may elicit ideas about vowel alternations, especially if you suggest that they pay attention to the vowel sounds in each word. Guide the students to the realization that each base word includes a long vowel that alternates to a short vowel in the derived form, as in *cave* and *cavity*. Ask them to identify the vowel alternation in each pair of words by underlining it. Add the headers and discuss the results, pointing out that just as with the consonant alternations, knowledge of vowel changes can help in spelling words. There are multiple ways to spell vowel sounds, but the spelling pattern tends to remain constant despite changes in sound. Therefore, knowing how to spell *please* helps to ensure *pleasant* as the correct spelling of the adjective, rather than *plesant*. Discuss any unfamiliar word meanings before closing the lesson. As an extension, you might assist students in identifying the various suffixes that have been added to the sort words, though without concern for how they were added.

Talking Points

- When a suffix is added to a base word, the sound of a vowel may change, but the spelling is likely to remain constant, as in *divide/division* and *crime/criminal*.

***Did You Know?* Volcano** takes its name from Vulcan, who was the Roman god of fire and metalworking. His forge was thought to be inside Mount Etna (located on the island of Sicily off the coast of Italy), which periodically belched fire and flames. Over time, this and other erupting mountains came to be named *volcanoes,* after Vulcan.

Athlete is derived from the Greek word *athlos,* meaning "prize," and *athlein,* "to compete for a prize." The word entered English in the 1500s. For a discussion of types of athletic competitions involving multiple events, see Sorts 26 and 27.

SORT 14. Long-Vowel to Schwa Changes

Sorting by Sound	
Long	Schwa
invite	**invitation**
admire	admiration
combine	combination
compete	competition
define	definition
deprive	deprivation
hesitate	hesitant
ignore	ignorant
narrate	narrative
organize	organization
relate	relative
social	society

Considerations: As a check on students' ability to transfer understandings of long- to short-vowel alternations to long-vowel to schwa alternations, and as an attention-getting way to introduce this sort, you might begin with a soft or ungraded quiz. Dictate five to seven of the words from the schwa category. Go over the spellings and discuss the results. Then, with the students' help, sort the words into long and schwa categories, using the header cards as a guide. Underline and discuss the vowel alternations of each pair, and review the talking points.

Talking Points

- Knowledge of related words can be especially helpful in spelling words with the schwa, as in *divide/dividend,* because despite changes in sound, the spelling is likely to remain constant.

Did You Know? **Define** is made up of two meaning units, or *morphemes*: the prefix, *de-*, and the word root, *fin*. Although *de-* has several meanings, here it acts as an intensifier; it emphasizes the meaning of the root, which is "boundary" or "limit." When we define something, we are setting limits on how people should think of the word. Imagine what our communication would be like if we did not define words! We find *fin* as a root in numerous other words, and it carries the same meaning—as, for example, in *confine,* which means "with boundaries," as when a person is confined to a hospital bed or an animal is confined to a cage. *Finish* and *finally* suggest that a person or thing has reached the limit, the end. Something that is *finite* has a limit. It does not go on forever, whereas something that is *infinite* (prefix *in-,* which means "no, not," + *fin,* which means "limit") has no limits. The etymologies of words provide this information; they tell the story or history of each word. An unabridged dictionary includes the information as part of the entry for the word.

SORT 15. Long- and Short-Vowel Changes with Schwa

Sorting by Pattern

Base Word	Derived Word
symbol	**symbolic**
contribute	contribution
declare	declaration
distribute	distribution
habit	habitual
incline	inclination
mandate	mandatory
migrate	migratory
mobile	mobility
preside	president
prohibit	prohibition
reside	resident

Sorting by Sound (Vowel Change)

Long	Schwa	Short	Schwa
migrate	**migratory**	**symbolic**	**symbol**
declare	declaration	contribute	contribution
incline	inclination	distribute	distribution
mandate	mandatory	habit	habitual
preside	president	mobility	mobile
reside	resident	prohibit	prohibition

Considerations: Because the schwa is so confusing to spell, this sort extends concepts from the previous sort. Here both long- and short-vowel alternations with schwa are explored. Begin by asking students to sort the words into two categories, base words and derived words, as shown in the pattern sort. Then tell students that in addition to long- to short-vowel and long-vowel to schwa alternations, there is another way that vowel sounds change when a suffix is added. Draw attention to the change in *migrate/migratory* in the sort just completed. Underline the vowel *a* in each word, and identify the sound it makes (long *a* in *migrate* and schwa in *migratory*). Set the pair of words aside, as shown in the sound sort. Follow the same process with *declare/declaration,* being sure to underline vowel *a* in each word and discuss the change in sound. Place the words under *migrate* and *migratory.* (If students wonder why it is not being called an *r*-controlled vowel, explain that when a vowel-plus-*r* pattern is in an unstressed syllable, as it is here, it is called a schwa.) Then place *symbolic* and *symbol* to the side of the other cards. Ask students to consider how the sound of the vowel changes. They should notice that it alters from a short *o* in *symbolic* to a schwa in *symbol*. Add the header cards, and proceed with the remaining words in a similar manner. Discuss the talking points, and clarify word meanings as needed. As an extension or follow-up, help students to identify the stressed syllable of each word (highlighting it is one way). Addition of the suffix causes the stress to shift, often turning a stressed syllable into an unstressed one, and therefore a long or short vowel into a schwa.

Talking Points

• Although suffixes sometimes cause a short or long vowel to become a schwa, thinking of the base word can clarify the spelling, as in *distribute/distribution*.

Did You Know? **Migrate** stems from a root meaning "to change one's place of living." The move is generally from one country or region to another; migrations are made by humans, birds, fish, and insects. Monarch butterflies, for example, migrate from their summer home in southern Canada to a winter range in central Mexico; many birds follow a similar pattern of behavior, often following similar routes, called *flyways*. Some fish migrate from one area of water to another, or, as salmon do, from freshwater to saltwater and back again. At many times over the centuries and millennia, large numbers of humans have migrated. Sometimes the migrations have been brought about because people were forced away, at other times because they were seeking a better life. Migrant workers move for yet another reason. Their moves are often cyclical: They move according to where there is work, such as crops to harvest, and often return to the same locations the following year. *Emigrate* and *immigrate* are two related words that are sometimes confused. They describe the permanent moves of people. *Emigrate* refers to the departure point, the place from which the person is exiting, and *immigrate* considers the place to which the person is coming. Other related words include *emigrant, immigrant,* and *émigré,* one who left a native country, especially for political reasons. Were your ancestors immigrants at one time? From what country did they emigrate?

Literature Links

Lawrence, J. (Illustrator). (1995). *The great migration: An American story.* New York: Harper Trophy. Chronicles the African American migration north in the early 20th century through a sequence of 60 paintings and accompanying captions.

Tan, S. (2007). *The arrival.* New York: Levine. A sophisticated wordless picture book that describes a man's departure from his wife and child and his travels to a new country across the ocean.

SORT 16. Vowel Alternations with Predictable Spelling Changes

Sorting by Pattern

Vowel Spelling Change	No Vowel Spelling Change
exclaim/exclamation	analyze/analysis*
explain/explanation	emphasize/emphasis
proclaim/proclamation	synthesize/synthesis
clarify/clarification	
justify/justification	
qualify/qualification	
deceive/deception	
perceive/perception	
receive/reception	

Considerations: The purpose of this sort is to familiarize students with some of the predictable spelling changes that can occur with vowel alternations. After discussing any unfamiliar words, introduce the sort by informing students that just as consonant alternations sometimes entail a predictable spelling change, some vowel alternations do also. Ask students to work with partners to categorize pairs of words under the header categories: vowel spelling change and no vowel spelling change. Explain that there may also be consonant spelling changes in some of the words, but that their focus is to be on the vowel pattern. Suggest that they underline or highlight letters that are involved in the spelling changes. When they are finished, discuss their results. Although all of the words involve vowel alternations, there is no spelling change for six of the words. Those that do change tend to do so in predictable ways: If you know how to spell one word in the family, you will likely be able to spell others. If students think about the words as four word families, each with common characteristics, learning to spell the words will be easier. Before ending the session, discuss any unfamiliar words.

> *Note.* Although spelling is consistent in *analyze* and *analysis*, because the vowel is *y* rather than *i*, students may choose to classify the words as oddballs.

Talking Points

- Some vowel alternations require a spelling change; however, these tend to be predictable, as in *deceive, perceive, receive* and *deception, perception, reception.*

Did You Know? Syn- is a prefix that means "like" or "together." It combines with roots of Greek origin, and when the combining root begins with *b, m,* or *p,* an alternative spelling for the prefix is used: *sym-,* as in *symbol, symmetry,* or *symphony.* **Synthesis** and *synthesize,* from the sort, literally mean "put together" (*thesis,* meaning "to put," + *syn-,* meaning "together"). Similarly, *synonym* means "like name" (*syn-,* meaning "like," + *-onym,* meaning "name"), and *synergy* means "work together" (*-ergy,* meaning "to work," + *syn-,* meaning "together"). Although *synthetic,* a related word, has been used for more than 300 years, the sense of something made artificially through a chemical process was not recorded until 1874. A few words carry the meaning of "synthetic" in the prefix, as, for example, *synfuel.*

SORT 17. Syllable Stress and Vowel Alternations

Sorting by Sound	
No Stress Change	Stress Change
(de**rive**)/de**riv**ative	a**cad**emy/**ac**ademic
(**labor**)/**lab**oratory	**com**edy/co**me**dian
se**rene**/se**ren**ity	(de**rive**)/deri**va**tion
	di**plo**macy/diplo**mat**ic
	indicate/in**dic**ative
	(**labor**)/la**bor**ious
	major/ma**jor**ity
	op**pose**/**op**posite
	per**spire**/perspi**ra**tion
	politics/po**lit**ical

Considerations: This sort focuses on syllable stress with vowel alternations. Clarify the meanings of any unfamiliar words, and then ask students to pair related words. Explain to them that they will be sorting the words according to whether there is a change in stress from the base word to the derived word. In the Sort 17 answer key, *labor* and *derive* are shown in parentheses because the cards for these words will need to be used twice, as there are two derived words for each; students can simply move them from one category to another as the words are discussed. When they are finished sorting, discuss the vowel alternations. There are many, as most of the words involve more than one alternation, and the *academy/academic* pair involves three: *academic/academy, academy/academic,* and *academic/academy!* Using red, green, and blue crayons or markers, you might invite students to identify an alternation and underline or circle the involved letter in each word. Color coding will allow long- to short-vowel, long-vowel to schwa, and short-vowel to schwa alternations to be marked in different colors. Finding all of the changes should not be an aim; awareness that multiple alternations can occur within a word should be. (The Sort 17 answer key shows sample responses.) Because a primary purpose of this sort is to increase awareness, repeated sorting of the words by students is unnecessary.

Talking Points

- Some words include multiple vowel alternations, as in *academy/academic*.

Did You Know? Derivational constancy (this spelling phase) is a period of spelling development that focuses on derived words, or words that come from the same source. We often associate the word *source* with rivers, as the place where they begin. The words **derive, derivation,** and **derivative** are actually developed from the Latin word *derivare,* which literally means to "draw off stream" (*de-,* meaning to "draw off," + *rivare,* meaning "stream"); in other words, something that is derived comes from a flowing or common source. Words that stem from the same word are said to *derive* from that word. They are *derivatives* of the word, as *labor, laborious,* and *laboratory* have all derived from the Latin word *labor;* they are derivatives of the word. *Rivulet* ("small stream") and *rival* ("one using the same stream as another") share *derive's* ancestry.

SORT 18. Consonant, Vowel, and Stress Changes with *c*

Sorting by Sound and Pattern (Consonant Alternations)

/k/ → /s/	/s/ → /sh/
authentic/authenticity	commerce/commercial
eccentric/eccentricity	finance/financial
public/publicity	office/official
	prejudice/prejudicial
critic/criticize	
italic/italicize	audacity/audacious
	ferocity/ferocious
	tenacity/tenacious

Considerations: This particular sort is reserved for the end of this section, because it involves stress changes and both vowel and consonant alternations. Also, the several suffixes involved will segue to some final work with suffixes and prefixes in the next section. The sort is intended to expand students' concept of a consonant alternation. Previous sorts with consonant changes dealt with the /shən/ ending, whereas this sort involves suffixes *-ize, -ity, -ial,* and *-ious.* Although the categories target alternations with *c,* addition of the suffix also brings about vowel and/or stress changes. Begin by discussing any unfamiliar words. Then ask students to pair related words. (Reserve the headers for later.) Once this is completed, give them an opportunity to review the paired list, speculate on the focus of the sort, and talk about their ideas with partners before sharing them with the whole group. Then explain that this set of words involves more consonant alternations, and ask students to sort the words in a way that will highlight them. Let students know that there may be more than one way to group the words. When they are finished, discuss their results; accept any groupings that are reasonably justified. Then guide students to notice that some of the words alter from /k/ to /s/ and others from /s/ to /sh/, and that the words under each type of consonant alternation may be grouped by families. Discuss each family of words and any spelling consistencies. As an extension, you might ask students to look for examples of vowel and stress changes in the sort.

Talking Points

- Other suffixes besides *-ion* can lead to consonant alternations; thinking of a related word can help with their spellings, as with *critic/criticize, public/publicity,* and others.
- Adding a suffix can cause vowel and stress changes, as well as consonant alternations, as in *office/official.*

Did You Know? In ancient Rome, the word for **office** originally meant "a kind or helpful act." It then became synonymous with *job,* and in the 1300s Chaucer used it in his *Canterbury Tales* in the sense we commonly associate it with today: a place of work. A related word, *officious,* when borrowed into English was used to describe someone eager to help or serve. However, as sometimes happens, it began taking on a negative connotation, describing the volunteering and involvement of a person whose services were neither asked for nor needed. In time, this negative meaning of "meddling" became the primary meaning. The original meaning is still recorded in dictionaries, but it is identified as *archaic,* which means that its use is rare. So though someday you may want to work as an official in an office, it probably would be best to avoid being officious.

SORT 13 Long- to Short-Vowel Changes

Long Vowel		Short Vowel
cave	cavity	division
revision	humanity	provide
crime	typical	athletic
assumption	volcanic	decide
volcano	divide	introduction
athlete	type	revise
introduce	provision	criminal
decision	humane	assume

Long-Vowel to Schwa Changes

Long Vowel		Schwa
invite	invitation	deprivation
ignorant	organize	combine
admiration	define	hesitant
compete	narrate	society
relate	combination	definition
hesitate	social	admire
narrative	deprive	organization
competition	relative	ignore

Long- and Short-Vowel Changes with Schwa

Long Vowel	Schwa	Short Vowel	Schwa
migrate	migratory		symbol
symbolic	distribute		president
declaration	mandate		prohibit
mobile	habitual		contribution
distribution	preside		inclination
habit	mandatory		declare
contribute	reside		prohibition
resident	incline		mobility

Spelling Change		No Spelling Change
exclaim	exclamation	deceive
reception	emphasis	qualify
justify	perception	synthesize
analyze	clarification	proclamation
qualification	explain	receive
proclaim	synthesis	clarify
emphasize	justification	deception
perceive	analysis	explanation

No Stress Change		Stress Change
derive	derivative	comedian
comedy	academic	academy
diplomacy	perspiration	political
indicate	majority	opposite
serene	labor	perspire
laborious	indicative	politics
oppose	diplomatic	laboratory
derivation	major	serenity

/k/ → /s/		/s/ → /sh/
authentic	authenticity	office
official	tenacity	commercial
prejudicial	critic	eccentric
tenacious	financial	ferocity
finance	audacious	public
publicity	criticize	ferocious
audacity	italic	prejudice
eccentricity	commerce	italicize

A Further Look at Suffixes and Prefixes
(DSA Features S and T)

This final section related to the study of patterns and meaning extends students' understanding of suffixes by examining several new ones: *-able* and *-ible*, *-ant* and *-ance*, as well as *-ent* and *-ence*, and provides a deeper investigation of *-ity* as a suffix (see Sort 18). Prefixes are also returned to in the context of *assimilated* or absorbed prefixes. Prefixes of this type lose the spellings we typically associate with them and take on new, sometimes unrecognizable spellings as they are absorbed into the letters that follow. Consider for example, the prefixes *in-* and *sub-* in *inactive* and *subway*, compared with their spelling in *illiterate* and *supplanted*. This final study is especially important because the remainder of this chapter deals with Greek and Latin roots, which often have several affixes attached to form longer, lower-frequency words.

SORT 19. Examining Suffixes (*-able* and *-ible*)

Sorting by Pattern and Meaning

-able	*-ible*	Oddball
acceptable	**edible**	?
avoidable	audible	digestible
comfortable	compatible	
dependable	feasible	
fashionable	horrible	
favorable	incredible	
laughable	indelible	
perishable	irascible	
predictable	plausible	
preferable		
questionable		
reasonable		
remarkable		

Considerations: Although this sort may be introduced as a structured sort with strong teacher guidance, you might try the following alternative: Introduce the sort with a soft (ungraded) quiz. Ask students to spell five to seven of the words. Be sure to include both *-able* and *-ible* words, but avoid the oddball for this purpose. After the dictation, distribute the template of words, including the headers. Students can use this to check their performance on the quiz. They are likely to have confused suffixes and misspelled some of the words. Ask them to sort the words under the headers and generate a hypothesis to explain when they should use the *-ible* suffix and when *-able*. Encourage them to team up with a partner or two, and make it clear that their theory needs to work with every word in a given category. Any problem words should be placed as oddballs. Let them know that after a reasonable time, they will have a chance to test their theory. As students work with the words, circulate and prompt their thinking. After adequate time, you might ask a volunteering team to explain their theory for when to use which suffix. Expand and clarify their thinking as needed. Once students understand the idea that *-able* usually attaches to base words and *-ible* to roots that cannot stand alone, give them an opportunity to write down the spelling of a transfer word, letting them know that your concern is with the suffix and not whether they can spell the entire word right. Alternatively, you might let each team collectively determine a spelling for the word. *Mandible* and *ostensible* are two possible transfer words, as are other -*ible* words not included in the sort. Discuss each word's spelling and strategies used to determine the correct suffix.

Talking Points

• Base words usually require -*able* and roots -*ible*, as in *favorable* and *feasible*.

Did You Know? Let's consider two of the -*ible* words: *irascible* and *horrible*. **Irascible** means "easily angered" and derives from the Latin word for *anger*. Other related words are *ire* and *irate*. The former refers to "anger," and the latter to being "extremely angry or enraged." **Horrible** was borrowed from the Latin word meaning "to bristle with fear, shudder." It is related to *horror, horrid, horrific, horrify, horrendous,* and *abhor,* which means to "regard something with loathing," to "shun" it (*ab-,* meaning "away," + *hor,* meaning "shudder"). If you've ever felt goosebumps or had your hair stand on end from fear, you've experienced *horipilation,* another member of this family.

SORT 20. Taking a Closer Look (-*able*)

Sorting by Pattern and Meaning

Base + -*able*	*e*-Drop + -*able*	Oddball
agreeable	**valuable**	**?**
accountable	admirable	amiable
affordable	adorable	
commendable	advisable	
considerable	believable	
knowledgeable	comparable	
manageable	debatable	
noticeable	desirable	
rechargeable	disposable	
replaceable	excusable	
	recognizable	
	reusable	

Considerations: As with the previous sort, begin with a soft quiz. Ask students to spell the following words: *considerable, advisable, knowledgeable, manageable, believable, affordable,* and *reusable.* Then distribute the template of words, and allow time for students to check their spellings. Because they are likely to have misspelled some of the words, tell them that adding -*able* to base words can be confusing—but, as they will discover, clues in the words themselves can help with the spelling. Discuss any unfamiliar words, and then ask the group to categorize the words under the appropriate headers. When they are finished, discuss each category, and be sure to talk about the spelling of the base word. This is especially important for a word such as *amiable,* which has no base word but is spelled with -*able* to avoid the situation of double *i*'s that would otherwise result (*amiible*). Point out the five words that retain the final -*e,* and ask students to consider why this is the case when normally the final -*e* is dropped. Provide time for them to discuss the possibilities with partners and to share their ideas. If it is not mentioned, point out that in all of the words that kept the *e,* a *c* or *g* immediately precedes it. If the *e* was dropped, the *a* in -*able* would cause the soft sound of *c* or *g* to become hard. (For more on hard and soft *c* and *g,* see Sort 37 of Chapter 4.)

Talking Points

- Base words drop the final *-e* before the *-able* suffix is added, unless this will cause a soft *c* or *g* sound to be hardened; in this case, the *e* is kept, as in *knowledgeable* and *noticeable*.

Did You Know? **Amiable,** which means "friendly, good-natured," stems from *amicus,* the Latin word for "friend." Because of its Latin origins, we find words from other languages that also derived from *amicus,* with similar meanings and spellings. For example, *friend* in French is *ami,* in Italian it is *amico,* and in Portuguese and Spanish it is *amigo.* These words are examples of *cognates,* or words related across languages (see Sort 58). There are many cognates. Other English words related to *amiable* include *amicable,* which means "showing good will, friendliness"; *amity,* which means "peaceful relations" (such as between countries); and the legal term *amicus curiae,* which literally means "friend of the court" and refers to a person who is asked to provide expertise on a topic affecting a court case but is not actually involved in the case itself. As a friendly end note to this word story, consider the following anonymous quote: "The best vitamin for making friends is B-1." Perhaps the person was thinking of the importance of being amiable as one of the ingredients.

SORT 21. Examining Suffixes (*-ant, -ance, -ent, -ence*)

Sorting by Pattern and Meaning

-ant	*-ance*	*-ent*	*-ence*
attendant	**attendance**	**different**	**difference**
important	importance	adolescent	adolescence
reluctant	reluctance	competent	competence
tolerant	tolerance	convenient	convenience
		independent	independence
		innocent	innocence
		negligent	negligence
		obedient	obedience

Considerations: By now, students have considerable experience working with longer, more complex, and lower-frequency words. If they need a slower entry into the concepts of this sort, you might introduce the *-ant/-ance* words first and then add the others. Otherwise, introduce the sort by dictating three to five words for the students to spell. Some students will likely misspell one or more of the endings. Explain that words with /ənt/ and /əns/ can be confusing to spell, because there is more than one way to represent the ending. This sort will provide some clues for choosing the correct ending. Distribute the template of words, and discuss any unfamiliar words. Be sure students understand the multiple meanings of *tolerance:* "ability to put up with pain" and "respect for the beliefs and practices of others." (For ideas on teaching the latter, see *www.tolerance.org.* The site offers a free magazine and other excellent materials for teachers.) Ask students to pair related words—*attendant/attendance, different/difference,* and so forth. Then ask them to examine the pairs for clues and share their observations. Words with *-ant* also use *-ance,* and words with *-ent* use *-ence.* This is an important observation and a good talking point.

Talking Points

- When trying to spell words ending in /ənt/ and /əns/, if you know how to spell one of the words, you can spell the other; thus *tolerant* becomes *tolerance*, not *tolerence*.

Did You Know? **Adolescent** and **adolescence** are both somewhat difficult words to spell, due to their homophonic final syllables—which the sounds suggest could be spelled *-scent*, *-sent*, or *-cent* and *-scence*, *-sense*, or *-cents*. Although spellings of *adolesent* and *adolecents* might seem easier than the correct spellings, they completely obscure the meaning connection. Although *adolescent* has nothing to do with a sense of smell, it has everything to do with becoming an adult. *Adolescent* and *adult* come from the same Latin word, just different forms of it. So the one literally means "growing up," whereas the other means "grown up." Numerous other words carry this sense of "growing." We can tell this by their *-escence* endings: for example, *convalescence*, which means "growing with strength," and *senescence*, which means "growing old." (See Sort 53 for other *-sen* words.)

SORT 22. Taking a Closer Look (-ant, -ance, -ent, -ence)

Sorting by Pattern and Meaning

-ant	-ance	-ent	-ence	Oddball
relevant	**relevance**	**excellent**	**excellence**	?
abundant	abundance	diligent	diligence	efficiency
assistant	assistance	efficient	equivalence	relevancy
significant	significance	equivalent	insistence	
		insistent	persistence	
		persistent	prominence	
		prominent		

Considerations: This sort provides further exposure to *-ant*, *-ance*, *-ent*, and *-ence*, and introduces students to a third member of these word families—namely, *-ancy* and *-ency*. In some cases all three forms exist, as in *relevant*, *relevance*, and *relevancy* and *equivalent*, *equivalence*, and *equivalency*. In others, just two exist; for example, there is no such word as *efficience*, just *efficient* and *efficiency*. There are many words with these endings; as students collect them in their notebooks and encounter them in their reading, they may realize that the *e*-family is more common. This realization is important in developing a best-guess strategy: If you don't know the spelling and can't find out, use *-ent*, *-ence*, or *-ency*. Before ending the session, be sure students clearly understand what the words mean.

Talking Points

- If the related word spelling is *-ent* or *-ence*, use *-ency*; if the spelling is *-ant* or *-ance*, use *-ancy*; keep in mind that many words do not include all three forms.

Did You Know? The original meaning of *sign* was "mark" or "indication"; we see this meaning connection carried into the word **significant** when we consider that something significant shows signs or indications of being important or meaningful. *Sign* has served as a building block for many other words. What words related to *sign* can you brainstorm, and what meaning connection can you uncover? (There are many possibilities, including the following: *signal*, *signage*, *signature*, *signet*, *assignment*, *consignment*, *countersign*, *cosign*, *designee*, *insignia*, *sign language*, and *resignation*.)

SORT 23. Examining Suffixes (-*ity*)

Sorting by Pattern and Meaning

No Change	e-Drop	Spelling Change
Base + -*ity*	e-Drop + -*ity*	-*ble* → *bil* + -*ity*
popular/popularity	**creative/creativity**	**available/availability**
familiar/familiarity	mature/maturity	eligible/eligibility
original/originality	sensitive/sensitivity	possible/possibility
peculiar/peculiarity		responsible/responsibility
personal/personality		

Considerations: This sort focuses on three ways to add -*ity* to base words: with no change, with *e*-drop, and with a spelling change. Ask students to begin by pairing base words with their derived forms. Then, with the headers as guides, tell them to work in pairs to categorize the pairs of words. As you discuss the results, ask students to look carefully at words in the spelling change category to determine what the change is. If needed, there are numerous additional examples, such as *accountable/accountability*, *adaptable/adaptability*, *capable/capability*, and *sustainable/sustainability*.

Talking Points

- When -*ity* is added to base words ending in -*ble*, the spelling changes to *bil* before the ending is added: *responsible/responsibility*.

Did You Know? In ancient Athens and other Greek cities, once a year citizens gathered in the marketplace for a **popular** vote. The focus of the meeting was to determine who, if anyone, should be banished from the city in order to improve it. Though the banishment was not permanent, the act was still one of disgrace. Each voter was given an *ostrakon*, a shell or pottery shard, as a ballot and asked to write the name of a person on it. If 6,000 or more votes were cast and the majority of them listed the same man, that person was cast out, or *ostracized*. Common use of the word today is no longer literal; instead of being banished, a person who is ostracized by others is likely to be excluded from social activities.

SORT 24. Examining Assimilated Prefixes (*in-*)

Sorting by Pattern

Not			
in-	*il-*	*im-*	*ir-*
inexpensive	**illegal**	**immature**	**irregular**
inappropriate	illegible	immeasurable	irrational
inconvenient	illiterate	immobile	irrefutable
indecisive	illogical	immortal	irrelevant
indefinite		immovable	irresistible
indescribable			irresponsible
indispensable			
inequality			
inexperienced			

Considerations: This is the first of two sorts on *assimilated prefixes*. As noted at the onset of this section, these are prefixes that are absorbed into the word or root to which they attach. What does this mean for reading and spelling? The altered spelling of the prefix, including the double consonants that usually result, obscures the identity of the prefix; this makes it difficult for readers and writers to understand and spell such words, especially when the prefix is attached to a root. Because roots and prefixes abound in the next section, in order to help students better understand assimilated prefixes, they are addressed here and in Sort 25 in the context of affixation to base words, which is more straightforward. Two awarenesses can make it easier for readers and writers to interpret assimilated prefixes. First, being familiar with regular suffixes helps students understand the range of possibilities for interpreting the prefix. Second, being skeptical of words that include a double consonant toward the beginning of the word helps, especially if some of the initial letters in the word are those of a known prefix. Take the word *surrender,* for example. The double consonants and *su-* initial letters suggest that the prefix *sub-* might be involved. Indeed, the word does include the prefix *sub-*, plus the root *render,* and literally means to "deliver under."

Introduce the words as a pattern sort, and ask students to use the headers as guides for sorting. When the sorts are completed, discuss the meaning of the words by applying "not" to the base word; for instance, *immeasurable* means "not measurable" or "you can't measure it." The same assimilations sometimes carry the other meaning of *in-*: "into," as in *immigrate.*

Talking Points

- The prefix *in-*, meaning "not," can also be spelled *il-* (illegal), *im-* (immortal), or *ir-* (irregular).

Did You Know? **Immature** is made up of *im-* (an assimilation of the prefix *in-*, here meaning "not" rather than "into") plus *mature* (which means "fully grown or developed"). Apples on a tree may be immature and not ready for picking; a person's behavior can be immature regardless of age; and animals and plants that are still growing and developing are also considered immature. Over time, different words have evolved to designate a still-developing plant or animal: for example, *sapling* for a young tree, and *seedling* for a young plant grown from a *seed*. Although the same word may be used to describe several different immature animals—such as *joey* for kangaroos, koalas, wallabies, and opossums—there tend to be different names for the young of different animals. For instance, young alligators are called *hatchlings*; young dogs are called *pups*, as are the young of bats; young bears and tigers are *cubs*; young cats are *kittens*, whereas young foxes, beavers, and ferrets are *kits*; young hares are *leverets*; young spiders are *spiderlings*; and young fish are *fry*. Young horses are *foals*, and pigs are *piglets*; young swans are *cygnets*, young turkeys are *poults*, and young pigeons are *squabs*. There are also *lambs, fawns, calves, ducklings, goslings,* and *tadpoles*; and, of course, among others, *infants* for monkeys, *babies* for apes, and *kids* for goats. What other words describe immature plants or animals?

SORT 25. Examining Assimilated Prefixes (*ad-, com-, ex-, ob-, sub-*)

Sorting by Pattern and Meaning

Toward	With	Out	To/Against	Under
ad-	*com-*	*ex-*	*ob-*	*sub-*
adjoin	**compliant**	**exchange**	**obligation**	**submarine**
accompany	colleague	emerge	oppress	subdivision
affix	commotion	enumerate		suffix
allure	connote			suppliant
annotate	cooperate			surreal
appointment	correspond			
assure				
attempt				

Considerations: This sort extends students' knowledge of prefix assimilation. It is not so important for students to understand the specific meaning of the individual prefixes and bases as it is important that they begin to recognize the "look" of various types of assimilated prefixes. For that reason, although this list is not all-inclusive, a wide variety of assimilations has been included for each prefix. Discuss the assimilations and word meanings. Also, for a few of the words with obvious connections, talk about the meaning of the prefix as it relates to the base word, as with *adjoin* (*ad-* meaning "to" + *join* = "join to"); *affix* (*ad-* meaning "to" + *fix* = "fix to," "attach"); *compliant* (*com-* meaning "with" + *pliant* = "flexible with"); *enumerate* (*ex-* meaning "out" + *numerate* = "number out"); and *subdivision* (*sub-* meaning "below" + *division* = "division below")—namely, not the main division, such as a town, but a smaller part. In the case of *ob-*, draw students' attention to the fact that the prefix has multiple meanings, two of which are nearly opposites, as in *obligation* (*ob-* meaning "to" + *ligation* = "bind to") and *oppress* (*ob-* meaning "against" + *press* = "press against"). Sentence context can help in determining which meaning to apply.

Talking Points

- The prefixes *ad-, com-, ex-, ob-,* and *sub-* assimilate to base words and roots, often resulting in double letters and changed spellings, as in *appoint, commission,* and *effort.*

Did You Know? **Accompany** means "to go with a companion." *Companion* derives from the Latin *com-,* "together," and *panin,* "bread." A companion is literally someone with whom you share bread. It is interesting to consider that *company,* which carries the same meaning connections, is in the literal sense a business made up of individuals who have the kind of close relationship that encourages them to sit down together to share their bread.

-*able*		-*ible*
acceptable	edible	remarkable
predictable	dependable	incredible
fashionable	indelible	questionable
compatible	avoidable	horrible
laughable	digestible	preferable
plausible	reasonable	favorable
comfortable	irascible	audible
feasible	perishable	?

SORT 20 Taking a Closer Look (-*able*)

Base + *-able*		e-Drop + *-able*
agreeable	valuable	disposable
comparable	advisable	affordable
noticeable	recognizable	debatable
adorable	considerable	reusable
rechargeable	excusable	knowledgeable
accountable	desirable	admirable
believable	replaceable	amiable
manageable	commendable	?

-ant	*-ance*	*-ent*	*-ence*

attendant	attendance	different
difference	tolerance	independent
convenient	innocence	reluctance
adolescent	negligent	competent
negligence	important	convenience
tolerant	adolescence	obedience
innocent	competence	reluctant
importance	obedient	independence

SORT 22

Taking a Closer Look (-*ant*, -*ance*, -*ent*, -*ence*)

-*ant*	-*ance*	-*ent*	-*ence*

relevant	relevance	excellent	
excellence	prominence	insistent	
diligent	efficient	significance	
abundant	insistence	abundance	
prominent	assistant	equivalence	
equivalent	efficiency	persistence	
diligence	persistent	assistance	
significant	relevancy	?	

SORT 23 Examining Suffixes (-*ity*)

No Change	*e*-Drop	Spelling Change
popular	popularity	creative
creativity	available	availability
familiar	personality	mature
originality	responsible	familiarity
possible	sensitivity	eligibility
peculiarity	eligible	peculiar
possibility	original	sensitive
maturity	responsibility	personal

in-	*il-*	*im-*	*ir-*

inexpensive	illegal	immature
irregular	immeasurable	irrelevant
indescribable	irrefutable	inappropriate
immortal	indispensable	illogical
indecisive	irresponsible	illegible
irrational	indefinite	irresistible
inequality	immobile	inexperienced
illiterate	inconvenient	immovable

Examining Assimilated Prefixes (*ad-, com-, ex-, ob-, sub-*)

ad-	com-	ex-	ob-	sub-

adjoin	compliant	exchange
obligation	submarine	colleague
suffix	assure	affix
annotate	commotion	enumerate
emerge	subdivision	appointment
connote	allure	suppliant
surreal	oppress	correspond
accompany	cooperate	attempt

Greek and Latin Word Elements

This final section of word study for derivational constancy spellers explores words largely through the lens of meaning. By now, students should have a firm grasp of sound–pattern associations (*phonics*); realize how words divide into syllables (*syllabication*); and understand the structure of compounds, base words, and various prefixes and suffixes and how they work together (*morphology*). They have also explored meaning through such features as homophones and homographs. When it comes to understanding the meanings of words, particularly the sophisticated vocabulary of the academic language found in middle school and high school texts, learners will benefit from understanding the Greek and Latin roots (along with prefixes and suffixes) that make up the words. By understanding individual units of meaning, called *morphemes,* and considering them in relation to other meaning chunks in the word, readers can comprehend many otherwise unfamiliar words. Take, for example, the longest word in any English dictionary. Despite its rather intimidating 45-letter length, most readers of this book will probably be able to approximate a meaning for the word by considering one meaning chunk at a time. In fact, a seventh-grade teacher found her students quite up to the challenge after a brief introduction to the study of roots. The Wordplay Web Site (*www.fun-with-words.com*) reports that the word is included in several dictionaries; it was coined in the 1930s by the president of the National Puzzlers' League. Why? Just to create a new "longest" word. So whether you think of this as a "little-engine-that-could" sort of word or more simply a chunking challenge, give it a try. When finished, check the answer in the box on the next page.

What does the following word mean?

pneumonoultramicroscopicsilicovolcanoconiosis

This section on word roots includes 32 sorts. It begins with an exploration of common Greek and Latin prefixes and a study of basic Greek roots, also known as *combining forms*. These elements are examined first because words generated from them tend to be semantically more transparent, and because many of the words occur with relative frequency beginning in the upper elementary grades and continuing through middle school and high school. Common Latin roots are then introduced, with a thorough look at the way meaning changes when prefixes are combined with the root. Following the study of common Greek and Latin roots, the focus shifts to less common roots. In these sorts, the roots may be all Greek, all Latin, or a combination of the two. Some sorts include two different roots with the same meaning. Because English includes borrowings from both Greek and Latin, we sometimes have roots for the same concept from each language. For example, we have *pod*, which comes from Greek, meaning "foot" (as in *tripod, gastropod, podium*), but we also have *ped* from Latin, which also means "foot" (as in *pedal, pedestrian, pedestal*). At times this has the potential to confuse readers, because the same spelling used for a root in one language may be used for a root with an entirely different meaning in the other language—*ped* in Latin means "foot," but in Greek means "child," as in *pediatrics*. The context of the sentence and the combining parts used with the word can help readers to determine the appropriate meaning.

Word elements for the 32 sorts in this section were selected and sequenced on the bases of utility or frequency, clarity of meaning, combinability with other word elements, interest, and topic. Each sort focuses on a theme, and the roots chosen for the sort reflect that particular theme. Examples of themes include numbers, size and amount, senses, actions, body parts, ruling and governing, and others. In most cases, I have refrained from including words with as-yet-unstudied roots. Although this was not always possible, it does help students to focus on a more limited number of new word parts, and it provides opportunity to review roots when students encounter words in later studies with roots they already know. Despite the progression laid out for the sorts in this section, most can be used flexibly to

> It is a lung disease caused by breathing
> in particles of volcanic dust.

fit with a particular content area or literature study. If they are going to be used out of order, I suggest that you first help students to build a foundation of knowledge through Sorts 26, 27, 29, 31, and 32, then identify particular themed sorts of interest for study. As part of your selection process, after building students' initial foundation knowledge, you might consider the 14 roots shown in Table 1.3 that can unlock the meanings of some 100,000 words (Brown, 1947). As students study Greek and Latin word elements, they will undoubtedly encounter words with which they are not familiar. Learning to unravel the meanings of such words and expanding vocabulary knowledge are really what this section is all about, with the hope that along the way, students will learn to savor the language as well.

Because the focus for studying Greek and Latin word elements is on building vocabulary, definitions and meaning connections replace the how-to information of earlier "Considerations" discussions. Also, instead of a separate "Talking Points" section for each sort, important information for students to understand and remember related to roots and their meanings is incorporated into the answer key for each sort.

The sorts can be introduced in various ways. One possibility is to ask students to categorize the words according to elements listed in the headers. Allow time for them to consider and talk about meaning connections among the words, as well as any unfamiliar words. If one aim is for them to try to determine the meanings of the various roots or prefixes, retain the headers until the discussion. Be sure that students have access to a good unabridged dictionary, so that they can investigate meanings and explore the etymologies of some of the words. Any unabridged dictionary will include etymological information, as well as definitions. Definitions in this section come from *The American Heritage College Dictionary* (4th ed., 2004), and from the larger *The American Heritage Dictionary of the English Language* (5th ed., 2011). If students are not already recording word study work in a notebook, this is an excellent time to start.

SORT 26. Greek and Latin Prefixes: Numbers (*mono-, bi-, tri-*)

One	Two	Three
mono-	*bi-*	*tri-*
monotone	**bicycle**	**triangle**
monolingual	biceps	triad
monolith	bicuspid	triathlon
monologue	biennial	trigonometry
monopoly	bifocals	trilogy
monorail	bimonthly	trio
monotonous	binary	triplets
	biweekly	triptych
		trivial

Considerations: This sort sets the stage for future discussions of word elements. The meaning of each word in the sort is made transparent by linking the meaning of the prefix to the meaning of the word root. This type of process can be applied to other sorts in this section, but **keep the idea sharing conversational;** it should not be a recitation of the meanings of prefixes and roots.

Ask students to categorize the words, using the headers as guides. Then suggest that they consider how the prefixes affect the meanings of the words in each category and share their ideas. They should realize some of the following connections, and you should draw others to their attention: *Monotone* means "one tone"—in other words, a tone with no variation; *monolingual* means "one language" (students may be familiar with *bilingual,* but not *monolingual*); a *monologue* is "a (long) speech by one person," whereas a dialogue involves two or more persons. You might ask students what they think *-logue* means. In *monopoly,* the prefix meaning "one" combines with a root that means "to sell." Whether in the game or in real life, a monopoly exists when a person or group has total control over selling or producing services and goods. A *monorail* is a system of transportation that relies on one rail instead of two. For a discussion of *monolith,* see "Did You Know?" for this sort.

Bicycle has a clear connection to *bi-* with its two wheels; *bifocals* are lenses that are corrected for two different types of seeing or focusing. *Bimonthly* and *biweekly* have multiple meanings that can be confusing; lexicographers urge writers to use the words to mean "happening every 2 months" or "2 weeks," respectively (not twice monthly or weekly; *semi-* is the prefix of choice for these meanings). *Bisect* means "cut into two parts." *Biceps* are muscles that attach in two places, so what must *triceps* be? *Bicuspids* are teeth with two sharp points, or cusps, located midway on each side of the mouth, top and bottom. *Biennial* stems from a root meaning "year," as does *annual*; it means "happening every other year" or "lasting for 2 years." *Binary* refers to something composed of two parts. For example, a binary number system uses just the numbers 0 and 1, rather than 0–9, as does our base-10 number system. Instead of counting 0, 1, 2, 3, 4, 5, . . . counting goes 0, 1, 10, 11, 100, 101, and so on.

The meaning connection to "three" is clear in *triangle, triplets,* and *trio,* but may not be in some of the words. A *triathlon* is an athletic competition that involves three events: swimming, bicycling, and running. *Trigonometry* is the study of triangles. A *triad* is a group of three (students may sometimes work in triads), and a *trilogy* is a group of three literary works that are united by a theme. (You might ask students if they have read any *trilogies.*) What about the word *triptych,* which may be unfamiliar to teachers and students? Invite students to guess possible meanings for the word before telling them "three folds." In ancient Rome, a triptych (**trĭp•**tĭk) was a hinged writing tablet with three leaves. It is also a piece of artwork consisting of three painted or carved panels that are hinged together. Most museums of art have examples on display. The last *tri-* word, *trivial,* stems from a word meaning "three roads" (*tri- + via*). Places where three roads met were sometimes very public. The "public" sense of the word evolved into "commonplace" and eventually to the modern meaning of something insignificant.

Did You Know? **Monolith** is derived from *mono-,* meaning "one," and *lith,* meaning "stone." It refers to a geological feature that is a single massive stone, as well as to something made of a large block of stone, such as a monument or sculpture. *Monolithic* rock formations are found on all of the continents, including Antarctica. *Trilithons* (trī•**lĭth•**ŏn), as the name suggests, have something to do with three stones. Trilithons, or *triliths,* are a type of prehistoric structure made of two large upright stones with a third placed across the top. The most famous trilithons are part of Stonehenge in England. The standing stones were placed in a circle more than 4,000 years ago, with an embankment and ditch surrounding the stones that is even older. Based on the circular design, archeologists believe that Stonehenge was used as a religious center and as an astronomical observatory.

SORT 27. Greek and Latin Prefixes: More Numbers (*quadr-, pent-, oct-, dec-, cent-*)

Four	Five	Eight	Ten	Hundred
quadr-	*pent-*	*oct-*	*dec-*	*cent-*
quadruple	**pentagon**	**octopus**	**decade**	**century**
quadrangle	pentad	octagon	decathlon	bicentennial
quadrant	pentathlon	octave	December	centenarian
quadruplets		octet	decimal	centigrade
		October	decimeter	centimeter
		octogenarian		percent

Considerations: Students may or may not make a connection between words with *quadr-* and words with *quart-* (not included in this sort), which have a related but different meaning. Words of the latter type (*quarter, quart, quarterly*) also have to do with the number four, but mean "one-fourth." A *pentad* is a group of five (providing opportunities for students to work in triads and pentads will help to reinforce the meanings of these two words). *Pentagon* is a shape with five sides and five angles, but when capitalized it refers to a building in which the U.S. Department of Defense is located. It takes its name from the shape of the building. A *pentathlon*, like the *triathlon* of the previous sort, is an athletic competition, in this case with five events. What, then, is a *decathlon*? What events make up each competition? An *octave* refers to a tone that is eight steps higher or lower than another tone, as well as to eight lines of poetry, and an *octet* usually refers to a group of eight singers. The *gen* in *octogenarian* means "ten times." If students apply their prior understanding of *-ian*, as well as knowledge of *gen* and *oct-*, they may deduce that an *octogenarian* is a person in his or her 80s (10 × 8 = 80). Then how old is a *centenarian*? Ask students what they think *bicentennial* means (happening every 200 years). See "Did You Know?" for discussions of *octopus, October,* and *December.*

Did You Know? **Octopuses** or **octopi** are marine mollusks with round, soft bodies and eight tentacles, often called "arms." A close look at the word *octopus* gives rise to a question: *Octo-* = "eight," but what about *pus*? Rather than meaning "arm," this root is a variation of the Greek root for "foot" (see "Considerations" for Sort 39), probably so called because the creature moves around on these, which is something we do not do with our arms.

You might be wondering: If *octo-* means "eight" and *dec-* means "ten," why is our tenth month called **October,** and why is **December,** with its meaning of "ten," used for the twelfth month? To understand how this came about, we must know more about the calendar. The first Roman calendar probably came into existence more than 2,700 years ago. At that time the year had 10 months, or 304 days. The calendar started with the spring equinox in March, ignoring 2 months of winter altogether, and a month went from one full moon to the next. The names of the months fit that early calendar, but some 700 years after the calendar was initiated, Julius Caesar, the famous Roman leader mentioned a few times in Chapter 4, hired an astronomer to identify ways to improve the calendar. Instead of a lunar-based calendar, the astronomer suggested one based on the sun. He allowed for leap year and moved the beginning of the year from March 1 to January 1. The calendar he devised is still the calendar we use today.

SORT 28. Greek and Latin Prefixes: Size and Amount (*semi-, poly-, multi-, micro-, mega-*)

Half, Partly	Many	Many	Small	Large
semi-	*poly-*	*multi-*	*micro-*	*mega-*
semisweet	**polysyllabic**	**multicultural**	**microphone**	**megaphone**
semicircle	polydactyl	multimedia	microbe	megabyte
semicolon	polygon	multinational	microchip	megalopolis
semifinals	polygraph	multiplication	microcosm	
semiskilled		multipurpose	microfilm	
semisolid			microscope	

Considerations: Most of the meaning connections for this sort are straightforward. *Polydactyl* is an unusual word. Though uncommon, *dactyl* is a word meaning "finger" or "toe"; it is derived from the Greek word for "finger." So *polydactyl* means "many-fingered" or "many-toed"; it refers to a person or animal having more than the usual number of fingers or toes. A *polygraph* is an instrument that can keep track of several bodily processes, such as blood pressure and breathing, at the same time. It is often used as a lie detector. A *microbe* is a microscopic organism. The word comes from *microscopic* and *bios* and literally means "small life." *Microcosm*, which comes from *micro-* and *cosm*, literally means "small world." A *megabyte* is a unit of computer memory equal to 1,000,000 bytes. So how much is a *byte?* It is the amount of computer memory it takes to store one character (the word *character* is composed of nine characters, so imagine how many characters there are in this book!). *Megalopolis* is discussed in the "Did You Know?" section for this sort.

Did You Know? Although the *mega-* in **megalopolis** stems from the same Greek word as the other listed words and means "large" or "great," its meaning is slightly different, referring to something of *abnormal* size or greatness. The root *-polis* means "city." When we combine it with *megal-*, we have "a city of abnormal size." A *megalopolis* is not a typical city. In fact, it is not an actual city at all; it is a "region made up of several large cities sufficiently close to be considered a single urban complex" (*The American Heritage Dictionary of the English Language*, 1996). In other words, people commute between the cities and may live in suburbs that are residential areas of more than one of the cities. For example, in the United States, the Boston to Washington, D.C., corridor is sometimes referred to as the "BosWash" megalopolis that includes the cities of Boston and Washington and also Hartford, Connecticut; New York City; Philadelphia, Pennsylvania; Baltimore, Maryland; and all of their surrounding areas, such as New Jersey, Delaware, and other areas. The biggest megalopolis is in Japan, but other parts of Asia, as well as Europe and Africa, also have megalopolises. By looking at a map, you might be able to tell where they are located.

SORT 29. Common Greek Elements (*auto-, bio-, geo-, graph, -meter/metr, therm*)

Self	Life	Earth	Write	Measure	Warm, Hot
auto-	*bio-*	*geo-*	*graph*	*-meter/metr*	*therm*
automatic	biology	geology	graphite	speedometer	thermostat
(autobiography)	antibiotics	geode	(autobiography)	barometer	(geothermal)
(autograph)	(autobiography)	(geography)	(autograph)	(geometry)	(thermometer)
automobile	biodegradable	(geometry)	(biography)	odometer	
	(biography)	(geothermal)	cartographer	(thermometer)	
	bionic		epigraph		
	biosphere		(geography)		
			homograph		

Considerations: Numerous words in this sort include elements from other words in the sort. For example, *autobiography* includes the prefixes *auto-* and *bio-* and the root *graph*. Such words are designated in the answer key by parentheses, and they are listed with each applicable word element. As you guide students through the sort, placement of these words into a particular category is not important; what is important is that students recognize that some of the words include multiple elements from the sort. Ask them to consider why all of this duplication exists. If they do not mention the possibility that the word elements are common and therefore found in lots of words, bring this to their attention. Encourage students to generate additional words for one of the roots; *graph*, in particular, is in many words, often as *-graphy*. Because *auto-* occurs at the beginning of words, a dictionary can easily be used to help generate words for that word element. With word roots this is more difficult, because roots often have prefixes and suffixes attached. Go over any unfamiliar words as you discuss meaning connections. You might invite students to speculate on the meaning of *automaton*. It derives from a word that means "self-acting" and refers to a robot. (See Chapter 4, Sort 21.) *Epigraph* and several words sometimes confused with it are discussed in the "Did You Know?" section.

Did You Know? The prefix *epi-* has several meanings, including "over," "around," "beside," "near," "after," and "on." For instance, the epicenter of an earthquake is on or at the center of the earthquake. There are several writing-related words with the prefix *epi-* that can be confusing: **epigraph** (included in this sort), *epigram*, *epithet*, and *epitaph*. *Epigraph* refers to the inscription on a statue and to a short saying at the beginning of a literary work related to the theme. *Epigrams* are short and often witty sayings. Samuel Taylor Coleridge, a poet, captured the meaning of *epigram* in the following epigram: "What is an epigram? A dwarfish whole; its body brevity, and wit its soul." Mark Twain often added a bit of humor to an epigram: "Cauliflower is nothing more than cabbage with a college education." An *epithet*, meaning literally "attributed to," is a term used to characterize a person or thing. Homer, an ancient Greek poet, for example, often called Hephaestus (the Greek name for Vulcan; see Sort 13) "the famous craftsman," and Poseidon, thought to be the god of water, earthquakes, and horses, "the earth-shaker." An *epitaph*, which literally means "on tomb," is an inscription on a tomb written in memory of someone buried there. Two examples follow. The first was written about the deceased Stanley Laurel, a famous English-born comedian who, with Oliver Hardy, was a Hollywood star between the 1930s and 1950s: "A master of comedy; his genius in the art of humour brought gladness to the world he loved." The second epitaph was written by Benjamin Franklin in anticipation of his death:

The body of Benjamin Franklin, Printer,
Like the covering of an old book
Its contents torn out and
Stript of its lettering and gilding
Lies here, food for worms;
Yet the work shall not be lost.
For it will (as he believed) appear once more
In a new and beautiful edition,
Corrected and amended by the author.

SORT 30. Common Greek and Latin Elements (*aud, phon, vis, -scope, tele-*)

Hear	Sound	See	See	Distance
aud	*phon*	*vis*	*-scope*	*tele-*
audience	**homophone**	**supervise**	**kaleidoscope**	**telegraph**
(audiovisual)	phonics	(audiovisual)	periscope	telecommunications
audition	phonograph	envision	stethoscope	telemarketing
auditorium	symphony	(television)	(telescope)	(telephone)
inaudible	(telephone)	visibility		(telescope)
		vista		telethon
				(television)

Considerations: Some students may be unfamiliar with the meaning of *phonograph,* a device on which "written sound" can be heard by means of a stylus and record or rotating disk. *Symphony* literally means "sound together"; a *vista* is a view, or "what you see"; and *kaleidoscope,* an apt name given the beautiful patterns created by the device, literally means "see beautiful." *Stethoscope,* a device used by a doctor to listen to a person's heart and lungs, quite literally means "see chest"; here viewing is used figuratively and refers to being able to take in information. A discussion of *television* and *telethon* follows.

Did You Know? The **television** was first revealed at the Chicago 1933 Century of Progress Exposition. How long do you suppose it was before the first TV dinner was created? Or before the first TV **telethon** was held? In *telethon,* the prefix *tele-* has been combined with a portion of *marathon,* which is a prolonged activity or event that usually involves endurance. *Telethon* first came into use in 1952, but before that there was *walkathon* (1932) and *talkathon* (1948). Since the early 1970s numerous *-thon* words have appeared: *bikeathon, hikeathon, readathon, singathon, workathon.* Words of this type with limited use have not yet made it into the dictionary and would be considered nonsense words. If you were going to coin a *-thon* word, what would it be?

SORT 31. Applying Prefix Knowledge to Common Latin Roots (*ject* and *tract*)

Throw	Draw, Pull
ject	*tract*
projector	**tractor**
abject	abstract
adjective	attract
conjecture	contraction
dejected	detract
eject	distracted
injection	extract
interject	intractable
objection	protracted
projectile	retraction
rejection	subtract
subjects	traction

Considerations: Prefixes play a critical role throughout the word studies in this section. Many of the words generated with a particular root involve no other word roots, just the addition of a prefix and/or suffix. Again and again, the same prefixes are attached to different roots. Although by now students have considerable experience affixing prefixes to base words, in this sort and the one that follows, attention turns to combining prefixes with word roots. By considering the meaning of the root and an attached prefix, students can approximate the meaning of an unfamiliar word. The table that follows illustrates this. It shows the word, the literal meaning of the prefix and root combined, and the actual meaning of the word. Because of the strong recurrence of these prefixes, take the time to discuss the meaning relationships, both literal and actual. Making comparisons across the two roots, which rely on many of the same prefixes, can help to make the connections clear. Invite students to think of sentence examples for the words; share and talk about these.

Begin by asking students to speculate on the literal meanings of *projector* and *tractor*. Explain that a projector is literally something that "throws forward" (in this case, light and an image), and a tractor is something that "pulls or draws." Ask what part of each word carries the meaning of "throw" or "pull." After talking about the roots, ask students to sort the word cards into two categories, using the headers as guides. Distribute copies of Appendix H, "Applying Prefix Knowledge to Common Latin Roots." Explain to students that you will be taking a close look at how prefixes affect the meaning of a root. Talk about the meaning of words in the sort categories that have prefixes. As you do so, ask students to add each word and its meaning to the table. (Although the literal or actual meaning listed in the following table may be used for recording, it will likely be more valuable to students to use a meaning that they articulate after discussing the word.) Continue the process for each word. If time is limited, continue the discussion at a later time. Appendix G, "Understanding Prefixes," may be helpful for this activity and other word studies in this section. After discussing information from the table, you might ask students to brainstorm additional words that could have been included but were not.

	ject *(throw)*			tract *(draw, pull)*	
Word	Literal meaning	*Actual meaning*	**Word**	Literal meaning	*Actual meaning*
abject	throw away, as in "outcast"	*wretched, contemptible*	**abstract**	draw away	*consider apart from*
adjective	throw to, as in "add to"	*added to (a noun)*	**attract***	pull to	*draw interest to*
conjecture*	throw together	*infer or guess*	**contraction***	draw together	*a pulling together*
dejected	throw down	*downcast*	**detract**	pull away	*divert attention, draw away*
—			**distracted**	draw apart	*diverted attention*
eject*	throw out	*force to leave*	**extract**	draw away from	*pull away, remove, derive*
injection	throw into	*something put in, as a shot*	**intractable**	not able to be pulled	*stubborn*
interject	throw between	*insert between*	—		
projectile	throw forth	*something that can be thrown*	**protracted**	draw forth	*drawn out*
rejection	throw back	*refusal*	**retraction**	draw back	*something taken back*
subjects	throw under	*persons under the power of another*	**subtract**	draw under	*take away*
—			**traction**	pull, draw	*act of pulling*

*Prefix is assimilated.

Did You Know? **Tractors,** as the name suggests, are vehicles used to pull. They come in various sizes suited to the job: from small garden tractors for mowing lawns and tilling gardens, to large tractors used in agriculture to plow fields, harvest crops, and pull heavy equipment. Work performed by the latter type of tractor was carried out by horses before the tractor's invention. In the mid-1800s, when horses pulled the farming machines, farmers would often boast about the strength of their horses. Horse pulling contests were held to test the strength and stamina of the animals. A sled was attached to the horse, and weight was added to see if the horse could pull it. If the horse moved the load, more weight was added. Sometimes the pulling was done by teams of horses. Although it has been suggested that this event gave rise to the term *horsepower,* the word actually was coined by James Watt, an inventor. Pulling events are still held, but now the boasting and comparing are done with tractors.

SORT 32. Applying Prefix Knowledge to More Common Latin Roots (*mis/mit, port*)

Send	Carry	
mis/mit	*port*	Oddball
mission	**portfolio**	**?**
admittance	comport	transatlantic
commission	deport	transit
dismiss	export	transplant
emissions	import	
intermittent	rapport	
missile	reporter	
omitted	supportive	
promise	transportation	
remittance		
submissive		
transmission		

Considerations: Like the previous sort, this one builds knowledge of meaning connections between specific prefixes and two word roots—in this case, *mis* or *mit* and *port*. In addition, students are introduced to *trans-*, a prefix that is used in two of the words. Discuss the meaning of *trans-* in relation to the words *transit, transplant,* and *transatlantic*; then talk about the two roots. The same process used in the previous sort can be used here. The time spent familiarizing students with prefixes and how they affect the meaning of roots will benefit them throughout their study of roots. Begin with *mission, missile,* and *portfolio,* which do not include prefixes, and talk about their meaning connection to the root, *mis/mit* or *port.* Students should understand that *mis* and *mit* are the same root but just have different spellings to fit different endings that may be attached to them. They may wonder about *rapport* and its prefix. This word, which is of French and Latin origins, actually reveals remnants of two prefixes (*re-* and *ad-*) plus the root *port.* As you discuss the words, watch for signs of carry-over from the previous sort. Are students able to suggest meanings for some of the prefixes? Are they able to use their knowledge to make sense of the word?

	mit/mis *(send)*			**port** *(carry)*	
Word	Literal meaning	*Actual meaning*	**Word**	Literal meaning	*Actual meaning*
admittance	send toward	*permission to enter*	—		
commission	send with	*persons allowed to perform certain duties*	**comport**	carry together	*behave oneself, agree with*
—			**deport**	carry away	*expel from a country; also, comport*
dismiss	send apart	*direct or allow to leave*	—		

Word	mit/mis *(send)* Literal meaning	*Actual meaning*	Word	port *(carry)* Literal meaning	*Actual meaning*
emissions*	send out	*substances released into the air*	**export**	carry out	*send out goods, cause an idea to spread*
—			**import**	carry in	*bring or carry in from an outside source*
intermittent	send between	*stopping and starting*	—		
omitted*	send away	*left out*	—		
promise	send forth	*a vow or pledge to do something*	—		
—			**rapport**	bring (carry) back toward	*relationship of mutual trust*
remittance	send back	*sending of money to someone at a distance*	**reporter**	carry back	*one who carries back and repeats to another*
submissive	send under	*inclined to yield to the will or power of another*	**supportive***	carry below	*give assistance to*
transmission	send across	*something sent from one place to another*	**transportation**	carry across	*means of carrying goods/ people from one place to another*

*Prefix is assimilated.

Did You Know? **Portmanteau** is another word that could be added to the *port* category. In one sense, it is a large suitcase with two compartments. This meaning is evident in the literal meaning of the roots of the word: *port* ("carry") and *manteau* ("cloak" or "coat"), which stem from French. However, in the latter half of the 19th century, Lewis Carroll (author of *Alice in Wonderland, Through the Looking Glass,* and other works) gave new meaning to *portmanteau* when he applied it to words. In *Through the Looking Glass,* Humpty Dumpty explains to Alice words from the poem "Jabberwocky." "Well, '*slithy*' means 'lithe and slimy.' . . . You see it's like a portmanteau—there are two meanings packed up into one word" (Carroll, 1971, p. 164). Additional examples from the poem include *chortle* (*chuckle* + *snort*), *mimsy* (*flimsy* + *miserable*), and *galumphing* (*gallop* + *triumphantly*). Other common examples of *portmanteau words* include *smog* (*smoke* + *fog*), *guesstimate* (*guess* + *estimate*), *Spanglish* (*Spanish* + *English*), and *infomercial* (*information* + *commercial*). Portmanteau words are *neologisms,* or new words. They are sometimes called *frankenwords,* which is itself a portmanteau word, composed of *Frankenstein* (named after the monster Frankenstein) + *words.* Of what do you think the Thanksgiving dish *turducken* might be made? Do you know of other portmanteau words?

SORT 33. Latin Roots: Senses (*dict, spect/spic, spir, tact/tag/tang*)

Speak	Look	Breathe	Touch
dict	*spect/spic*	*spir*	*tact/tag/tang*
contradict	**spectator**	**spirited**	**contact**
dictate	aspect	aspiration	contagious
dictator	inspector	conspire	tactful
dictionary	perspective	expire	tactile
edict	perspicacious	inspiration	tangent
	spectacle	respiratory	tangible
	specter		

Considerations: After the words have been categorized by root, discuss the meaning connections of several words. An *edict* ("speak out") is a proclamation or command issued by an authority and often enforceable by law. *Aspect* is made up of the prefix *ad-* (here assimilated), meaning "to," plus *spect,* literally meaning "to look to"; it refers to the appearance of something to the eye—a person might have a pleasing aspect, for instance. *Per-* warrants discussion. It means "through" or "thoroughly." *Perspective* literally means "look through," as when you consider your perspective from a hilltop or on an issue. Before talking about the meaning of *perspicacious,* you might ask students if they consider themselves to be perspicacious. This will allow them to attempt to apply knowledge of the prefix *per-* and the root. The word literally means having the quality of being able to "look through" and actually means "clear-sighted," as having acute mental discernment. When discussing the meaning connections for *tact,* caution students that *tact* can have a different meaning—namely, "to arrange," as in *tactics* or *tactical.*

Did You Know? The first American dictionary of the English language was published in 1806 by Noah Webster, who was, among other things, a *lexicographer* ("one who compiles dictionaries") and a spelling reformer. He used his role as a lexicographer to institute changes in spelling; for example, he changed the spelling of words ending in *-re* to *-er,* as in *centre* to *center,* and those ending in *-our,* such as *colour* and *honour,* to *color* and *honor.* Rather than prescribe changes to the language as Noah Webster's dictionary did, most dictionaries describe the language as it exists at the time. Today there are many different kinds of dictionaries, and they appear in electronic as well as printed forms. An online Wikipedia search for **dictionary** brings up an article on dictionaries, which at the end provides links to several online dictionaries, including links for searching etymologies, translating words, and creating and submitting new words or pseudowords.

SORT 34. Latin Roots: Actions Set 1 (*fract/frag, rupt, flect/flex, vers/vert*)

Break	Break	Bend	Turn
fract/frag	*rupt*	*flect/flex*	*vers/vert*
fracture	**eruption**	**flexible**	**avert**
fraction	abrupt	deflect	adversity
fragile	bankrupt	reflection	advertise
fragment	disrupt	reflex	anniversary
infraction	interrupt		controversy
	rupture		invert
			versatile
			versus
			vertigo

Considerations: This is the first of four sorts (one follows this one, and two are presented later) that focus on roots pertaining to actions. Most of the meaning connections for the first three roots are straightforward. *Bankrupt,* which has obscure connections, is discussed under "Did You Know?" The literal meaning connection of "turn toward" in *adversity* seems unexpected, considering that the word means "misfortune." Perhaps the connection has more to do with a person's reaction to times of adversity—namely, to turn toward assistance. *Anniversary* literally means "turn year." Before talking about *vertigo* ("dizziness"), you might tell students that people sometimes suffer from vertigo, and ask what they think it means. Although *vertebrate* is not included in the sort, you might also ask students to consider the meaning connection in the word.

Did You Know? Most of the *rupt* words show an obvious meaning connection to "break"—for example, *eruption,* "a breaking out"; *interrupt,* "break between"; and *disrupt,* "break apart." But what about the word **bankrupt?** More than one person has mistakenly speculated that when you're bankrupt, you're "breaking the bank." Although the finances of a person who is bankrupt are "broken," one person's bankruptcy is unlikely to lead to the fall of an entire bank. So what is the story? Origins of the word take us back to Italian medieval times, when moneylenders, the precursors of our bankers, carried out their business on a small bench (*banca*) in the marketplace. If their business failed, they were obligated to break up their benches. This *banca rupta* evolved into English *bankrupt.*

SORT 35. Latin Roots: Actions Set 2 (*fac/fact, fer, mot, struct, ven/vent*)

Make	Carry/Bear	Move	Build	Come
fac/fact	*fer*	*mot*	*struct*	*ven/vent*
factory	**ferry**	**promote**	**construction**	**convention**
artifact	conifer	demoted	destruction	adventure
facilitate	inference	emotion	infrastructure	avenue
facsimile	transfer	motivate	instruct	intervene
satisfaction		motorist	obstruction	prevention

Considerations: This is the second set of roots whose meanings relate to actions. An *artifact* refers to something that is made or shaped by human abilities, as, for example, a tool used in ancient times. *Satisfaction* is the noun form of *satisfy,* meaning "to make sufficient." *Facsimile,* which means to "make the same," is discussed under "Did You Know?", as is *infrastructure*. You might ask students to speculate on the connection between *conifer* and "carry." They may or may not recognize *coni-* as meaning "cone"; the word literally means "carry cone" or "cone-bearing." Meaning connections for several of the *ven* words are straightforward. However, students may wonder about *avenue*. This word and *adventure* are related to *advent* ("to come to"), and their literal meanings all have to do with arriving. What might the connection be? *Obstruction* refers to the result of "piling up or building against" (*struct*, "build," + *ob-*, "against").

Did You Know? Two words in this sort that may be somewhat unfamiliar are *infrastructure* and *facsimile*, though both are integral parts of our everyday living. The *infra-* in **infrastructure** means "under," so the word's literal meaning is "structure below." Just what this refers to differs depending on the context, but usually the word refers to roads, bridges, airports, and utilities—the underlying structure of a city or other area, sometimes called *public works*. The *infrastructure* is something people do not tend to think much about until a disaster occurs that disrupts the workings of the infrastructure, as with such happenings as a tornado, hurricane, earthquake, or war.

A *facsimile* is an exact copy (*fac*, meaning "make," + *simile*, meaning "same"). It is often called a *fax* and refers to a printed copy sent electronically to someone, though the process of faxing is being used less and less as people send more documents as .pdfs through email. We find the meaning of "like" or "same" in other words, such as *similar, simile,* and *simulate* or *simulation*.

SORT 36. Greek and Latin Elements: Air, Land, Water, and Light (*aero-, aster, hydr, naut/nav, photo-, terra*)

Air	Star	Water	Ship	Light	Earth
aero-	*aster*	*hydr*	*naut/nav*	*photo-*	*terra*
aerobic	**astronomy**	**hydrant**	**navigate**	**photograph**	**terrain**
aerial	asterisk	dehydrated	(aeronautics)	photosynthesis	Mediterranean
aerodynamic	asteroid	hydroelectric	nautical	telephoto	subterranean
(aeronautics)	astronaut	hydroplane	navigable		terrace
	disaster				territory

Considerations: An asterisk (*) resembles a star, but what about *disaster*? If the sun, our star, fell apart or even moved away from Earth, it would mean the end of our planet. The word *disaster* literally means "star apart" or "star asunder." *Asunder* means "in separate pieces." It is not surprising that when disaster strikes, we often say that things are falling to pieces. *Photograph* is sometimes mistakenly thought to literally mean "picture writing." However, it is light that is causing the image, so the literal translation is actually "light writing." You might ask students if they are familiar with any other terms with *terra*, such as *terra cotta* ("baked earth"); *terra firma* ("solid earth"), *terrestrial*, and *extraterrestrial*. What is the meaning connection to earth for each? *Nausea* is another word that is actually related to the *nav/naut* words in this sort. For a discussion of the connection, see Chapter 4, Sort 46, "Did You Know?"

Did You Know? Important civilizations, such as ancient Greece and Rome, flourished in the area around the **Mediterranean** Sea, which is nearly enclosed by land: Europe on the north, Africa on the south, and Asia on the east. It connects to the Atlantic Ocean on the west by way of a narrow strait (the Strait of Gibraltar is just 9 miles wide). The Mediterranean Sea covers nearly a million square miles. Its name literally means "middle of" or "heart of" "land." Although the Mediterranean is situated far inland, the name probably carried more of the connotation of "center of" rather than "surrounded by" land. It was the center of the world to those who lived there.

SORT 37. Greek and Latin Elements: Round and Around (*circum-, peri-, centr, circ, vol[v]*)

Around	Near, Around	Center	Circle	Roll
circum-	*peri-*	*centr*	*circ*	*vol(v)*
circumference	**perimeter**	**central**	**circular**	**revolving**
circumnavigate	perihelion	concentration	circa	convoluted
circumspect	periodic	concentric	circuit	evolve
circumvent	periodical	egocentric	circuitous	involvement
	periphery		circulation	revolution
				volume

Considerations: This sort examines two prefixes, *circum-* and *peri-*, and three roots with related meanings, *centr, circ,* and *volv.* Roots from previous studies are found in several of the words, as in *circumference, circumnavigate, circumspect, circumvent,* and *perimeter.* Students are likely to be unfamiliar with several of the words in this sort, including some of those just listed. Provide an opportunity for them to work in dyads or triads to try to figure out the meanings of some of the more difficult ones. Discuss their ideas, and demonstrate the meaning connection for any words that are still unknown. For example, *circumvent* literally means to "come, or go, around." When you go around something, you avoid it, which is one of the meanings of *circumvent.* It often carries the sense of doing so artfully, as in "He tried to circumvent the review process but found he could not." *Peri-* also means "around" or "near." Its meaning should be familiar in *perimeter. Perihelion* literally means "near the sun"; it refers to the point at which the earth (or any other orbiting planet or celestial body) is closest to the sun. How do the other words in that category relate to "near" or "around"? As an extra challenge, students might ponder whether the name Cyclops, a mythological figure, has any connection to *cycle,* and if so, what? (The name actually comes from *cycl,* meaning "circle," and *op,* meaning "eye." For more *opt* words, see Sort 40.) *Convoluted* literally means "with rolls or coils." Seashells are sometimes described as convoluted, with their many overlapping spirals. A complicated argument might also be said to be convoluted.

Did You Know? The first books used by the ancients of Egypt, Greece, and Rome were actually rolls made from the papyrus plant. The Greeks called the plant *biblos* after the city of Byblos, which exported papyrus. By contrast, the Romans named their rolls after the word for the action of rolling, *volumen.* The books or **volumes** were made by pasting sheets of papyrus together, edge to edge, and then rolling the lengthy strip around a cylinder with projecting ends. Text was written on only one side of the material due to its thinness, and it was written from left to right in columns. To read such a book, a person had to hold the roll in the right hand, read a column, and then roll up what was read with the left hand while unrolling a new portion with the right. When finished reading, instead of merely closing a cover, the reader had to reroll the entire *volumen.* This form of book fell from use in the 400s when parchment (made from the skins of animals) replaced papyrus. The new material had several advantages: It was stronger, could be used on both sides, and could be folded and bound.

Literature Link

Fritz, J. (1994). *Around the world in a hundred years.* New York: Putnam & Grosset. Read about explorers who tried to circumnavigate the world.

SORT 38. Greek and Latin Roots: Reading and Writing (*gram, leg, lit, scrib/script*)

Write, Letter, Line	Read	Letter	Write
gram	*leg*	*lit*	*scrib/script*
monogram	**legend**	**literate**	**scribble**
anagram	legendary	alliteration	ascribe
cryptogram	legible	literal	circumscribe
diagram		literature	inscription
epigram		obliterate	nondescript
grammar			prescription
parallelogram			scripture
telegram			subscribe

Considerations: The words listed for *gram* all derive from the same root, but because the root existed before the Greek language, several Greek words were derived from it—each with related but different meanings, such as "write," "letter," "line," and even "draw." The words listed in this sort are derived from the various Greek words. Because spelling of the root is identical and the meanings are somewhat related, they are examined as a group. An *anagram* is a word or phrase formed of reordered letters, as in *read → dear*. It comes from the prefix *ana-*, meaning "up" and "back" (see also Sort 52), and *gram*, which here means "letter." The letters of anagrams are sometimes in scrambled order, as in *here come the dots* for "the Morse code." An *epigram*, it may be recalled, is a short, witty poem or saying (see Sort 29), such as the following by Benjamin Franklin: "Little strokes fell big oaks." What is the message of this epigram? *Crypto-* is a Greek prefix that means "hidden" or "secret." A cryptogram is writing that is in code. When you obliterate something you get rid of it completely, so that there is no trace. The word literally means "over letter," as when you rub or wipe over letters to erase them. *Nondescript* is often used to refer to animals and places that lack distinctive qualities, as in "A nondescript dog has been frequenting our backyard." *Scripture* refers to a sacred writing or book, or a passage from such a book.

Did You Know? **Aliteracy** is a relatively new term that refers to people who *can* read but choose not to (prefix *a-*, meaning "without," + *literacy*). Many people view aliteracy as a problem. Why? The following saying by Mark Twain provides a clue: "The man who does not read good books has no advantage over the man who cannot read them." Mark Twain may be thinking about the fact that people can gain knowledge through reading, develop their vocabularies, and enjoy themselves. Do you agree or disagree with this quote? Why or why not? What might be reasons that some people lack motivation for reading? What could be tried to motivate them?

SORT 39. Greek and Latin Roots: Body Language (*man, ped, pod, ped*)

Hand	Foot	Foot	Child
man	*ped*	*pod*	*ped*
manual	**centipede**	**tripod**	**pediatric**
manacle	expedite	antipodes	encyclopedia
manage-	expedition	podiatrist	pedagogue
ment	impede	podium	pedagogy
maneuver	pedestal		pedantic
manipulate	pedestrian		pediatrician
manufacture	quadruped		
manure			

Considerations: This is the first of two sorts to highlight body language. In this sort the focus is on "hand," *man*, and "foot," which, as pointed out in the introduction to this section, can be either *ped* or *pod*, depending on its origins (Latin or Greek). Because there is also a Greek root spelled *ped*, meaning "child," it too is included in this sort. Students can often use context to determine which *ped* is being referred to; if not, they should consult a dictionary. Because many of the words in this sort have clear meaning connections but may be unfamiliar words, it is worthwhile to go over them. *Manacles*, which are metal rings attached to a chain, were often used to restrain prisoners or slaves. *Expedite* literally means "out foot," or in other words, "free from entanglements," a situation that would indeed expedite an action. As you discuss *quadruped*, you might ask students, "If a horse is a quadruped, what are humans?" (*bipeds*). *Antipodes* (ăn•tĭp´•ǝ•dēz´) is literally "opposite feet"; it refers to any two things that are exact opposites, such as the North and South Poles. *Encyclopedia* is composed of *en-*, meaning "in"; *cyclo*, meaning "circle"; and *ped*, meaning "child." Together, *encyclo-* means "circular" or, more loosely, "general," and *-pedia* means "education." By reading the encyclopedia, you can gain a general education. *Pedagogue* is made up of *ped* plus *gogue*, which comes from a root meaning to "lead." "Child leader" refers to a "teacher." As sometimes happens, this word has come to have a negative connotation, one associated with a narrow concern for rules and book learning, as in the word *pedantic*. By contrast, *pedagogy* simply refers to the "art or profession of teaching."

Did You Know? Although we associate manufacturing with industry, machines, and other mechanical devices, **manufacture** literally means "hand made." Actually, manufactured articles can be made by hand or machine. Even ideas and excuses can be manufactured, as in "They manufactured an excuse to avoid being grounded." **Manure** is a relative, though perhaps not an obvious one. The word first meant "to work with the hands"—in other words, to do manual labor, such as tilling the soil, with various tools. When a more polite word was needed for *dung*, which was often worked into the soil as fertilizer, *manuere*, the verb for the act of cultivating, was applied as a euphemism or polite substitution for excrement.

SORT 40. Greek and Latin Roots: More Body Language (*cap, cord, corp, dent/don, derm, ocu/opt*)

Head	Heart	Body	Tooth	Skin	Eye, Vision
cap	*cord*	*corp*	*dent/don*	*derm*	*ocu/opt*
captain	**accord**	**corpse**	**dentures**	**epidermis**	**optical**
capitalize	concord	corps	dentils	dermatology	binoculars
capitol	cordially	corporation	dentist	pachyderm	optometry
decapitate	discord	corpulent	orthodontist		
per capita		incorporate			

Considerations: Most of the meaning connections in this sort are straightforward. *Per capita*, like the previously discussed *terra firma* and *terra cotta* (Sort 36), is a Latin phrase and literally means "per head." *Per capita* refers to something figured per person; it is a phrase often used in discussions about expenditures. Although *cap* often means "head," it can also mean "seize," as in *capture*. *Corpulent* means "with body" and is used to describe someone who is obese. The "body" in *corporation* refers to a body or group of people. *Pachyderm* refers to animals such as the *elephant*, *rhinoceros*, and *hippopotamus*. It is the "thick" (*pachy*) "skin" (*derm*) of these animals that affords them entry to the group. You might ask students to share their ideas on *pachyderm* before delving into the meaning of individual parts.

Did You Know? We have the French to thank for **dentist** and *dandelion*, both of which relate to "tooth." The meaning connection of the former is clear, but what about *dandelion?* Lions do have big teeth, but that is not the connection. In French, the word is *dent de lion* ("tooth of lion") and refers to the deeply serrated leaf edges of the plant. Although both of these words can be traced to Latin origins, the Greek root for "tooth," *don*, is also represented in English words related to teeth, as in *orthodontist*—in which *ortho* means "straight" or "correct," as it also does in *orthography*, a rather sophisticated word for spelling ("straight" or "correct" + "writing").

"What about **dentils?**" you might be wondering. Dentils are a type of molding or trim sometimes found in architecture, including homes. The molding is made up of a series of small, rectangular blocks that resemble teeth. It is sometimes used under the rooflines of houses, as well as under the mantels of fireplaces. There are other architectural features whose names are also associated with the body, as, for example, *capital* and *oculus*. The former (not surprisingly, given its root meaning "head") is the name for the top part of a pillar or column. The latter is the term for a round window in a wall or at the top of a dome. Have you ever seen an oculus, or "eye" window?

SORT 41. Greek and Latin Roots: People (*dem, greg, pol/polis, pop/pub, civ*)

People	Flock, Herd	City	People	Citizen
dem	*greg*	*pol/*polis	*pop/pub*	*civ*
democratic	**congregation**	**metropolis**	**population**	**civics**
demographics	desegregate	cosmopolitan	populace	civil
endemic	egregious	police	publication	civilian
epidemic	gregarious	policy	publicize	civility
	segregation	politician		civilization
				uncivilized

Considerations: *Endemic* ("in people") is used to describe something that is common or peculiar to a particular group of people or to a region, as in a disease that is *endemic* to the tropics. *Epidemic* ("on people") usually refers to a disease or infection that spreads rapidly among people. A person who is *gregarious* "belongs to the herd," or is sociable. *Segregation* literally means "apart from the flock," as when people are separated from the main body or group. The word element *se-* often means "apart," as it does in *segregation* and also in *separate, secret,* and *seclusion*. *Congregation* means "together herd," as when people assemble. See "Did You Know?" for a discussion of *egregious*. *Cosmopolitan* is made up of the root *cosm*, meaning "universe" or "world," and *poli*, which means "city." English is sometimes said to be a *cosmopolitan language*, meaning that it is common around the world. A *cosmopolitan problem* would be one with worldwide relevance. The root *polis* is often combined in the names of cities, as in *Annapolis, Indianapolis,* and *Minneapolis*. Ask students if they know of any other cities with the root.

Did You Know? **Egregious** stems from a Latin word meaning "outstanding." The assimilated prefix, *e(x)*, + the root, *greg*, literally mean "out of the flock." A person or act characterized by exceptionally good qualities (namely, characteristics that make him, her, or it stand out from others) was considered *egregious*. However, today the word has a completely opposite meaning and denotes something "conspicuously bad or offensive." How did such a turnaround in meanings come about? The change may be the result of an ironic use of the original meaning, as occurred in one of Shakespeare's plays, which then became popular. Whatever the case, the negative meaning that was first recorded in the mid-1500s is still used today.

SORT 42. Greek and Latin Elements: Ruling and Governing (*-archy, -cracy, dom, reg*)

Rule, Government	Government, Rule	Lord	Rule
-archy	*-cracy*	*dom*	*reg*
monarchy	**democracy**	**dominate**	**regulation**
anarchy	aristocracy	domain	regime
hierarchy	autocracy	dominant	regimen
matriarchy	bureaucracy	domineering	regiment
oligarchy	plutocracy	dominion	region
patriarchy	technocracy	predominate	
	theocracy		

Considerations: Many of the words in the first two categories of this sort are likely to be unfamiliar to students, though they may have heard of some of them. To introduce the sort, ask students to pair up and identify words they think they know by noting the meaning on the back of each word card. Then discuss the words and verify or clarify the meanings with dictionaries. The literal meanings follow:

> *-cracy:* *aristocracy,* "best rule"; *autocracy,* "self-rule"; *bureaucracy,* "office rule"; *democracy,* "people rule"; *plutocracy,* "wealth rule"; *technocracy,* "skill rule" (technical); *theocracy,* "God rule."
> *-archy:* *anarchy,* "without ruler"; *hierarchy,* "high priest (rank) rule"; *matriarchy,* "mother (women) rule"; *monarchy,* "one rule"; *oligarchy,* "few rule"; *patriarchy,* "father (men) rule." (Other words with *matr-* and *patr-* are highlighted in Sort 52.)

Dictionaries also include the word *mobocracy.* You might ask students to speculate on the word's meaning, or to consider other possible *-cracy* or *-archy* words that might one day be coined. Words with *dom* require caution when interpreting; this spelling pattern can also mean "house," as in *domicile* and *domesticate. Reg* also has another meaning, "regal."

Did You Know? As other stories have illustrated, word meanings change over time. **Hierarchy** is an example of the gradual and sometimes surprising changes that occasionally occur. *Hierarchy* was first used to describe the ranks of angels. This earliest meaning is evident in the word elements: *hier-,* which stems from the Greek word for "holy, powerful," and *-archy,* which means "leader, rule." From the angel-related meaning evolved reference to rule by an authoritarian group. The political meaning developed into the sense of classifying the populace according to wealth, social standing, or ability—a meaning that seems unrelated to the earlier political sense. One explanation put forth for the change is that because *hier-* sounded like *higher,* people confused the two meanings (Barnhart, 2005). Eventually, the meaning came to encompass ordered classification of a group of elements or objects, as when scores are listed in a hierarchical series from strongest to weakest.

SORT 43. Greek and Latin Roots: Truth or Consequences (*jud, mon, ques/quir/quis, leg, ver*)

Judge	Warn	Seek	Law	True
jud	*mon*	*ques/quir/quis*	*leg*	*ver*
judicial	**admonish**	**inquiry**	**legality**	**verdict**
adjudge	monitor	acquire	legislation	verification
injudicious	monster	inquisitive	legitimate	verify
judgmental	monstrosity	questionnaire	privilege	very
	premonition	requirement		
	remonstrate			
	summon			

Considerations: *Adjudge* means to "rule" or "decide" a case, as in *He adjudged the man not guilty of the charges. Adjudicate*, a word not included in the sort, is related; it means to "hear and settle a case by judicial procedure." *Privilege* comes from *privi*, meaning "single," and *leg*, which means "law"; in effect, the word means "a law affecting one person." *Private* shares the same meaning of "single" and the same root. To *admonish* someone is literally to "warn toward," as when someone is scolded for something or reminded of a forgotten item. In turn, the scolded person might *remonstrate* or "warn back" by presenting an objection. *Premonition* means "warn before"; it is a forewarning of something to happen. *Monstrosity* and *monster* stem from an early meaning of *monster*, which meant a "warning" or "portent"; in other words, an indication of something terrible about to occur. *Monstrosity* has a somewhat softened meaning today, referring to something frightful, ugly, or exceptionally large, as in *The vase we received is truly a monstrosity.* Caution is needed when interpreting words with *leg*, as there are different meanings for this spelling—for example, "gather" (*legion*), "dispute" (*legacy, allegations, college*), and "read" (*legend, legible*).

Did You Know? In Saxon England (England before 1066), trials were often used to determine a person's innocence or guilt, but they were trials of a different sort from those we associate with the modern-day judicial system. Instead of being presumed innocent until proven guilty, the accused individual often had to undergo an ordeal involving a physical test. For instance, the person might be plunged into water, be expected to place a bare arm in boiling water, or be required to handle a very hot object. If the accused could perform the test without getting hurt, he or she was **adjudged** innocent; if not, the person was found guilty. Sometimes trials were decided by jury. In this process, an accused person could be freed if enough people came forward to swear that they believed the person to be innocent. In 1066 Saxon England was conquered by French-speaking Normans, who made French the official language for more than a century. The French influence brought many legal terms into the language. One example is **verdict,** which means "truly said" (*ver + dict*).

SORT 44. Greek and Latin Word Elements: Opposites (*ante-, post-, bene, mal, hyper-, hypo-*)

Before	After	Good	Bad	Over, Beyond	Under, Below
ante-	*post-*	*bene*	*mal*	*hyper-*	*hypo-*
anterior	**posterior**	**benefit**	**malfunction**	**hypersensitive**	**hypothermia**
ante meridiem	post meridiem	benefactor	dismal	hyperbole	hypochondriac
anteroom	posterity	beneficial	malaria	hypercritical	hypocrite
	posthumous		malnutrition	hyperventilate	hypodermic
	postscript		malpractice		

Considerations: Because this sort includes three different pairs of word categories, you may want to stagger their introduction, discussing one pair each day for a series of days. Several words in this sort include roots from previous word studies: *script, fac, derm,* and *therm.* As they are discussed, notice which students seem to recall their meanings. You might ask students to search the dictionary for additional words to add to the discussion. *Bene* and *mal* mean "good" and "bad," respectively. A *benefactor,* then, is literally one who "makes or does good." Though it is not included in the sort, ask students to consider what a *malefactor* is. The literal meaning of *malaria* is "bad air," and of *dismal,* "bad day." *Dis* looks like a prefix in this word and may fool students, but it actually comes from the Latin word for day, *dies.* Though students have probably heard of *hyperbole,* they may not have a clear understanding of its meaning. It is a figure of speech that uses exaggeration for emphasis, as in *I'm so hungry I could eat a horse.*

Several of the *ante-* and *post-* words may be unfamiliar to most students. *Anterior* refers to "before" in the sense of either time or location, just as *posterior* refers to "after" in relation to time or place. An *anteroom* is an outer room, such as a waiting room. *Ante meridiem* is the phrase behind the abbreviation A.M., just as *post meridiem* is for P.M. The two Latin phrases literally mean "before midday" and "after midday," *midday* referring to "noon." *Postscript* is another Latin word; it is synonymous with P.S. *Posthumous* refers to something occurring after a person's death, such as the posthumous publication of a person's memoir. Its origins are a little unclear; *humous* stems either from the Latin word for to "bury" (*humare*) or from a word meaning "earth, ground" (*humus*). Other words derived from the latter include *exhume,* meaning to "remove from a grave," and *humus,* a type of rich soil.

Did You Know? **Hypocrite** stems from the Greek word *hypocrites,* referring to an onstage actor. Over time the word evolved to mean a different sort of actor, a pretender, such as one who claims to have certain beliefs, opinions, or virtues but does not. This meaning of "falseness" was first recorded in the 1200s, though with a slightly different spelling—*ypocrite.*

SORT 45. Latin Roots: Conflicts (*bell, cede/cess, pug, vinc/vict, val*)

War	Go, Yield	Fight	Conquer	Be Strong
bell	*cede/cess*	*pug*	*vinc/vict*	*val*
rebellion	**concede**	**pugnacious**	**victory**	**valiant**
antebellum	excessive	impugn	conviction	convalesce
bellicose	intercede	pugnacity	convince	evaluate
belligerent	recede	repugnant	evict	invalid
	secede		invincible	prevalent
	secession			

Considerations: Several of the *bell* words are likely to be unfamiliar to students. Begin with *rebellion,* a known word, and apply the meaning of the root "war," then add on the prefix until you have the literal meaning of "war back." Ask students how this meaning relates to the actual meaning of *rebellion.* *Antebellum* ("before war") refers to something belonging to the period before a war—usually the American Civil War, as in *antebellum slavery* or *antebellum architecture. Belligerent* literally means to "make war"; it describes someone who is hostile and aggressive. Words stemming from *cede/cess* and *vinc/vict* have fairly straightforward meaning connections but still should be discussed. The *se-* in *secede* and *secession* means "apart." *Pugnacious* is synonymous with *belligerent.* It stems from a Latin word meaning "fist." *Impugn* (ĭm•pūn) means to "challenge in argument," as to impugn the record of a political candidate. Something repugnant might be so repulsive that you would "fight against" it.

Did You Know? "Strong" is evident in all of the *val* words included in this sort. **Valiant** means "courageous"; **convalesce** means to "become strong"; **evaluate** means "to bring out the strength or value of something"; **invalid** (in both senses of this homograph) means "without strength"; and **prevalent** means "stronger," though the literal sum of its parts does not lead to this whole. Several other words not included in this sort are related—for example, *valedictorian,* meaning "one who gives a farewell speech" (in other words, a speech in which strength and worth are highlighted); *valid,* meaning "something strongly grounded, with legal force"; *valor,* meaning "boldness"; and *value,* meaning "worth, strength." When you are considering words with a *val* spelling, it is important to think carefully about the meaning and context. Some words that include the spelling pattern stem from other sources and have different meaning connections, as in *valentine, valet,* and *valley.*

SORT 46. Latin Roots: Actions Set 3 (*clud/clus, duc/duct, pend, scend, tend*)

Close	Lead	Hang	Climb	Stretch
clud/clus	*duc/duct*	*pend*	*scend*	*tend*
exclude	**conductor**	**pendulum**	**ascend**	**tendon**
inclusive	abduct	appendage	condescend	distend
preclude	aqueduct	appendix	descend	extensive
recluse	deduction	impending	transcend	intensify
secluded	induction	pendant		superintendent

Considerations: Most of the meaning connections in this sort are apparent when the meaning of the prefix is applied to the root meaning. A few warrant discussion. In *secluded,* as in *secession* from the previous sort, the *se-* means "apart." Something that is secluded is shut off or apart from other things. Ask students what a *recluse* might be. *Aqueduct* may be unfamiliar to students. Ask what they think this means. Although *aqueducts* were devised earlier in other parts of the world, the most famous ones are the Roman aqueducts, some of which were built as early as the 7th century B.C. They formed an extensive network for carrying water, not only in Rome but also in other parts of the Roman Empire, from Germany to Africa. They were an amazing feat of engineering. After discussing *aqueduct,* ask students what they think a *viaduct* is.

Did You Know? **Appendix** refers to a collection of supplementary material that is sometimes placed at the end of a book in a separate section, such as the appendices in this book. It also describes a part of the human anatomy that no longer serves a real purpose, but that sometimes becomes inflamed and must be removed (see Sort 51 for *appendicitis*). Although the word *appendicitis* was in use in 1885, it was not included in the *Oxford English Dictionary* of the times because lexicographers were uncertain about including scientific words of recent origin, so they omitted it. In 1902, the soon-to-be-crowned King Edward VII of Great Britain had to have his appendix removed, and the operation delayed his coronation. The incident was much talked about and brought the word into widespread use. As is usually the case, if a word is used enough by enough people, whether or not to include it in a dictionary is no longer a question.

SORT 47. Latin Roots: Actions Set 4 (*flu, junct, mod, press, sect*)

Flow	Join	Measure	Press	Cut
flu	*junct*	*mod*	*press*	*sect*
fluid	**conjunction**	**modular**	**pressure**	**dissect**
confluence	adjunct	accommodate	compression	bisect
fluctuate	junction	commodious	irrepressible	insect
fluent	juncture	moderate	oppression	intersection
influence		modify		
influenza				
superfluous				

Considerations: Students have considerable experience with combinations of roots and prefixes at this point; they should be able to grasp at least a literal meaning for most of the words that may be unfamiliar. You might ask them to speculate on the meaning connection to *influenza* before explaining that this word for an acute, infectious illness was borrowed from an Italian word with the same spelling, meaning "epidemic." Epidemics were originally thought to be due to the influence of the stars. When talking about the *mod* words, caution students that this spelling can also mean "manner," as it does in *modern.* As you discuss the root *sect,* you might ask students to brainstorm other words with the root (such as *section* and *sector*), as well as words with *cis,* another Latin root that means "to cut" (as in *incision, decision, incisor, incisive*). The Greeks also have a word for "cut," which we see reflected in the suffix *-tomy,* meaning "act of cutting," as in the surgical procedures *tonsillectomy* and *appendectomy.*

Did You Know? **Superfluous** and **accommodate** are often misspelled, even by literate adults. In the former case, the *l* and *u* are often reversed in order (*superfulous*), and in the latter instance an *m* is often omitted (*accomodate*). A careful look at the spelling–meaning connections of these two words can make spelling them easier. *Super-* (see Sort 7) means "over," and *flu* means "flowing," so something that is *superfluous* is "beyond what is needed." To understand how *accommodate* works, we can also look at its parts: the assimilated prefix *ad* + *commodus*. The latter is really our word **commodious,** which means "spacious enough" or "suitable" (*com-,* meaning "with," + *mod,* meaning "measure"). When we *accommodate* someone, we make the situation "suitable" or "fitting" for them.

SORT 48. Latin Roots: Peace and Good Will (*fid, grac/grat, pac, sens/sent, sol*)

Faith, Trust	Pleasing	Peace	Feel	Alone
fid	*grac/grat*	*pac*	*sens/sent*	*sol*
fidelity	**gratifying**	**pacify**	**sensible**	**solitude**
affidavit	congratulate	Pacific Ocean	consensus	desolate
bona fide	gracious	pacifier	sensational	solitaire
confident	gratitude	pacifist	sensibility	solitary
confidential	ingratiate		sentimental	
perfidious				

Considerations: Although all of the words should be discussed, a few of the words in the *fid* column may be unfamiliar to students. Though most will have heard of *fidelity,* their understanding of the meaning may be somewhat vague. You might ask them why banks sometimes include the word in their name. What message does this send to potential patrons? An *affidavit* is a written pledge made under oath in the presence of an authorized person. *Bona fide* is another direct borrowing from Latin (like *per capita*). It literally means "good faith" and refers to something said or done with sincerity, something genuine, as in *She made a bona fide attempt to complete the project on time. Perfidious* literally means "through faith," but in the sense of wronging someone, as a deliberate breach of faith. *Ingratiate* may also need explanation. Although its meaning is indeed "to bring oneself into favor," it is important for students to realize that the act is often deliberate and therefore the connotation is negative. Though not in the sort, *ingrate* is another related word, but here the *in-* bears the meaning of "not." An ingrate is an ungrateful person.

Did You Know? The **Pacific Ocean** was named by Ferdinand Magellan when much of the world was being explored. Why did Magellan call the world's largest ocean *Pacificum?* At the time of his voyage, the ocean was relatively calm and free of violent storms, so the name seemed appropriate. This same meaning of "peaceful" is obvious in the word *pacifier,* an object that babies like to suck on that generally has a calming influence. The word *appease* ("to bring peace or quiet") is descended from the same root, *pax,* as is *pay.* In the latter instance, the connection to peace is not readily apparent. It stems from the practice of paying debts in order to pacify creditors.

On a related note, the Atlantic Ocean takes its name from Mount Atlas, a mountain in West Africa, on which, according to Greek mythology, the heavens were thought to rest. Actually, a Greek Titan or giant was believed to be responsible for holding them up. By the 1500s, *Atlas* was synonymous in English with "someone who bears a heavy burden." Mercator, a 16th-century cartographer, included a picture of Atlas holding up the heavens on the title page of a book of maps and called the book *Atlas,* a name that is still used today to designate a collection of maps.

SORT 49. Latin Roots: Speaking (*lingu, loc/loq, voc/vok, verb*)

Tongue	Speak	Call	Word
lingu	*loc/loq*	*voc/vok*	*verb*
bilingual	**eloquent**	**vocalize**	**verbalize**
lingo	circumlocution	advocate	adverb
linguini	colloquial	provoke	verbatim
linguistics	elocution	revoke	verbiage
multilingual	loquacious	vocabulary	verbose
sociolinguist	soliloquy	vocation	
		vociferous	

Considerations: Though students may initially be unfamiliar with several of the words, the meanings of most become transparent when the meanings of the prefixes and roots are applied. Because we use our tongues to speak, the connection of "tongue" to the various language-related words is clear. *Linguine* requires more thought; this pasta takes its name from its tongue-like shape. *Lingo* may require explanation; it refers to the specialized vocabulary of a particular field—baseball lingo, technology lingo, medical lingo, and so forth. Meaning connections with the *loc/loq* words include *eloquent* ("speak out"); *circumlocution* ("speak around," sometimes with the meaning of "wordiness"); *colloquial* ("speak with," as in informal speech); *elocution* ("speak out," in the sense of public speaking and the qualities associated with it—gesture, production, delivery); *loquacious* ("talkative"); and *soliloquy* ("speak alone"; although this word can mean to talk to oneself, it usually refers to a character's revealing of his or her thoughts during a dramatic production). You might invite students to speculate on the meaning of *vociferous* ("voice carry"; namely, "loud and noisy") before discussing it.

Did You Know? **Vocabulary** derives from a Latin word with the same meaning. The word was first recorded in the early 1500s. You may be wondering how many words there are in English. It's difficult to say, because new words are coined and old ones fall out of use on a constant basis. Although an average person uses only about 3,000 words in everyday communication, research has shown that about 90,000 different words are used in school texts in grades 3–9. Robert Hendrickson's (2004) *Facts on File Encyclopedia* suggests that with "words from many other disciplines, jargons of professions and trades, and slang expressions from England and America, the total must come to at least between 15 and 20 million" (p. 703).

SORT 50. Greek and Latin Roots: Wisdom and Wonder
(*anima, cogn, mem, mir/marv, sci, soph*)

Mind, Soul	Know, Learn	Mindful	Wonderful	Know	Wise
anima	*cogn*	*mem*	*mir/marv*	*sci*	*soph*
unanimous	**recognize**	**memorize**	**miracle**	**conscience**	**philosophy**
animated	cognition	immemorial	marvelous	conscientious	sophisticated
inanimate	cognizant	memento	miraculous	prescience	sophomore
	incognito	memoir	mirage	subconsciously	
		memorandum			
		remember			

Considerations: Be sure that students understand that the *un-* in *unanimous* means "one" rather than "not." Ask them to brainstorm other words with this prefix and inquire whether they recall another prefix with the same meaning (*mono-*). *Prescience*, which means "foresight," is similar in meaning to the previously studied *premonition* (Sort 43 in this chapter). Talk about the nuances of their meanings. The word *science* has been discussed at the syllable juncture stage (Chapter 4, Sort 18); how does it fit with the other words in this category? As students analyze the meanings of words in this sort, you might discuss other related words, such as *commemorate* and *admirable*.

Did You Know? **Philosophy,** which means "love of wisdom," is composed of two roots: *phil*, meaning "love," and *soph*, meaning "wisdom." We have the Greeks to thank for this word. It was borrowed in 1340. Numerous other words relate to *phil*, as, for example, *Philadelphia* ("city of brotherly love"); *philharmonic* ("love of music"); *audiophile* ("one who loves sound"); *bibliophile* ("one who loves books"); *philanthropy* ("love of humankind"); *philodendron* ("love of trees," said because of the plant's tendency to twine around branches); and, perhaps in the future, *logophile* ("one who loves words"). On a final note, the *soph* in *philosophy* is also found in *sophomore*, in which it means "wise." However, the *more* refers to "foolish"; this creates an interesting contradiction—"wise" and "foolish." What might be the connection?

Literature Link

Madden, D. (1989). *Incognito mosquito: Private insective.* New York: Random House Books for Young Readers. Other books in this series include *Incognito Mosquito: Flies* and *Incognito Mosquito Makes History* (ages 9–12).

SORT 51. Greek and Latin Elements: Care and Illness (*cur, path, -phobia, -itis, vol*)

Care	Suffer, Feel	Fear	Inflammation	Will, Willing
cur	*path*	*-phobia*	*-itis*	*vol*
manicure	**empathy**	**claustrophobia**	**arthritis**	**volunteer**
pedicure	antipathy	acrophobia	appendicitis	benevolent
security	apathetic	agoraphobia	bronchitis	malevolent
	pathetic	xenophobia	laryngitis	volition
	pathology		tonsillitis	voluntary
	sympathetic			
	telepathy			

Considerations: Students should be able to identify the meanings of these words, although a dictionary will likely be needed for the *-phobia* group. Thinking of *acrobat* may help to determine the meaning of *acrophobia* ("fear of heights"). Other *-phobia* words include *agoraphobia* ("fear of open, public spaces"), *claustrophobia* ("fear of closed spaces"), and *xenophobia* ("fear of strangers"). Encourage students to brainstorm other illness-related endings besides *-phobia* and *-itis*. The former word part is discussed further under "Did You Know?" Students may already know *manicure* and *pedicure*. If not, their knowledge from earlier word studies can be applied to figure out the words. *Security* ("without care") is less transparent; students may need to consult the etymology section of a dictionary. As with *segregation* (Sort 41 in this chapter), the *se-* element carries meaning, here "without." Though several of the words with *path* may be new, with the exception of *pathology*, the meanings are clear. *Pathology* extends the sense of "suffering" to a cause; *pathology* is the study of diseases. The *vol* words are fairly easy to grasp. If you do something of your own *volition*, you do it willingly, voluntarily. As students consider *benevolent* and *malevolent*, they should recall the meanings of *bene* and *mal* (Sort 44 in this chapter) and be able to apply them to *vol* to realize that the words refer to people or other beings characterized by "good will" and "bad will." Students may wonder about the meaning connection between "mother" and *matrix* or *matriculate*. *Matrix* refers to "a situation or surrounding substance in which something else originates, develops, or is contained." A sense of beginning is also associated with *matriculate*: "to be admitted to a group." If you have not already done so, you might present students with the "longest word" from the introductory matter of this section to see whether they can decipher its meaning.

Did You Know? A **phobia** is a strong fear of or aversion to something; the fear can have a legitimate source but can also be irrational, as when it causes a person to avoid something despite awareness that the "something" is harmless. Because we all tend to have our own fears, it is not surprising that many names for phobias have been coined. A collection found at *www.phobialist.com* requires that a listed word be referenced in some text in order to be included, and it identifies more than 530 different phobias! Unless you suffer from *technophobia*, it is a list well worth browsing. Although *-phobia* is derived from Greek, contributions to the list from the medical profession, which relies heavily on Latin for its terminology, have led to the inclusion of many words with Latin roots affixed to the Greek suffix.

SORT 52. Greek and Latin Roots: Time and Family (*chron, mat/matr, pat/patr, onym, doc*)

Time	Mother	Father	Name	Teach
chron	*mat/matr*	*pat/part*	*onym*	*doc*
chronic	**maternal**	**paternal**	**pseudonym**	**doctor**
anachronism	matriarch	patriarch	acronym	docent
chronicle	matriculate	patriotic	anonymous	documentary
chronology	matrimony	patronize	antonym	indoctrinate
synchronize	matrix	(patronymic)	eponym	
			(patronymic)	

Considerations: *Anachronism,* like *anagram* (Sort 38 in this chapter), includes the prefix *ana-,* which here means "out of," as in "out of time." Including a cell phone in a story about medieval times would be an *anachronism.* Students should be familiar with several members of the *onym* family: *homonym* ("same name"); *synonym* ("similar name"); *antonym* ("opposite name"); *acronym* ("beginning name"), such as NASA for National Aeronautics and Space Administration; *eponym* (*epi-,* meaning "after" + *onym,* meaning "name"), as a place or word derived from a person's name, such as *pasteurize* after Louis Pasteur; and *pseudonym* ("false name"). *Patronymic* ("father name") may be new. It refers to a name derived from one's father, as, for example, a person's surname in the United States.

Did You Know? Another interesting *onym* word besides those included in this sort was coined by Franklin Pierce Adams, an early 20th-century American columnist. *Aptronym,* a term meaning "label name," refers to names that writers sometimes give to their characters to reveal something about their personality or occupation. Writers have long engaged in the practice. John Bunyan's *Pilgrim's Progress,* written in the 1600s, includes two such characters: Mr. Worldly Wiseman and Mr. Talkative. The works of Charles Dickens abound with examples. Children's authors also make use of aptronyms. For example, there is little doubt that Joan Aiken's (1963) "Miss Slighcarp" is an unlikable character in *The Wolves of Willoughby Chase,* and can you tell which school staff member to side with in Roald Dahl's (1990) *Matilda*—"Miss Honey" or "Miss Trunchbull"? Have you used aptronyms in your writing?

SORT 53. Latin Roots: Beginnings and Endings (*nov, sen, mort, nat, gen*)

New	Old	Death	Be Born	Birth
nov	*sen*	*mort*	*nat*	*gen*
novelty	**senator**	**mortal**	**native**	**genetic**
innovation	senile	mortality	cognate	generation
novice	senility	mortgage	innate	engender
renovation	seniority	mortified	national	indigenous
		mortuary	nativity	progeny
			natural	

Considerations: Most of the words in this sort have obvious meaning connections to their root. *Mortgage,* which does not, is discussed in "Did You Know?" The concept of *cognate,* first introduced in this chapter in Sort 20, should be reviewed. The word literally means "born with"; it is the name for words from different languages that are descended from the same ancestral root, such as the Indo-European roots that many languages share. The roots *matr* and *patr* from Sort 52, just above, are examples of words that have cognates in other languages. *Gen* is a root that can also mean "kind," as in *general, generalize,* and *genre. Progeny,* literally "forward birth," means "offspring." *Indigenous* is synonymous with "native" (literally "born in"). It should not be confused with a similarly spelled word, *indigent,* which stems from a different root with the meaning of "lacking." *Indigent* is used to describe someone who is impoverished.

Did You Know? Few people have enough money to pay for property (such as a house, land, business) outright. Instead, they usually have to take out a **mortgage,** an agreement in which the borrower promises to complete payment by a certain date (sometimes as long into the future as 30 years) or otherwise forfeit the property and all money paid toward purchasing it. Sometimes property that is already owned is used as security for another debt. In either case, the mortgage is literally a "dead pledge." It is called this because the debt is "dead" or void when the pledge is paid off. The words *engage* and *engagement* also include a pledge or promise in their meanings, as evident from the *gage* root.

SORT 54. Greek and Latin Elements: Order (*equa/equi, medi, prim, proto-, secu/sequ*)

Equal	Middle	First	First	Follow
equa/equi	*medi*	*prim*	*proto-*	*secu/sequ*
equator	**medium**	**primary**	**prototype**	**sequential**
equality	intermediary	primate	protocol	consecutive
equanimity	intermediate	primer	protozoan	consequence
equilibrium	median	primeval		prosecute
equinox	mediocre	primitive		subsequent
equivocate				

Considerations: Of the roots presented in this sort, *equa/equi* may present the most difficulties for students in terms of unfamiliar words. As you discuss this category, ask students what known roots they see in the words. They should notice *anim* ("mind") in *equanimity,* which literally means "equal mind"—a meaning that is close to the actual meaning of "even-tempered, composed." They should also notice *voc* in *equivocate.* Ask students to speculate on the meaning of this word before checking in a dictionary. *Equilibrium* literally means "equal balance," as in *When nature is in balance, there is equilibrium. Nox* in *equinox* means "night"; *equinox* refers to 1 of 2 days a year when there are approximately equal hours of daylight and darkness (there is a spring equinox and a fall equinox). *Nox* can also mean "harm," as in a *noxious* substance or *obnoxious* behavior. (Other words related to night with a different spelling, *noc,* are discussed in Sort 56.) The two elements in this sort with the meaning of "first" have different sources: *prim* stems from Latin, whereas *proto-* comes from Greek. Thinking of *zoo* or *zoology* may help students to understand the meaning of *protozoan.*

Did You Know? **Medium** is by no means a mediocre word, despite its ancestral relationship with the word *mediocre.* Instead, it is a word rich in meanings. When *medium* became part of the English language in the 1500s, it referred to the middle placement of an object or person. Since then it has acquired diverse other meanings, including a "conveyance" (as in a *medium of transportation*), a "situation or environment in which something can thrive" (*potting soil is a perfect medium for a violet*), an "artistic technique" (*oil paints are his favorite medium*), a "way of communication" (often used in the plural, as in *newspapers, radio, and television are part of the mass media*), and a "person used to communicate with the dead" (*a medium was used to try to communicate with her dead friend*).

SORT 55. Greek and Latin Elements: All or Nothing (*nihil/nil/null, omni-, pan-, plen/plet, vac*)

Zero, Nothing	All	All	Full	Empty
nihil/nil/null	*omni-*	*pan-*	*plen/plet*	*vac*
nil	**omnipresent**	**pandemic**	**plentiful**	**evacuate**
annihilate	omnipotence	panacea	completed	vacancy
nullify	omniscient	pandemonium	depletion	vacation
	omnivore	pangram	plethora	vacuous
		panoply	replenish	vacuum
		panorama		
		pantomime		

Considerations: The word *nil* is actually a contraction of the root *nihil*, meaning "nothing," as in *What did I do today? Nil.* Students will likely be familiar with *omniscient* as a narrator who is "all-knowing." Remind them that the *sci* root is what carries the meaning of "knowing," and that *omni-* means "all" in the word. In *omnipotent*, which means "having unlimited power or ability," *pot* is a root meaning to "be able to." The same root is found in words such as *potent* and *potential*, and even *possible* and *possibility*. *Omnivore* also includes a root that is likely to be unfamiliar, *vor*. It is discussed in the "Did You Know?" section for this sort. Most of the meaning connections for *pan-* are straightforward; *panacea* is not. It literally means "cure-all," or a remedy to fix anything and everything. A *pangram* is a "sentence that uses all letters of the alphabet." You might invite students to create their own pangrams or to search the Web for examples. A *panoply* is literally a "complete suit of armor," but now also "a splendid or striking array." Also as part of the discussion of the *plen* words, you might ask students to guess the meaning of *plenipotentiary* ("full power," as in a dignitary or diplomat who has the power to act on behalf of a government).

Did You Know? **Omnivore** literally means "devour all" (*omni-*, meaning "all," + *vor*, "devour"). Omnivores, including humans, have a distinct advantage over animals that are carnivores ("meat eaters") or herbivores ("plant eaters"), in that they can live on plants *and* animals. If one food supply is limited, they can turn to the other. There are many different types of omnivores, including some fish and various mammals and birds. Some creatures are insectivores and feed mainly at night. Others, such as earthworms, feed on decomposed matter. What do you suppose they are called? As a final thought about *vor*, have you ever had a voracious appetite? What was it like?

SORT 56. Latin Roots: Light and Dark; Day and Night (*cand/chand, jour, luc/lum, noc, omb/umbr*)

Shine	Day	Light	Night	Shade
cand/chand	*jour*	*luc/lum*	*noc*	*omb/umbr*
candlelight	**journal**	**lucid**	**nocturnal**	**umbrella**
candelabra	adjourned	elucidate	nocturne	adumbrate
candid	journey	illuminated		somber
candidate	photojournalism	luminary		sombrero
candor	sojourner	luminosity		umbrage
chandelier		translucent		

Considerations: The only word likely to need additional explanation, besides those discussed in "Did You Know?", is *sojourner.* The word takes its name from *sub-,* meaning "under" or "until," and *jour,* meaning "day." It literally means "one who spends the day" or "one who stays or dwells for a while."

Did You Know? Although we think of an **umbrella** as protection from rain, it was first used to protect people from the sun's hot rays. It comes from the Latin word for shade (*umbra*) and, when considered with its ending, means a "little shade." Although the umbrella has long been used in England to provide shade, it has been keeping people dry for only about 250 years. *Sombrero* is a related word; it comes from the Spanish word for "shade," *sombra.*

    Candidate was borrowed from a Latin word that originally meant "clothed in white." During ancient Roman times, a candidate seeking office wore a white toga to suggest that his character and reputation were unstained, and that he was worthy of the office for which he was campaigning.

SORT 57. Latin Roots: Odds and Ends (*loc, pos, mut, magn, min*)

Place	Put	Change	Great	Lessen
loc	*pos*	*mut*	*magn*	*min*
dislocated	**disposal**	**mutation**	**magnify**	**minimize**
allocate	composite	commuter	magnanimous	diminish
locality	compost	immutable	magnate	mince
locomotive	exposure	permutation	magnificent	minimum
	imposition		magnitude	minuscule
				minutia

Considerations: Note that *miniscule* is an alternative spelling for *minuscule. Minutia* (mĭ•nōo•shē•ə) refers to a small or trivial detail. The plural is *minutiae,* as in "People sometimes have to deal with *minutiae* as part of their work." Students should be able to identify the meanings of each word in this sort by considering the meaning of the word elements involved. If they have doubts as you discuss them, suggest that they consult a dictionary.

Did You Know? The phenomenon of someone shuttling back and forth between home and work every day is American. Although most people probably associate **commuters** with the 20th and 21st centuries, the word originated in 1865. Railroads made commuting possible, and the 1840s invention of the multiple-ride ticket, called the *commutation ticket,* made commuting easier and less expensive. The word *commuter* evolved from the commutation ticket: Riders involved in exchanging individual tickets for a less expensive, collective one were called *commuters.* Multiple-ride tickets remain the preference of commuters for the same reasons they were desirable in the 1800s.

SORT 58. Latin Roots: "Stand," Alone (*sist, stab, stan, stat, stit*)

			Stand		
sist	*stab*	*stan*	*stat*	*stit*	*?*
consistent	**establish**	**stance**	**statue**	**institution**	**obstacle**
resistance	destabilize	circumstances	statistics	constitution	obstinate
subsist	instability	instant	stature	destitute	stamina
		standard	status	restitution	
		substance		substitute	

Considerations: Depending on the group, engage students in an open sort, or ask them to sort the words by using the headers. In the latter case, explain that there may be oddballs despite the absence of a *?* card. After the sorting, discuss the categories and the relationship of each of the words to "stand." In some cases a dictionary may be of help; in others, it may require a guess. Incorporate the following "Did You Know?" into the discussion.

Did You Know? All of the words in this sort share a common ancestor, the root *sta*, meaning "to stand." However, unlike nearly all of the other roots discussed in this chapter, *sta* is much older. It is an Indo-European root and goes back to a language that was spoken about 7,000 years ago in an area somewhere between the eastern part of Europe and western Asia. The Indo-European language gave rise to many other languages. English and most of the languages of Europe and south, southeast, and central Asia descended from it. Because many languages arose from a common ancestor, certain words across languages descended from the same root; as previously noted, these words are called **cognates**. For example, consider "mother," for which there are numerous cognates: Spanish and Italian, *madre*; German, *mutter*; Swedish, *moder*; Greek, *meter*; Russian, *mat*; and Dutch, *moeder*. Knowing the word in one language can sometimes help with understanding the word in another. For example, though you may not know Spanish, you can probably guess the English word for all or nearly all of the following cognates: *automóvil, teléfono, octubre, miniature, importante, familia, foto,* and *vegetales.* Can you think of other cognates?

mono-	bi-	tri-
monotone	bicycle	triangle
biennial	trivial	biceps
triathlon	biweekly	trigonometry
monolingual	trio	bifocals
triad	bimonthly	monopoly
binary	monotonous	triptych
monologue	triplets	monolith
bicuspid	monorail	trilogy

quadr-	*pent-*	*oct-*	*dec-*	*cent-*
quadruple	pentagon	octopus		
decade	century	decimal		
octogenarian	decathlon	octagon		
percent	quadrant	centenarian		
octave	pentathlon	October		
December	centimeter	quadruplets		
quadrangle	decimeter	pentad		
bicentennial	octet	centigrade		

Greek and Latin Prefixes: Size and Amount
(*semi-*, *poly-*, *multi-*, *micro-*, *mega-*)

semi-	*poly-*	*multi-*	*micro-*	*mega-*

semisweet	polysyllabic	multicultural
microphone	megaphone	polygon
semicolon	multipurpose	microchip
microfilm	megabyte	polygraph
multiplication	semicircle	multinational
polydactyl	microscope	semiskilled
semisolid	megalopolis	microbe
microcosm	multimedia	semifinals

SORT 29

Common Greek Elements
(*auto-*, *bio-*, *geo-*, *graph*, *-meter/metr*, *therm*)

auto-	*bio-*	*geo-*	*graph*	*-meter/ metr*	*therm*
automatic		biology		geology	
graphite		speedometer		thermostat	
biosphere		geothermal		geode	
homograph		bionic		odometer	
geometry		cartographer		epigraph	
biodegradable		barometer		autobiography	
thermometer		automobile		biography	
autograph		antibiotics		geography	

Common Greek and Latin Elements
(*aud, phon, vis, -scope, tele-*)

aud	*phon*	*vis*	*-scope*	*tele-*

audience   homophone   supervise

kaleidoscope   telegraph   periscope

phonics   visibility   audiovisual

audition   telescope   symphony

telethon   inaudible   telephone

envision   stethoscope   auditorium

phonograph   television   vista

telecommunications   telemarketing

SORT 31

Applying Prefix Knowledge to Common Latin Roots
(*ject* and *tract*)

ject		*tract*
projector	tractor	protracted
extract	subjects	conjecture
dejected	traction	projectile
subtract	interject	detract
injection	attract	abject
distracted	rejection	retraction
adjective	intractable	eject
contraction	objection	abstract

Applying Prefix Knowledge to More Common Latin Roots
(*mis/mit, port*)

mis/mit	*port*	**?**
mission	portfolio	transplant
transportation	omitted	reporter
deport	transit	dismiss
commission	remittance	submissive
export	rapport	intermittent
missile	admittance	transatlantic
supportive	transmission	comport
emissions	import	promise

Latin Roots: Senses (*dict, spect/spic, spir, tact/tag/tang*)

dict	*spect/ spic*	*spir*	*tact/tag/ tang*
contradict	spectator		spirited
contact	respiratory		tactile
inspector	conspire		dictionary
edict	tangent		perspicacious
inspiration	dictate		expire
perspective	specter		spectacle
tactful	contagious		aspect
dictator	aspiration		tangible

Latin Roots: Actions Set 1
(*fract/frag, rupt, flect/flex, vers/vert*)

fract/ frag	rupt	flect/flex	vers/ vert
fracture	eruption		flexible
avert	reflex		interrupt
fragile	rupture		adversity
bankrupt	advertise		abrupt
versatile	fragment		vertigo
infraction	versus		anniversary
controversy	fraction		reflection
disrupt	deflect		invert

SORT 35

Latin Roots: Actions Set 2
(*fac/fact, fer, mot, struct, ven/vent*)

fac/ fact	fer	mot	struct	ven/ vent
factory		ferry		promote
construction		convention		conifer
instruct		emotion		adventure
prevention		facsimile		demoted
inference		transfer		destruction
satisfaction		motorist		facilitate
motivate		intervene		avenue
infrastructure		artifact		obstruction

aero-	aster	hydr	naut/ nav	photo-	terra
aerobic		astronomy		hydrant	
navigate		photograph		terrain	
subterranean		hydroplane		asterisk	
nautical		aerodynamic		Mediterranean	
asteroid		territory		telephoto	
hydroelectric		disaster		aeronautics	
aerial		navigable		terrace	
photosynthesis		astronaut		dehydrated	

SORT 37
Greek and Latin Elements: Round and Around
(*circum-, peri-, centr, circ, vol[v]*)

circum-	peri-	centr	circ	vol(v)

circumference	perimeter	central
circular	revolving	periodical
circuit	periphery	circa
concentric	involvement	circumnavigate
perihelion	evolve	circulation
convoluted	circumspect	egocentric
revolution	volume	periodic
circumvent	concentration	circuitous

gram	*leg*	*lit*	*scrib/ script*
monogram	legend		literate
scribble	literal		epigram
parallelogram	inscription		legible
subscribe	telegram		scripture
legendary	prescription		diagram
ascribe	cryptogram		alliteration
grammar	circumscribe		nondescript
obliterate	anagram		literature

Greek and Latin Roots: Body Language (*man, ped, pod, ped*)

man	ped	pod	ped
manual	centipede		tripod
pediatric	quadruped		expedition
pedagogue	expedite		maneuver
management	podiatrist		pediatrician
pedestal	manure		podium
manufacture	encyclopedia		pedantic
impede	pedestrian		manacle
manipulate	antipodes		pedagogy

From *Mindful of Words, Second Edition*, by Kathy Ganske. Copyright © 2021 The Guilford Press. Permission to photocopy this form is granted to purchasers of this book for personal use or use with students (see copyright page for details). Enlarge 135% to fill letter-size paper, 175% for 11″ × 17″ paper.

cap	*cord*	*corp*	*dent/ don*	*derm*	*ocu/ opt*

captain	accord	corpse
dentures	epidermis	optical
cordially	capitalize	dentist
dentils	corporation	decapitate
capitol	pachyderm	corpulent
dermatology	discord	optometry
incorporate	binoculars	concord
per capita	corps	orthodontist

SORT 41

Greek and Latin Roots: People
(*dem, greg, pol/polis, pop/pub, civ*)

dem	*greg*	*pol/ polis*	*pop/ pub*	*civ*
democratic	congregation		metropolis	
population	civics		publicize	
civilization	policy		desegregate	
egregious	civility		cosmopolitan	
populace	endemic		epidemic	
segregation	police		uncivilized	
civil	gregarious		politician	
demographics	publication		civilian	

SORT 42
Greek and Latin Elements: Ruling and Governing
(*-archy, -cracy, dom, reg*)

-archy	*-cracy*	*dom*	*reg*
monarchy	democracy		dominate
regulation	regimen		aristocracy
theocracy	technocracy		domineering
oligarchy	regime		hierarchy
autocracy	domain		bureaucracy
regiment	anarchy		region
dominion	plutocracy		predominate
matriarchy	dominant		patriarchy

Greek and Latin Roots: Truth or Consequences
(jud, mon, ques/quir/quis, leg, ver)

jud	*mon*	*ques/quir/ quis*	*leg*	*ver*
judicial		admonish		inquiry
legality		verdict		privilege
inquisitive		requirement		premonition
monstrosity		very		injudicious
legislation		questionnaire		summon
verify		monster		judgmental
legitimate		acquire		remonstrate
monitor		adjudge		verification

SORT 44

Greek and Latin Word Elements: Opposites
(*ante-*, *post-*, *bene*, *mal*, *hyper-*, *hypo-*)

ante-	*post-*	*bene*	*mal*	*hyper-*	*hypo-*
anterior		posterior		benefit	
malfunction		hypersensitive		hypothermia	
posthumous		hypocrite		dismal	
hypercritical		anteroom		malpractice	
beneficial		hyperbole		post meridiem	
malnutrition		benefactor		hypochondriac	
ante meridiem		hypodermic		postscript	
hyperventilate		posterity		malaria	

SORT 45 — Latin Roots: Conflicts (*bell, cede/cess, pug, vinc/vict, val*)

bell	*cede/ cess*	*pug*	*vine/ vict*	*val*
rebellion	concede		pugnacious	
victory	valiant		excessive	
prevalent	impugn		convince	
intercede	evaluate		bellicose	
conviction	secede		repugnant	
antebellum	invincible		recede	
invalid	pugnacity		convalesce	
secession	belligerent		evict	

SORT 46
Latin Roots: Actions Set 3
(*clud/clus, duc/duct, pend, scend, tend*)

clud/ clus	due/duct	pend	scend	tend
exclude		conductor		pendulum
ascend		tendon		abduct
appendix		descend		superintendent
recluse		pendant		inclusive
intensify		aqueduct		extensive
condescend		distend		impending
deduction		transcend		preclude
secluded		appendage		induction

SORT 47

Latin Roots: Actions Set 4 (*flu, junct, mod, press, sect*)

flu	*junct*	*mod*	*press*	*sect*

fluid	conjunction	modular
pressure	dissect	fluent
superfluous	junction	intersection
juncture	commodious	fluctuate
modify	adjunct	compression
irrepressible	influenza	bisect
insect	accommodate	confluence
moderate	influence	oppression

Latin Roots: Peace and Good Will
(*fid, grac/grat, pac, sens/sent, sol*)

fid	*grac/ grat*	*pac*	*sens/ sent*	*sol*
fidelity	gratifying			pacify
sensible	solitude			sensational
confident	desolate			gratitude
pacifist	congratulate			bona fide
ingratiate	sensibility			solitary
consensus	affidavit			pacifier
solitaire	gracious			perfidious
confidential	Pacific Ocean			sentimental

SORT 49 Latin Roots: Speaking (*lingu, loc/loq, voc/vok, verb*)

lingu	*loc/loq*	*voc/vok*	*verb*
bilingual	eloquent	vocalize	
verbalize	soliloquy	linguini	
loquacious	verbatim	colloquial	
adverb	sociolinguist	provoke	
circumlocution	verbose	vocabulary	
vocation	lingo	advocate	
linguistics	vociferous	verbiage	
multilingual	revoke	elocution	

SORT 50

Greek and Latin Roots: Wisdom and Wonder
(*anima, cogn, mem, mir/marv, sci, soph*)

anima	*cogn*	*mem*	*mir/marv*	*sci*	*soph*
unanimous		recognize			memorize
miracle		conscience			philosophy
incognito		marvelous			memento
mirage		cognizant			subconsciously
memorandum		sophomore			animated
prescience		immemorial			conscientious
inanimate		miraculous			memoir
remember		cognition			sophisticated

SORT 51 Greek and Latin Elements: Care and Illness
(*cur, path, -phobia, -itis, vol*)

cur	*path*	*-phobia*	*-itis*	*vol*

manicure	empathy	claustrophobia
arthritis	volunteer	pathetic
volition	pedicure	antipathy
security	appendicitis	benevolent
acrophobia	pathology	agoraphobia
tonsillitis	malevolent	sympathetic
apathetic	bronchitis	voluntary
xenophobia	telepathy	laryngitis

chron	*mat/ matr*	*pat/ patr*	*onym*	*doc*
chronic	maternal			paternal
pseudonym	doctor			matrimony
patronize	antonym			synchronize
anachronism	matrix			indoctrinate
patriarch	chronology			acronym
docent	eponym			matriculate
anonymous	documentary			patriotic
matriarch	patronymic			chronicle

SORT 53

Latin Roots: Beginnings and Endings
(*nov, sen, mort, nat, gen*)

nov	sen	mort	nat	gen

novelty	senator	mortal
native	genetic	natural
mortgage	senility	progeny
engender	seniority	mortality
mortuary	innate	renovation
nativity	indigenous	national
senile	novice	generation
cognate	mortified	innovation

Greek and Latin Elements: Order
(*equa/equi, medi, prim, proto-, secu/sequ*)

equa/ equi	medi	prim	proto-	secu/ sequ
equator		medium		primary
prototype		sequential		prosecute
consequence		equilibrium		median
equivocate		primate		protozoan
primeval		consecutive		equanimity
intermediate		equinox		subsequent
protocol		mediocre		primer
equality		primitive		intermediary

SORT 55

Greek and Latin Elements: All or Nothing
(*nihil/nil/null, omni-, pan-, plen/plet, vac*)

nihil/ nil/null	omni-	pan-	plen/ plet	vac
nil		omnipresent		pandemic
plentiful		evacuate		completed
replenish		panoply		vacuum
panacea		vacancy		omniscient
vacuous		depletion		pandemonium
omnipotence		plethora		nullify
pantomime		vacation		panorama
annihilate		pangram		omnivore

SORT 56

Latin Roots: Light and Dark; Day and Night
(*cand/chand, jour, luc/lum, noc, omb/umbr*)

cand/ chand	jour	luc/lum	noc	omb/ umbr
candlelight	journal	lucid		
nocturnal	umbrella	adumbrate		
sojourner	candidate	translucent		
somber	luminary	candid		
candelabra	journey	elucidate		
umbrage	luminosity	chandelier		
adjourned	sombrero	nocturne		
illuminated	candor	photojournalism		

SORT 57

Latin Roots: Odds and Ends (*loc, pos, mut, magn, min*)

loc	*pos*	*mut*	*magn*	*min*

dislocated	disposal	mutation
magnify	minimize	exposure
minuscule	locality	magnate
magnitude	commuter	mince
diminish	locomotive	permutation
compost	magnificent	minutia
magnanimous	composite	allocate
imposition	minimum	immutable

SORT 58

Latin Roots: "Stand," Alone (*sist, stab, stan, stat, stit*)

sist	*stab*	*stan*	*stat*	*stit*

consistent	establish	stance
statue	institution	substance
destitute	status	instability
establish	stamina	restitution
stature	resistance	statistics
circumstances	instant	standard
obstinate	destabilize	substitute
constitution	obstacle	subsist

Appendices

APPENDIX A Performance Records

Name

Category	Subcategory	#	Feature
Compounds and inflectional endings		1	Introducing compound words
		2	-ing: no change and e-drop
		3	-ed: no change and e-drop
		4	-ing: no change, e-drop, and double
		5	-ed: no change, e-drop, and double
		6	-ed: r-controlled no change, e-drop, and double
		7	-ed and -ing: no change, e-drop, and double
		8	Plurals: -s and -es
		9	More plurals
		10	-er and -est: no change, e-drop, double, and -y to i
Syllable juncture	Open and closed syllables	11	VCV and VCCV (doublet)
		12	VCV and VCCV (doublet or different)
		13	VCV, VCCV (doublet or different), and VV
		14	More VCV, VCCV (doublet or different)
		15	VCV (long or short), VCCV (doublet or different)
	Vowel patterns in stressed syllables	16	Long and short a
		17	Long and short e
		18	More long and short e
		19	Long and short i
		20	More long and short i
		21	Long and short o
		22	Long and short u
		23	r-controlled Vre
		24	r-controlled o
		25	r-controlled a
		26	r-controlled /ûr/
		27	r-controlled e
		28	Abstract vowels with o
		29	Abstract vowels with a
	Unstressed syllables	30	Final syllables with long-a
		31	Final syllables with /ən/
		32	Final syllables with /ər/
		33	More final syllables with /ər/
		34	Final syllables with /chər/ and /zhər/
		35	Final syllables with /əl/
		36	Initial syllables
	Consonant extensions	37	Hard and soft c and g
		38	Final /k/
		39	ch and ph
		40	gu(e) and qu(e)
		41	Vowel i

From *Mindful of Words, Second Edition*, by Kathy Ganske. Copyright © 2021 The Guilford Press. Permission to photocopy this form is granted to purchasers of this book for personal use or use with students (see copyright page for details). Purchasers can download enlarged versions of this form (see the box on page xviii).

363

Performance Records (p. 2 of 3)

Category	Subcategory	#	Sort
Derivational constancy	**Vowel alternations**	18	Consonant, vowel, and stress changes with c
		17	Syllable stress and alternations
		16	With predictable spelling changes
		15	Long and short to schwa
		14	Long to schwa
		13	Long to short
	Consonant alternations	12	Adding -ion: predictable spelling changes
		11	Adding -ion: e-drop
		10	Adding -ion and -ian: no spelling change
		9	Adding -ion: no spelling change
		8	Silent and sounded consonants
	Revisiting prefixes and suffixes	7	Prefixes (inter-, mid-, sub-, super-)
		6	Prefixes (mis-, en-, de-, anti-)
		5	Prefixes (un-, dis-, in-)
		4	Suffixes with final -y (-ier, -iness, -ious, -ily, -ied)
		3	Doubling and no change with various suffixes
		2	Doubling and no change with -ed and -ing
		1	e-drop and no change with -ed and -ing
Syllable juncture	**Additional sorts**	63	States stress break
		62	Hyphenated compounds with repeated elements
		61	Hyphenated compounds
		60	Compounds with color words
		59	Compounds with food words
		58	Compounds with weather words
		57	Compounds with position words
		56	Compounds with around-the-home words
		55	Compounds with opposite words
		54	Compounds with space words
		53	Compounds with substance words
		52	Homographs set 2
		51	Homographs set 1
		50	Homophones set 3
		49	Homophones set 2
		48	Homophones set 1
	Prefixes and suffixes	47	Putting it all together
		46	Suffix -y: no change, e-drop, and double
		45	Suffixes (-ful, -less, -ly, -ness)
		44	Prefixes (in-, in-, non-, pre-)
		43	Prefixes (dis-, fore-, mis-)
		42	Prefixes (un- and re-)

Name

Performance Records *(p. 3 of 3)*

Derivational constancy

			Name
A further look at suffixes and prefixes	19	Suffixes (*-able* and *-ible*)	
	20	Taking a closer look (*-able*)	
	21	Suffixes (*-ant, -ance, -ent, -ence*)	
	22	Taking a closer look (*-ant, -ance, -ent, -ence*)	
	23	Suffixes (*-ity*)	
	24	Assimilated prefixes (*in-*)	
	25	Assimilated prefixes (*ad-, com-, ex-, ob-, sub-*)	
Greek and Latin word elements	26	Numbers (*mono-, bi-, tri-*)	
	27	More numbers (*quadr-, pent-, oct-, dec-, cent-*)	
	28	Size and amount (*semi-, poly-, multi-, micro-, mega-*)	
	29	Common elements (*auto-, bio-, geo-, graph, -meter/metr, therm*)	
	30	Common elements (*aud, phon, vis, -scope, -tele-*)	
	31	Applying prefixes to roots (*ject* and *tract*)	
	32	Applying prefixes to roots (*mis/mit, port*)	
	33	Senses (*dict, spect/spic, spir, tact/tag/tang*)	
	34	Actions set 1 (*tract/trag, rupt, flect/flex, vers/vert*)	
	35	Actions set 2 (*fac/fact, fer, mot, struct, ven/vent*)	
	36	Air, land, water, light (*aero-, aster-, hydr, naut/nav, photo-, terra*)	
	37	Round and around (*circum-, peri-, cent-, circ, voll/v*)	
	38	Reading and writing (*gram, leg, lit, scrib/script*)	
	39	Body language (*man, ped, pod, ped*)	
	40	More body language (*cap, cord, corp, dent/don, derm, ocu/opth*)	
	41	People (*dem, greg, pol/polis, pop/pub, civ*)	
	42	Ruling and governing (*-archy, -cracy, dom, reg*)	
	43	Truth or consequences (*jud, mon, ques/quir/quis, leg, ver*)	
	44	Opposites (*ante-, post-, bene, mal, hyper-, hypo-*)	
	45	Conflicts (*bell, cede/cess, pug, vinc/vict, val*)	
	46	Actions set 3 (*clud/clus, duc/duct, pend, scend, tend*)	
	47	Actions set 4 (*flu, junct, mod, press, sect*)	
	48	Peace and good will (*fid, grac/grat, pac, sens/sent, sol*)	
	49	Speaking (*lingu, loc/log, voc/vok, verb*)	
	50	Wisdom and wonder (*anima, cogn, mir/marv, sci, soph*)	
	51	Care and illness (*cur, path, -phobia, -itis, vol*)	
	52	Time and family (*chron, mat/matr, pat/patr, onym, doc*)	
	53	Beginnings and endings (*nov, sen, nat, gen*)	
	54	Order (*equa/equi, medi, prim, proto-, secu/sequ*)	
	55	All or nothing (*nihil/nil/null, omni-, pan-, plen/plet, vac*)	
	56	Light/dark, day/night (*cand/chand, jour, luc/lum, noc, omb/umbr*)	
	57	Odds and ends (*loc, pos, mut, magn, min*)	
	58	"Stand," alone (*sist, stab, stan, stat, stit*)	

3-D figures	**2-D figures**	**Operations**	**Measurement**
cone	circle	addend	acre
cube	circumference*	addition	area
cylinder	congruent	computation	capacity
faces	diameter*	difference	centimeter
hexagon	intersecting	divide	distance
pentagon	obtuse	dividend	gallon
plane	parallel	divisor	gram
polygon	perpendicular	equation	foot
prism	quadrilateral	minus	height
pyramid	radius*	multiple	kilometer
rhombus	ray	multiply	length
sphere	rectangle	product	liter
three-dimensional	symmetry	quotient	mass
trapezoid	two-dimensional	subtraction	measure
triangle		sum	meter
	Other	total	mile
Numbers	array		millimeter
data	axis		minute
decimal	bisect		perimeter
denominator	coordinates		pint
digit	grid		pound
equivalent	horizontal		quart
estimation	interval		second
even	matrix		temperature
formula	mean		volume
fraction	median		weight
numeral	mode		width
numerator	probability		yard
odd	proportion		
percent	range		
pi	scale		
prime	segment		
probability	ratio		
random	vertical		
rounding			
simplify			
solve			
variable			

*Applicable to 3-D figures also.

APPENDIX C Sampling of 100+ Important Science Words

Biology	Astronomy	Physical science	Earth science	Other
adaptation	asteroid	acids	cloud	classification
amphibians	celestial	bases	conservation	environment
birds	constellation	circuit	core	extinct
cell	eclipse	compound	crust	magnify
decompose	galaxy	concave lens	earthquake	observation
diversity	lunar	conductor	erosion	prehistoric
ecosystem	meteor	convex lens	evaporation	properties
edible	meteorite	dissolving	force	reasoning
endangered	moon	elements	fossils	renewable
fish	nebula	friction	gravity	scientist
habitat	orbit	gas	igneous	vibration
inherit	phases	liquid	mantle	
invertebrates	planet	machine	metamorphic	
life cycle	radiation	magnet	ocean	
mammals	reflection	matter	plate tectonics	
metamorphosis	revolution	mixture	pollution	
offspring	rotation	molecule	precipitation	
organism	solar system	nucleus	seasons	
osmosis	space	plasma	sedimentary	
photosynthesis	universe	solid	thermometer	
predatory	wavelength	solution	volcano	
prey		velocity	water cycle	
reptiles			weather	
respiration				
shelter				
species				
threatened				
thriving				
traits				
vertebrates				

Families/communities	Geography	Government	History	Economy
ancestors	borders	amendments	ancient	agriculture
community	boundary	Bill of Rights	civilization	boycott
cooperate	climate	census	colonial	consumer
culture	coast	citizen	Civil Rights	economy
custom	compass rose	city	Civil War	export
neighborhood	continent	Congress	expansion	famine
population	desert	Constitution	expedition	global
respect	equator	country	explorers	goods
responsibility	geography	Declaration of Independence	Great Depression	import
rural	globe	democracy	immigration	industry
settlement	hemisphere	document	independence	monopoly
suburban	latitude	election	Louisiana Purchase	produce
tradition	longitude	executive branch	migration	product
urban	map legend (key)	government	Native American	resources
volunteer	mountains	governor	pioneer	tariff
	mouth	judicial branch	religion	
	ocean	justice	republic	
	plains	laws	Revolutionary War	
	plateau	legislative branch	segregation	
	prime meridian	mayor	settlers	
	region	President	slavery	
	source	Representative	suffrage	
	tidal basin	rights	treaty	
	tributary	Senator	World War	
	valleys	state		
	vegetation	Supreme Court		

accept	I plan to **accept** their invitation to the party.
addition	**Addition** is used to find the sum of numbers. The family put an **addition** on their house after the baby was born.
affect	Will the change in schedule **affect** you?
allowed	We're **allowed** to stay up as long as we want on Friday nights.
aloud	The teacher read the story **aloud** to the class.
ascent	His **ascent** to the top of the mountain made him famous.
assent	Dad finally gave his **assent,** so I can go to the game.
bazaar	There were lots of interesting things to buy for cheap prices at the church **bazaar.**
berry	My favorite **berry** is the strawberry.
bizarre	That was one of the most **bizarre** movies I've ever seen, strange . . . really strange.
boarder	The **boarder** paid his rent and left.
border	There was a **border** around the bulletin board. Mexico **borders** the United States.
borough	A **borough** is another name for a town in some states, such as New Jersey.
burrow	Animals such as gophers, prairie dogs, woodchucks, moles, and rabbits dig underground tunnels called **burrows** for shelter.
bury	We will **bury** the dead bird.
capital	Begin the sentence with a **capital** letter. Washington, D.C., is the **capital** of the United States. To start a business, you need **capital**—in other words, money.
capitol	The state government meets in the state **capitol.** The U.S. Congress meets in the **Capitol** in Washington, D.C.
carat	**Carat** is the unit of measure used for diamonds and gold.
caret	When I revise my work, I use a **caret** (^) to show that I want to insert more information.
carrot	Do you want me to put a **carrot** in the stew?
ceiling	They looked up to see how high the **ceiling** was.
cellar	The **cellar** was used as an underground shelter from storms and to store items; it had an outside entrance.
cent	A penny is worth one **cent.**
cereal	I have **cereal** for breakfast every morning.
choral	For the **choral** reading, everyone read the same piece aloud at once.

(continued)

colonel	He is a **colonel** in the army and hopes to become a general one day.
complement	This angle is a **complement** to that one; together they equal 90º. I have new shelves in my room; now all I need is a **complement** of books to fill them.
compliment	I appreciated the **compliment** about my work.
coral	**Coral** are marine creatures that produce rocklike deposits that are pinkish or red-orange in color.
council	The student **council** met to discuss the problem.
counsel	My brother's always trying to **counsel** me on how to improve my game.
currant	There's a **currant** bush behind my grandmother's house; she uses the berries to make great jelly.
current	I listen or read about the news every day to know about **current** events. Water in the river's **current** was fast-moving.
cymbal	I love to hear the crash of the **cymbals** when the percussion instruments play.
desert	After the battle was lost, the soldier decided to **desert** the army. To go to jail is a just **desert** for breaking certain laws.
dessert	The chocolate **dessert** was unbelievably tasty.
dual	I have a **dual** role in the play: Dr. Jekyll and Mr. Hyde.
duel	In olden times, two people sometimes fought a **duel** to preserve their honor.
edition	That company puts out both a morning and an evening **edition** of the newspaper.
effect	Being able to read independently in school had a positive **effect** on their reading interest. The special lighting **effects** surprised everyone.
except	I'd go **except** that I have to watch my brother and sister. Everyone is going **except** me.
fairy	Which **fairy** tale is your favorite?
ferry	They crossed the wide river on a **ferry.**
flew	A bird suddenly **flew** out of the tree.
flu	They had to close the school because so many people were sick with the **flu**.
flue	We need to get a chimney sweep to come and clean the **flue** before a fire starts in it.
frees	Having no class tomorrow **frees** me to work on my project.
freeze	Water will **freeze** at temperatures of 32º Fahrenheit or 0º Celsius.
frieze	A **frieze** is an architectural decoration located above columns on a building or wall.
hangar	The airplane **hangar** held six planes.
hanger	Please hang your suit on a **hanger**.
kernel	Corn on the cob is delicious, but I have a **kernel** of corn stuck between my teeth.

(continued)

lessen	An ice pack might **lessen** the swelling from your bump.
lesson	The **lesson** on plate tectonics was fascinating.
manner	His **manner** of speaking was clear and relaxed.
manor	The **manor** house on the plantation was a mansion.
marry	The couple decided to **marry.**
medal	The soldier was awarded a **medal** for his bravery.
meddle	Some people love to **meddle** in other people's business.
merry	If you have a **merry** time, it's a fun time.
metal	There's a lot of **metal** in an automobile.
miner	The **miner** put on his hard hat and headed down the deep shaft with a pick and shovel.
minor	He was released from the hospital after his **minor** accident. You are considered a **minor** until you reach full legal age.
morning	We'll leave in the **morning**, sometime before noon.
mourning	They were **mourning** the death of their old dog.
muscle	She exercises every day to keep her **muscles** toned.
mussel	Clams are a kind of **mussel.**
palate	She doesn't like bread that sticks to your **palate**—you know, the roof of your mouth—when you eat it.
palette	The artist spread paint on the **palette**.
pallet	Cargo from the ship was unloaded onto wooden **pallets.**
patience	I hate waiting for things, but I guess **patience** is something we all have to learn.
patients	Six **patients** were ahead of me in the doctor's waiting room.
peak	The climber made it to the top of the mountain **peak.** Most athletes reach their **peak** at an early age.
pedal	It can be difficult to **pedal** a bike uphill.
peddle	It used to be very common for people to **peddle** or sell goods door to door.
peek	Let's take a **peek** at the next chapter. Spring flowers were beginning to **peek** through the snow.
petal	The flower **petal** was ruffled around the edge.
pique	The odors drifting from the restaurant **pique** my interest; let's check it out.
principal	The **principal** starts the day with announcements. She is the **principal** dancer in her organization.
principle	Do you understand the **principles** we discussed in class?
profit	Businesses have to make a **profit,** or they can't afford to stay in business.

(continued)

372

prophet	The words of the **prophet** inspired the people.
rain	The **rain** poured for three days.
raise	I need to **raise** the height of this shelf. My boss gave me a **raise.**
rays	The **rays** of the sun streamed across the sky.
raze	I didn't know what the newsperson meant by "They will **raze** the old building on Monday," but then my friend told me that that kind of **raze** means *to demolish*.
reign	The **reign** of King Henry VI started when he was an infant and lasted for nearly 40 years.
rein	The rider controlled the horse by pulling on the **reins.** (*Reindeer* includes the same spelling but is unrelated in meaning.)
roomer	Because they had extra space, the family decided to take in a **roomer.**
rumor	A **rumor** is just hearsay and may or may not be true.
scent	Bears have a very keen or strong **scent.**
sealing	We are **sealing** this package in order to mail it.
seas	The stormy **seas** were rough and choppy.
sees	He **sees** my point, but still won't let me go. With her new glasses, she **sees** better than ever.
seize	He **seized** his backpack and raced to the bus stop.
seller	The **seller** had just about every product you could imagine.
sent	I **sent** her a postcard on my vacation.
serial	I like **serial** novels the best, because after the first one you can read another and another and so on.
stationary	You can't move the birdhouse because it's **stationary.**
stationery	When I write a thank-you note, I like to use **stationery.**
symbol	Lots of **symbols** are used in math, such as +, −, $, %, >, and <, to name a few.
tidal	The storm created a huge **tidal** wave.
title	I need a **title** for my story that will grab the reader's interest.
vain	Your efforts to complete the project before tomorrow when you haven't even started it will be in **vain.** My sister's **vain** about her looks; she's always admiring herself in the mirror.
vane	The weather **vane** on top of the shed turned in the wind.
vein	The **veins** of a person carry blood to the heart; the lines on the leaf are also called **veins;** and streaks of gold or other ore in rock are **veins,** too.
weather	The **weather** today is supposed to be sunny and breezy.
whether	I don't know **whether** we'll go with them or not.

APPENDIX G Understanding Prefixes

Prefix	Meaning	Prefix	Meaning
ab-	away from	mis-	badly, wrongly
acro-	top, height, beginning (*acr-*)	mono-	one (*mon-*)
ad-	to, toward (*ac-, af-, ag-, al-, ap-, as-, at-*)	multi-	many
ante-	before	neo-	new
anti-	opposing, against (*ant-*)	non-	not
auto-	self (*aut-*)	ob-	against, away, over, (toward) (*oc-, of-, op-, o-*)
bi-	two	omni-	all
centi-	hundred	pan-	all
com-	together, with (*co-, col-, con-, cor-*)	para-	beside, beyond, similar to (*par-*)
contra-	against	penta-	five (*pent-*)
de-	out, off, apart, away, down (*des-*)	per-	through, thoroughly
di-	two	peri-	around, near
dia-	through, across (*di-*)	poly-	many
dis-	not, opposite of, apart (*dif-, dis-, di-*)	post-	after
en-	put into, cause to (*em-*)	pre-	before
epi-	on, over, near, after (*ep-*)	pro-	before, in front of, forth
eu-	good, well	proto-	first, earliest (*prot-*)
ex-	out, away from (*ec-, ef-, e-*)	pseudo-	false (*pseudo-*)
fore-	before	quadri-	four, square (*quadru-, quadr-*)
homo-	same	re-	back, again
hyper-	over, beyond	retro-	backward, back
hypo-	below, under (*hyp-*)	semi-	half, partial
in-	not (*il-, im-, ir-*)	sub-	below, under (*suc-, suf-, sug-, sum-, sup-, sur-, sus-*)
in-	into (*il-, im-, ir-*)		
inter-	between, within, mutual	super-	above, over
kilo-	thousand	syn-	together, with, similar (*sym-, syl-*)
mega-	large	tele-	distant, from afar (*tel-*)
micro-	small (*micr-*)	trans-	across, beyond, through
mid-	middle	tri-	three
milli-	thousand	un-	not, opposite of
		uni-	one, single

APPENDIX H Applying Prefix Knowledge to Common Latin Roots

Root:		
Word	**Literal Meaning**	**Actual Meaning**

Instructions

Academic Vocabulary: This is a 5- to 10-minute lesson prior to a small-group session to teach academic vocabulary, usually to the whole class. Show students the new word; then invite them to read the word with you and to call out the word's spelling. Introduction of the word might include an invitation to speculate on the word's meaning. It should include student talk, examples of the word being used, and a synthesis of the discussion that makes clear the word's meaning. Once introduced, apply the word in the weekly small-group lesson and at other appropriate times; encourage students to use the word and previously taught academic vocabulary words.

Materials: What do you need for this lesson, including images to support vocabulary teaching/learning?

Orthographic Feature Focus for This Week: What feature are you targeting for instruction?

Connect the New to the Known: What do students already know related to the feature you've listed above that will help them with new learning in this lesson? It may be the feature you focused on last week.

Words from the Categorization That May Need to Be Taught: Draw on what you know about students' vocabulary knowledge, and invite their questions about unfamiliar words, to identify new words to discuss and words with multiple meanings the students may not know. Acting out each word's meaning and showing images of the word's meaning are two ways to support language minority students' understanding.

Survey (and Sort): If this lesson builds on the previous lesson, it is helpful to begin by asking students to recall what they learned about in that lesson. After discussing unfamiliar vocabulary, engage students in sorting the word cards. A gradual-release-of-responsibility approach will help to ensure that all students in the group can actively participate. Whatever your approach, be sure that students are cognitively engaged. Namely, don't just tell them where to place word cards; involve them in actively considering where to place each card.

Analyze: There should be lots of student talk here. Encourage students to think and talk with prompts, such as these:

- Do the words in each category go together? Did you appropriately place the words? Do you need to modify any of the placements?
- How are the words similar in each category?
- Do you detect any problems?
- Do we need continue to refine the placement of any of the words?
- What do you think each category has in common?

Interpret: The take-aways or <u>insights</u> should be about the orthographic <u>features</u>, but also, ideally, will be about the vocabulary. As students think about what their take-aways or <u>insights</u> are and any <u>strategies</u> they used to help them, encourage them to provide <u>evidence</u> to support or <u>justify</u> their thinking. Also, ask them to <u>clarify</u> their thinking by telling more; encourage them to ask each other to <u>clarify</u> when needed. Guide students to articulate their <u>insights</u> or take-aways from the lesson today, and to be as <u>explicit</u> as possible.

Prompts that might be useful include the following:

- What did you learn from our categories; how do you interpret them?
- We need you to justify your idea. What evidence in the sort makes you think as you do?
- Can you be more explicit?

Note: Your use of the academic vocabulary words (<u>underlined</u>) that have been taught is important.

Link: You might present students with a sentence or paragraph that includes a couple of non-sort words with the same feature as targeted in the lesson, to check their understanding and ability to read the sentence. Or you might dictate a sentence that includes sort words or non-sort words with the targeted feature and ask students to write it. Discuss their results. Close the lesson with a recapping of what students learned that will enable them to become better readers and/or writers.

(continued)

Preparing for the Lesson

Academic Vocabulary *Teach New Vocabulary to Expand Knowledge of Word Meanings:*	**Group:**
	Date:
Orthographic Feature Focus for This Week *Connect the New to the Known:*	**Materials:**

Words from the Categorization That May Need to Be Taught

Teaching the SAIL Lesson

Survey (and Sort) *Key purpose: Introduce the words and discuss meanings; then categorize the words or pictures.*

(continued)

Teaching the SAIL Lesson *(continued)*

Analyze

Key purpose: Have students check closely to see that they have placed the words in the way they think best, and encourage talking/conferring with partners or the group to aid their analysis.

Interpret

Key purpose: Uncover what students have learned; clarify or add to those understandings; identify or imply take-aways that they can use in reading and/or writing.

Link

Key purpose: To bring meaningful closure to the lesson through synthesis, and to afford students opportunity to apply and link understandings through reading and/or writing.

Reflecting on the Lesson
- What remarkable learning did you hear or observe during this lesson?
- What went well?
- What would you like to improve on next week?
- What did the students learn? Who learned what?
- What did the students, or some of them, not grasp?
- What can you do to make the learning more effective?
- Can you write down the academic vocabulary words you have heard each child use? Or are you the only one using the academic vocabulary? If the latter, what can you do to change this?
- Were students engaged in the lesson? Why or why not?
- What percentage of the time was teacher talk, and what percentage of the time was student talk?

ANITA C. HERNÁNDEZ
JOSÉ A. MONTELONGO
New Mexico State University

English–Spanish cognate pairs are words that are spelled identically (or nearly identically) and have the same meaning (or nearly the same meaning) in both English and Spanish. Sometimes the spelling is transparent, in words such as the English *idea* and the Spanish *idea*. In other cases, the spelling similarity is not as transparent as in the cognate pairs: *space* and *espacio*. Even in such pairs, however, the relationship between the English and Spanish words is evident. This makes cognates among the easiest vocabulary words for Spanish-speaking Latinx English learners (ELs) to understand, because of the transparency in spelling and meaning. Moreover, Spanish–English cognates allow students to learn vocabulary simultaneously—a form of *translanguaging,* where students can use their two languages to enhance their own learning (Garcia, Ibarra-Johnson, & Seltzer, 2017). The word cards should be presented in random order. To make checking easier, the answer keys have been alphabetized.

Cognates are an important linguistic category of words that should be taught. There are more than 20,000 English–Spanish cognates (Nash, 1997) and many of them are academic words that intermediate students read in their science, social studies, and mathematics textbooks. For Latinx ELs, English–Spanish cognates open the door to learning academic language, as many of the cognate vocabulary words are found in the glossaries of their content area textbooks. Cognates also tap into Latinx ELs' linguistic funds of knowledge and stimulate them to learn more about their two languages. Once teachers introduce this category of words, students begin to see them everywhere in their classrooms and in their texts. Cognate vocabulary enhances their motivation to learn, and they become much more interested in word study.

Note: Not all Spanish–English words are cognates; the noncognate words are translations.

Once Latinx students who are ELs have an understanding of cognates, teachers can then instruct them to recognize cognates through the rich morphological relationships between English and Spanish. Typically, cognates consist of a root word or word root plus a prefix and/or suffix. For example, the English word *inaudible* is composed of a prefix, *in-,* a word root, *aud-,* and a suffix, *-ible*—just as its Spanish cognate, *inaudible,* is.

The morphological relationships between English words and their Spanish cognates are not random, but rule-governed. Just as it is incumbent upon teachers to have their students learn the transformational rules for changing verbs from one tense to another, or for changing nouns from singular to plural, it is important for teachers to have their Latinx ELs learn the rules for transforming English words to their Spanish cognates and vice versa using morphology. Purposeful word sorts can be used both to help students learn these transformational rules and to reinforce their learning and expand their vocabulary. Below we suggest three morphological strategies.

Strategy 1: Cognate Recognition and Categorization through Latin and Greek Prefixes

Teachers can promote the development of a cognate recognition strategy by teaching Latinx ELs that certain Latin and Greek prefixes are identical or similar in both English and Spanish. This is evident in the English–Spanish cognate pairs that are presented in Sort 1 of this appendix, below.

We illustrate the teaching and sorting of cognates by prefixes with the list of nine words in Sort 1. The first step is to have the students match each English word with its Spanish cognate. Next, have the students group the words by their prefixes: *uni-*, *bi-*, and *tri-*. Discuss with the students the meanings of the prefixes and the meanings of the English and Spanish words. Point out that many words in English have Spanish cognates that have the same prefixes.

SORT 1. Cognate Prefixes (*uni-*, *bi-*, *tri-*)

English Cognates	Spanish Cognates
bicycle	*bicicleta*
bilingual	*bilingüe*
binoculars	*binoculares*
triangle	*triángulo*
tricycle	*triciclo*
trilingual	*trilingüe*
unicorn	*uniciclo*
unicycle	*unicornio*
uniform	*uniforme*

Results for Sort 1 are as follows:

uni- prefix in English . . .	. . . is also the *uni-* prefix in Spanish
unicorn	*unicornio*
unicycle	*uniciclo*
uniform	*uniforme*

bi- prefix in English . . .	. . . is also the *bi-* prefix in Spanish
bicycle	*bicicleta*
bilingual	*bilingüe*
binoculars	*binoculares*

tri- prefix in English . . .	. . . is also the *tri-* prefix in Spanish
triangle	*triángulo*
tricycle	*triciclo*
trilingual	*trilingüe*

Considerations: Draw attention to the idea that these English prefixes are the same or nearly the same in Spanish in both spelling and meaning.

Sort 2 below provides another list of nine words with three different prefixes. First, have the students match each English word with its Spanish cognate. Next have the students group the words by their prefixes: *trans-*, *tele-*, and *inter-*. Discuss with the students the meanings of the prefixes and the meanings of the English and Spanish words: *trans-* means "across"; *tele-* means "distant"; *inter-* means "between." Remind students that many words in English have Spanish cognates that have the same prefixes.

SORT 2. Cognate Prefixes (*trans-*, *tele-*, *inter-*)

English Cognates	Spanish Cognates
intercept	*interceptar*
interfere	*interferir*
interrupt	*interrumpir*
telephone	*teléfono*
telescope	*telescopio*
television	*televisión*
transfer	*transferir*
transmit	*transmitir*
transport	*transportar*

Results for Sort 2 are as follows:

trans- prefix in English . . .	. . . is also the *trans-* prefix in Spanish
transfer	*transferir*
transmit	*transmitir*
transport	*transportar*

tele- prefix in English . . .	. . . is also the *tele-* prefix in Spanish
telephone	*teléfono*
telescope	*telescopio*
television	*televisión*

inter- prefix in English . . .	. . . is also the *inter-* prefix in Spanish
intercept	*interceptar*
interfere	*interferir*
interrupt	*interrumpir*

Many books and web pages provide listings of Latin and Greek prefixes, along with example words. To check whether a particular word is or is not an English–Spanish cognate, a teacher or student can consult the Find-A-Cognate Database (Montelongo, Hernández, & Herter, 2011) at *www.angelfire.com/ill/monte/findacognate.html.*

Strategy 2: Cognate Recognition Using Latin and Greek Roots

Many academic words in English contain roots that are derived from Latin and Greek. Words such as *dictionary, homograph,* and *automatic* carry meaning-transparent clues in their roots. When Latinx ELs are taught that *dict-* means "to say or speak," that *-graph* means "to write," and that *auto-* means "self," as well as the meanings of many other cognate roots, they are often able to make sense of previously unknown words. Knowledge of Latin and Greek roots can be used to recall or generate words related to each other by virtue of being derived from the same root. Words such as *contradict, dictionary,* and *prediction* are all related to "say/speak."

Contradict means "to speak against" or "to say the opposite," *dictionary* means "a book in which (spoken) words are defined," and *predict* means "to say what will happen before it occurs." Similarly, words with *-graph* have meanings associated with "letters," "to write," or "to record," such as *homograph* and *photograph.* Words with *auto-* have meanings associated with "self," such as *automatic* meaning "self-acting," *automobile* meaning "a car that moves by itself," and *autograph* meaning "a signature written by a person him- or herself."

Teachers can create morphology mini-lessons with sorts of cognate words with Latin and Greek roots. In doing so, teachers provide their Latinx ELs with yet another potent strategy for recognizing cognates. A sample set of nine Latin and Greek roots is presented in Sort 3. First, have students match each English word with its Spanish cognate. After the students have matched the English words with their Spanish cognates, ask students to group the words by their roots (*dict-*, *-graph*, and *auto-*) and try to figure out the meanings of the words. Discuss the meanings of the roots and the meanings of the English and Spanish cognates. Here, as earlier, point out that many English words have Spanish cognates with the same word roots.

SORT 3. Cognate Roots (*dict-*, *-graph*, *auto-*)

English Cognates	Spanish Cognates
autograph	*autografía*
automatic	*automático*
automobile	*automóvil*
calligraphy	*caligrafía*
contradict	*contradecir*
dictionary	*diccionario*
homograph	*homógrafo*
photograph	*fotografía*
prediction	*predicción*

Results for Sort 3 are as follows:

dict- root in English . . .	. . . is the *dic-* root in Spanish
dictator	*dictador*
dictionary	*diccionario*
prediction	*predicción*

-graph root in English . . .	. . . is the *-graf* root in Spanish
calligraphy	*caligrafía*
homograph	*homógrafo*
photograph	*fotografía*

auto- root in English . . .	. . . is also the *auto-* root in Spanish
autograph	*autografía*
automatic	*automático*
automobile	*automóvil*

Considerations: Discuss the meaning of the roots in Sort 3: *dict-* ("to say"), *-graph* ("to write"), and *auto-* ("self"). Draw attention to the idea that these English word roots are the same or nearly the same in Spanish in both spelling and meaning.

Another variation of the root sorts is to engage students in a cognate sort with both English and Spanish words that begin with any of the roots. Reassure students that several roots in English can be translated reliably into Spanish. You can provide the English roots first and have the students read them and discuss the root. Next, provide the Spanish words and instruct students to match the Spanish cognates with the English cognates. Discuss the similarities in spelling of the English and Spanish cognates. To extend the learning, ask students to brainstorm other words possessing the same roots. Other examples using the roots *tele-*, *dict-*, and *auto-* include *telegraph–telegráfo*, *telegram–telegrama*, *dictation–dictado*, *dictate–dictar*, and *autobiography–autobiografía*.

As is the case with cognate prefixes, there are many Latin and Greek word roots in addition to those included here. Many language books and web pages can be consulted for root meanings and examples of words that follow those rules. Once again, the Find-A-Cognate Database (Montelongo et al., 2011) can be used to check whether a particular word is or is not an English–Spanish cognate.

Strategy 3: Cognate Recognition Using Cognate Suffixes

A particularly fruitful set of resources for enabling Latinx ELs to develop cognate recognition strategies is the set of rule-governed suffix or word-ending patterns that exist between English and Spanish. Thousands of English words can be transformed into their Spanish cognates by knowing a few rule-governed word-ending patterns (Means, 2003). For example, English words ending in the suffix *-ic* can be converted into Spanish cognates ending in *-ico*, as seen in the pair *magic–mágico*. English adverbs possessing the ending *-ly*, which means "like," become Spanish cognates having the *-mente* ending (e.g., *possibly–posiblemente*). English adjectives with the suffix *-ous*, which means "possessing, full of a given quality," become Spanish cognates having the *-oso* ending (e.g., generous–*generoso*). Generally, suffixes change the meaning of words. Picture books contain many cognates that can be converted from English to Spanish (and vice versa) using word-ending patterns (e.g., Hernández, Montelongo, & Herter, 2016; Montelongo, Hernández, & Herter, 2014). Examples of the cognate words and the word-ending rules are presented in Sort 4.

In the list of nine words in Sort 4, have the students match each English word with its Spanish cognate. Then ask students to group the words by their word endings or suffixes: *-ic/-ico*, *-ly/-mente*, and *-ous/-oso*. Discuss the meaning of the suffixes and the words.

SORT 4. Cognate Suffixes and Word-Ending Regularities (*-ic/-ico, -ly/-mente, -ous/-oso*)

English Words	Spanish Words
famous	*famoso*
fantastic	*fantástico*
generous	*generoso*
magic	*mágico*
perfectly	*perfectamente*
plastic	*plástico*
possibly	*posiblemente*
precious	*precioso*
totally	*totalmente*

Results for Sort 4 are as follows:

-ic words in English . . .	. . . are *-ico* words in Spanish
fantastic	*fantástico*
magic	*mágico*
plastic	*plástico*

-ly suffix in English . . .	. . . is the *-mente* suffix in Spanish
perfectly	*perfectamente*
possibly	*posiblemente*
totally	*totalmente*

-ous suffix in English . . .	. . . is the *-oso* suffix in Spanish
famous	*famoso*
generous	*generoso*
precious	*precioso*

Considerations: Discuss the effect of the word-ending patterns or suffixes on the words in Sort 4: *-ic/-ico, -ly/-mente,* and *-ous/-oso.* In addition to reinforcing the idea that these words are English–Spanish cognates, draw attention to the idea that these English word-ending patterns or suffixes change the parts of speech of the root words.

Engage students in a cognate sort with both English and Spanish words that contain any of the word-ending patterns. You can present the English words first and have the students read them, notice each suffix in the word, and discuss the word. Next, present the Spanish words and instruct students to match the Spanish cognates with the English cognates. Compare and contrast the spellings of the English and Spanish cognates. To extend the learning, ask students to brainstorm other words possessing the suffix or word-ending patterns. For further study, continue to consult language books and web pages for Latin and Greek suffixes and to use the Find-A-Cognate Database (Montelongo et al., 2011) to check whether other words students may generate are English–Spanish cognates.

In sum, teaching Spanish–English cognates and their morphological patterns represents an "assets" approach to literacy instruction for Latinx ELs—one that builds on knowledge that students bring to schools. This is in contrast to a deficit approach, which assumes ELs are deficient because they lack English proficiency. The cognate word sorts allow students to simultaneously leverage their metalinguistic knowledge while enhancing their own literacies.

Translated by
ANITA C. HERNÁNDEZ
JOSÉ A. MONTELONGO

Note: Most words are English–Spanish cognates; those that are not cognates or are translations have an asterisk.

MORE DIFFICULT (see Chapter 1, Table 1.4)

Survey

academic	*académico*	distinction	*distincción*
analogous	*análogo*	elements	*elementos*
*approach	*enfoque*	explicit	*explícito*
aspects	*aspectos*	indicate	*indicar*
collapse	*colapso*	monitor	*monitorear*
complex	*complejo*	notion	*noción*
components	*componentes*	precise	*preciso*
contribution	*contribución*	*prior	*previo*
definite	*definitivo*	scenario	*escenario*
denote	*denotar*	specified	*especificado*
derived	*derivado*	*survey	*encuesta* or *estudio*

Analyze

adjacent	*adyacente*	criteria	*criteria*
alter	*alterar*	detected	*detectar*
analysis	*análisis*	deviation	*desviación*
analyze	*analizar*	eliminate	*eliminar*
apparent	*aparente*	excluded	*excluido*
assume	*asumir*	incorporated	*incorporado*
coincide	*coincidir*	modified	*modificado*
*comprise	*comprender* or *consistir en*	predominantly	*predominante*
confirmed	*confirmado*	presumption	*presunción*
consistent	*consistente*	stress	*estrés*
convinced	*convencido*		

*Words are translations and are also non-cognate words.

(*continued*)

MORE DIFFICULT *(continued)*

Interpret

abstract	*abstracto*	isolated	*aislado*
*acknowledged	*reconocido* or *admitido*	implies	*implica*
adequate	*adecuado*	inclination	*inclinación*
affect	*afectar*	interpretation	*interpretación*
alternative	*alternativo*	justification	*justificación*
ambiguous	*ambiguo*	*nonetheless	*sin embargo* or *no obstante*
arbitrary	*arbitrario*	*notwithstanding	*no obstante*
attributed	*atribuir*	perceived	*percibido*
clarity	*claridad*	perspective	*perspectiva*
conceived	*concebido*	preliminary	*preliminario*
contrary	*contrario*	primary	*primario*
*conversely	*a la inversa* or *en cambio*	principle	*principio*
deduction	*deducción*	process	*proceso*
encountered	*encontrado*	solely	*solo*
factors	*factores*	*straightforward	*directo*
impact	*impacto*	theory	*teoría*
implications	*implicaciones*	*underlying	*subyacente*

Link

compiled	*compilado*	option	*opción*
differentiation	*diferenciación*	relevant	*relevante*
facilitate	*facilitar*	substitution	*sustitución*
generated	*generado*	sufficient	*suficiente*
integration	*integración*	*ultimately	*finalmente* or *en última estancia*
*link	*enlace*		

EASIER (see Chapter 1, Table 1.5)

Survey

definitely	*definitivamente* or *seguro*	different	*diferente*
definition	*definición*	differs	*difiere*
describe	*describir*	disagree	*discrepar* or *no estar de acuerdo*
descriptive	*descriptivo*	discussion	*discusión*

(continued)

EASIER *(continued)*			
exactly	*exactamente*	obvious	*obvio*
explain	*explicar*	provide	*proveer*
identify	*identificar*	refer	*referir*
illustrate	*ilustrar*	specifics	*específicos* or *detalles específicos*
interruption	*interrupción*	*survey	*encuesta* or *estudio*

Analyze

*accurate	*preciso*	definitely	*definitivamente* or *seguro*
*agree	*de acuerdo*	detect	*detectar*
*agreement	*acuerdo*	detectives	*detectives*
analyze	*analizar*	determine	*determinar*
categories	*categorías*	examine	*examinar*
column	*columna*	*features	*caracteristicas*
confer	*conferir*	located	*localizado* or *situado*
correspond	*corresponder*	refine	*refinar*

Interpret

alters	*altera*	*highlight	*resaltar*
appropriate	*apropiado*	*insights	*ideas*
clarify	*aclarar*	interpret	*interpretar*
common	*común*	justify	*justificar*
consider	*considerar*	observations	*observaciones*
consult	*consultar*	*overlaps	*superposiciones*
evidence	*evidencia*	*understanding	*comprensión*

Link

apply	*aplicar*	expression	*expresión*
*challenge	*desafío* or *el reto*	focus	*enfocar*
compare	*comparar*	imagine	*imaginar*
context	*contexto*	reasoning	*razonamiento*
decide	*decidir*	record	*grabar*
demonstrate	*demostrar*	strategies	*estrategias*
difficult	*difícil*	transfer	*transferir*
discovered	*descubierto*		

References

Professional Literature

Adams, M. J. (2004). Modeling the connections between word recognition and reading. In R. B. Ruddell & N. J. Unrau (Eds.), *Theoretical models and processes of reading* (5th ed., pp. 1219–1243). Newark, DE: International Reading Association.

Allen, J. (1999). *Words, words, words*. York, ME: Stenhouse.

The American Heritage® College Dictionary (4th ed.). (2004). Boston: Houghton Mifflin.

The American Heritage® Dictionary of the English Language (3rd ed.). (1996). Boston: Houghton Mifflin.

The American Heritage® Dictionary of the English Language (5th ed.). (2011). Boston: Houghton Mifflin.

The American Heritage® Dictionary of the English Language (5th ed., online version). (2020). Boston: Houghton Mifflin Harcourt. Retrieved from *https://ahdictionary.com/word/search.html*.

Ammer, C. (1997). *The American Heritage dictionary of idioms*. Boston: Houghton Mifflin.

Anderson, R. C., & Nagy, W. E. (1992, Winter). The vocabulary conundrum. *American Educator, 16,* 14–18, 44–47.

Anglin, J. M. (1993). Knowing versus learning words. *Monographs of the Society for Research in Child Development, 58*(10), 176–186.

Applebee, A. N., Langer, J. A., Nystrand, M., & Gamoran, A. (2003). Discussion-based approaches to developing understanding: Classroom instruction and student performance in middle and high school English. *American Educational Research Journal, 40*(3), 685–730.

Archer, A, L., & Hughes, C. A. (2011). *Explicit instruction: Effective and efficient teaching.* New York: Guilford Press.

August, D., Carlo, M., Dressler, C., & Snow, C. (2005). The critical role of vocabulary development for English language learners. *Learning Disabilities Research and Practice, 20,* 50–57.

Baratta, A. M. (2010). Nominalization development across an undergraduate academic degree program. *Journal of Pragmatics, 42,* 1017–1036.

Barnhart, R. K. (Ed.). (2005). *Chambers dictionary of etymology.* New York: Chambers.

Baumann, J. F., Edwards, E. C., Font, G., Tereshinski, C. A., Kame'enui, E. J., & Olejnik, S. (2002). Teaching morphemic and contextual analysis to fifth-grade students. *Reading Research Quarterly, 37*(2), 150–178.

Baumann, J. F., & Graves, M. F. (2010). What is academic vocabulary? *Journal of Adolescent and Adult Literacy, 54*(1), 4–12.

Baumann, J. F., Jones, L. A., & Seifert-Kessell, N. (1993). Using think alouds to enhance children's comprehension monitoring abilities. *The Reading Teacher, 47,* 184–193.

Baumann, J. F., Kame'enui, E. J., & Ash, G. (2003). Research on vocabulary instruction: Voltaire redux. In J. Flood, D. Lapp, J. R. Squire, & J. Jensen (Eds.), *Handbook of research on teaching the English language arts* (2nd ed., pp. 752–785). Mahwah, NJ: Erlbaum.

Bear, D., Invernizzi, M., Templeton, S., & Johnston, F. (2016). *Words their way: Word study for phonics, spelling, and vocabulary instruction* (6th ed.). Boston: Pearson.

Beck, I. L., & McKeown, M. G. (1991). Conditions of vocabulary acquisition. In P. D. Pearson (Ed.), *Handbook of reading research* (Vol. 2, pp. 789–814). New York: Longman.

Beck, I. L., McKeown, M. G., & Kucan, L. (2013). *Bringing words to life: Robust vocabulary instruction* (2nd ed.). New York: Guilford Press.

Berkeley, S., Mastropieri, M. A., & Scruggs, T. E. (2011). Reading comprehension strategy instruction and attribution retraining for secondary students with learning and other mild disabilities. *Journal of Learning Disabilities, 44,* 18–32.

Biemiller, A. (2001). Teaching vocabulary: Early, direct, and sequential. *American Educator, 25,* 24–26.

Biemiller, A. (2005). Size and sequence in vocabulary

development: Implications for choosing words for primary grade vocabulary instruction. In E. H. Hiebert & M. Kamil (Eds.), *Teaching and learning vocabulary: Bringing research to practice* (pp. 223–242). Mahwah, NJ: Erlbaum.

Blachowicz, C. L. Z. (1986). Making connections: Alternatives to the vocabulary notebook. *Journal of Reading, 29,* 643–649.

Blevins, W. (2001). *Teaching phonics and word study in the intermediate grades.* New York: Scholastic.

Block, C. C., & Mangieri, J. N. (2003). *Exemplary literacy teachers: Promoting success for all children in grades K–5.* New York: Guilford Press.

Bowers, P. N., Kirby, J. R., & Deacon, S. H. (2010). The effects of morphological instruction on literacy skills: A systematic review of the literature. *Review of Educational Research, 80*(2), 144–179.

Boyle, J. R., & Kennedy, M. J. (2019). Innovations in classroom technology for students with disabilities. *Intervention in School and Clinic, 55*(2), 67–70.

Branch, G. F., Hanushek, E. A., & Rivkin, S. G. (2013). School leaders matter. *Education Next, 13*(1), 63–69. Retrieved September 3, 2019, from *www.educationnext.org/school-leaders-matter.*

Brown, B. A., Ryoo, K., & Rodriguez, J. (2010). Pathway towards fluency: Using 'disaggregate instruction' to promote science literacy. *International Journal of Science Education, 32,* 1465–1493.

Brown, J. I. (1947). Reading and vocabulary: 14 master words. In M. J. Herzberg (Ed.), *Word study* (pp. 1–4). Springfield, MA: G. & C. Merriam.

Bruner, J., Goodnow, J. J., & Austin, G. A. (1956). *A study of thinking.* New York: Wiley.

Bruner, J., Goodnow, J. J., & Austin, G. (1986). *A study of thinking.* Piscataway, NJ: Transaction.

Bryant, D. P., Goodwin, M., Bryant, B. R., & Higgins, K. (2003). Vocabulary instruction for students with learning disabilities: A review of the research. *Learning Disability Quarterly, 26,* 117–128.

Carlisle, J. F. (2010). Effects of instruction in morphological awareness on literacy achievement: An integrative review. *Reading Research Quarterly, 45*(4), 464–483.

Carroll, L. [C. L. Dodgson]. (1971). *Alice in Wonderland and through the looking glass.* New York: Norton.

Cary, S. (2000). *Working with second language learners: Answers to teachers' top ten questions.* Portsmouth, NH: Heinemann.

Cazden, C. B. (2001). *Classroom discourse: The language of teaching and learning.* Portsmouth, NH: Heinemann.

Ciullo, S., Ely, E., McKenna, J. W., Alves, K. D., & Kennedy, M. J. (2019). Reading instruction for students with learning disabilities in grades 4 and 5: An observation study. *Learning Disability Quarterly, 42*(2), 67–79.

Copland, M. A. (2004). Distributed leadership for instructional improvement: The principal's role. In D. S. Strickland & M. Kamil (Eds.), *Improving reading achievement through professional development* (pp. 213–231). Norwood, MA: Christopher-Gordon.

Cotton, K. (2003). *Principals and student achievement: What the research says.* Alexandria, VA: Association for Supervision and Curriculum Development.

Coxhead, A. (2000). A new academic word list. *TESOL Quarterly, 34*(2), 213–238.

Dale, E. (1965). Vocabulary measurement: Techniques and major findings. *Elementary English, 42,* 82–88.

Dingle, M. P., Brownell, M. T., Leko, M. M., Boardman, A. G., & Haager, D. (2011). Developing effective special education reading teachers: The influence of professional development, context, and individual qualities. *Learning Disability Quarterly, 34,* 87–103.

Dockrell, J. E., & Messer, D. J. (2004). Lexical acquisition in the early school years. In R. A. Berman (Ed.), *Language development across childhood and adolescence* (pp. 35–52). Amsterdam, the Netherlands: John Benjamins.

Durkin, D. D. (1978). What classroom observations reveal about reading comprehension. *Reading Research Quarterly, 14,* 481–533.

Ebbers, S. M., & Denton, C. A. (2008). A root awakening: Vocabulary instruction for older students with reading difficulties. *Learning Disabilities Research and Practice, 23,* 90–102.

Ehri, L. C., & Rosenthal, J. (2007). Spelling of words: A neglected facilitator of vocabulary learning. *Journal of Literacy Research, 39*(4), 389–409.

Elleman, A. M., Lindo, E. J., Morphy, P., & Compton, D. L. (2009). The impact of vocabulary instruction on passage-level comprehension of school-age children: A meta-analysis. *Journal of Research on Educational Effectiveness, 2,* 1–44.

Fang, Z. (2012). Language correlates of disciplinary literacy. *Topics in Language Disorders, 32*(1), 19–34.

Fang, Z., Lamme, L., & Pringle, R. (2010). *Language and literacy in inquiry-based science classrooms, grades 3–8.* Thousand Oaks, CA: Corwin.

Feldon, D. F. (2007). Cognitive load and classroom teaching: The double-edged sword of automaticity. *Educational Psychologist, 42,* 123–137.

Francis, D. J., Shaywitz, S. E., Stuebing, K. K., Shaywitz, B. A., & Fletcher, J. M. (1996). Developmental lag versus deficit models of reading disability: A longitudinal, individual growth curves analysis. *Journal of Educational Psychology, 88,* 3–17.

Fuchs, F., Fuchs, L. S., & Vaughn, S. (2014). What is intensive instruction and why is it important? *Teaching Exceptional Children, 46*(4), 13–18.

Ganske, K. (1999). The Developmental Spelling

Analysis: A measure of orthographic knowledge. *Educational Assessment, 6*(1), 41–70.

Ganske, K. (2006). *Word sorts and more: Sound, pattern, and meaning explorations K–3.* New York: Guilford Press.

Ganske, K. (2014). *Word journeys: Assessment-guided phonics, spelling, and vocabulary instruction* (2nd ed.). New York: Guilford Press.

Ganske, K. (2016). SAIL: A framework for promoting next generation word study. *The Reading Teacher, 70*(3), 337–346.

Ganske, K. (2017). Lesson closure: An important piece of the student learning puzzle. *The Reading Teacher, 71*(1), 95–100.

Ganske, K. (2018). *Word sorts and more: Sound, pattern, and meaning explorations K–3* (2nd ed.). New York: Guilford Press.

Garcia, O., Ibarra-Johnson, S., & Seltzer, K. (2017). *The translanguaging classroom: Leveraging student bilingualism for learning.* Philadelphia: Caslon.

Goodwin, A. P., & Ahn, S. (2010). A meta-analysis of morphological interventions: Effects on literacy achievement of children with literacy difficulties. *Annals of Dyslexia, 60*(2), 183–208.

Goodwin, A. P., & Ahn, S. (2013). A meta-analysis of morphological interventions in English: Effects on literacy outcomes for school-age children. *Scientific Studies of Reading, 17*(4), 257–285.

Goodwin, A. P., Cho, S. J., & Nichols, S. (2016). Ways to 'WIN' at vocabulary learning. *The Reading Teacher, 70*(1), 93–97.

Goodwin, A. P., Gilbert, J. K., & Cho, S. J. (2013). Morphological contributions to adolescent word reading: An item response approach. *Reading Research Quarterly, 48*(1), 39–60.

Goodwin, A. P., Gilbert, J. K., Cho, S. J., & Kearns, D. M. (2014). Probing lexical representations: Simultaneous modeling of word and person contributions to multidimensional lexical representations. *Journal of Educational Psychology, 106*(2), 448–468.

Goodwin, A. P., Lipsky, M., & Ahn, S. (2012). Word detectives: Using units of meaning to support literacy. *The Reading Teacher, 65*(7), 461–470.

Goodwin, A. P., & Perkins, J. (2015). Word detectives: Morphological instruction that supports academic language. *The Reading Teacher, 68*(7), 504–517.

Goodwin, A. P., Petscher, Y., Carlisle, J. F., & Mitchell, A. M. (2017). Exploring the dimensionality of morphological knowledge for adolescent readers. *Journal of Research in Reading, 40*(1), 91–117.

Graham, S. (2013). Writing standards. In L. M. Morrow, K. K. Wixson, & T. Shanahan (Eds.), *Teaching with the Common Core Standards for English language arts, grades 3–5* (pp. 88–106). New York: Guilford Press.

Graham, S., & Santangelo, T. (2014). Does spelling instruction make students better spellers, readers, and writers?: A meta-analytic review. *Reading and Writing, 27*(9), 1703–1743.

Graves, M. F. (2006). *The vocabulary book: Learning and instruction.* New York: Teachers College Press.

Graves, M. F., August, D., & Mancilla-Martinez, J. (2013). *Teaching vocabulary to English language learners.* New York: Teachers College Press.

Gunuc, S. (2014). The relationship between student engagement and their academic achievement. *International Journal on Trends in Education and Their Implications, 5*(5), 216–231.

Harris, M. L., Schumaker, J. B., & Deshler, D. D. (2011). The effects of strategic morphological analysis instruction on the vocabulary performance of secondary students with and without disabilities. *Learning Disability Quarterly, 34*(1), 17–33.

Harris, T. L., & Hodges, R. E. (1995). *The literacy dictionary: The vocabulary of reading and writing.* Newark, DE: International Reading Association.

Hart, B., & Risley, T. R. (1995). *Meaningful differences in the everyday experiences of young American children.* Baltimore: Brookes.

Heaney, S. (2000). *Beowulf: A new verse translation* (bilingual ed.). New York: Farrar, Straus & Giroux.

Henderson, E. H. (1981). *Learning to read and spell: The child's knowledge of words.* DeKalb: Northern Illinois University Press.

Hendrickson, R. (2004). *Facts on file encyclopedia: Word and phrase origins.* New York: Checkmark Books.

Herbert, P. (1991). *Humor in the classroom: Theories, functions, and guidelines.* Chicago: Central States Communication Association.

Hernández, A. C., Montelongo, J. A., & Herter, R. J. (2016). Using Spanish–English cognates in *Children's Choices* picture books to develop Latino English learners' linguistic knowledge. *The Reading Teacher, 70*(2), 233–239.

Hughes, C. A., Morris, J. R., Therrien, W. T., & Benson, S. K. (2017). Explicit instruction: Historical and contemporary contexts. *Learning Disabilities Research and Practice, 32*, 140–148.

Jeder, D. (2015). Implications of using humor in the classroom. *Procedia—Social and Behavioral Sciences, 180*, 828–833.

Jitendra, A. K., Edwards, L. L., Sacks, G., & Jacobson, L. A. (2004). What research says about vocabulary instruction for students with learning disabilities. *Exceptional Children, 70*, 299–322.

Johnson, E. S., Humphrey, M., Mellard, D. F., Woods, K., & Swanson, H. L. (2010). Cognitive processing deficits and students with specific learning disabilities: A selective meta-analysis of the literature. *Learning Disability Quarterly, 33*, 3–18.

Kelley, J. G., Lesaux, N. K., Kieffer, M. J., & Faller, S. E. (2010). Effective academic vocabulary instruction in the urban middle school. *The Reading Teacher, 64,* 5–14.

Kennedy, M. J., Deshler, D. D., & Lloyd, J. W. (2015). Effects of multimedia vocabulary instruction on adolescents with learning disabilities. *Journal of Learning Disabilities, 48,* 22–38.

Kennedy, M. J., Rodgers, W. J., Romig, J. E., Mathews, H. M., & Peeples, K. (2018). Introducing the Content Acquisition Podcast Professional Development (CAP-PD) process: Supporting vocabulary instruction for inclusive middle school science teachers. *Teacher Education and Special Education, 41,* 140–157.

Kennedy, M. J., Thomas, C. N., Meyer, J. P., Alves, K. D., & Lloyd, J. W. (2014). Using evidence-based multimedia to improve vocabulary performance of adolescents with LD. *Learning Disability Quarterly, 37,* 71–86.

Kennedy, M. J., & Wexler, J. (2013). Helping students succeed within secondary-level STEM content: Using the "T" in STEM to improve literacy skills. *Teaching Exceptional Children, 45*(4), 26–33.

Klingner, J. K., Urbach, J., Golos, D., Brownell, M. T., & Menon, S. (2010). Teaching reading in the 21st century: A glimpse at how special education teachers promote reading comprehension. *Learning Disability Quarterly, 33,* 59–74.

Knapp, M. S., & Associates. (1995). *Teaching for meaning in high-poverty classrooms.* New York: Teachers College Press.

Kuder, S. J. (2017). Vocabulary instruction for secondary students with reading disabilities: An updated research review. *Learning Disability Quarterly, 40,* 155–164.

Lawrence, E., & Seifert, D. (2016). *The Test of Semantic Reasoning.* Novato, CA: Academic Therapy Publications.

Lawrence, J. F., Crosson, A. C., Paré-Blagoev, E. J., & Snow, C. E. (2015). Word Generation randomized trial: Discussion mediates the impact of program treatment on academic word learning. *American Educational Research Journal, 52,* 750–786.

Lawrence, J. F., White, C., & Snow, C. E. (2010). The words students need. *Educational Leadership, 68*(2), 23–26.

Leithwood, K., Seashore Louis, K., Anderson, S., & Wahlstrom, K. (2004). *How leadership influences student learning.* New York: Wallace Foundation. Retrieved September 3, 2019, from *www.wallacefoundation.org/knowledge-center/Documents/How-Leadership-Influences-Student-Learning.pdf.*

Lesaux, N. K., Kieffer, M. J., Faller, S. E., & Kelley, J. (2010). The effectiveness and ease of implementation of an academic vocabulary intervention for linguistically diverse students in urban middle schools. *Reading Research Quarterly, 45,* 198–230.

Lesaux, N. K., Kieffer, M. J., Kelley, J., & Russ, J. (2014). Effects of academic vocabulary instruction for linguistically diverse adolescents: Evidence from a randomized field trial. *American Educational Research Journal, 51,* 1159–1194.

Lindström, E. R., Gesel, S. A., & Lemons, C. J. (2019). Data-based individualization in reading: Tips for successful implementation. *Intervention in School and Clinic, 55*(2), 113–119.

Marinellie, S. A., & Johnson, C. J. (2002). Definitional skill in school-age children with specific language impairment. *Journal of Communication Disorders, 35*(3), 241–259.

Marzano, R. J. (2004). *Building background knowledge for academic achievement.* Alexandria, VA: Association for Supervision and Curriculum Development.

Mayer, R. E. (2008). Applying the science of learning: Evidence-based principles for the design of multimedia instruction. *American Psychologist, 63,* 760–769.

McDermott, P. C., & Rothenberg, J. J. (1999, April). *Teaching in high poverty urban schools: Learning from practitioners and students.* Paper presented at the annual meeting of the American Educational Research Association, Montreal, Quebec, Canada.

McGregor, K. K., Oleson, J., Bahnsen, A., & Duff, D. (2013). Children with developmental language impairment have vocabulary deficits characterized by limited breadth and depth. *International Journal of Language and Communication Disorders, 48*(3), 307–319.

McKeown, M. G., Crosson, A. C., Moore, D. W., & Beck, I. L. (2018). Word knowledge and comprehension effects of an academic vocabulary intervention for middle school students. *American Educational Research Journal, 55*(3), 572–616.

McNeely, R. (n.d.). *Using humor in the classroom: Laughter has the power to fuel engagement and help students learn.* Washington, DC: National Education Association. Retrieved from *www.nea.org/tools/52165.htm.*

Means, T. (2003). *Instant Spanish vocabulary builder.* New York: Hippocrene Books.

The Merriam-Webster new book of word histories. (1991). Springfield, MA: Merriam-Webster.

Mitchell, A., & Savill-Smith, C. (2004). *The use of computer and video games for learning: A review of the literature.* London: Learning Skills Development Agency.

Mitchell, A. M., Truckenmiller, A., & Petscher, Y. (2015). Computer-adaptive assessments: Fundamentals and considerations. *Communique, 43*(8), 1–22.

Moats, L. (2005–2006, Winter). How spelling supports reading: And why it is more regular and predictable than you may think. *American Educator,* pp. 12–16, 20–22, 42–43.

Montelongo, J. A., Hernández, A. C., & Herter, R. J. (2011). Identifying cognates to scaffold instruction for Latino ELs. *The Reading Teacher, 65*(2), 161–164.

Montelongo, J. A., Hernández, A. C., & Herter, R. J. (2014). English–Spanish cognates and the Pura Belpre Children's Award Books: Reading the word and the world. *Multicultural Perspectives, 16,* 170–177.

Mueller, B. M. (2015). Analysis of nominalization in elementary and middle school science textbooks. *School of Education Student Capstone Theses and Dissertations, 247.* Retrieved from *https://digitalcommons.hamline.edu/hse_all/247.*

Murphy, P. K., Wilkinson, I. A., Soter, A. O., Hennessey, M. N., & Alexander, J. F. (2009). Examining the effects of classroom discussion on students' comprehension of text: A meta-analysis. *Journal of Educational Psychology, 101*(3), 740–764.

Nagy, W. E. (2005). Why instruction needs to be long-term and comprehensive. In E. H. Hiebert & M. L. Kamil (Eds.), *Teaching and learning vocabulary: Bringing research to practice* (pp. 27–44). Mahwah, NJ: Erlbaum.

Nagy, W. E., & Anderson, R. C. (1984). How many words are there in printed school English? *Reading Research Quarterly, 19,* 304–330.

Nagy, W. E., Carlisle, J. F., & Goodwin, A. P. (2014). Morphological knowledge and literacy acquisition. *Journal of Learning Disabilities, 47*(1), 3–12.

Nagy, W. E., & Scott, J. A. (2000). Vocabulary processes. In M. Kamil, P. Mosenthal, P. D. Pearson, & R. Barr (Eds.), *The handbook of reading research* (Vol. 3, pp. 269–284). New York: Longman.

Nagy, W. E., & Townsend, D. (2012). Words as tools: Learning academic vocabulary as language acquisition. *Reading Research Quarterly, 47,* 91–108.

Nash, R. (1997). *NTCs dictionary of Spanish cognates thematically organized.* New York: McGraw Hill Education.

National Academies of Sciences, Engineering, and Medicine. (2018). *How people learn II: Learners, contexts, and cultures.* Washington, DC: National Academies Press.

National Center for Education Statistics. (2015). *The National Assessment of Educational Progress: Reading.* Washington, DC: U.S. Department of Education. Retrieved from *https://nces.ed.gov/nationsreportcard/reading.*

National Center for Education Statistics. (2019). *Digest of education statistics, 2017* (NCES 2018-070). Washington, DC: U.S. Department of Education.

National Council for the Social Studies. (2013). *The College, Career, and Civic Life (C3) Framework for Social Studies State Standards: Guidance for enhancing the rigor of K–12 civics, economics, geography, and history.* Silver Springs, MD: Author.

National Governors Association Center for Best Practices & Council of Chief State School Officers. (2010). *Common Core State Standards for English language arts and literacy in history/social studies, science, and technical subjects.* Washington, DC: Authors.

National Reading Panel. (2000a). *Report of the National Reading Panel: Teaching children to read: An evidence-based assessment of the scientific research literature on reading and its implications for reading instruction.* Washington, DC: National Institute of Child Health and Human Development, National Institutes of Health.

National Reading Panel. (2000b). *Report of the National Reading Panel: Teaching children to read: An evidence-based assessment of the scientific research literature on reading and its implications for reading instruction: Reports of the subgroups.* Washington, DC: National Institute of Child Health and Human Development, National Institutes of Health.

Nelson, K. L., Dole, J. A., Hosp, J. L., & Hosp, M. K. (2015). Vocabulary instruction in K–3 low-income classrooms during a reading reform project. *Reading Psychology, 36,* 145–172.

Nevada Department of Education. (2018). *Nevada Academic Content Standards for social studies.* Carson City: Author.

Nippold, M. A. (2002). Lexical learning in school-age children, adolescents, and adults: A process where language and literacy converge. *Journal of Child Language, 29,* 474–478.

Nunes, T., & Bryant, P. (Eds.). (2006). *Improving literacy by teaching morphemes.* New York: Routledge.

Oldfather, P. (1995). Commentary: What's needed to maintain and extend motivation for literacy in the middle grades. *Journal of Reading, 38,* 420–422.

Pacheco, M. B., & Goodwin, A. P. (2013). Putting two and two together: Middle school students' morphological problem solving strategies for unknown words. *Journal of Adolescent and Adult Literacy, 56*(7), 541–553.

Peeples, K. N., Hirsch, S. E., Gardner, S. J., Keeley, R. G., Sherrow, B. L., McKenzie, J. M., et al. (2019). Using multimedia instruction and performance feedback to improve preservice teachers' vocabulary instruction. *Teacher Education and Special Education, 42*(3), 227–245.

Perfetti, C. (2007). Reading ability: Lexical quality to comprehension. *Scientific Studies of Reading, 11*(4), 357–383.

Perfetti, C. A., & Hart, L. (2002). The lexical quality hypothesis. In L. Verhoeven, C. Elbro, & P. Reitsma (Eds.), *Precursors of functional literacy* (pp. 190–213). Philadelphia: John Benjamins.

Phillips Galloway, E., Dobbs, C., Olivo, M., & Madigan, C. (2019). 'You can . . . ': An examination of linguistically-diverse learners' development of metalanguage and agency as language users within academic language units. *Linguistics and Education, 50,* 13–24.

Phillips Galloway, E., & McClain, J. (2020). *Examining the role of classroom talk in later language development.* Manuscript submitted for publication.

Phillips Galloway, E., & Uccelli, P. (2019). Examining developmental relations between core ademic language skills and reading comprehension for English learners and their peers. *Journal of Educational Psychology, 111*(1), 15–31.

Phillips Galloway, E., Uccelli, P., Aguilar, G., & Barr, C. D. (2020). Exploring the cross-linguistic contribution of Spanish and English academic language skills to English text comprehension for middle-grade dual language learners. *AERA Open, 6*(1).

Pianta, R. C., Hamre, B. K., & Allen, J. P. (2012) Teacher–student relationships and engagement: Conceptualizing, measuring, and improving the capacity of classroom interactions. In S. Christenson, A. L. Reschly, & C. Wylie (Eds.), *Handbook of research on student engagement* (pp. 365–386). New York: Springer.

Rotgans, J. I., & Schmidt, H. G. (2011). Cognitive engagement in the problem-based learning classroom. *Advances in Health Sciences Education: Theory and Practice, 16*(4), 465–479.

Rutherford, P. (2002). *Why didn't I learn this in college?* Alexandria, VA: Just ASK.

Schleppegrell, M. J. (2004). *The language of schooling: A functional linguistics perspective.* Mahwah, NJ: Erlbaum.

Schleppegrell, M. J. (2007). The linguistic challenges of mathematics teaching and learning: A research review. *Reading and Writing Quarterly, 23,* 139–159.

Scott, J. A., Jamieson-Noel, D., & Asselin, M. (2003). Vocabulary instruction throughout the day in twenty-three Canadian upper-elementary classrooms. *The Elementary School Journal, 103,* 269–286.

Sebastian, J., Allensworth, E., & Huang, H. (2016). The role of teacher leadership in how principals influence classroom instruction and student learning. *American Journal of Education, 123*(1), 69–108.

Silverman, R. D., Proctor, C. P., Harring, J. R., Doyle, B., Mitchell, M. A., & Meyer, A. G. (2013). Teachers' instruction and students' vocabulary and comprehension: An exploratory study with English monolingual and Spanish–English bilingual students in grades 3–5. *Reading Research Quarterly, 49,* 31–60.

Snow, C. E., Burns, S., & Griffin, P. (1998). *Preventing reading difficulties in young children.* Washington, DC: National Academy Press.

Snow, C. E., Griffin, P., & Burns, M.S. (Eds.). (2005). *Knowledge to support the teaching of reading: Preparing teachers for a changing world.* San Francisco: Jossey-Bass.

Snow, C. E., Lawrence, J. F., & White, C. (2009). Generating knowledge of academic language among urban middle school students. *Journal of Research on Educational Effectiveness, 2*(4), 325–344.

Snow, C. E., & Uccelli, P. (2009). The challenge of academic language. In D. R. Olson & N. Torrance (Eds.), *The Cambridge handbook of literacy* (pp. 112–133). New York: Cambridge University Press.

Spear-Swerling, L., & Zibulsky, J. (2014). Making time for literacy: Teacher knowledge and time allocation in instructional planning. *Reading and Writing, 27,* 1353–1378.

Stanovich, K. E. (1986). Matthew effects in reading: Some consequences of individual differences in the acquisition of literacy. *Reading Research Quarterly, 21,* 360–407.

Stanovich, K. E. (2000). *Progress in understanding reading: Scientific foundations and new frontiers.* New York: Guilford Press.

Taylor, B. M., Pearson, P. D., Peterson, D. S., & Rodriguez, M. C. (2003). The reading growth in high-poverty classrooms: The influence of teacher practices that encourage cognitive engagement in literacy learning. *The Elementary School Journal, 104*(1), 3–28.

Templeton, S. (1983). Using the spelling/meaning connection to develop word knowledge in older students. *Journal of Reading, 27,* 8–14.

Thomas, C. N., Peeples, K. N., Kennedy, M. J., & Decker, M. (2019). Riding the special education technology wave: Policy, obstacles, recommendations, actionable ideas, and resources. *Intervention in School and Clinic, 54,* 295–303.

Torgesen, J. K., & Burgess, S. R. (1998). Consistency of reading-related phonological processes throughout early childhood: Evidence from longitudinal–correlational and instructional studies. In J. Metsala & L. Ehri (Eds.), *Word recognition in beginning reading* (pp. 161–188). Hillsdale, NJ: Erlbaum.

Townsend, D. (2015). Who's using the language?: Supporting middle school students with content area academic language. *Journal of Adolescent and Adult Literacy, 58*(5), 376–387.

Watts, S. M. (1995). Vocabulary instruction during reading lessons in six classrooms. *Journal of Reading Behavior, 27,* 399–424.

Webb, S. (2005). Receptive and productive vocabulary learning. *Studies in Second Language Acquisition, 27,* 33–52.

White, T. G., Sowell, J., & Yanagihara, A. (1989). Teaching elementary students to use word-part clues. *The Reading Teacher, 42,* 302–308.

Wright, T. S., & Neuman, S. B. (2014). Paucity and disparity in kindergarten oral vocabulary instruction. *Journal of Literacy Research, 46,* 330–357.

Zeno, S. M., Ivens, S. H., Millard, R. T., & Duvvuri, R. (1995). *The educator's word frequency guide.* Brewster, NY: Touchstone Applied Science.

Zwiers, J. (2014). *Building academic language: Meeting Common Core Standards across disciplines* (2nd ed.). San Francisco: Jossey-Bass.

Children's Literature

Aiken, J. (1963). *The wolves of Willoughby Chase*. Garden City, NY: Doubleday.

Barrett, J. (1978). *Cloudy with a chance of meatballs*. New York: Scholastic.

Clements, A. (1996). *Frindle*. New York: Simon & Schuster.

Clements, A. (1997). *Double trouble in Walla Walla*. Brookfield, CT: Millbrook Press.

D'Aulaire, I., & D'Aulaire, E. P. (1967). *D'Aulaires' book of Norse myths*. New York: Doubleday.

D'Aulaire, I., & D'Aulaire, E. P. (1992). *D'Aulaires' book of Greek myths*. New York: Delacorte Books for Young Readers.

Dahl, R. (1990). *Matilda*. New York: Puffin Books.

DiCamillo, K. (2003). *Tale of Despereaux*. Cambridge, MA: Candlewick Press.

Editors of *Time for Kids*. (2006). *Butterflies!* New York: HarperCollins.

Fritz, J. (1994). *Around the world in a hundred years*. New York: Putnam & Grosset.

Heller, R. (1989). *Many luscious lollipops: A book about adjectives*. New York: Grosset & Dunlap.

Lawrence, J. (Illustrator). (1995). *The great migration: An American story*. New York: Harper Trophy.

Libbrecht, K. (2007). *The art of the snowflake: A photographic album*. St. Paul, MN: Voyageur Press.

Macaulay, D. (1990). *Black and white*. Boston: Houghton Mifflin.

Madden, D. (1989). *Incognito mosquito: Private insective*. New York: Random House Books for Young Readers.

Martin, J. B. (1998). *Snowflake Bentley*. Boston: Houghton Mifflin.

Muñoz Ryan, P. (2000). *Esperanza rising*. New York: Scholastic.

National Geographic Society. (2019a). The conservation of matter during physical and chemical changes. *National Geographic Society/Newsela*. Retrieved from *https://newsela.com/read/natgeo-conservation-matter-changes/id/50293*.

National Geographic Society. (2019b). Regional economy and the American Revolution. *National Geographic Society/Newsela*. Retrieved from *https://newsela.com/read/natgeo-regional-economy-american-revolution/id/51265*.

O'Neill, M. (1989). *Hailstones and halibut bones*. New York: Doubleday.

Palatini, M. (1995). *Piggie Pie!* New York: Clarion.

Sczieska, J. (1992). *The stinky cheese man and other fairly stupid tales*. New York: Viking.

Still, J. (1991). *Amazing butterflies and moths*. New York: Knopf.

Tan, S. (2007). *The arrival*. New York: Levine.

Terban, M. (1988). *Guppies in tuxedos: Funny eponyms*. New York: Clarion.

Terban, M. (1996). *Scholastic dictionary of idioms*. New York: Scholastic.

Truss, L. (2006). *Eats, shoots and leaves: Why commas really do make a difference*. New York: G. P. Putnam's Sons.

U'Ren, A. (2003). *Mary Smith*. New York: Farrar, Straus & Giroux.

Vinge, J. P. (1999). *The Random House book of Greek myths*. New York: Random House for Young Readers.

Websites

edHelper.com's United States Theme Unit—50 States: *www.edhelper.com/geography/Fifty_States.htm*

Ethnologue: Languages of the World: *www.ethnologue.com*

Instant Online Puzzle Maker: *www.puzzle-maker.com*

Miss Spelling's Spelling Center: *www.alphadictionary.com/articles/misspelling.html*

Phobia List: *www.phobialist.com*

Southern Poverty Law Center's Site for Teaching Tolerance: *www.tolerance.org*

Spellzone: *www.spellzone.com*

U.S. Census Bureau's U.S. and World Population Clock: *www.census.gov/popclock*

Wordplay Web Site: *www.fun-with-words.com*

Index of Words Used in the Sorts